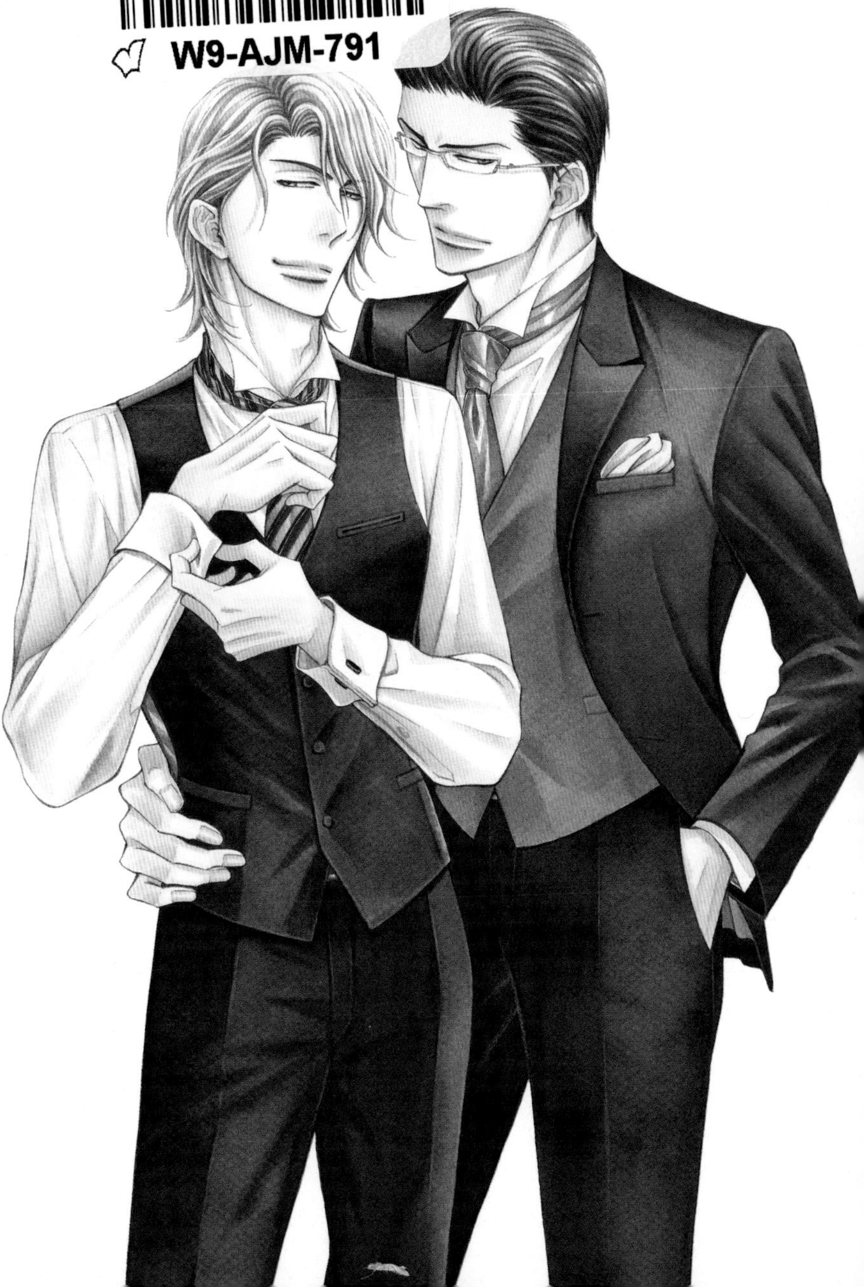

Hide and Seek

Story and Art by **Yaya Sakuragi**   volume **1**

CONTENTS

SUBLIME
SuBLime Manga Edition

ASUKA COMICS CL-DX

秘めごとあそび

1

桜城やや
YAYA SAKURAGI

Hide and Seek

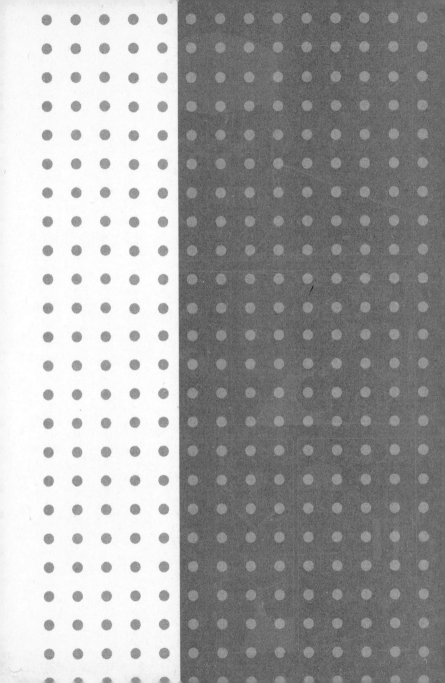

Hide and Seek: Act 1

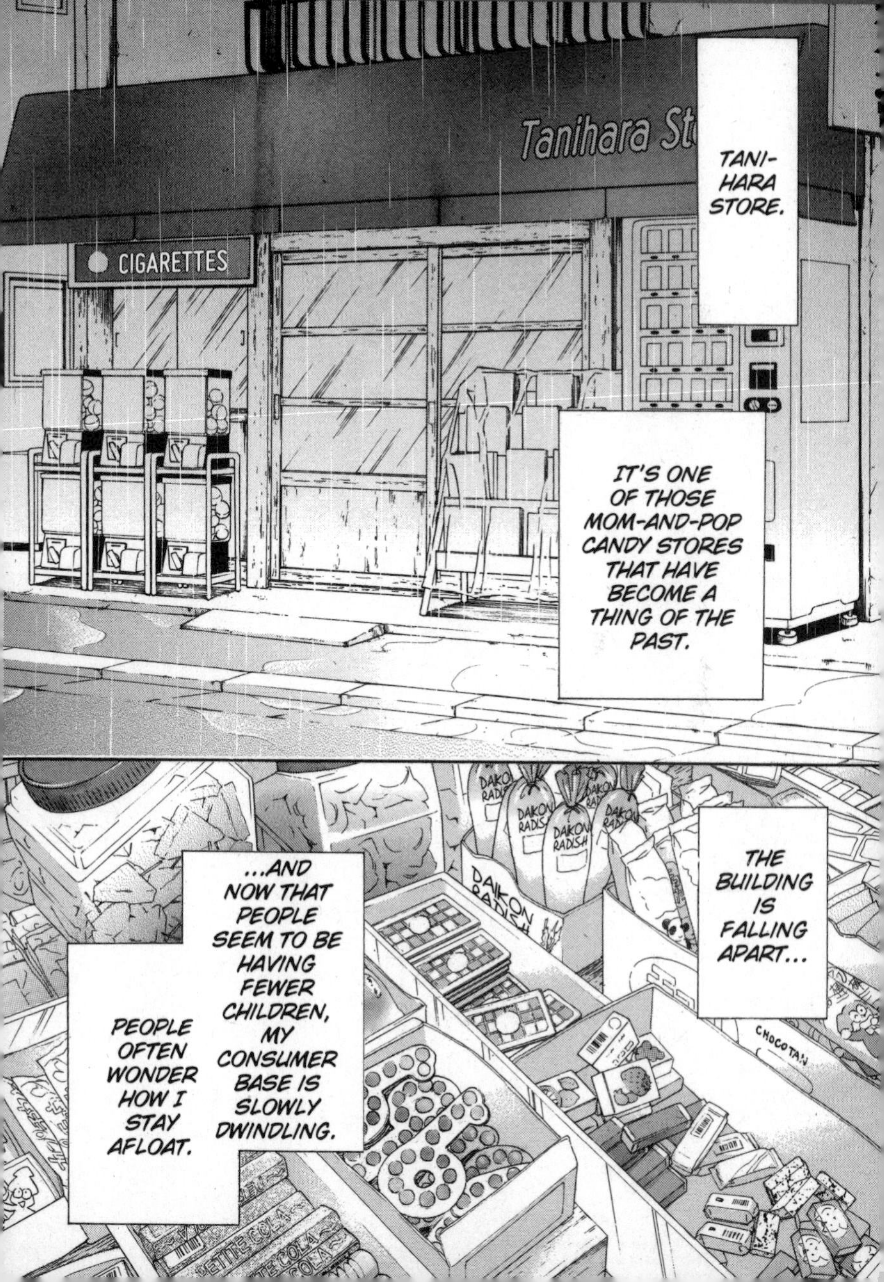
TANI-HARA STORE.
IT'S ONE OF THOSE MOM-AND-POP CANDY STORES THAT HAVE BECOME A THING OF THE PAST.
CIGARETTES
THE BUILDING IS FALLING APART...
...AND NOW THAT PEOPLE SEEM TO BE HAVING FEWER CHILDREN, MY CONSUMER BASE IS SLOWLY DWINDLING.
PEOPLE OFTEN WONDER HOW I STAY AFLOAT.
DAIKON RADISH
CHOCOTAN

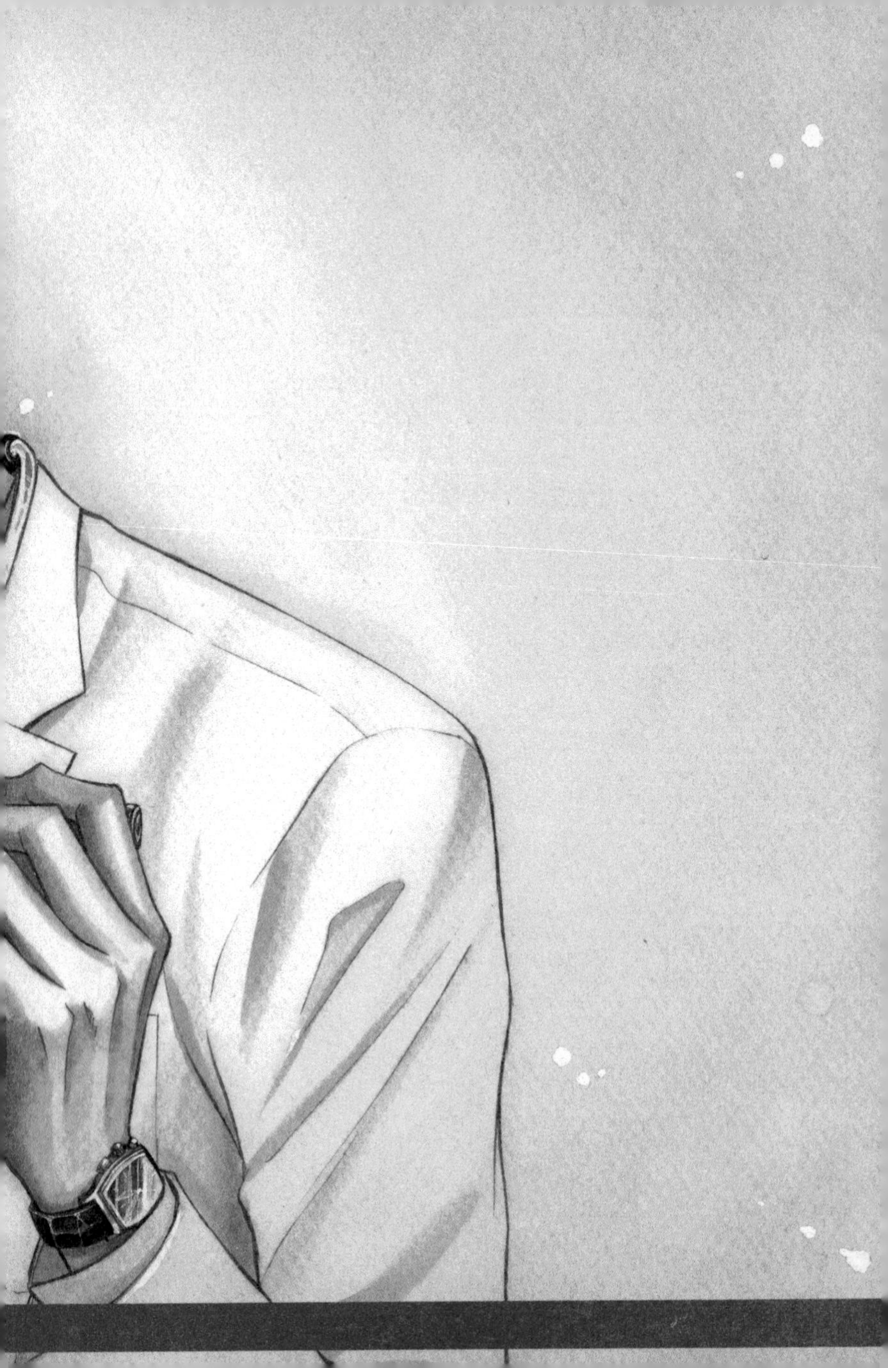

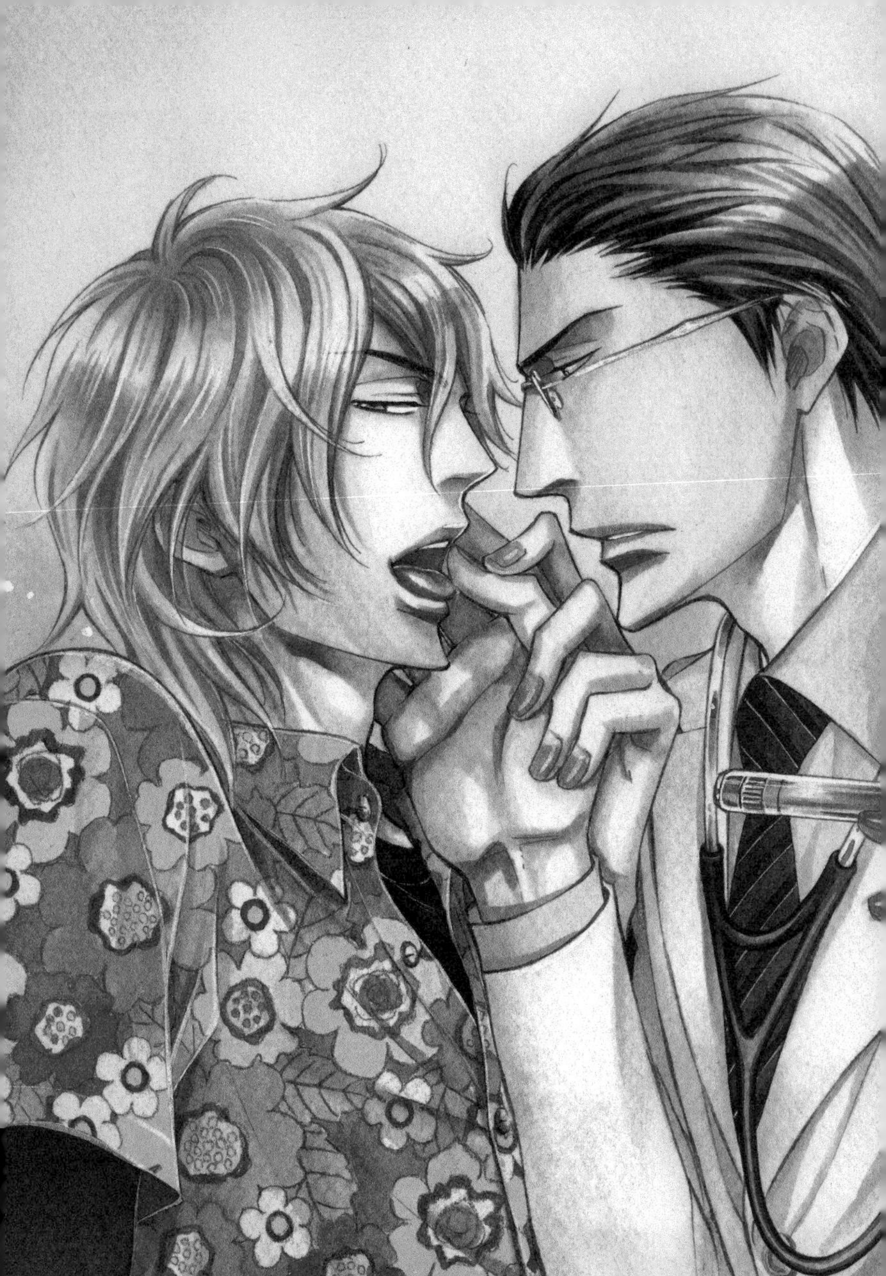

Hide and Seek: Act 1

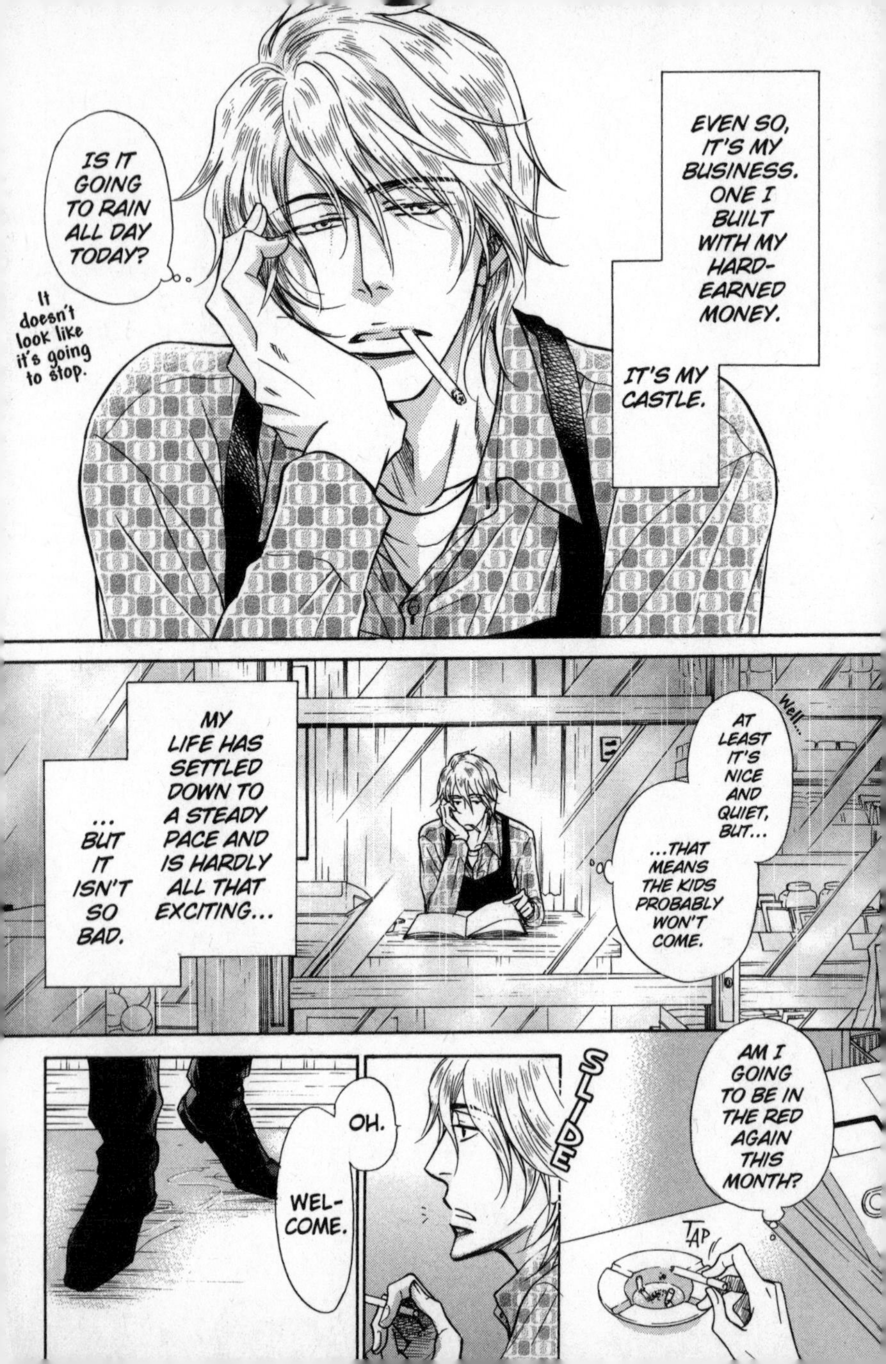
EVEN SO, IT'S MY BUSINESS. ONE I BUILT WITH MY HARD-EARNED MONEY.
IT'S MY CASTLE.
IS IT GOING TO RAIN ALL DAY TODAY?
It doesn't look like it's going to stop.
Well...
AT LEAST IT'S NICE AND QUIET, BUT...
...THAT MEANS THE KIDS PROBABLY WON'T COME.
MY LIFE HAS SETTLED DOWN TO A STEADY PACE AND IS HARDLY ALL THAT EXCITING...
...BUT IT ISN'T SO BAD.
AM I GOING TO BE IN THE RED AGAIN THIS MONTH?
TAP
SLIDE
OH.
WEL-COME.

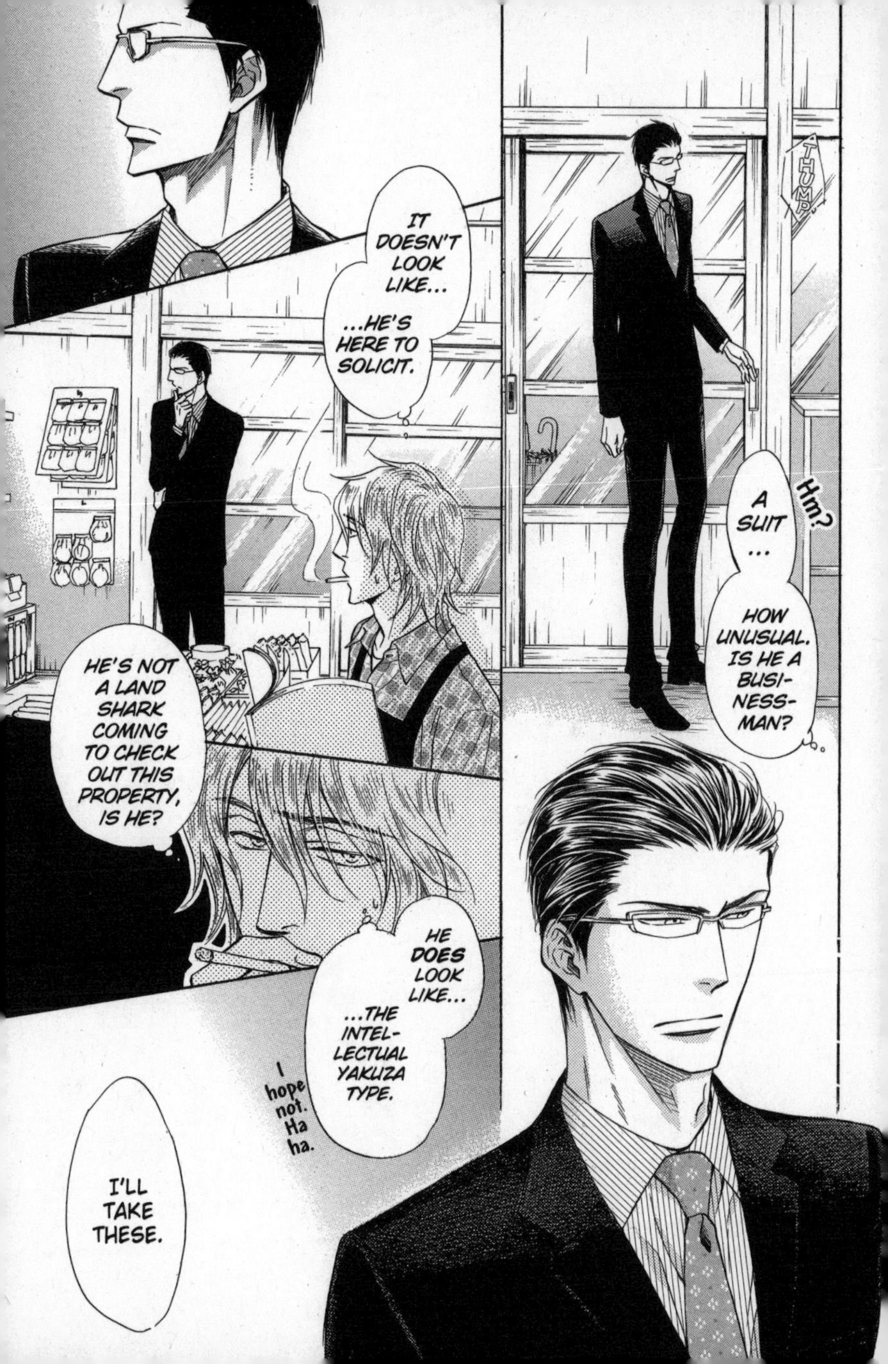
THUMP
Hm?
A SUIT...
HOW UNUSUAL. IS HE A BUSINESSMAN?
IT DOESN'T LOOK LIKE...
...HE'S HERE TO SOLICIT.
HE'S NOT A LAND SHARK COMING TO CHECK OUT THIS PROPERTY, IS HE?
HE DOES LOOK LIKE...
...THE INTELLECTUAL YAKUZA TYPE.
I hope not. Ha ha.
I'LL TAKE THESE.

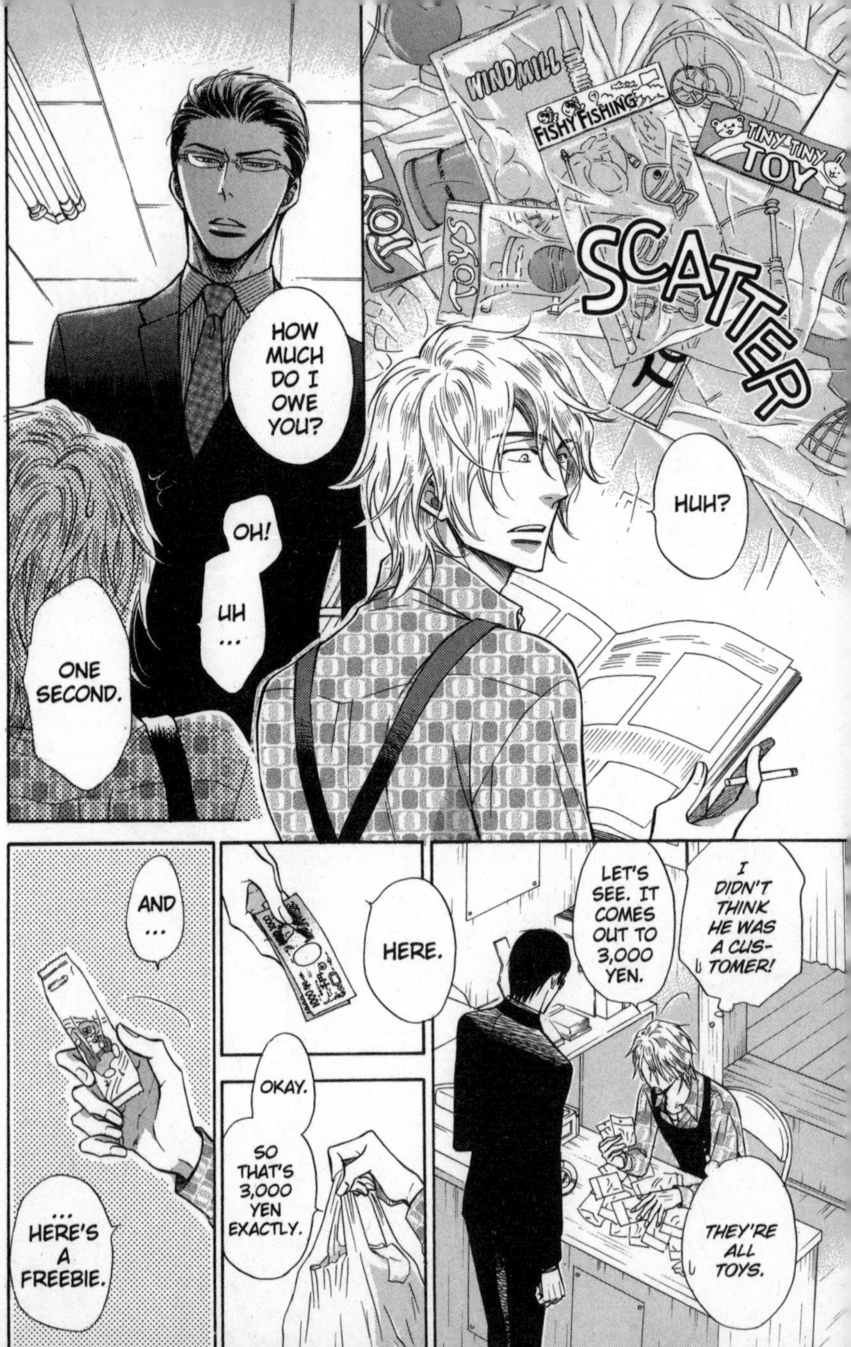
WINDMILL
FISHY FISHING
TINY-TINY TOY
SCATTER
HUH?
HOW MUCH DO I OWE YOU?
OH!
UH ...
ONE SECOND.
I DIDN'T THINK HE WAS A CUS-TOMER!
LET'S SEE. IT COMES OUT TO 3,000 YEN.
THEY'RE ALL TOYS.
HERE.
OKAY.
SO THAT'S 3,000 YEN EXACTLY.
AND ...
... HERE'S A FREEBIE.

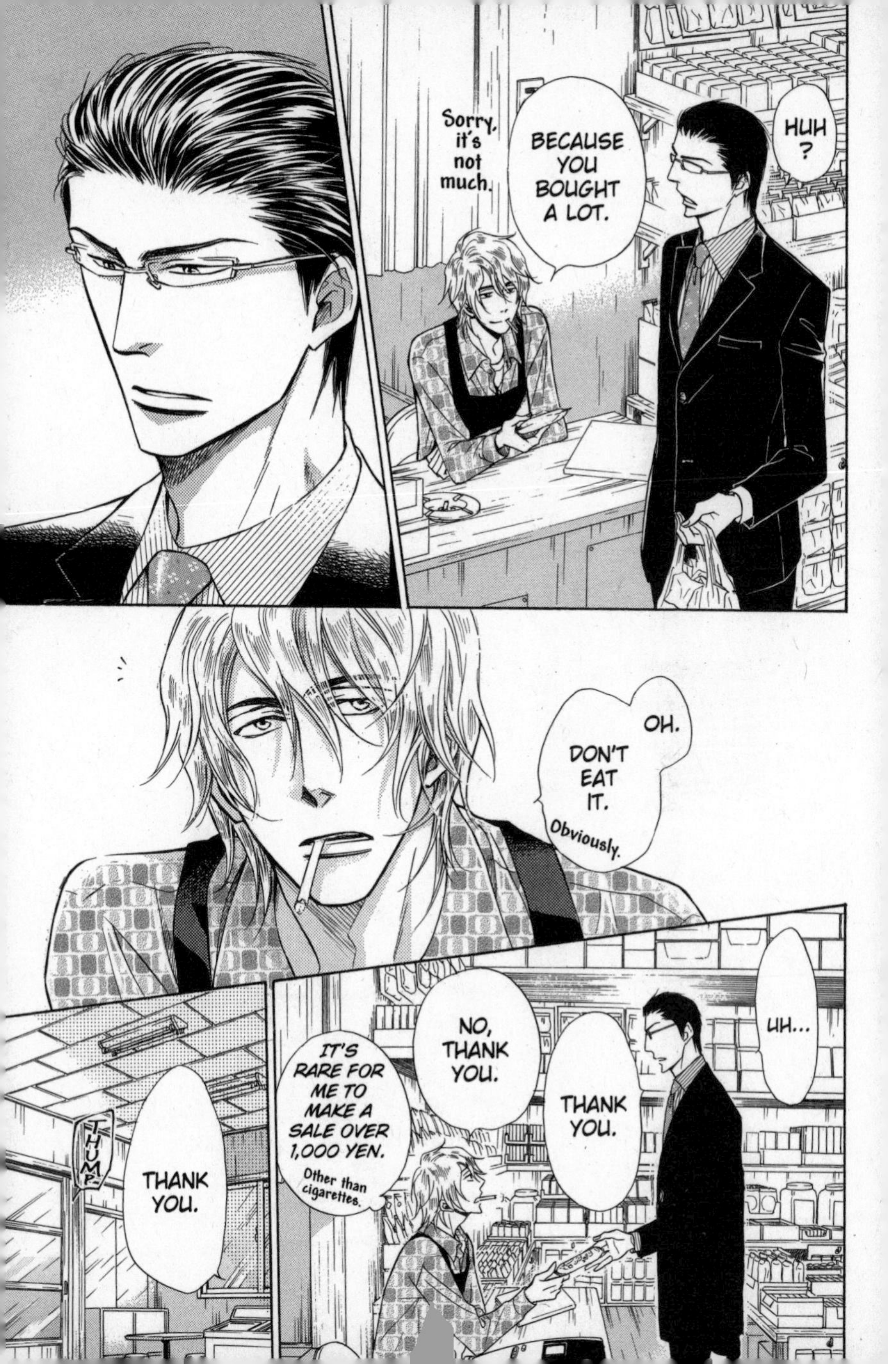
HUH?
BECAUSE YOU BOUGHT A LOT.
Sorry, it's not much.
OH.
DON'T EAT IT.
Obviously.
UH...
THANK YOU.
NO, THANK YOU.
IT'S RARE FOR ME TO MAKE A SALE OVER 1,000 YEN.
Other than cigarettes.
THUMP
THANK YOU.

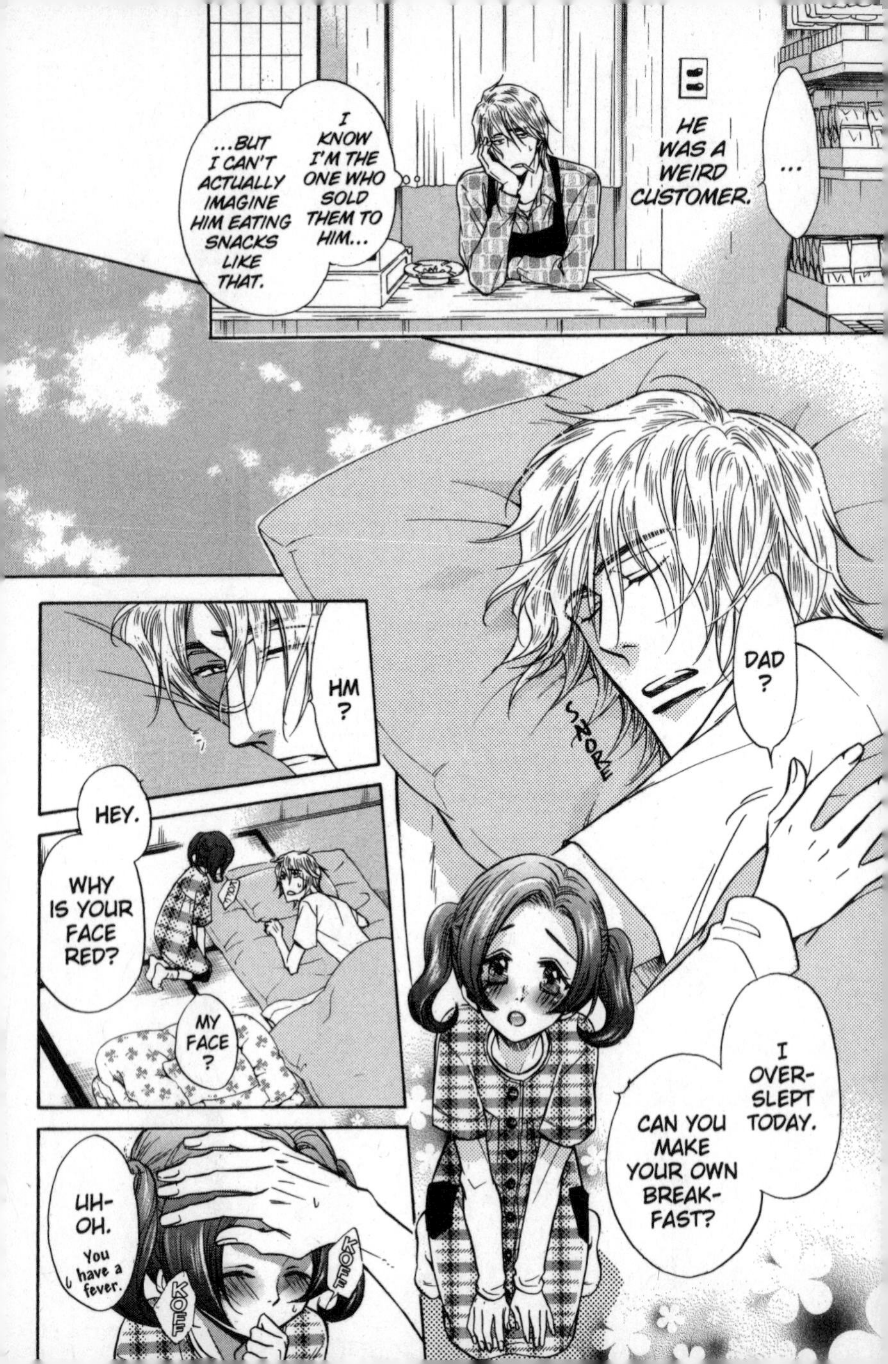
...
HE WAS A WEIRD CUSTOMER.
I KNOW I'M THE ONE WHO SOLD THEM TO HIM...
...BUT I CAN'T ACTUALLY IMAGINE HIM EATING SNACKS LIKE THAT.
DAD?
SNORE
I OVERSLEPT TODAY.
CAN YOU MAKE YOUR OWN BREAKFAST?
HM?
HEY.
WHY IS YOUR FACE RED?
MY FACE?
UH-OH.
You have a fever.
KOFF
KOFF

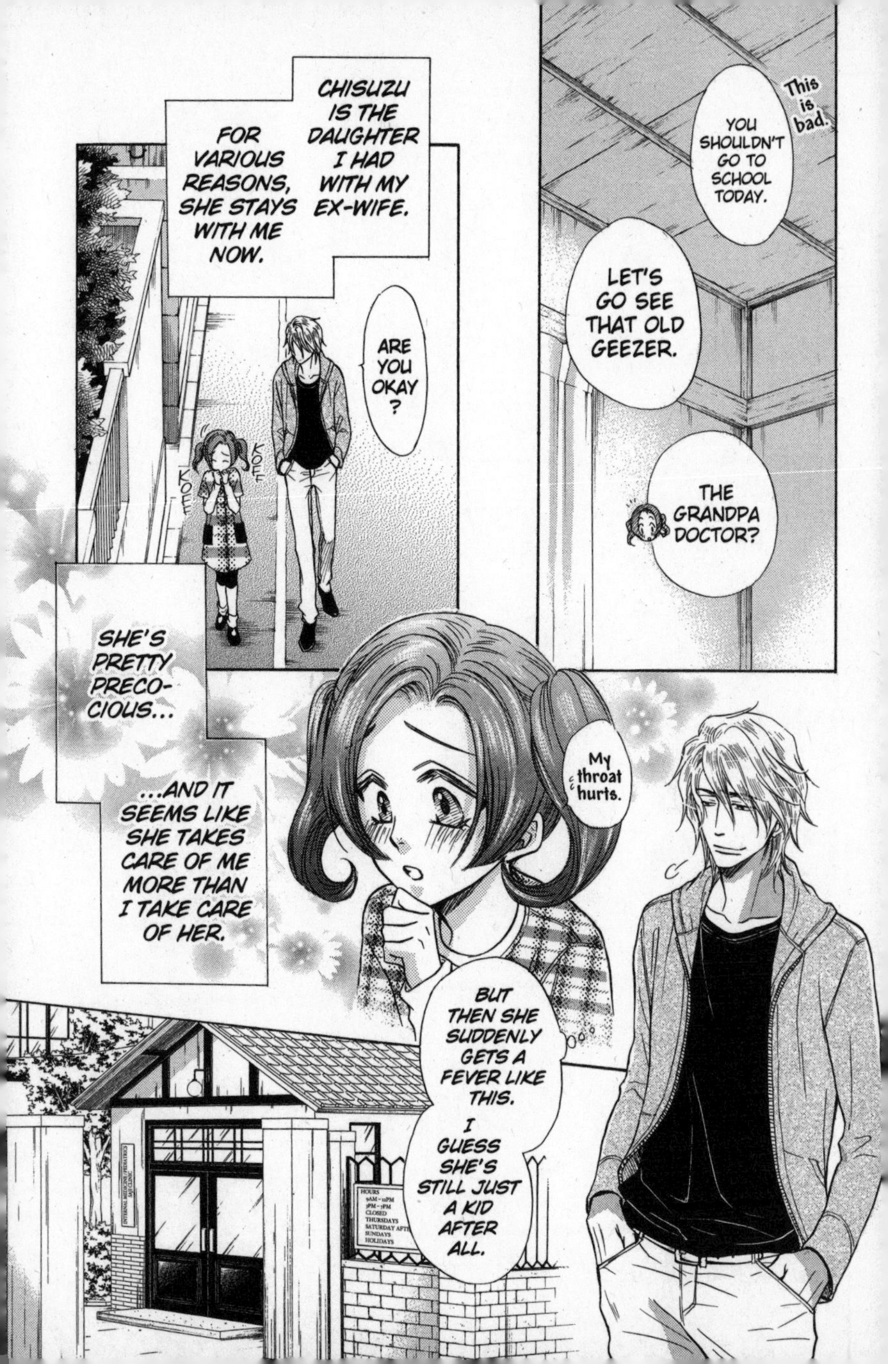
This is bad.
YOU SHOULDN'T GO TO SCHOOL TODAY.
LET'S GO SEE THAT OLD GEEZER.
THE GRANDPA DOCTOR?
CHISUZU IS THE DAUGHTER I HAD WITH MY EX-WIFE.
FOR VARIOUS REASONS, SHE STAYS WITH ME NOW.
ARE YOU OKAY?
KOFF
KOFF
SHE'S PRETTY PRECOCIOUS...
...AND IT SEEMS LIKE SHE TAKES CARE OF ME MORE THAN I TAKE CARE OF HER.
My throat hurts.
BUT THEN SHE SUDDENLY GETS A FEVER LIKE THIS.
I GUESS SHE'S STILL JUST A KID AFTER ALL.
HOURS
9AM–12PM
3PM–7PM
CLOSED
THURSDAYS
SUNDAYS
HOLIDAYS

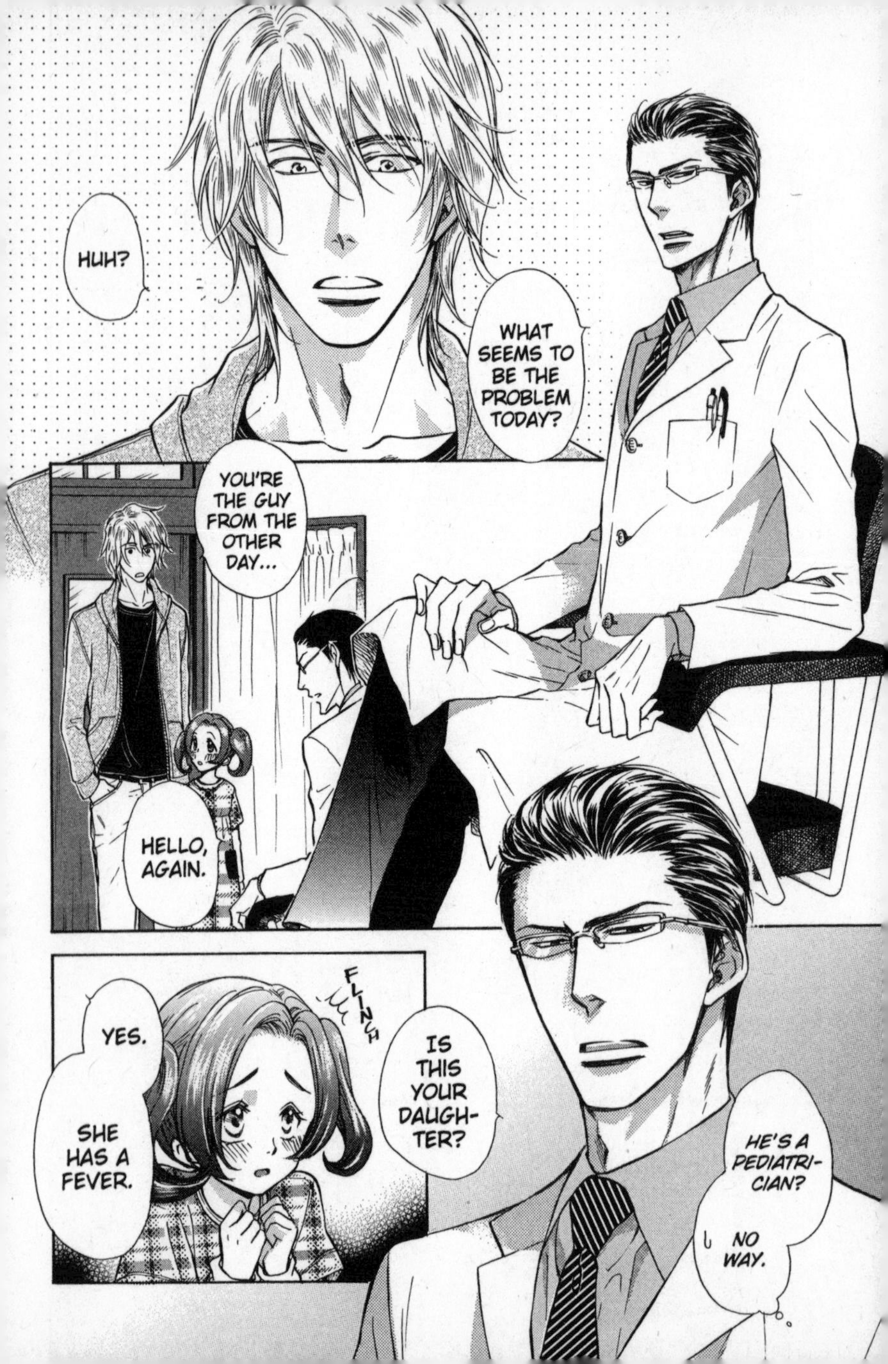
WHAT SEEMS TO BE THE PROBLEM TODAY?
HUH?
YOU'RE THE GUY FROM THE OTHER DAY...
HELLO, AGAIN.
HE'S A PEDIATRICIAN?
NO WAY.
IS THIS YOUR DAUGHTER?
FLINCH
YES.
SHE HAS A FEVER.

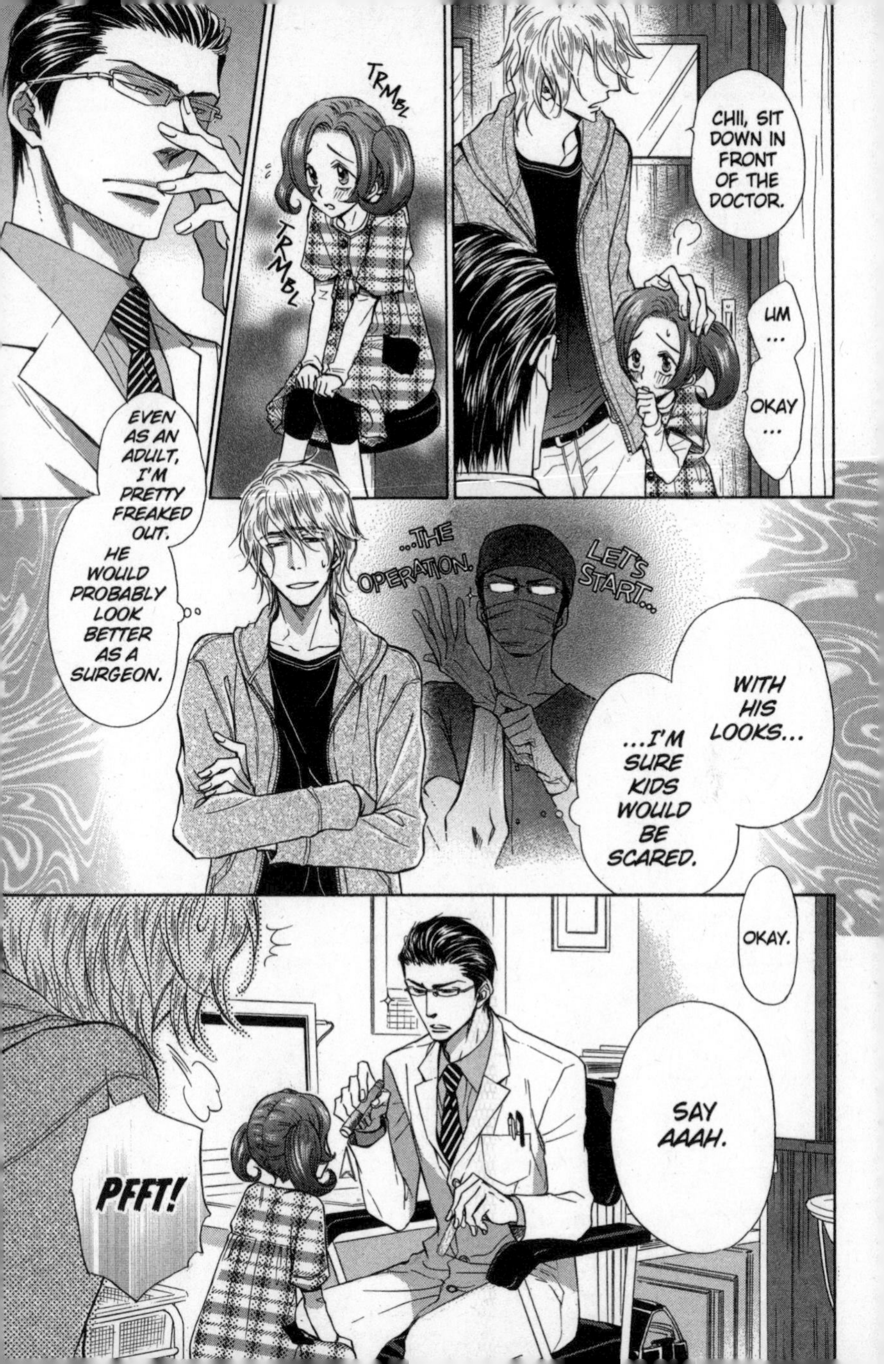
CHII, SIT DOWN IN FRONT OF THE DOCTOR.
UM ... OKAY ...
TRMBL
TRMBL
WITH HIS LOOKS...
...I'M SURE KIDS WOULD BE SCARED.
LET'S START...
...THE OPERATION.
EVEN AS AN ADULT, I'M PRETTY FREAKED OUT.
HE WOULD PROBABLY LOOK BETTER AS A SURGEON.
OKAY.
SAY AAAH.
PFFT!

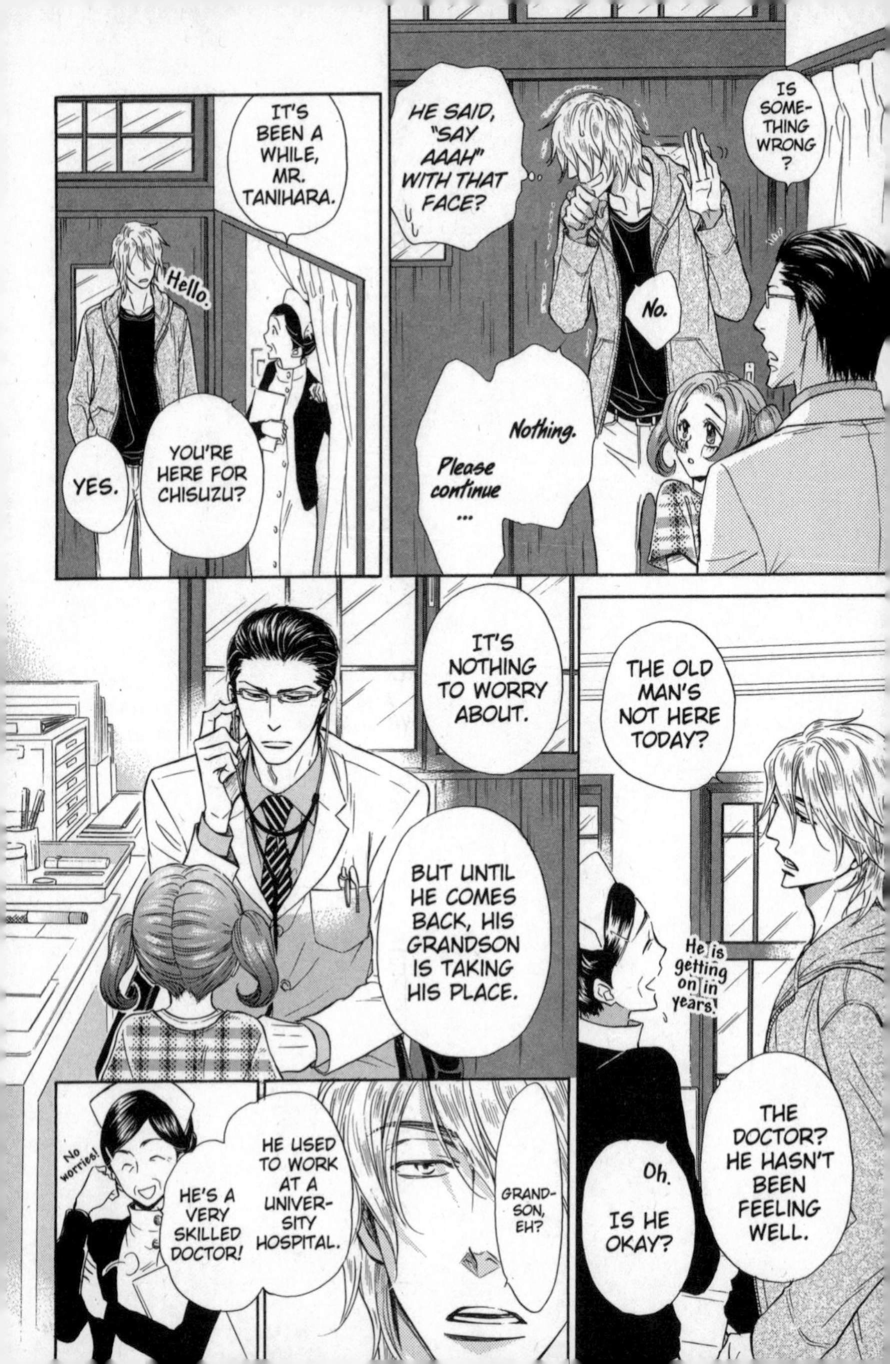
IS SOMETHING WRONG?
HE SAID, "SAY AAAH" WITH THAT FACE?
No.
Nothing.
Please continue...
IT'S BEEN A WHILE, MR. TANIHARA.
Hello.
YOU'RE HERE FOR CHISUZU?
YES.
THE OLD MAN'S NOT HERE TODAY?
He is getting on in years!
THE DOCTOR? HE HASN'T BEEN FEELING WELL.
Oh.
IS HE OKAY?
IT'S NOTHING TO WORRY ABOUT.
BUT UNTIL HE COMES BACK, HIS GRANDSON IS TAKING HIS PLACE.
GRANDSON, EH?
HE USED TO WORK AT A UNIVERSITY HOSPITAL.
HE'S A VERY SKILLED DOCTOR!
No worries!

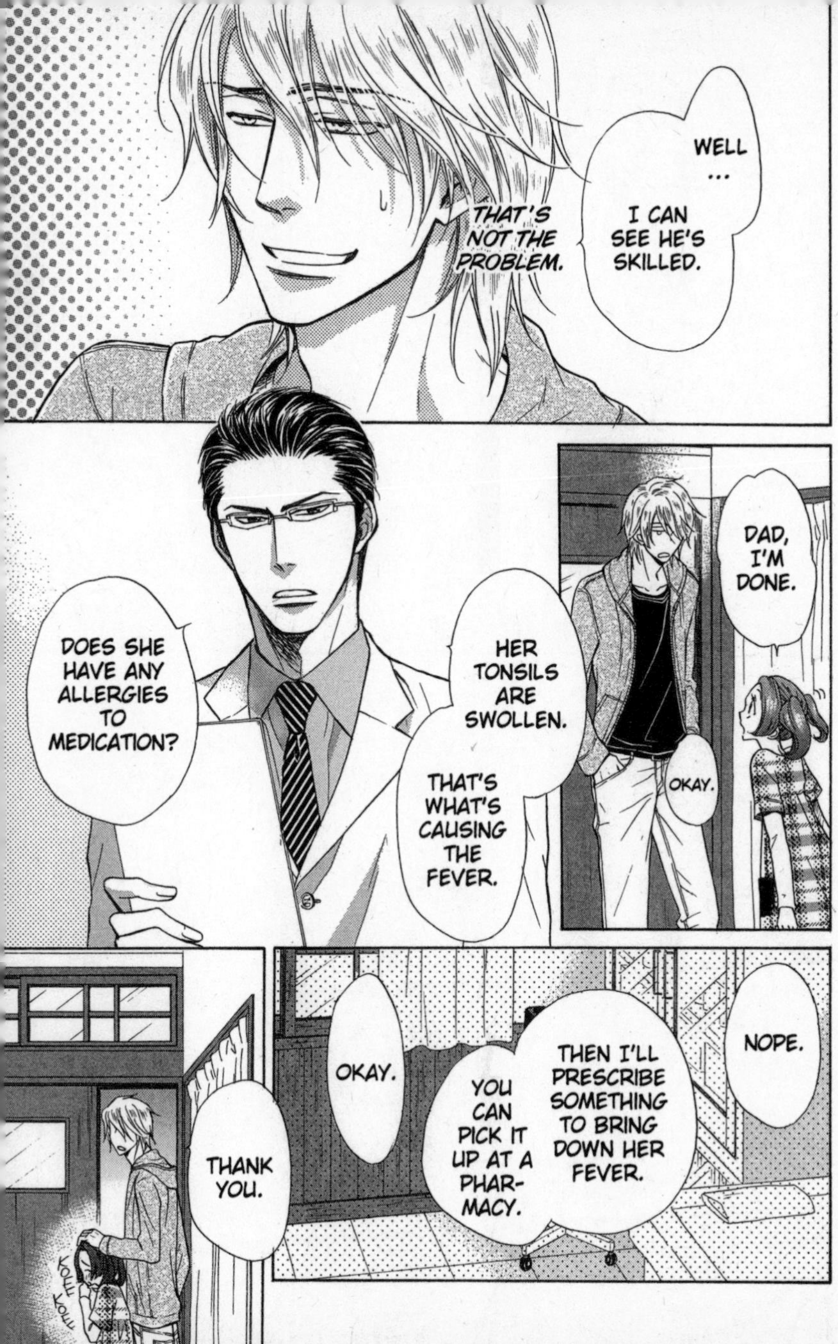
WELL ...
I CAN SEE HE'S SKILLED.
THAT'S NOT THE PROBLEM.
DAD, I'M DONE.
OKAY.
HER TONSILS ARE SWOLLEN.
THAT'S WHAT'S CAUSING THE FEVER.
DOES SHE HAVE ANY ALLERGIES TO MEDICATION?
NOPE.
THEN I'LL PRESCRIBE SOMETHING TO BRING DOWN HER FEVER.
YOU CAN PICK IT UP AT A PHAR-MACY.
OKAY.
THANK YOU.
KOFF KOFF

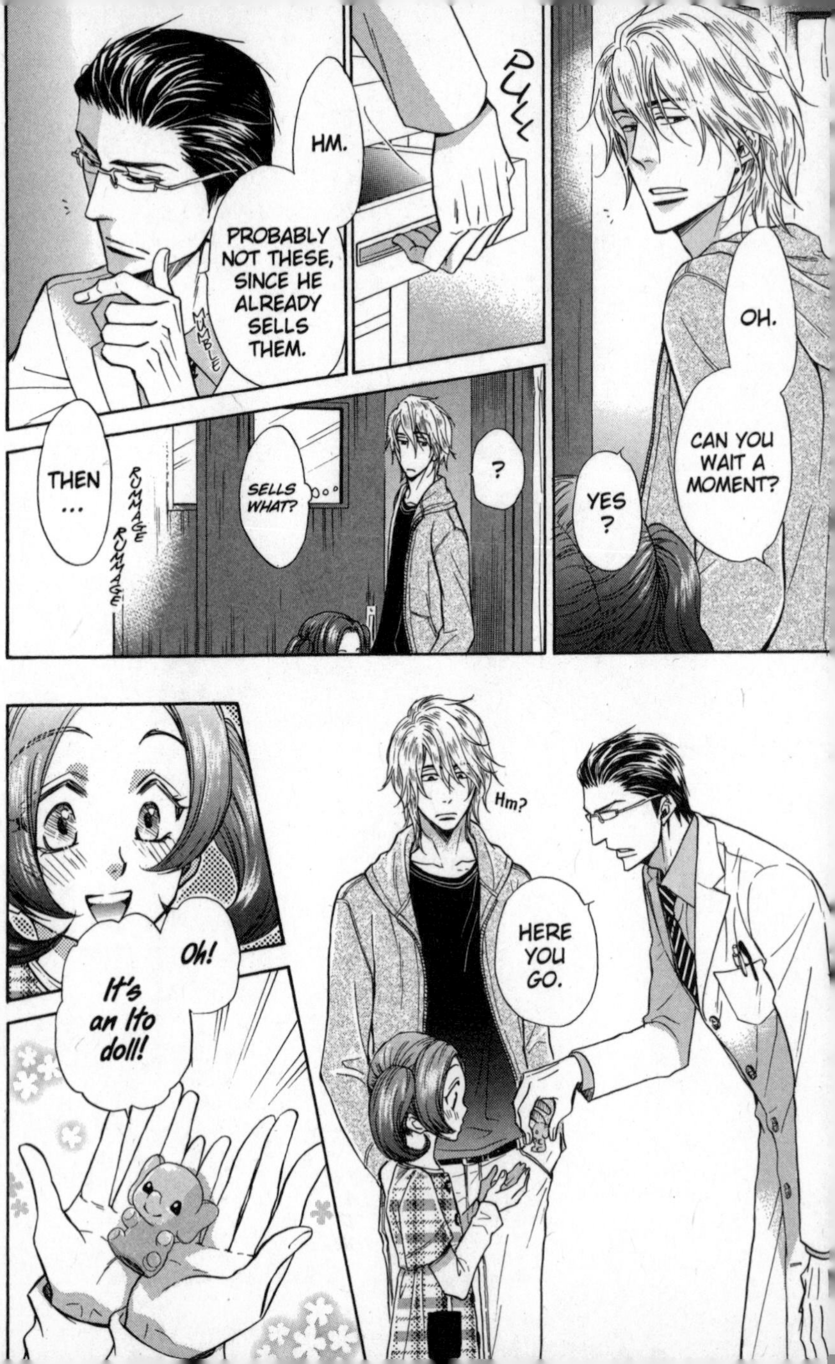
OH.
CAN YOU WAIT A MOMENT?
YES?
PULL
HM.
PROBABLY NOT THESE, SINCE HE ALREADY SELLS THEM.
MUMBLE
?
SELLS WHAT?
THEN...
RUMMAGE RUMMAGE
Hm?
HERE YOU GO.
Oh!
It's an Ito doll!

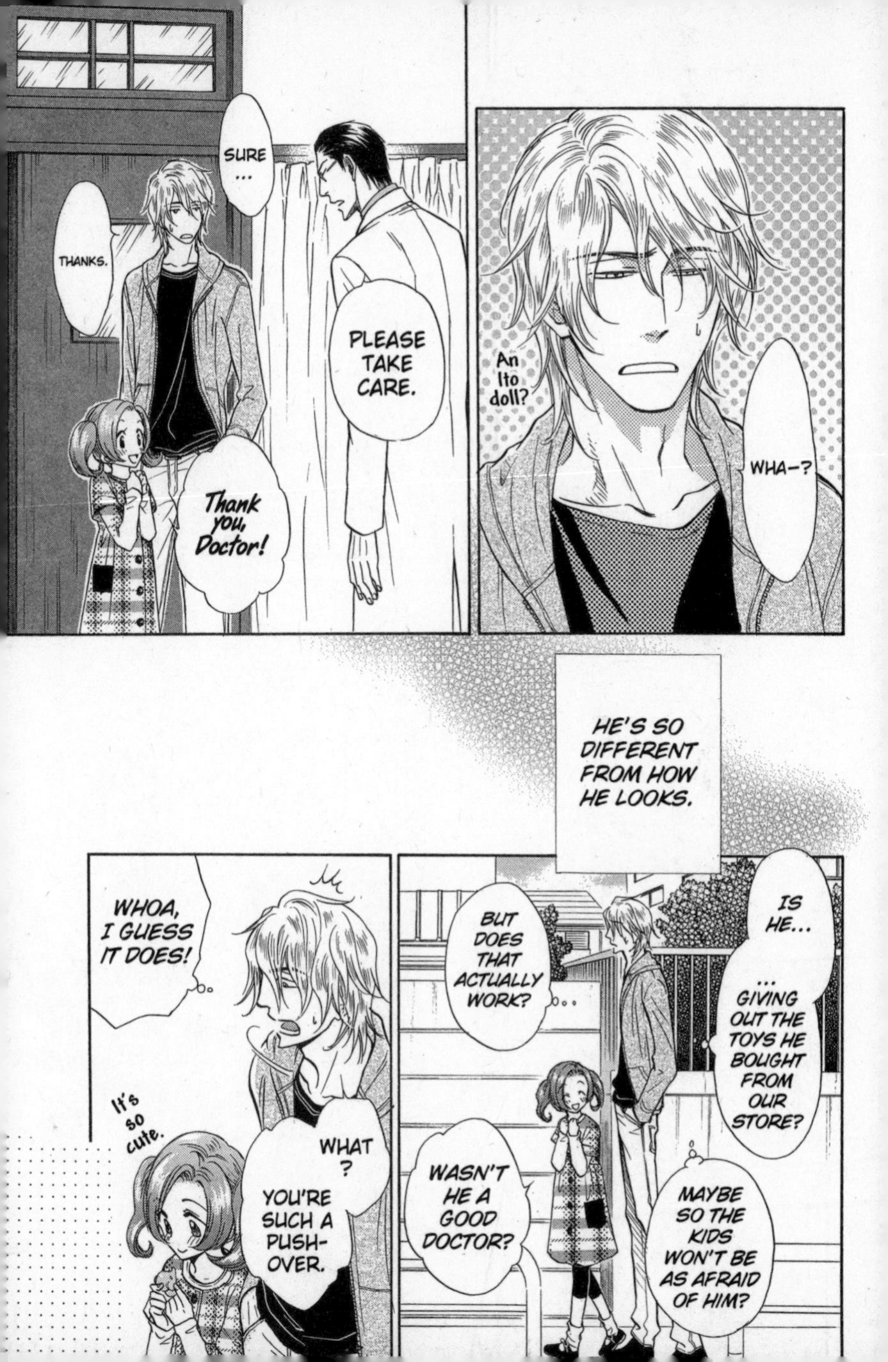
WHA-?
An Ito doll?
SURE ...
PLEASE TAKE CARE.
THANKS.
Thank you, Doctor!
HE'S SO DIFFERENT FROM HOW HE LOOKS.
IS HE...
... GIVING OUT THE TOYS HE BOUGHT FROM OUR STORE?
MAYBE SO THE KIDS WON'T BE AS AFRAID OF HIM?
BUT DOES THAT ACTUALLY WORK?
WASN'T HE A GOOD DOCTOR?
WHOA, I GUESS IT DOES!
WHAT?
YOU'RE SUCH A PUSH-OVER.
It's so cute.

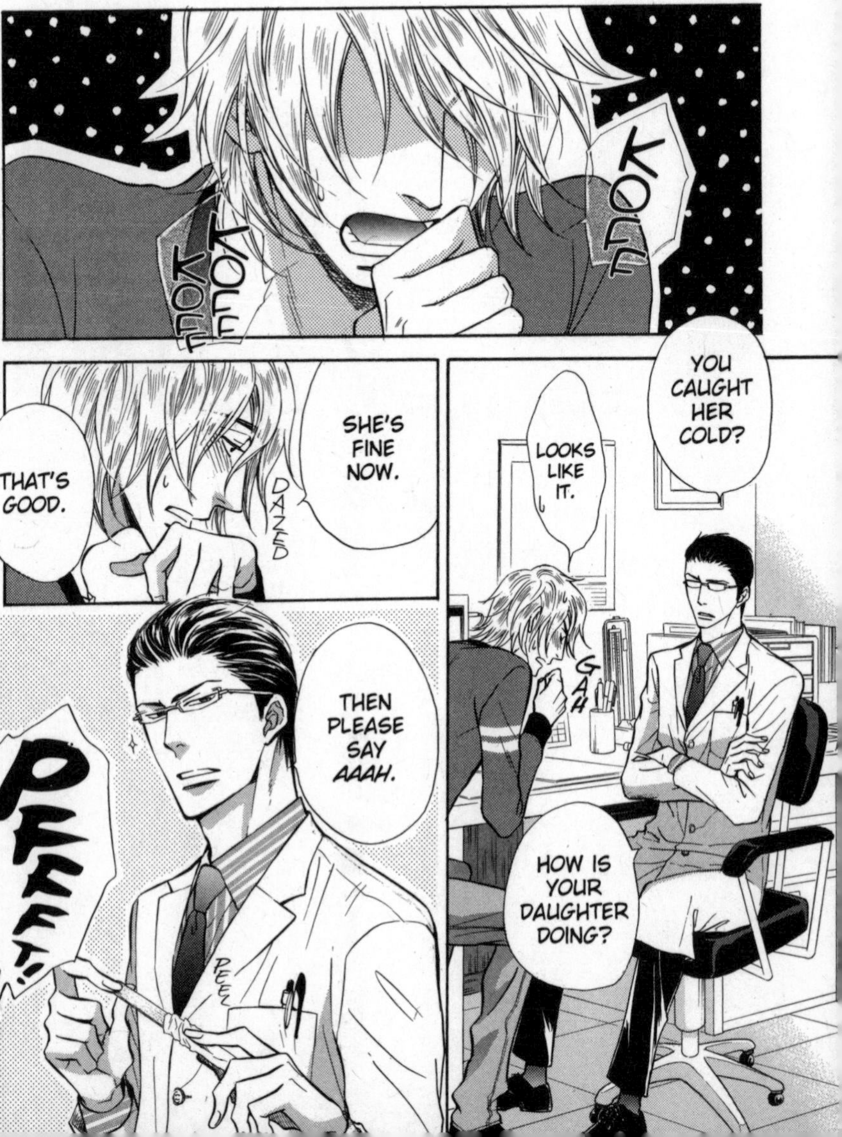
KOFF
KOFF KOFF
YOU CAUGHT HER COLD?
LOOKS LIKE IT.
GAH
HOW IS YOUR DAUGHTER DOING?
SHE'S FINE NOW.
DAZED
THAT'S GOOD.
THEN PLEASE SAY *AAAH*.
PEEL
PFFFT!!

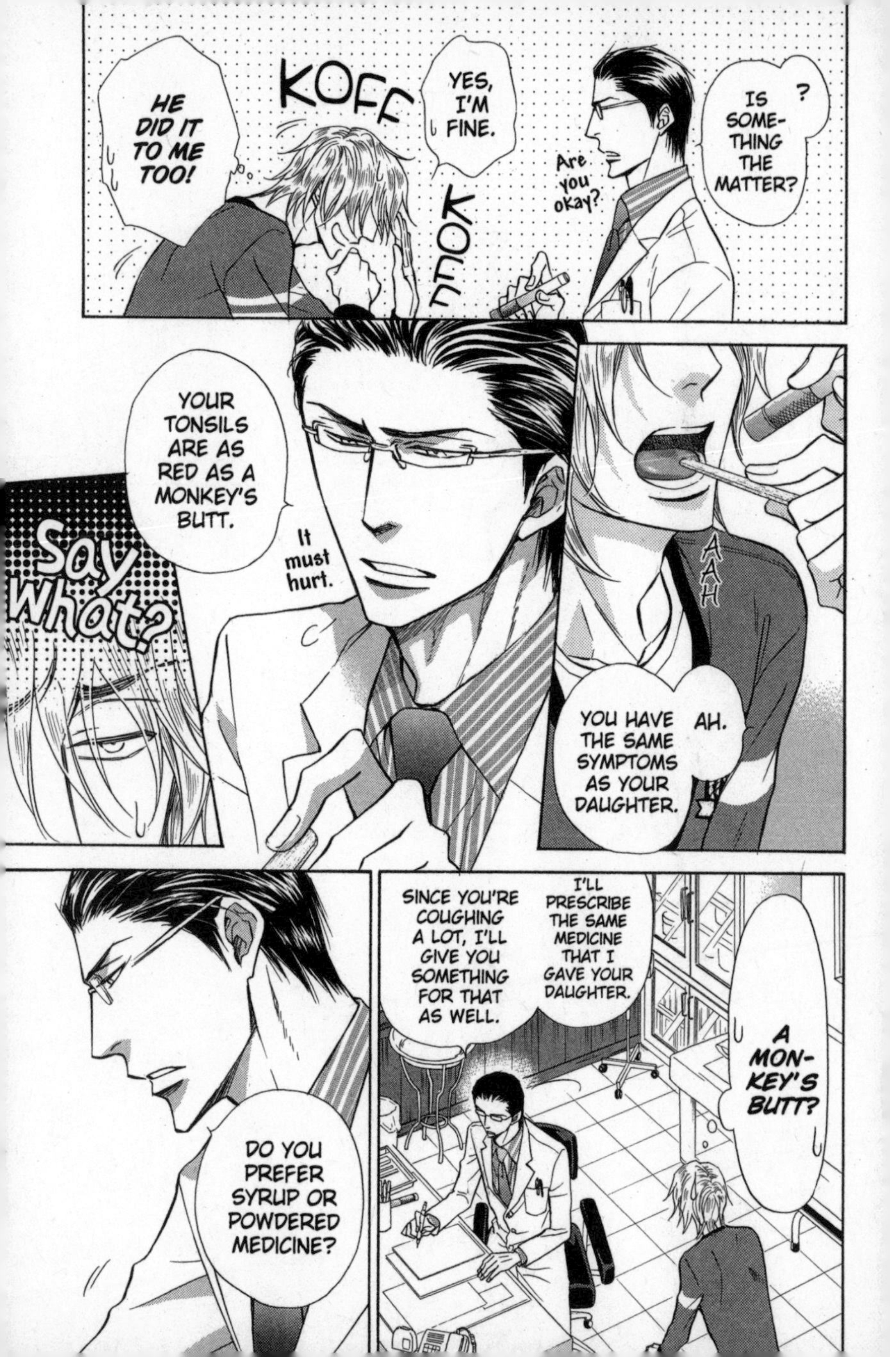
?
IS SOMETHING THE MATTER?
Are you okay?
YES, I'M FINE.
KOFF
KOFF
HE DID IT TO ME TOO!
AAH
AH.
YOU HAVE THE SAME SYMPTOMS AS YOUR DAUGHTER.
It must hurt.
YOUR TONSILS ARE AS RED AS A MONKEY'S BUTT.
Say what?
A MONKEY'S BUTT?
I'LL PRESCRIBE THE SAME MEDICINE THAT I GAVE YOUR DAUGHTER.
SINCE YOU'RE COUGHING A LOT, I'LL GIVE YOU SOMETHING FOR THAT AS WELL.
DO YOU PREFER SYRUP OR POWDERED MEDICINE?

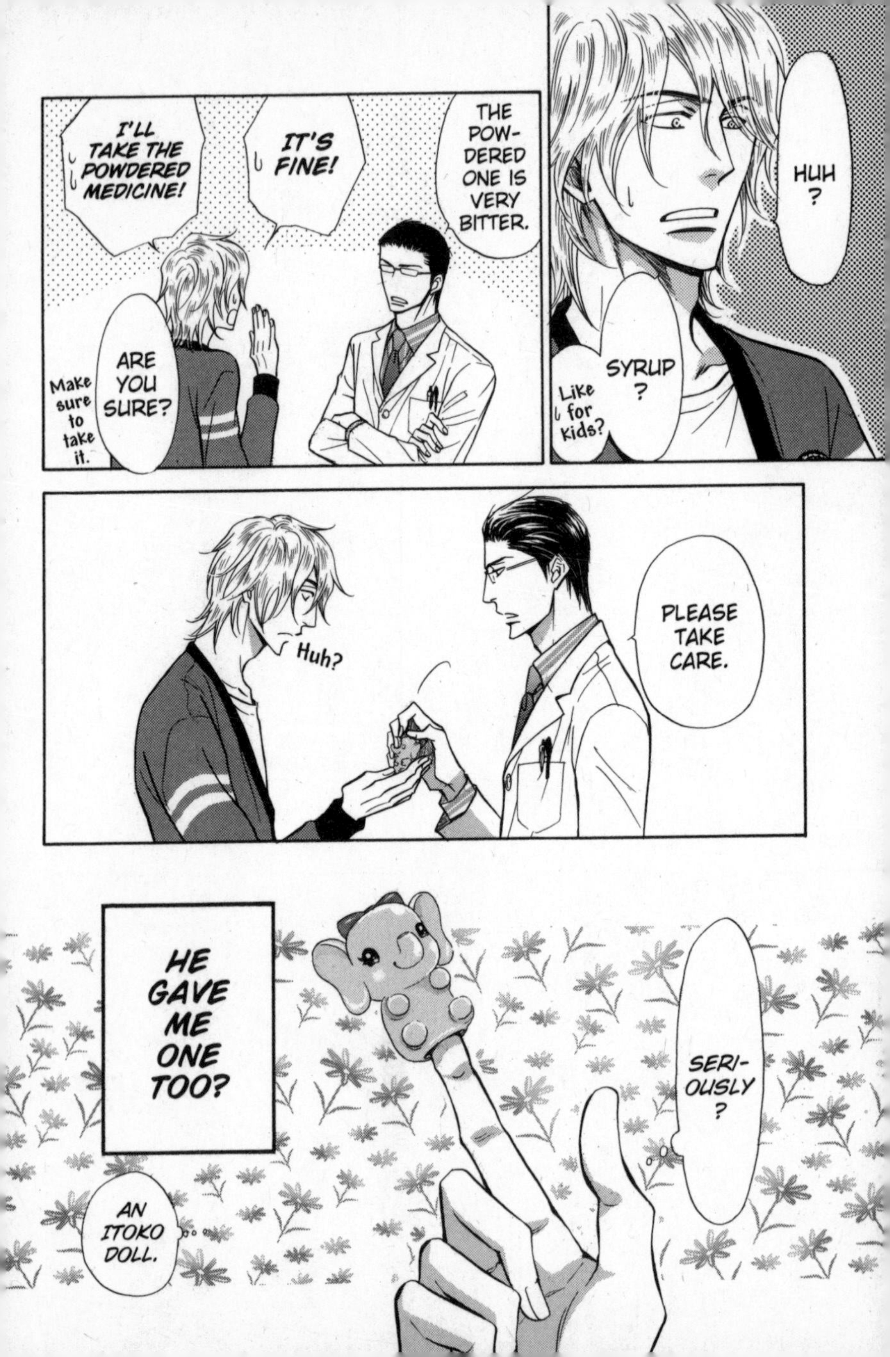
HUH?
SYRUP?
Like for kids?
THE POW-DERED ONE IS VERY BITTER.
IT'S FINE!
I'LL TAKE THE POWDERED MEDICINE!
ARE YOU SURE?
Make sure to take it.
PLEASE TAKE CARE.
Huh?
SERI-OUSLY?
HE GAVE ME ONE TOO?
AN ITOKO DOLL.

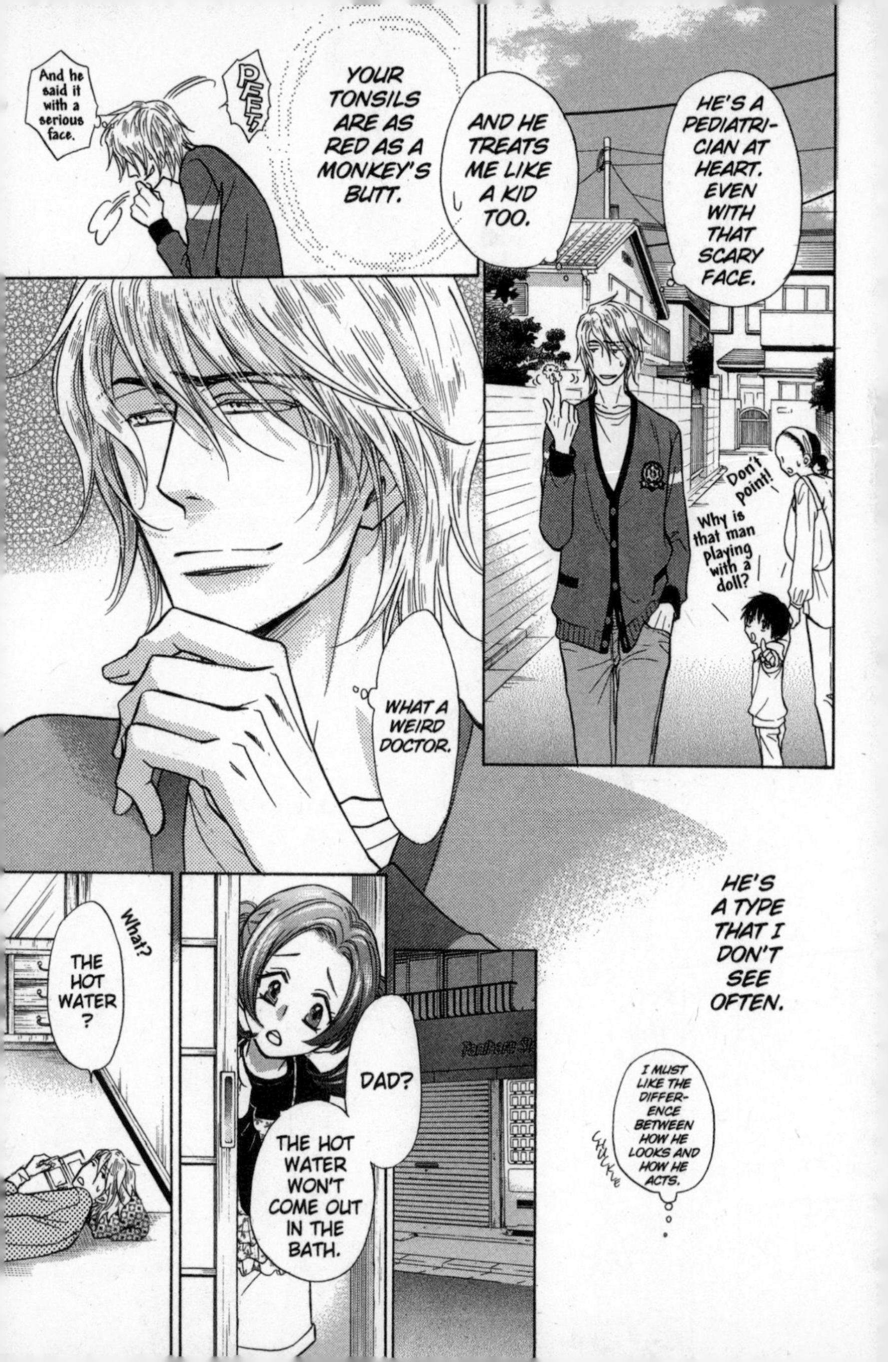
HE'S A PEDIATRICIAN AT HEART. EVEN WITH THAT SCARY FACE.
AND HE TREATS ME LIKE A KID TOO.
Don't point!
Why is that man playing with a doll?
YOUR TONSILS ARE AS RED AS A MONKEY'S BUTT.
PFFT
And he said it with a serious face.
WHAT A WEIRD DOCTOR.
HE'S A TYPE THAT I DON'T SEE OFTEN.
I MUST LIKE THE DIFFERENCE BETWEEN HOW HE LOOKS AND HOW HE ACTS.
CHUCKLE
DAD?
THE HOT WATER WON'T COME OUT IN THE BATH.
What?
THE HOT WATER?

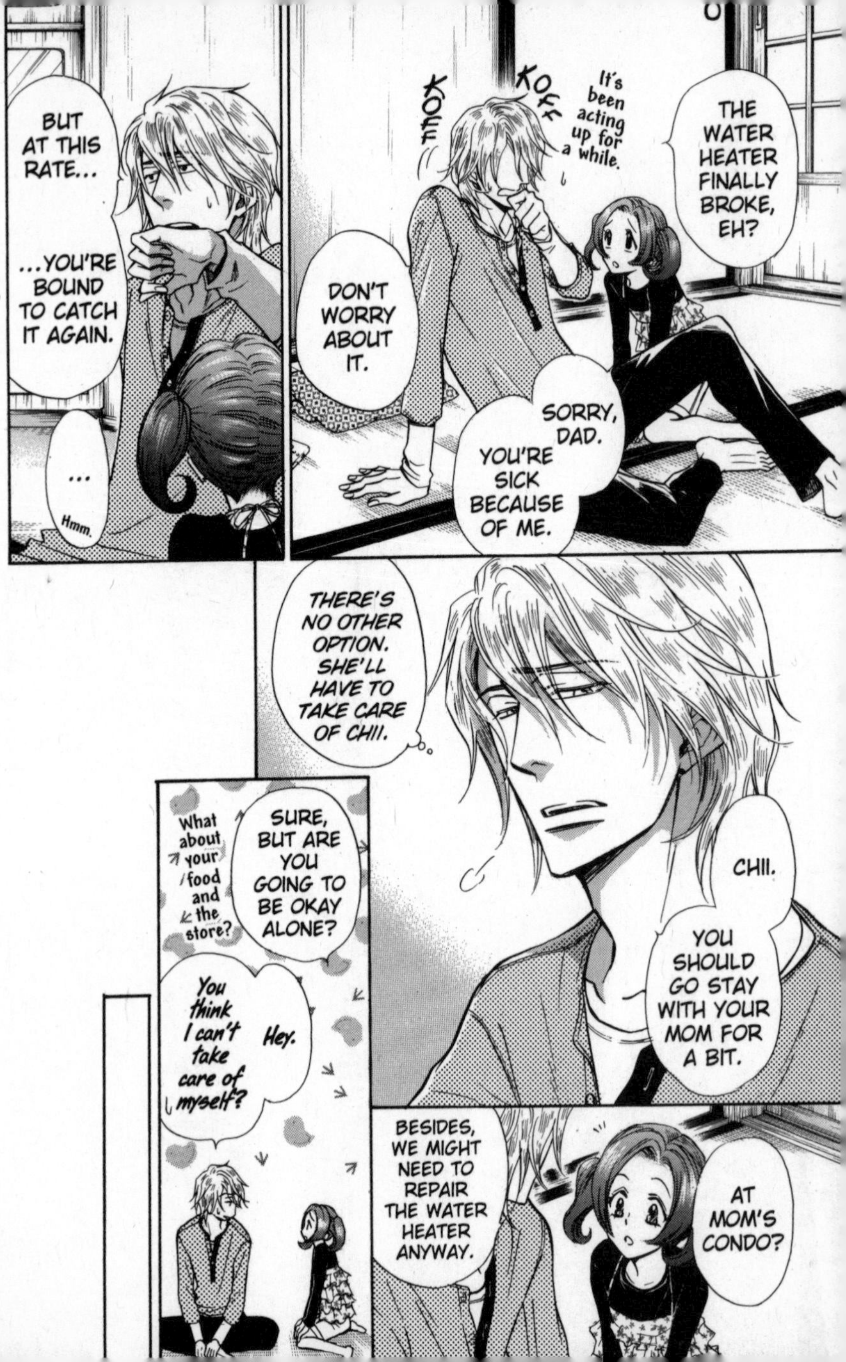
THE WATER HEATER FINALLY BROKE, EH?
It's been acting up for a while.
KOFF
KOFF
SORRY, DAD. YOU'RE SICK BECAUSE OF ME.
DON'T WORRY ABOUT IT.
BUT AT THIS RATE...
...YOU'RE BOUND TO CATCH IT AGAIN.
...
Hmm.
THERE'S NO OTHER OPTION. SHE'LL HAVE TO TAKE CARE OF CHII.
CHII.
YOU SHOULD GO STAY WITH YOUR MOM FOR A BIT.
AT MOM'S CONDO?
BESIDES, WE MIGHT NEED TO REPAIR THE WATER HEATER ANYWAY.
SURE, BUT ARE YOU GOING TO BE OKAY ALONE?
What about your food and the store?
Hey.
You think I can't take care of myself?

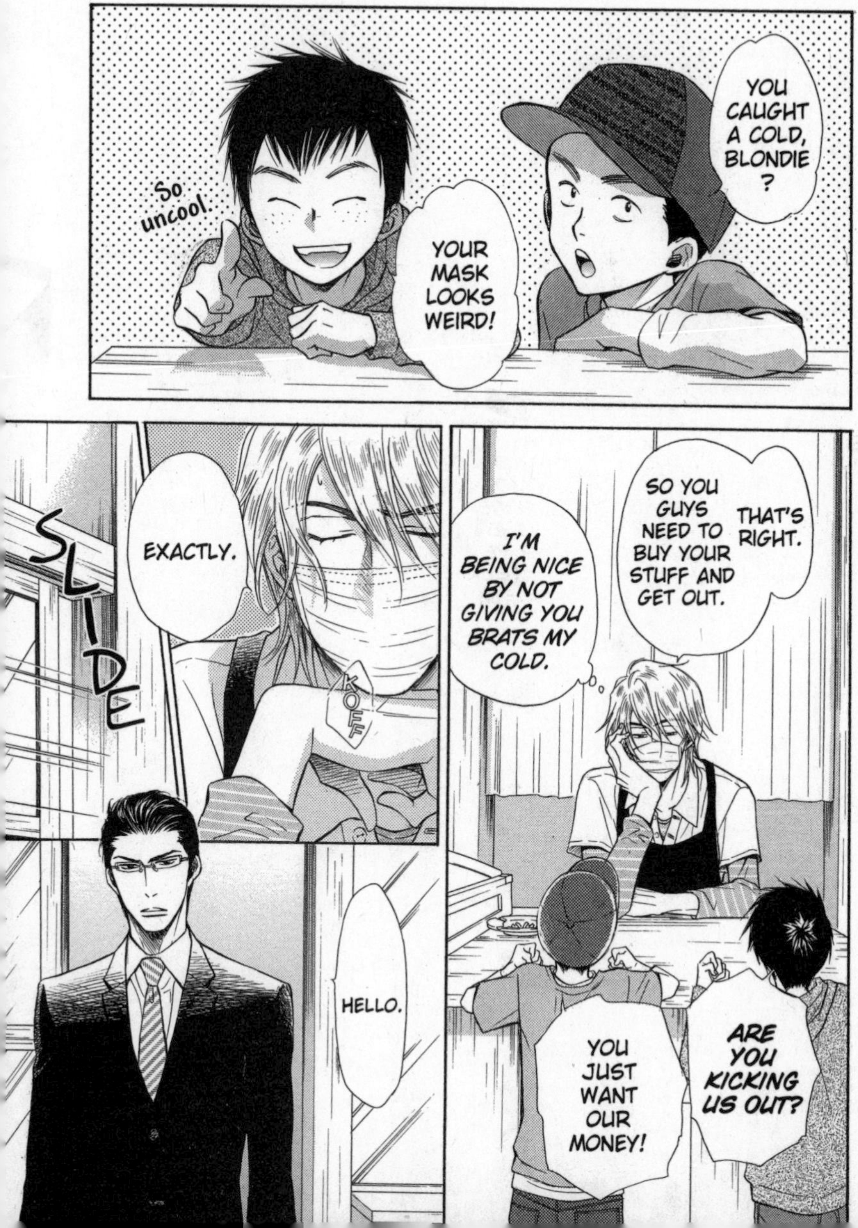
YOU CAUGHT A COLD, BLONDIE?
YOUR MASK LOOKS WEIRD!
So uncool.
THAT'S RIGHT.
SO YOU GUYS NEED TO BUY YOUR STUFF AND GET OUT.
I'M BEING NICE BY NOT GIVING YOU BRATS MY COLD.
ARE YOU KICKING US OUT?
YOU JUST WANT OUR MONEY!
EXACTLY.
KOFF
SLIDE
HELLO.

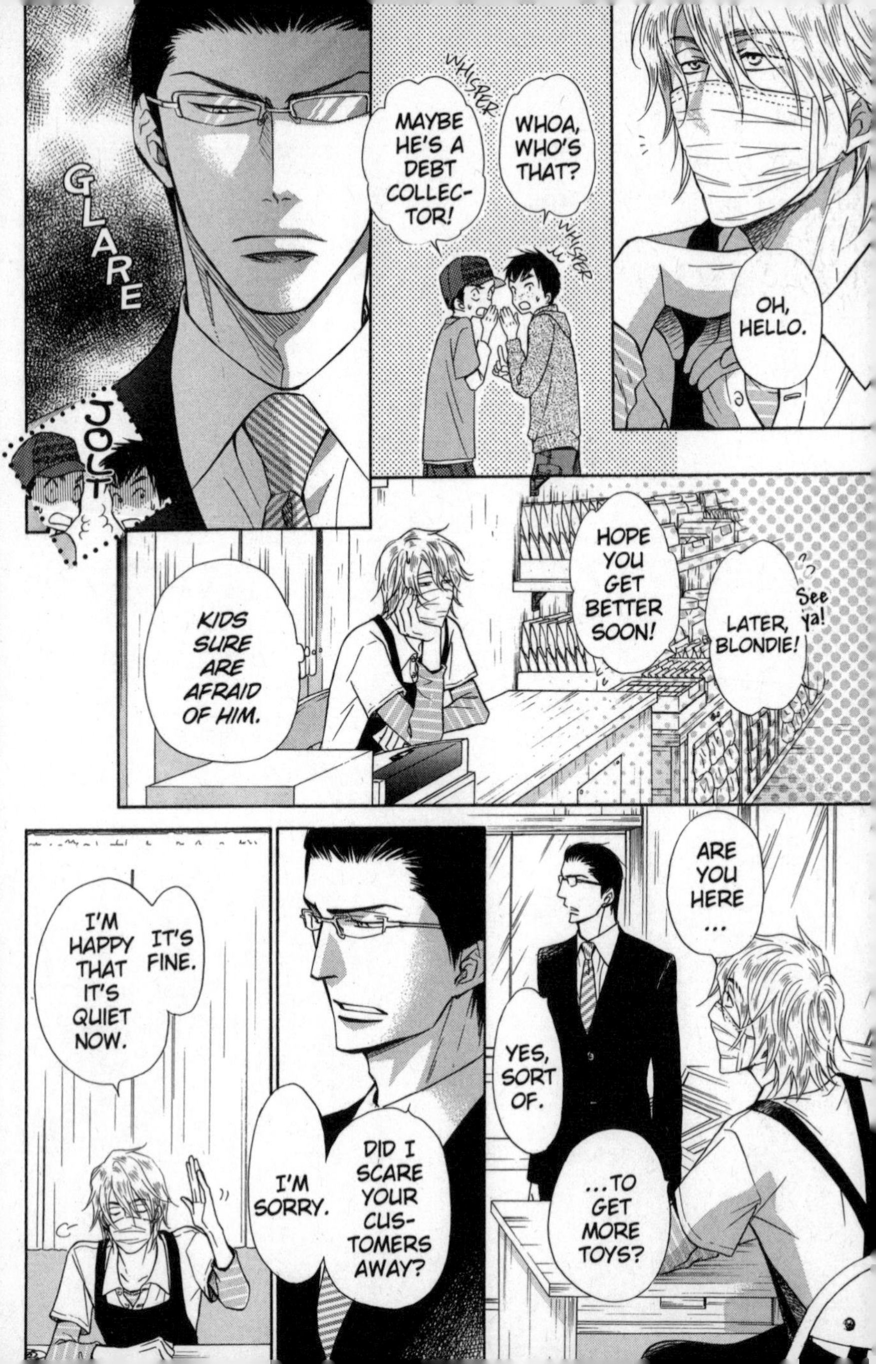
OH, HELLO.
WHISPER
WHOA, WHO'S THAT?
WHISPER
MAYBE HE'S A DEBT COLLECTOR!
GLARE
JOLT
See ya!
LATER, BLONDIE!
HOPE YOU GET BETTER SOON!
KIDS SURE ARE AFRAID OF HIM.
ARE YOU HERE...
YES, SORT OF.
...TO GET MORE TOYS?
DID I SCARE YOUR CUSTOMERS AWAY?
I'M SORRY.
IT'S FINE.
I'M HAPPY THAT IT'S QUIET NOW.

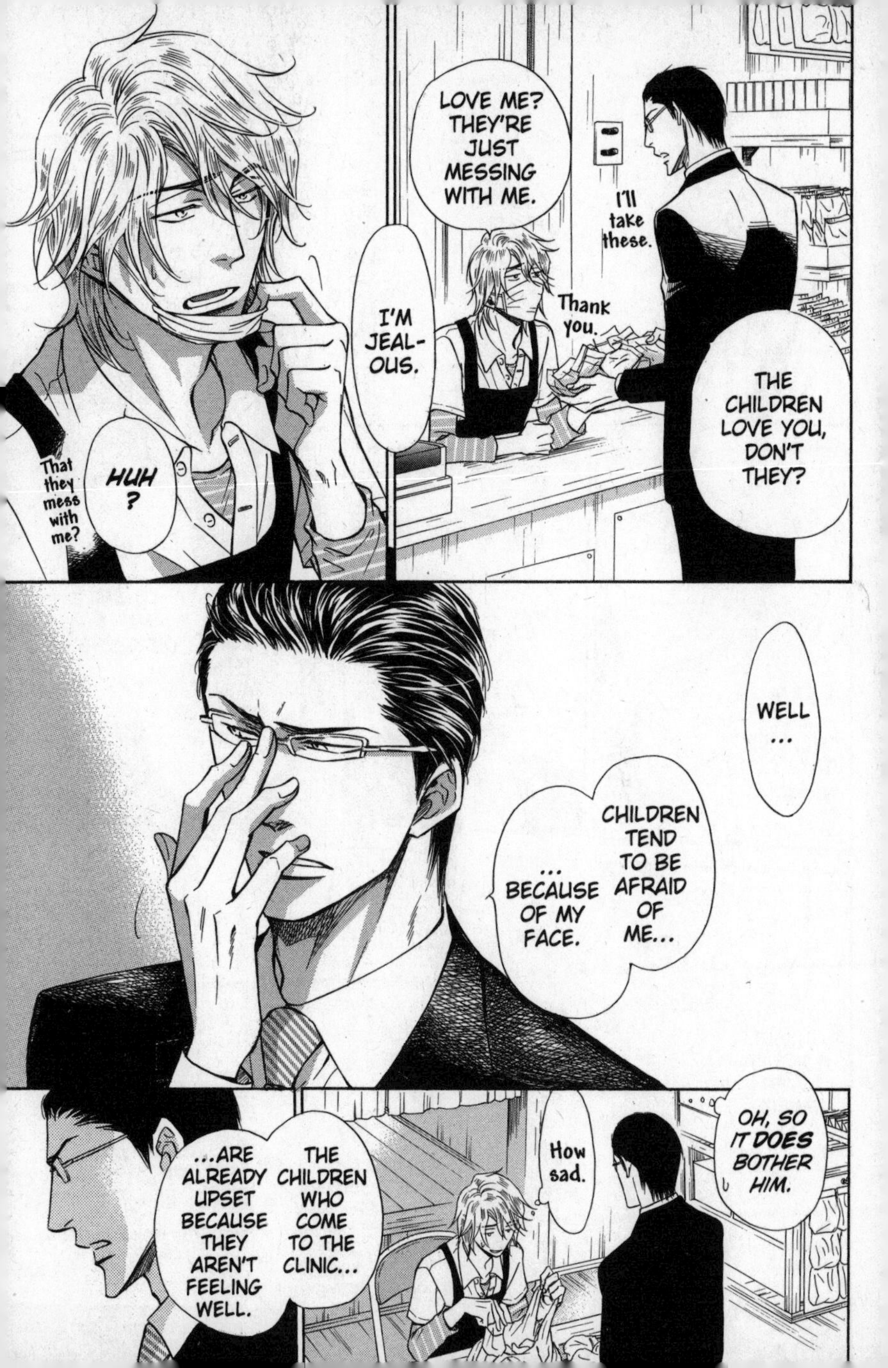
I'll take these.
Thank you.
THE CHILDREN LOVE YOU, DON'T THEY?
LOVE ME? THEY'RE JUST MESSING WITH ME.
I'M JEAL-OUS.
HUH?
That they mess with me?
WELL...
CHILDREN TEND TO BE AFRAID OF ME...
...BECAUSE OF MY FACE.
OH, SO IT DOES BOTHER HIM.
How sad.
THE CHILDREN WHO COME TO THE CLINIC...
...ARE ALREADY UPSET BECAUSE THEY AREN'T FEELING WELL.

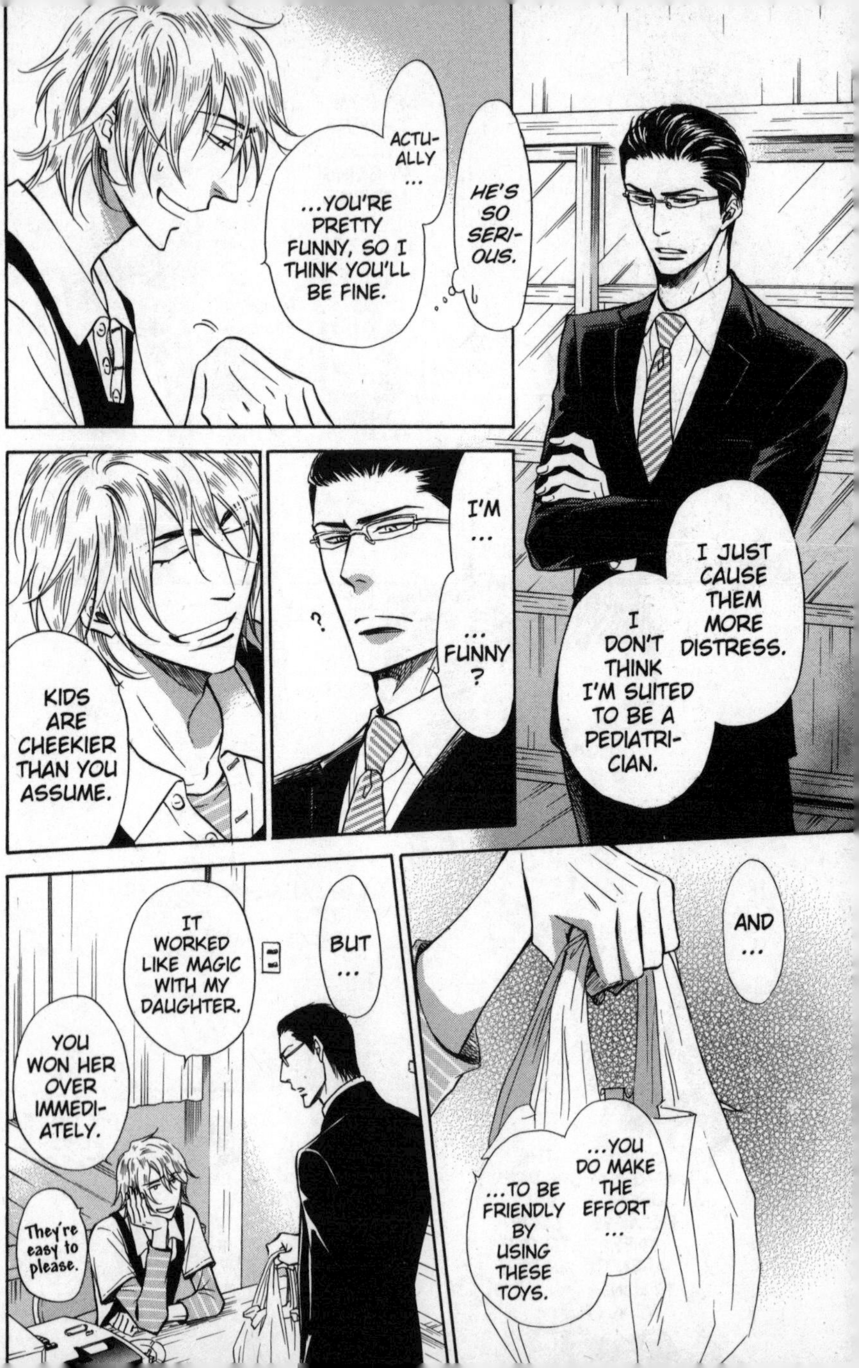
I DON'T THINK I'M SUITED TO BE A PEDIATRICIAN.
I JUST CAUSE THEM MORE DISTRESS.
HE'S SO SERIOUS.
ACTUALLY...
...YOU'RE PRETTY FUNNY, SO I THINK YOU'LL BE FINE.
I'M...
...FUNNY?
KIDS ARE CHEEKIER THAN YOU ASSUME.
AND...
...YOU DO MAKE THE EFFORT...
...TO BE FRIENDLY BY USING THESE TOYS.
BUT...
IT WORKED LIKE MAGIC WITH MY DAUGHTER.
YOU WON HER OVER IMMEDIATELY.
They're easy to please.

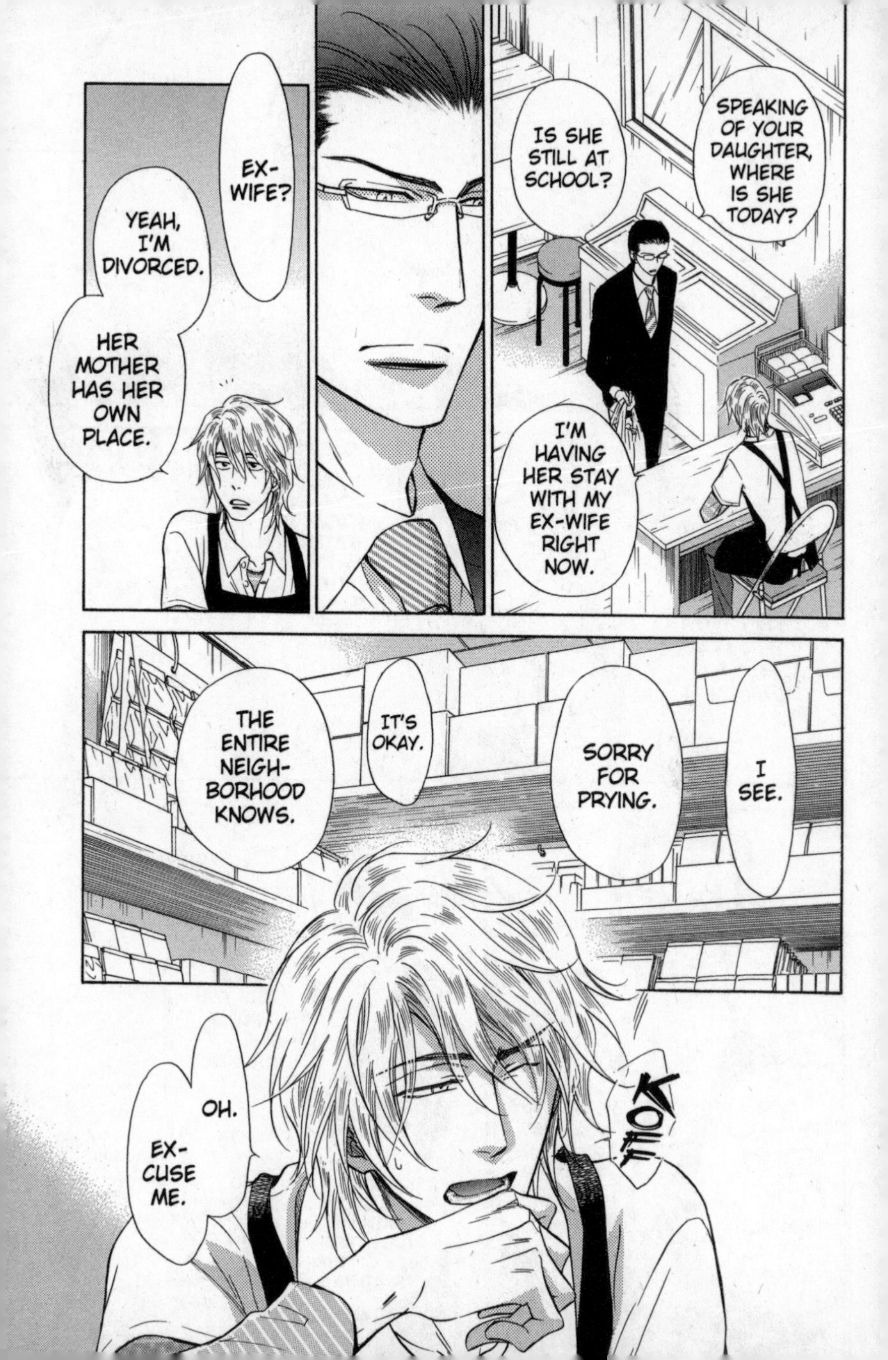
SPEAKING OF YOUR DAUGHTER, WHERE IS SHE TODAY?
IS SHE STILL AT SCHOOL?
I'M HAVING HER STAY WITH MY EX-WIFE RIGHT NOW.
EX-WIFE?
YEAH, I'M DIVORCED.
HER MOTHER HAS HER OWN PLACE.
I SEE.
SORRY FOR PRYING.
IT'S OKAY.
THE ENTIRE NEIGH-BORHOOD KNOWS.
KOFF
OH.
EX-CUSE ME.

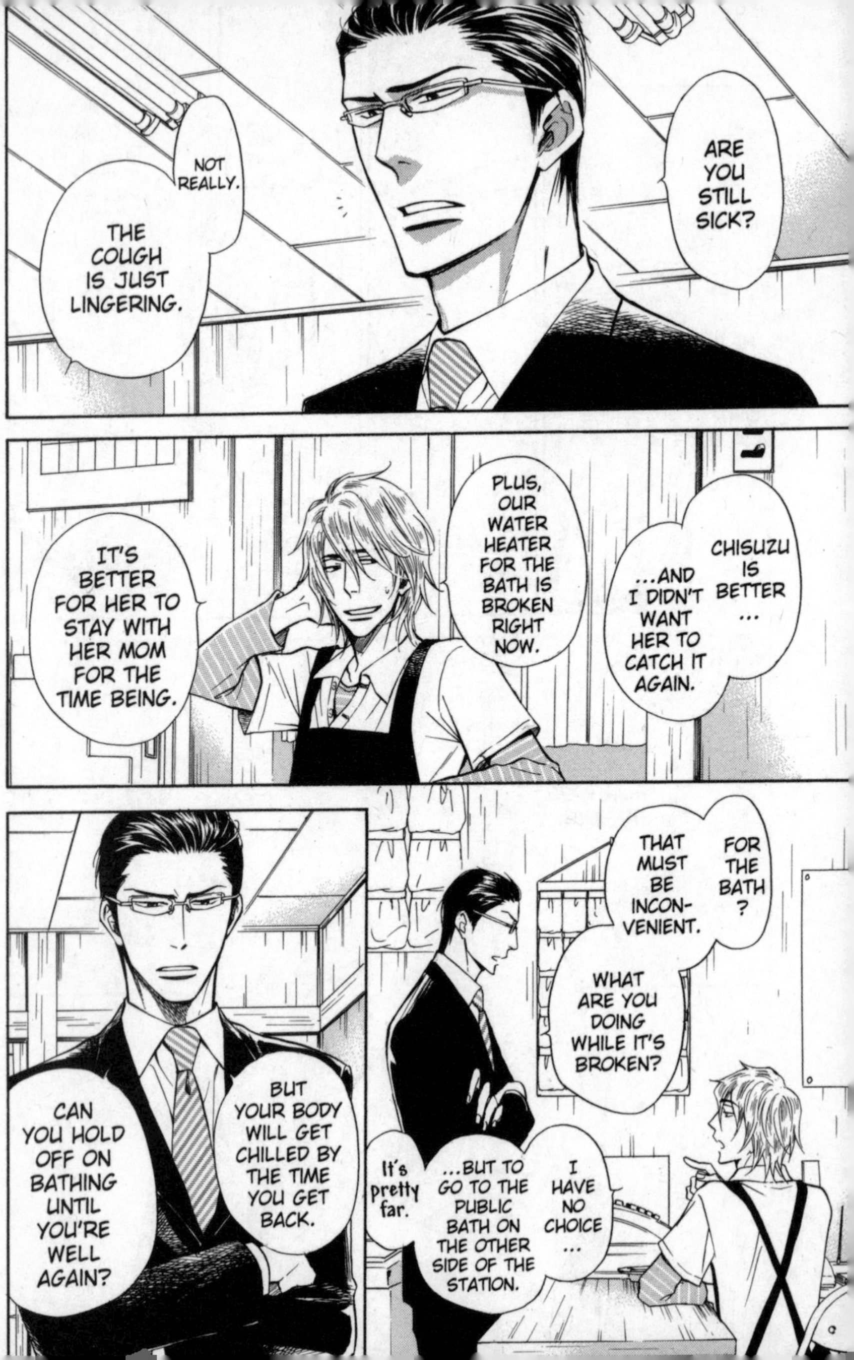
ARE YOU STILL SICK?
NOT REALLY.
THE COUGH IS JUST LINGERING.
CHISUZU IS BETTER...
...AND I DIDN'T WANT HER TO CATCH IT AGAIN.
PLUS, OUR WATER HEATER FOR THE BATH IS BROKEN RIGHT NOW.
IT'S BETTER FOR HER TO STAY WITH HER MOM FOR THE TIME BEING.
FOR THE BATH?
THAT MUST BE INCONVENIENT.
WHAT ARE YOU DOING WHILE IT'S BROKEN?
I HAVE NO CHOICE...
...BUT TO GO TO THE PUBLIC BATH ON THE OTHER SIDE OF THE STATION.
It's pretty far.
BUT YOUR BODY WILL GET CHILLED BY THE TIME YOU GET BACK.
CAN YOU HOLD OFF ON BATHING UNTIL YOU'RE WELL AGAIN?

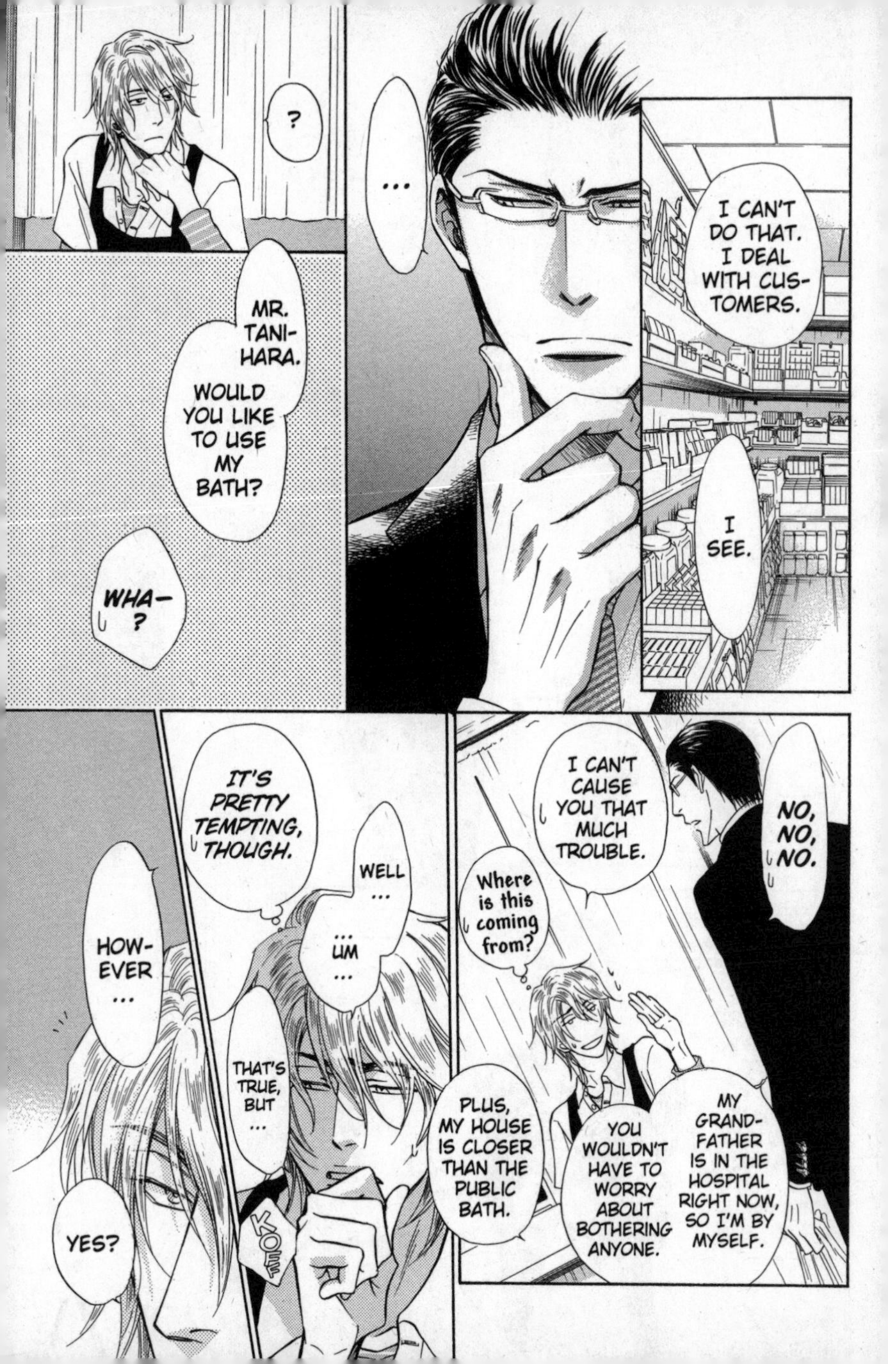
I CAN'T DO THAT. I DEAL WITH CUS-TOMERS.
I SEE.
...
?
MR. TANI-HARA.
WOULD YOU LIKE TO USE MY BATH?
WHA—?
NO, NO, NO.
I CAN'T CAUSE YOU THAT MUCH TROUBLE.
Where is this coming from?
MY GRAND-FATHER IS IN THE HOSPITAL RIGHT NOW, SO I'M BY MYSELF.
YOU WOULDN'T HAVE TO WORRY ABOUT BOTHERING ANYONE.
PLUS, MY HOUSE IS CLOSER THAN THE PUBLIC BATH.
IT'S PRETTY TEMPTING, THOUGH.
WELL ...
... UM ...
THAT'S TRUE, BUT ...
KOFF
HOW-EVER ...
YES?

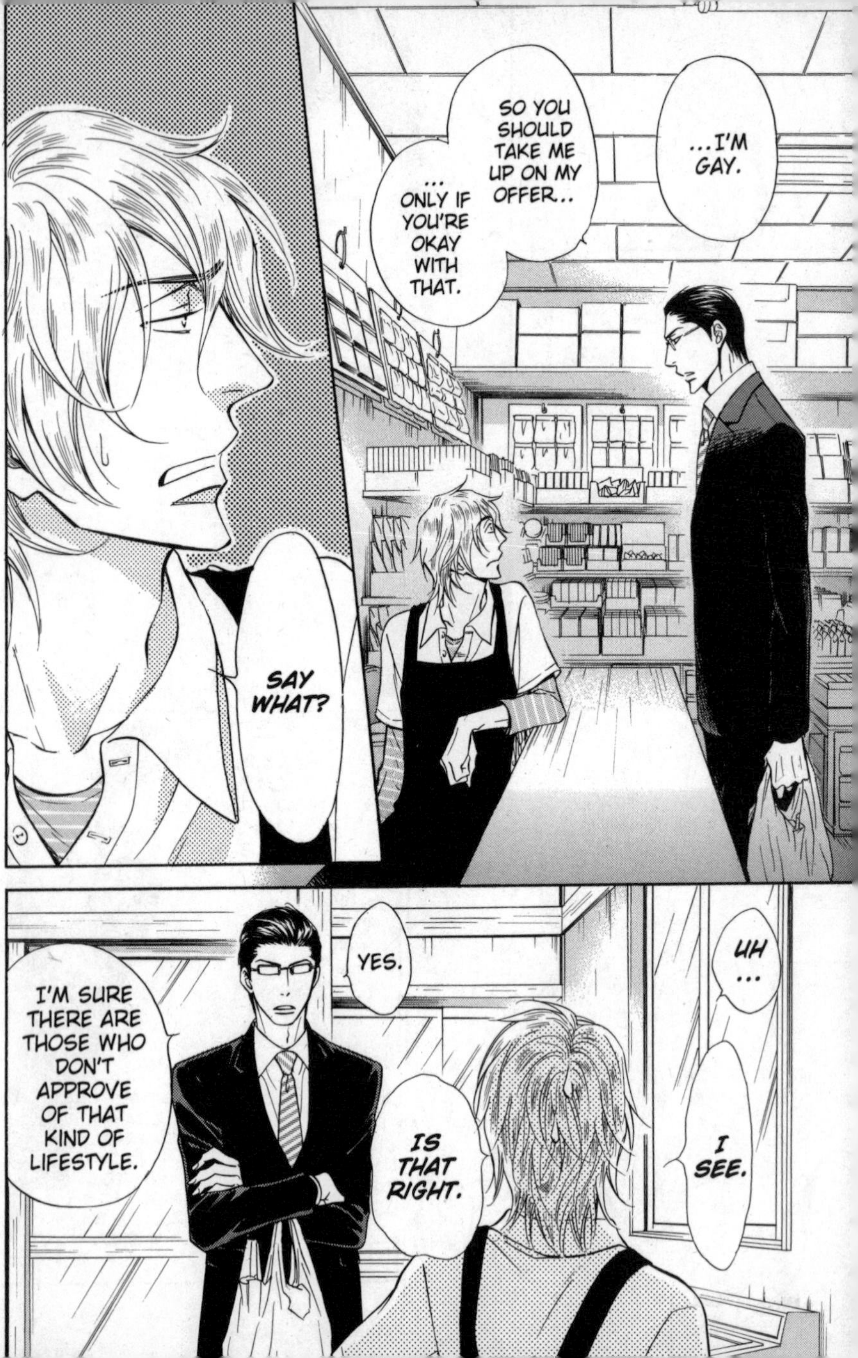
...I'M GAY.
SO YOU SHOULD TAKE ME UP ON MY OFFER...
...ONLY IF YOU'RE OKAY WITH THAT.
SAY WHAT?
UH ...
I SEE.
IS THAT RIGHT.
YES.
I'M SURE THERE ARE THOSE WHO DON'T APPROVE OF THAT KIND OF LIFESTYLE.

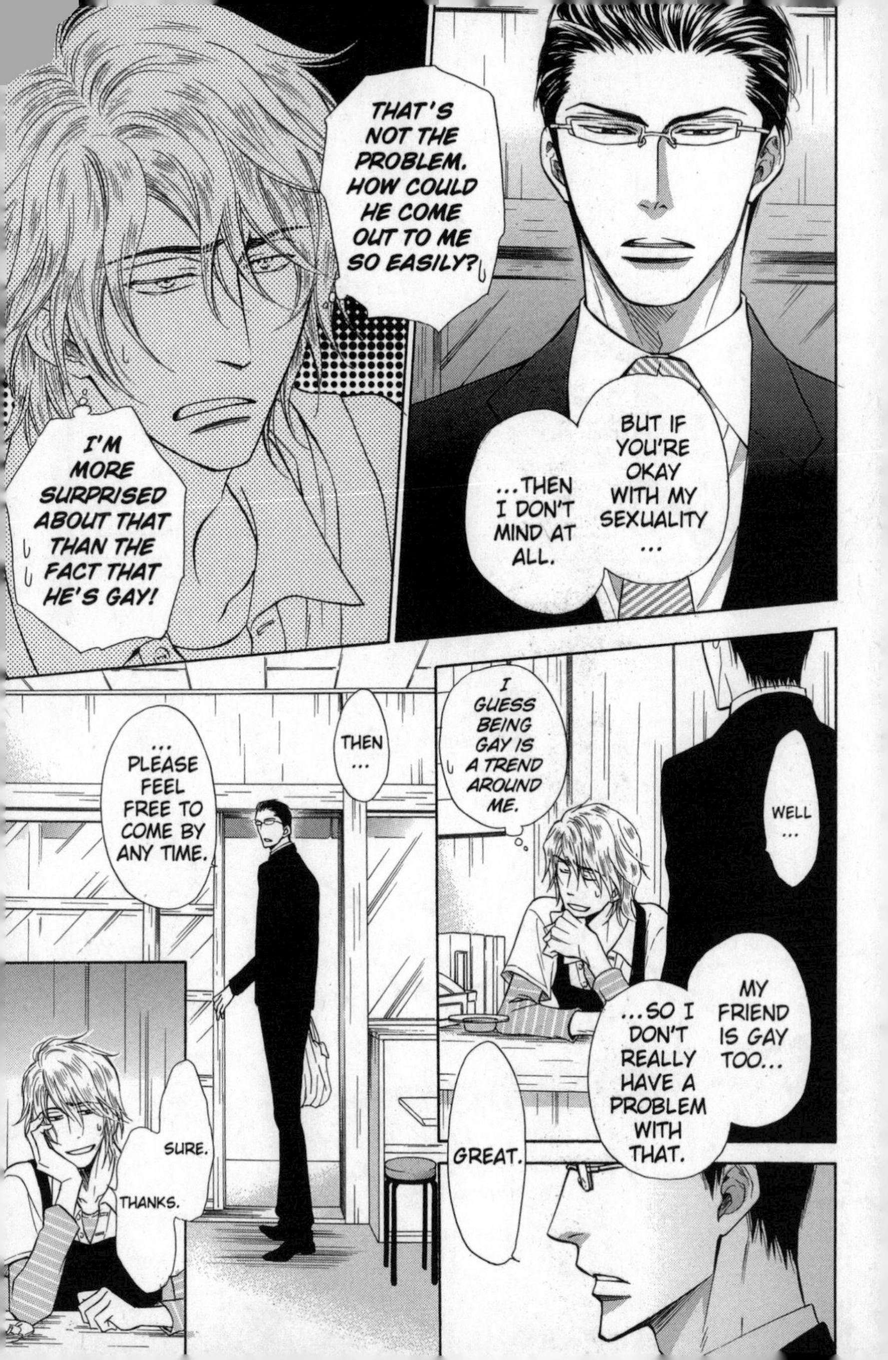
BUT IF YOU'RE OKAY WITH MY SEXUALITY...
...THEN I DON'T MIND AT ALL.
THAT'S NOT THE PROBLEM. HOW COULD HE COME OUT TO ME SO EASILY?
I'M MORE SURPRISED ABOUT THAT THAN THE FACT THAT HE'S GAY!
WELL...
MY FRIEND IS GAY TOO...
...SO I DON'T REALLY HAVE A PROBLEM WITH THAT.
I GUESS BEING GAY IS A TREND AROUND ME.
GREAT.
THEN...
...PLEASE FEEL FREE TO COME BY ANY TIME.
SURE.
THANKS.

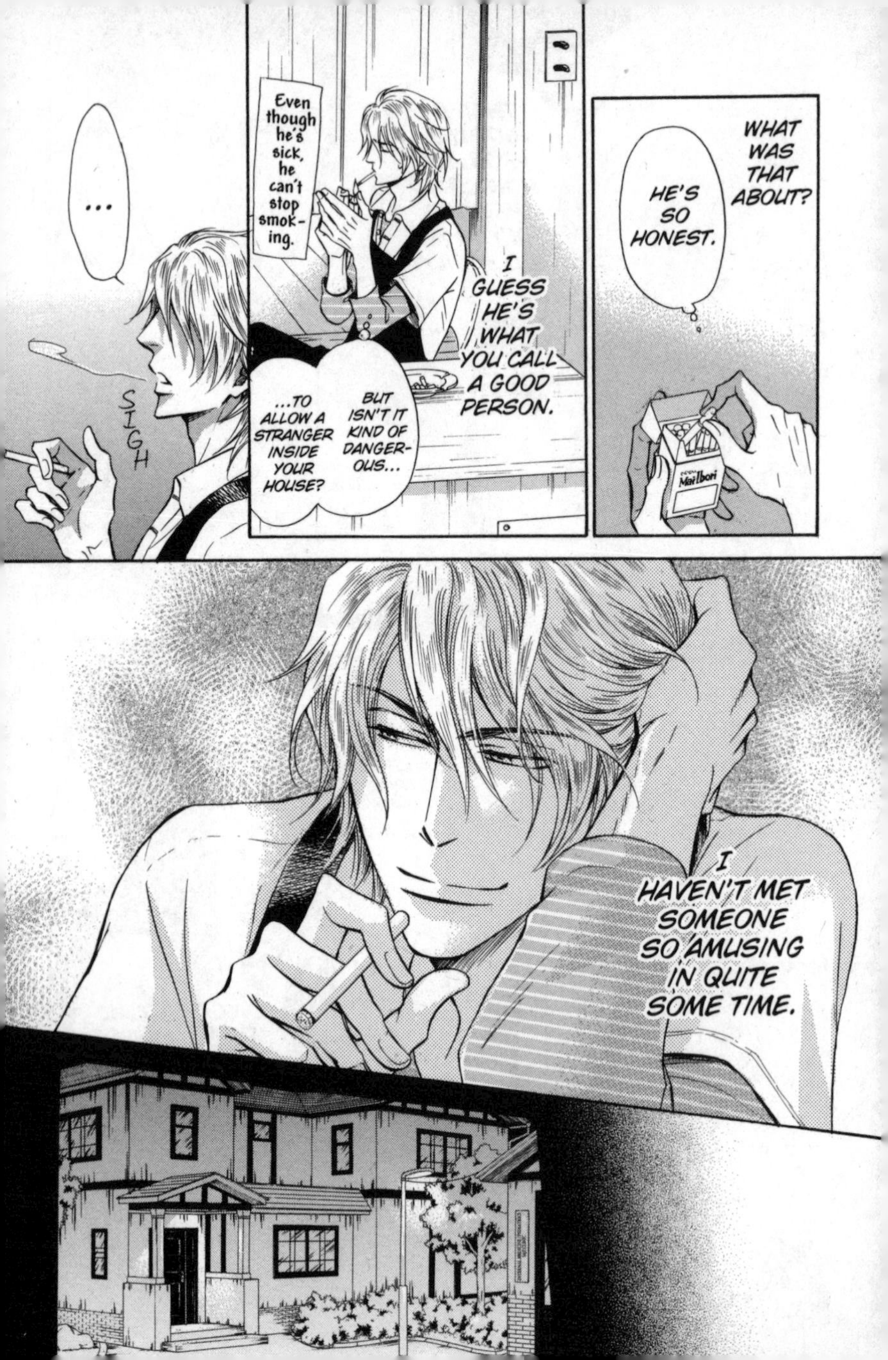
WHAT WAS THAT ABOUT?
HE'S SO HONEST.
Even though he's sick, he can't stop smoking.
I GUESS HE'S WHAT YOU CALL A GOOD PERSON.
BUT ISN'T IT KIND OF DANGEROUS...
...TO ALLOW A STRANGER INSIDE YOUR HOUSE?
...
SIGH
I HAVEN'T MET SOMEONE SO AMUSING IN QUITE SOME TIME.

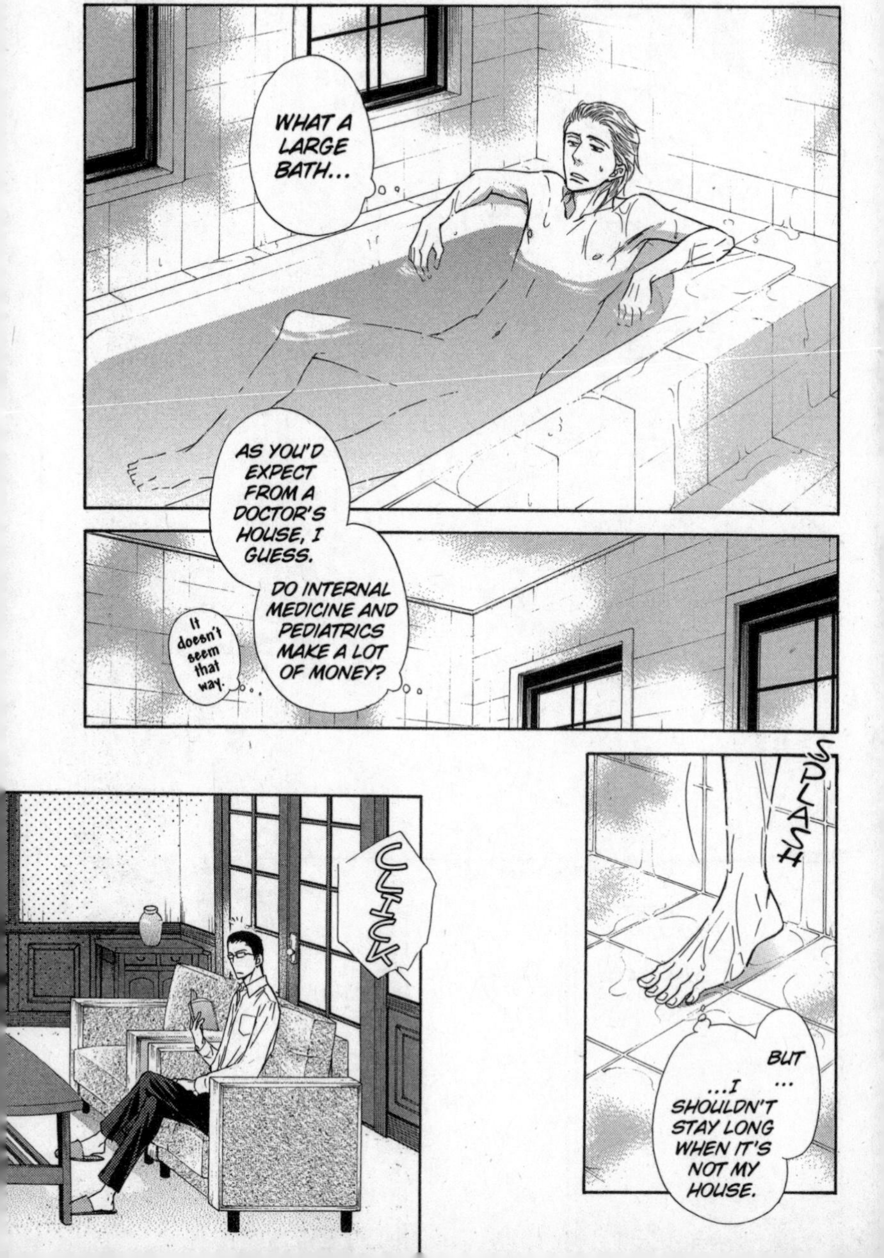
WHAT A LARGE BATH...
AS YOU'D EXPECT FROM A DOCTOR'S HOUSE, I GUESS.
DO INTERNAL MEDICINE AND PEDIATRICS MAKE A LOT OF MONEY?
It doesn't seem that way.
SPLASH
BUT... ...I SHOULDN'T STAY LONG WHEN IT'S NOT MY HOUSE.
CLICK

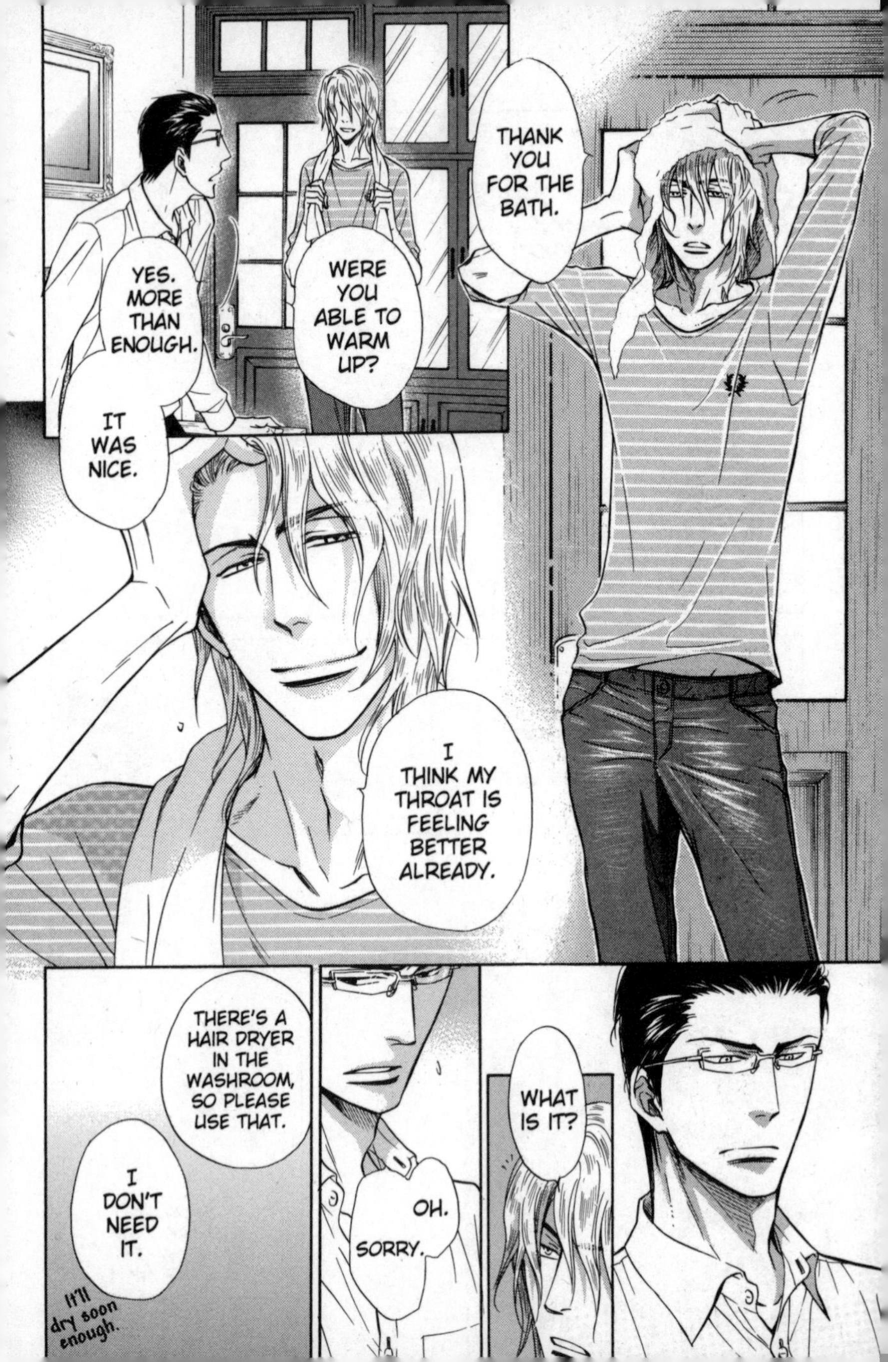
THANK YOU FOR THE BATH.
WERE YOU ABLE TO WARM UP?
YES. MORE THAN ENOUGH.
IT WAS NICE.
I THINK MY THROAT IS FEELING BETTER ALREADY.
WHAT IS IT?
OH.
SORRY.
THERE'S A HAIR DRYER IN THE WASHROOM, SO PLEASE USE THAT.
I DON'T NEED IT.
It'll dry soon enough.

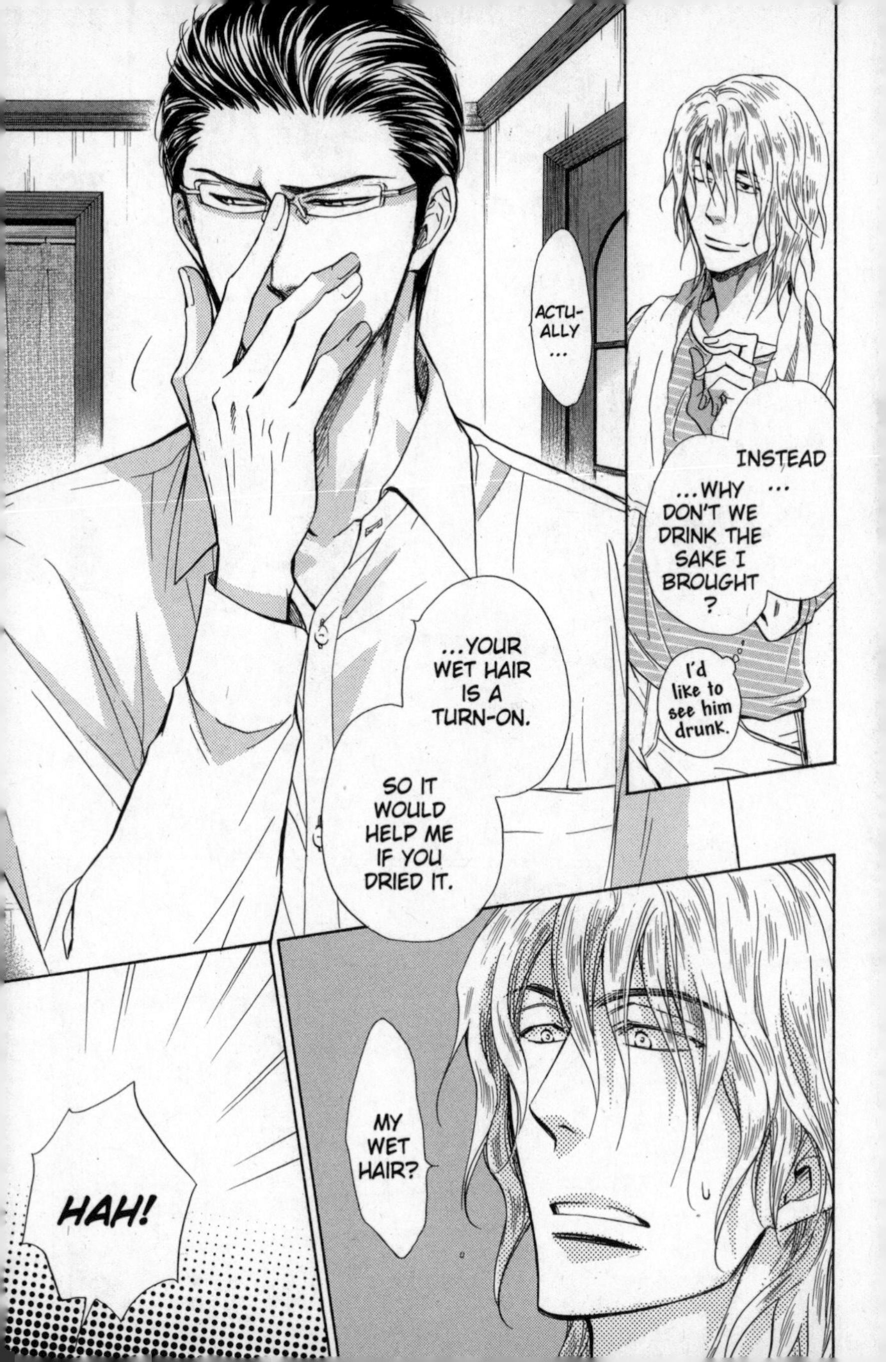
INSTEAD...
...WHY DON'T WE DRINK THE SAKE I BROUGHT?
I'd like to see him drunk.
ACTU-ALLY...
...YOUR WET HAIR IS A TURN-ON.
SO IT WOULD HELP ME IF YOU DRIED IT.
MY WET HAIR?
HAH!

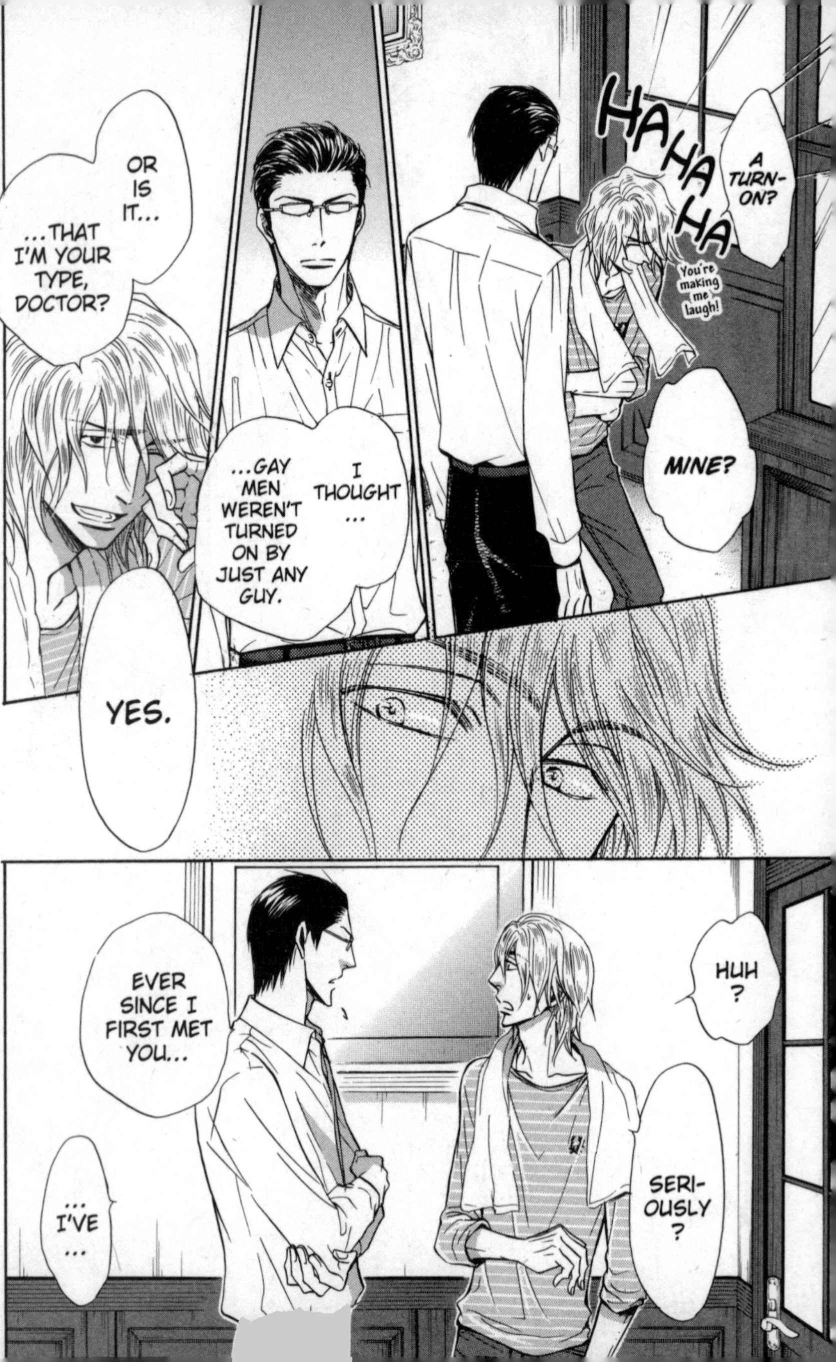
A TURN-ON?
HAHAHA
You're making me laugh!
MINE?
I THOUGHT...
...GAY MEN WEREN'T TURNED ON BY JUST ANY GUY.
OR IS IT...
...THAT I'M YOUR TYPE, DOCTOR?
YES.
HUH?
SERIOUSLY?
EVER SINCE I FIRST MET YOU...
...I'VE...

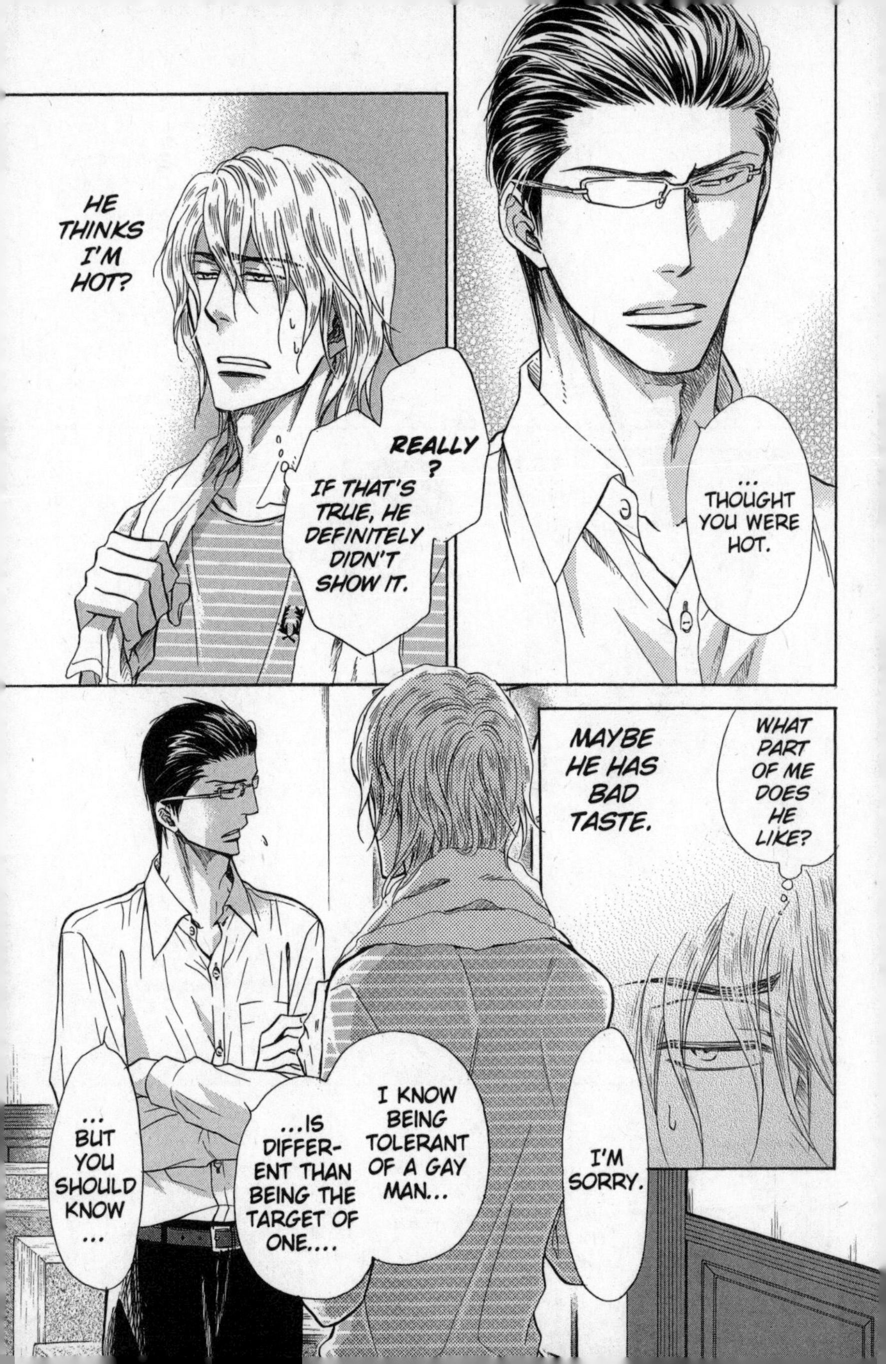

...THOUGHT YOU WERE HOT.
HE THINKS I'M HOT?
REALLY? IF THAT'S TRUE, HE DEFINITELY DIDN'T SHOW IT.
WHAT PART OF ME DOES HE LIKE?
MAYBE HE HAS BAD TASTE.
I'M SORRY.
I KNOW BEING TOLERANT OF A GAY MAN...
...IS DIFFER-ENT THAN BEING THE TARGET OF ONE....
...BUT YOU SHOULD KNOW...

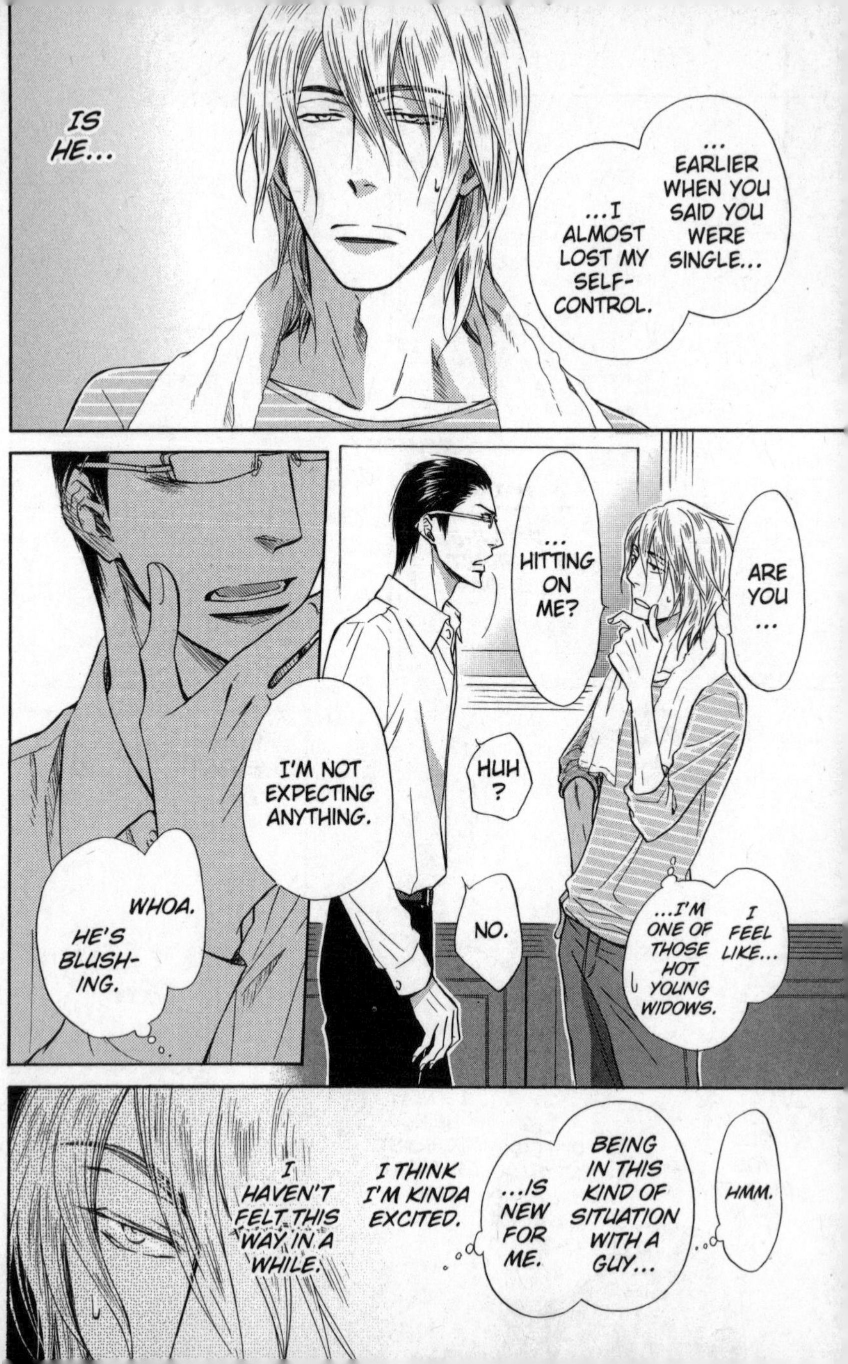
... EARLIER WHEN YOU SAID YOU WERE SINGLE... ...I ALMOST LOST MY SELF-CONTROL.
IS HE...
ARE YOU ...
... HITTING ON ME?
I FEEL LIKE... ...I'M ONE OF THOSE HOT YOUNG WIDOWS.
HUH?
NO.
I'M NOT EXPECTING ANYTHING.
WHOA. HE'S BLUSH-ING.
HMM.
BEING IN THIS KIND OF SITUATION WITH A GUY...
...IS NEW FOR ME.
I THINK I'M KINDA EXCITED.
I HAVEN'T FELT THIS WAY IN A WHILE.

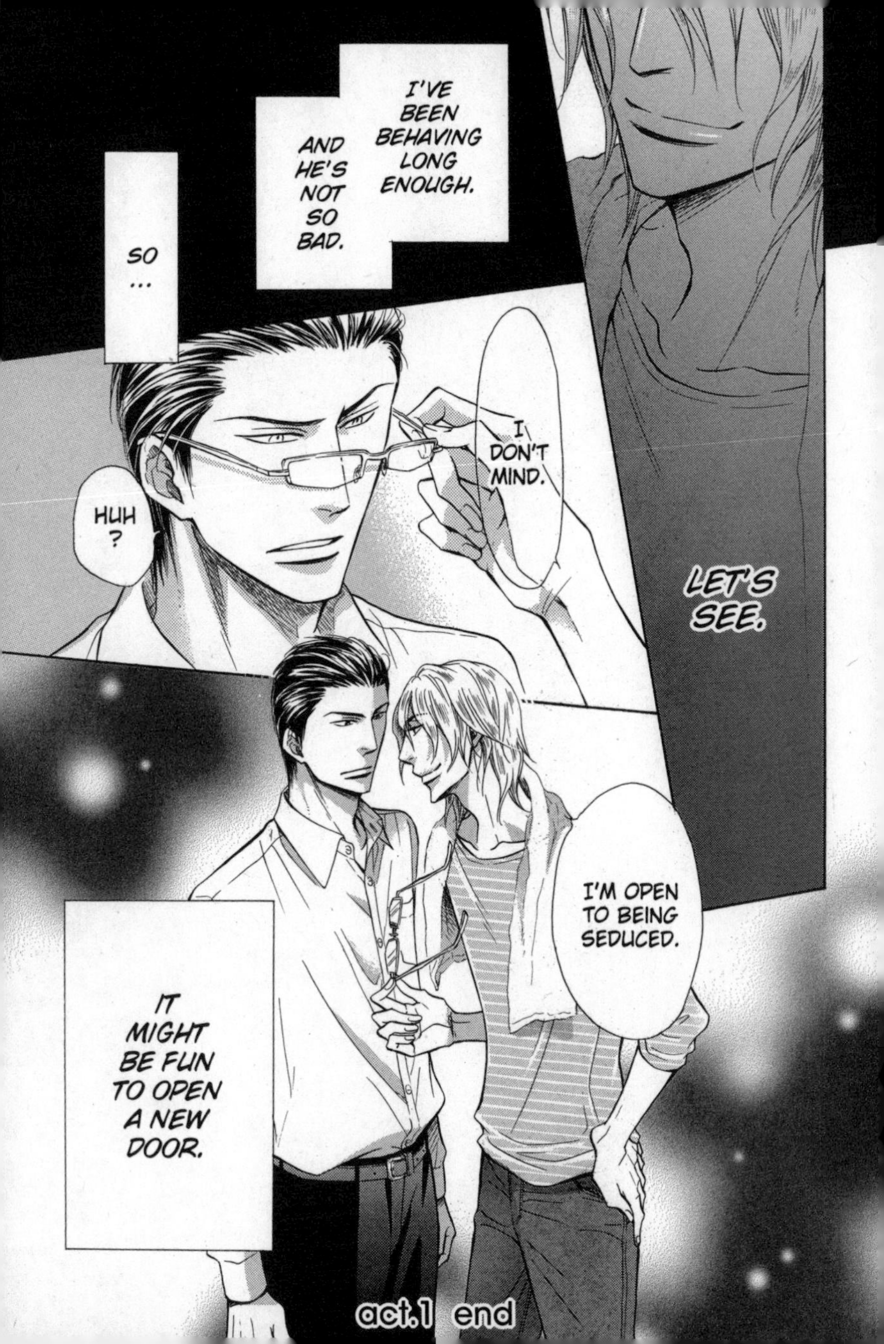
I'VE BEEN BEHAVING LONG ENOUGH.
AND HE'S NOT SO BAD.
SO ...
I DON'T MIND.
HUH?
LET'S SEE.
I'M OPEN TO BEING SEDUCED.
IT MIGHT BE FUN TO OPEN A NEW DOOR.
act.1 end

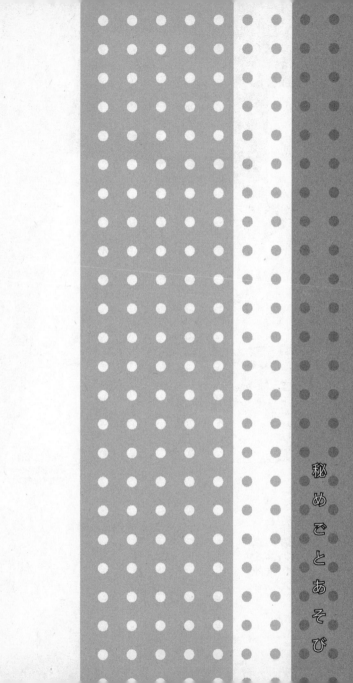

秘めごとあそび

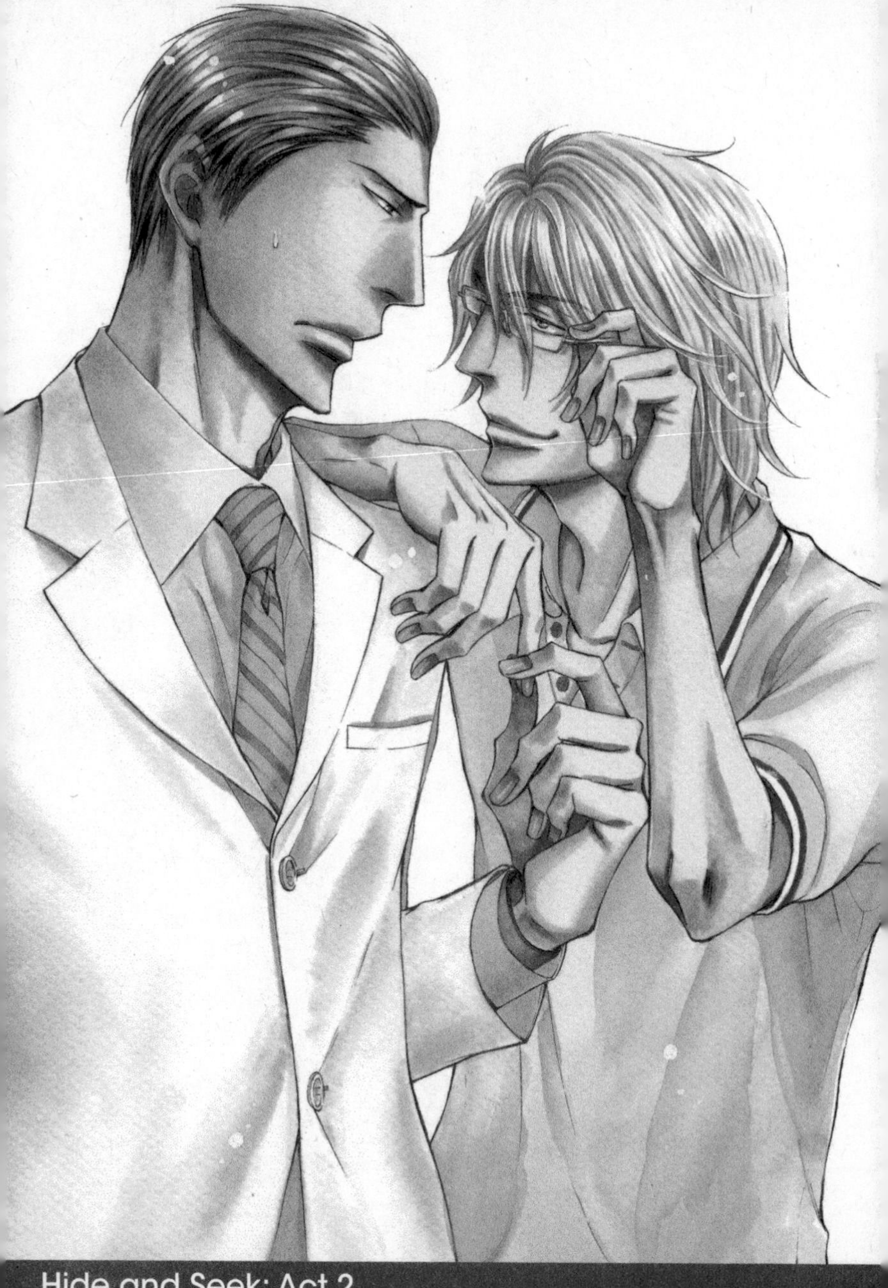

Hide and Seek: Act 2

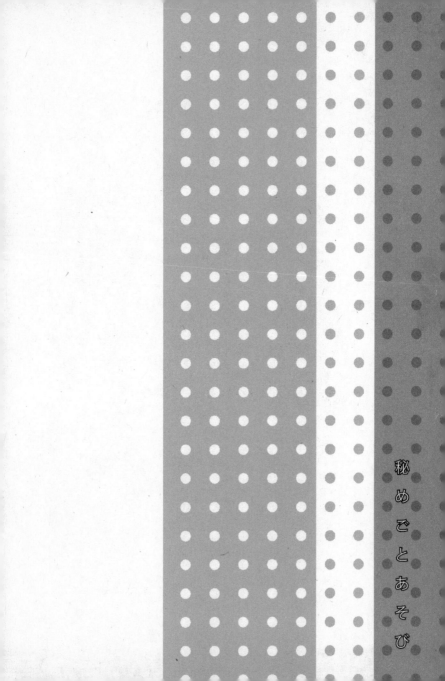

秘めごとあそび

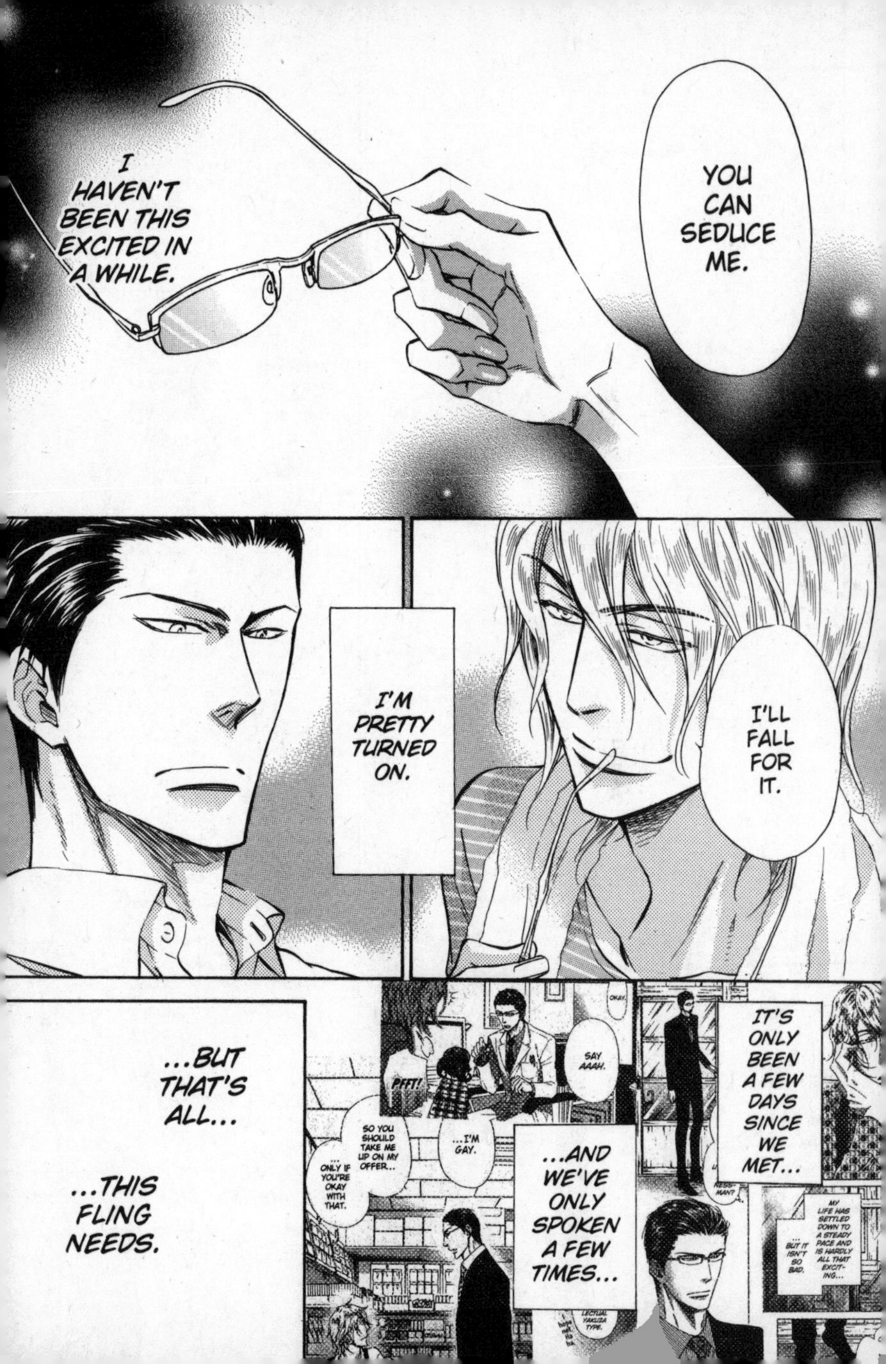
YOU CAN SEDUCE ME.
I HAVEN'T BEEN THIS EXCITED IN A WHILE.
I'LL FALL FOR IT.
I'M PRETTY TURNED ON.
IT'S ONLY BEEN A FEW DAYS SINCE WE MET...
MY LIFE HAS SETTLED DOWN TO A STEADY PACE AND IS HARDLY ALL THAT EXCITING...
...BUT IT ISN'T SO BAD.
...AND WE'VE ONLY SPOKEN A FEW TIMES...
OKAY.
SAY AAAH.
PFFT!
...I'M GAY.
SO YOU SHOULD TAKE ME UP ON MY OFFER...
...ONLY IF YOU'RE OKAY WITH THAT.
...BUT THAT'S ALL...
...THIS FLING NEEDS.

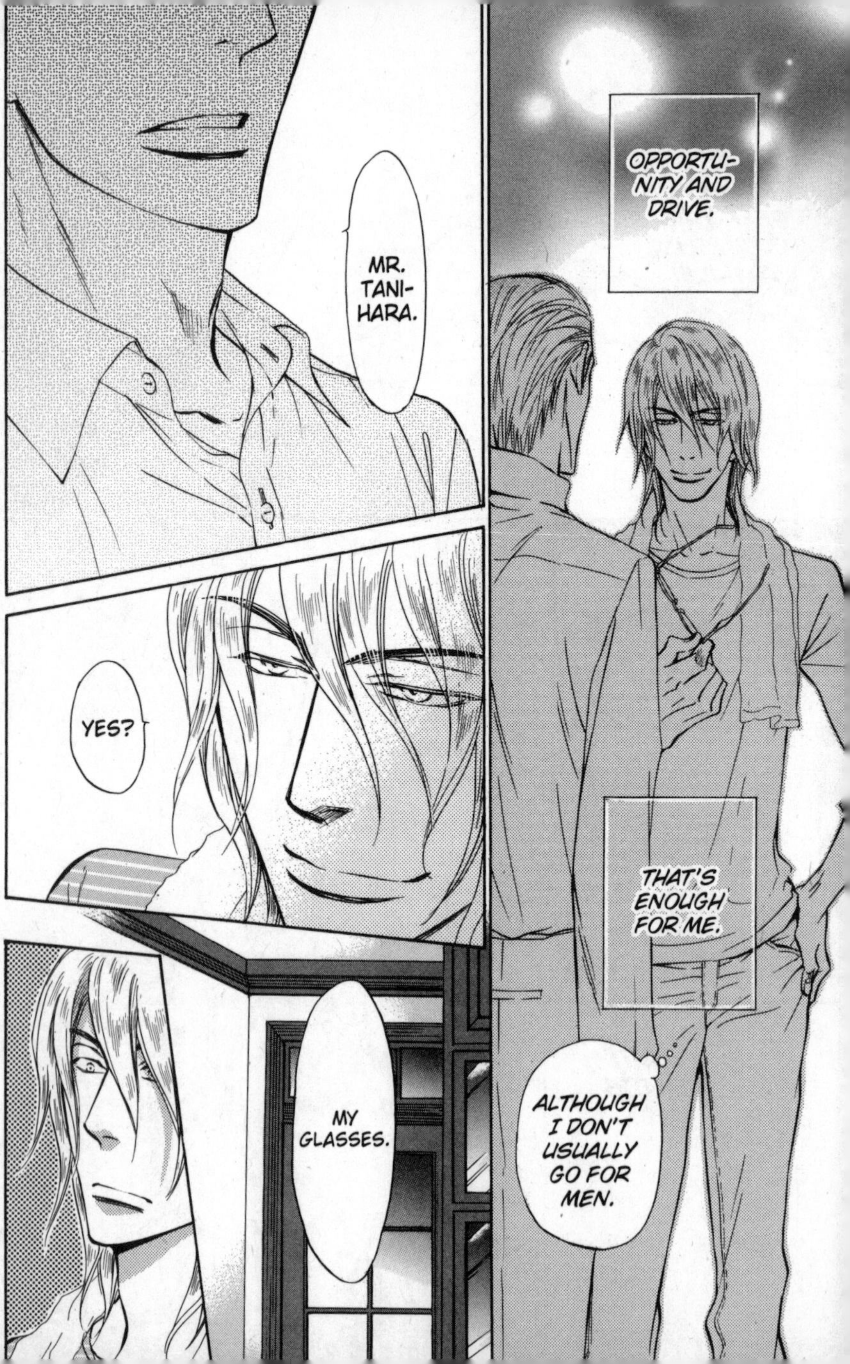
OPPORTUNITY AND DRIVE.
THAT'S ENOUGH FOR ME.
ALTHOUGH I DON'T USUALLY GO FOR MEN.
MR. TANIHARA.
YES?
MY GLASSES.

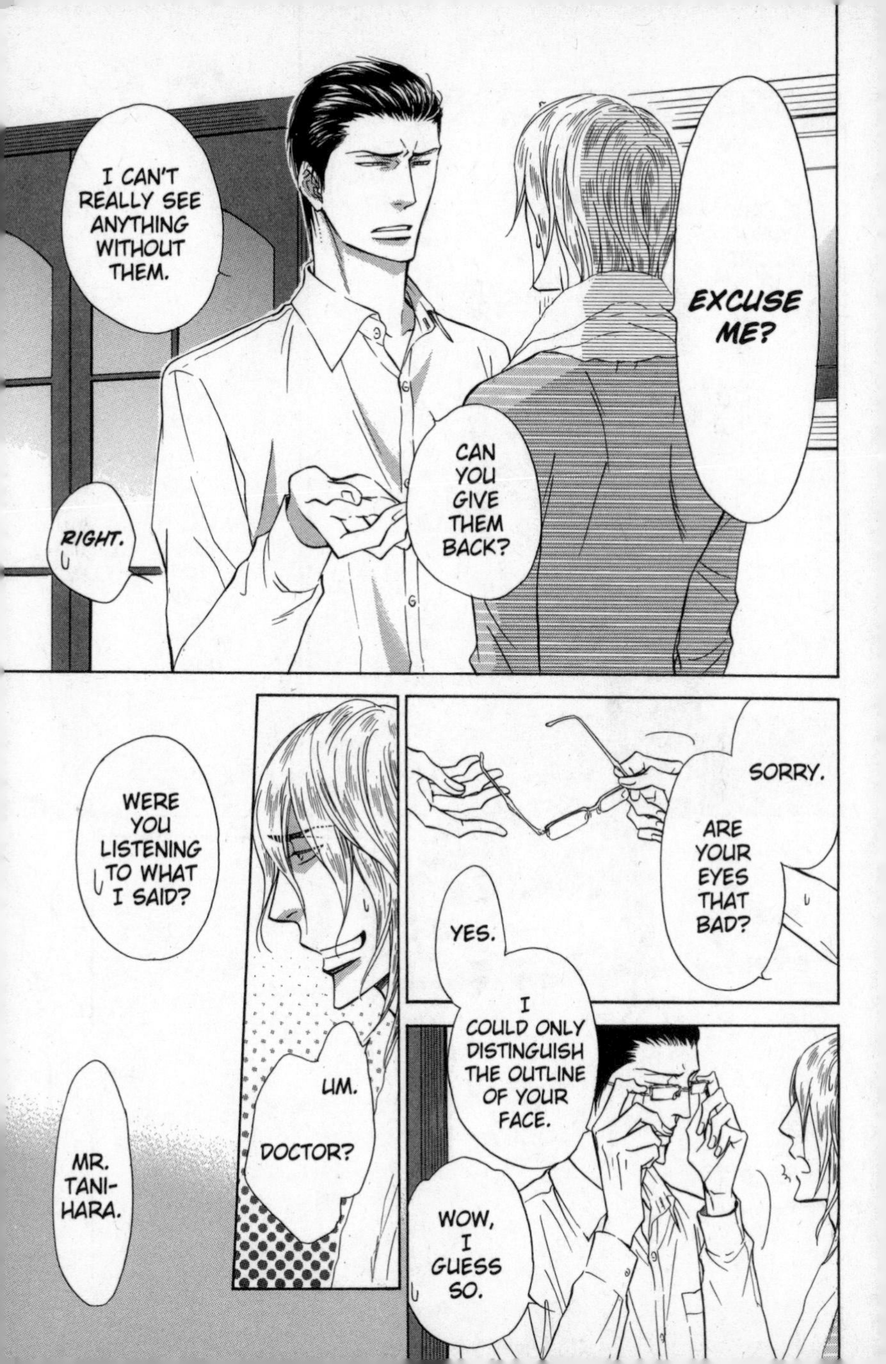
EXCUSE ME?
I CAN'T REALLY SEE ANYTHING WITHOUT THEM.
CAN YOU GIVE THEM BACK?
RIGHT.
SORRY.
ARE YOUR EYES THAT BAD?
YES.
I COULD ONLY DISTINGUISH THE OUTLINE OF YOUR FACE.
WOW, I GUESS SO.
WERE YOU LISTENING TO WHAT I SAID?
UM.
DOCTOR?
MR. TANI-HARA.

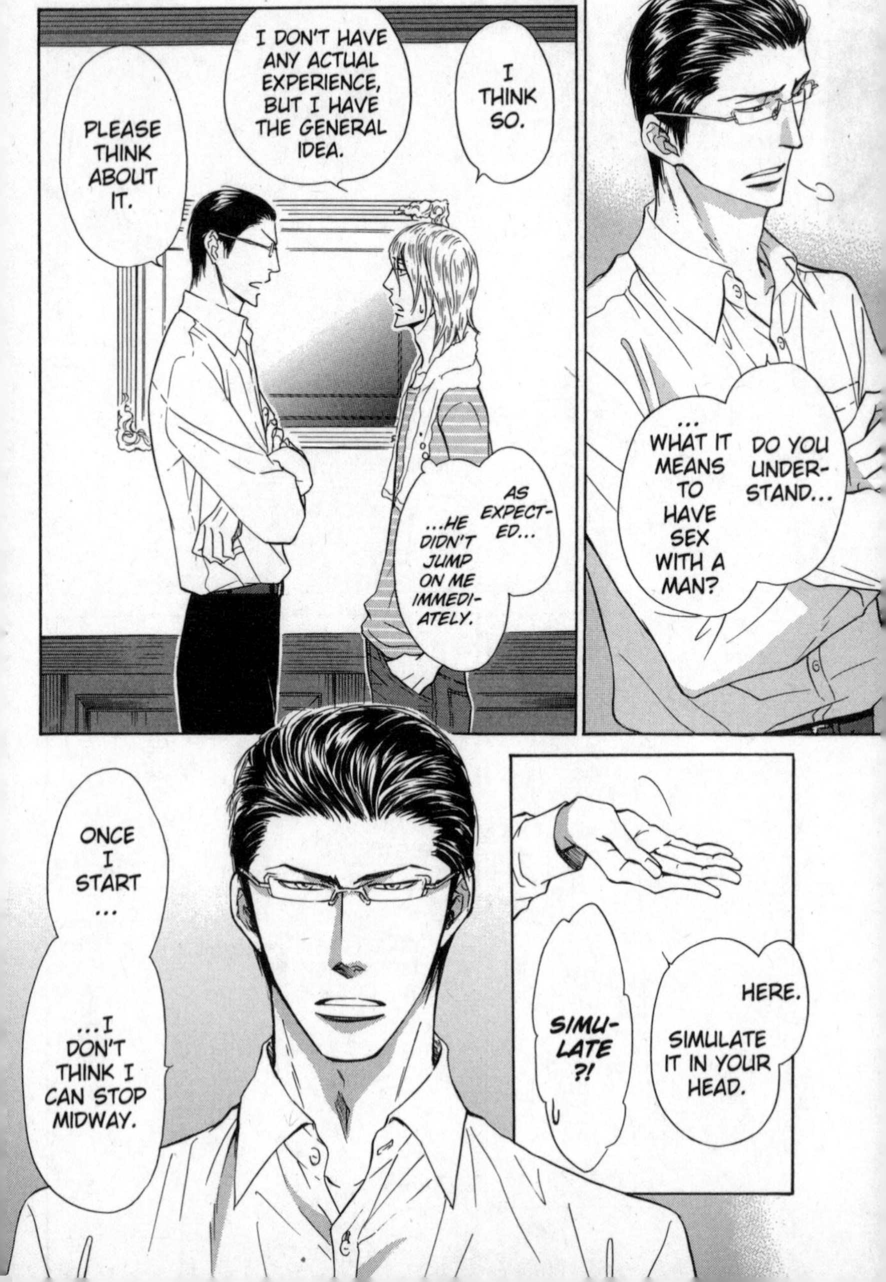
DO YOU UNDERSTAND...
...WHAT IT MEANS TO HAVE SEX WITH A MAN?
I THINK SO.
I DON'T HAVE ANY ACTUAL EXPERIENCE, BUT I HAVE THE GENERAL IDEA.
PLEASE THINK ABOUT IT.
AS EXPECTED...
...HE DIDN'T JUMP ON ME IMMEDIATELY.
HERE.
SIMULATE IT IN YOUR HEAD.
SIMULATE?!
ONCE I START...
...I DON'T THINK I CAN STOP MIDWAY.

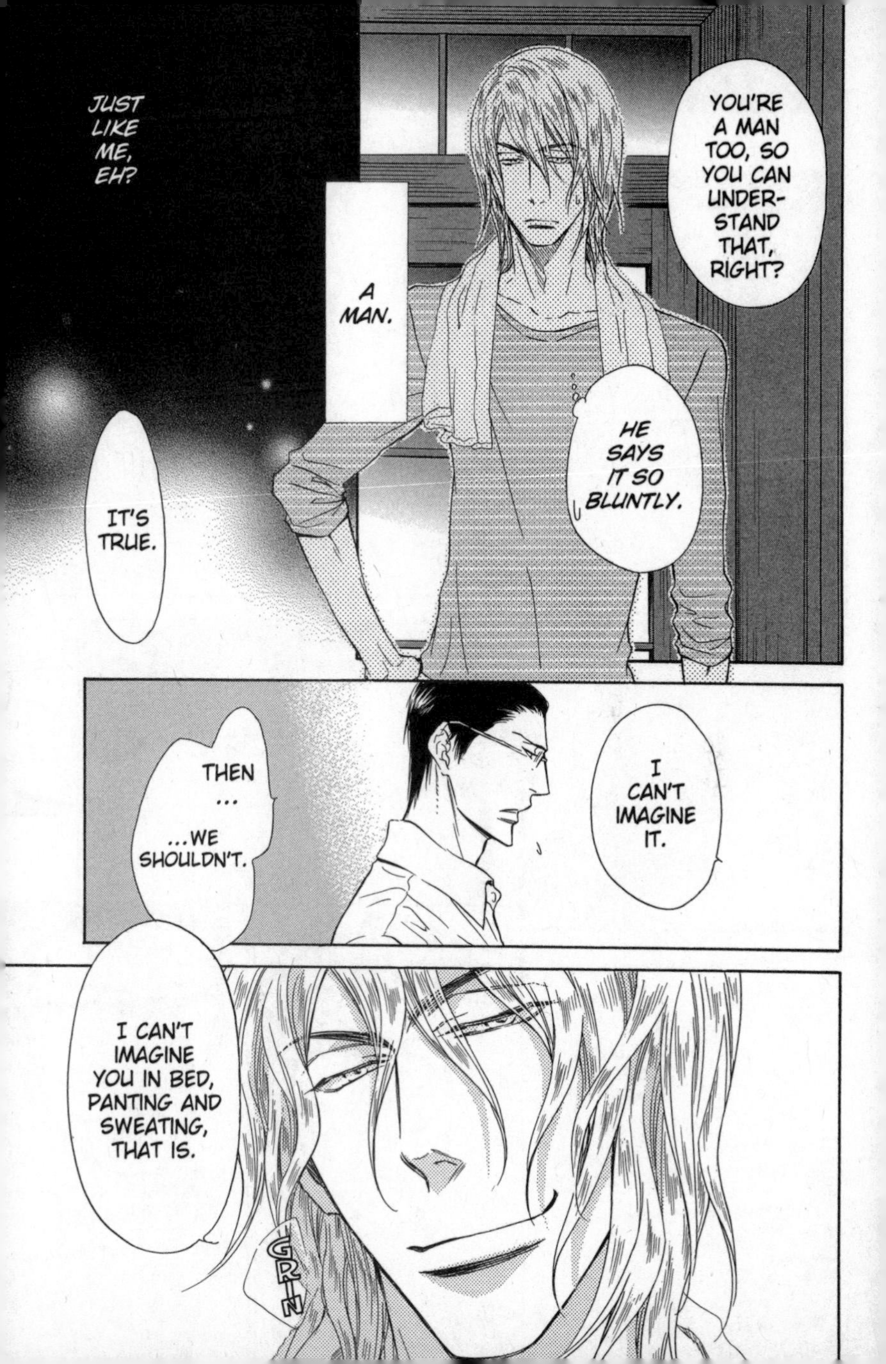
YOU'RE A MAN TOO, SO YOU CAN UNDER-STAND THAT, RIGHT?
JUST LIKE ME, EH?
A MAN.
HE SAYS IT SO BLUNTLY.
IT'S TRUE.
I CAN'T IMAGINE IT.
THEN ...
...WE SHOULDN'T.
I CAN'T IMAGINE YOU IN BED, PANTING AND SWEATING, THAT IS.
GRIN

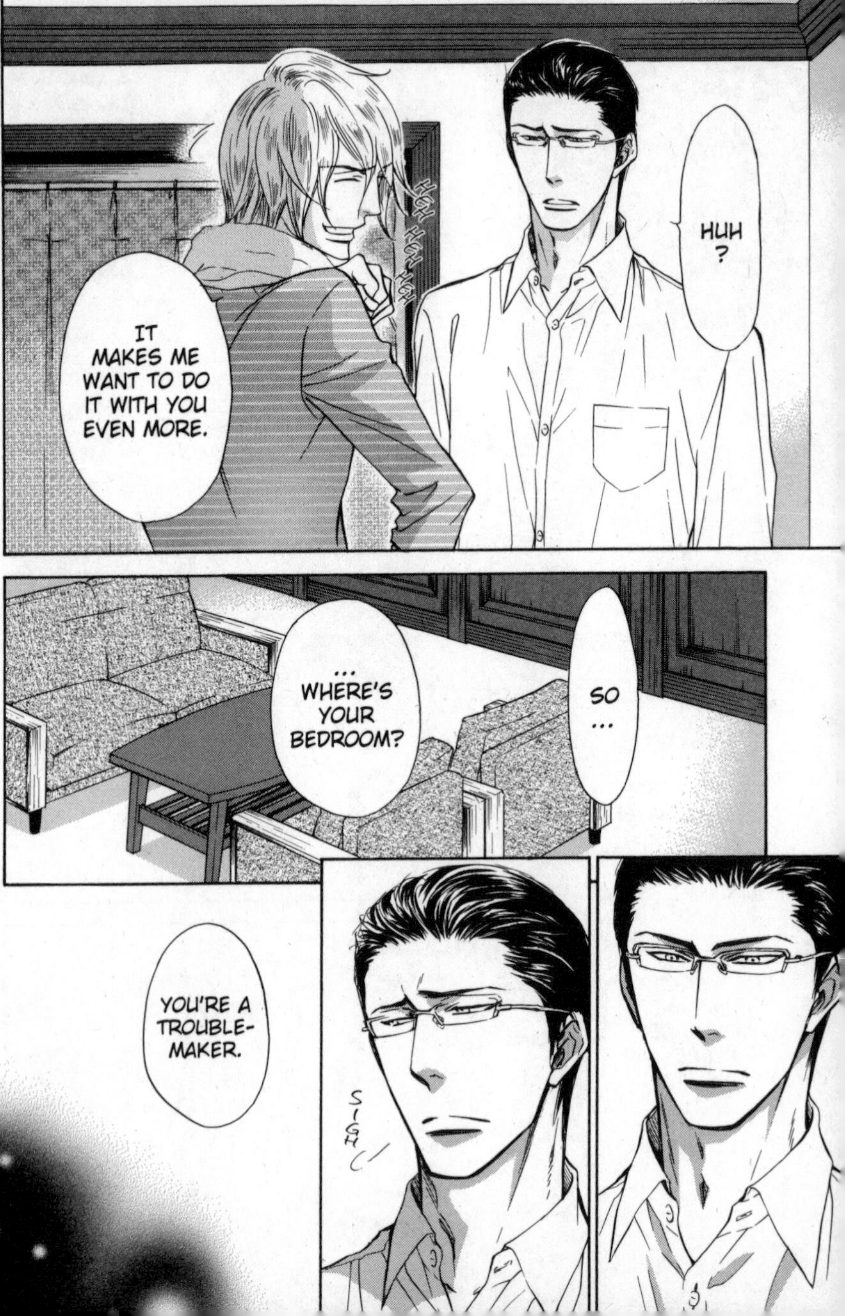
HUH?
HGH HGH HGH
IT MAKES ME WANT TO DO IT WITH YOU EVEN MORE.
SO...
...WHERE'S YOUR BEDROOM?
SIGH
YOU'RE A TROUBLE-MAKER.

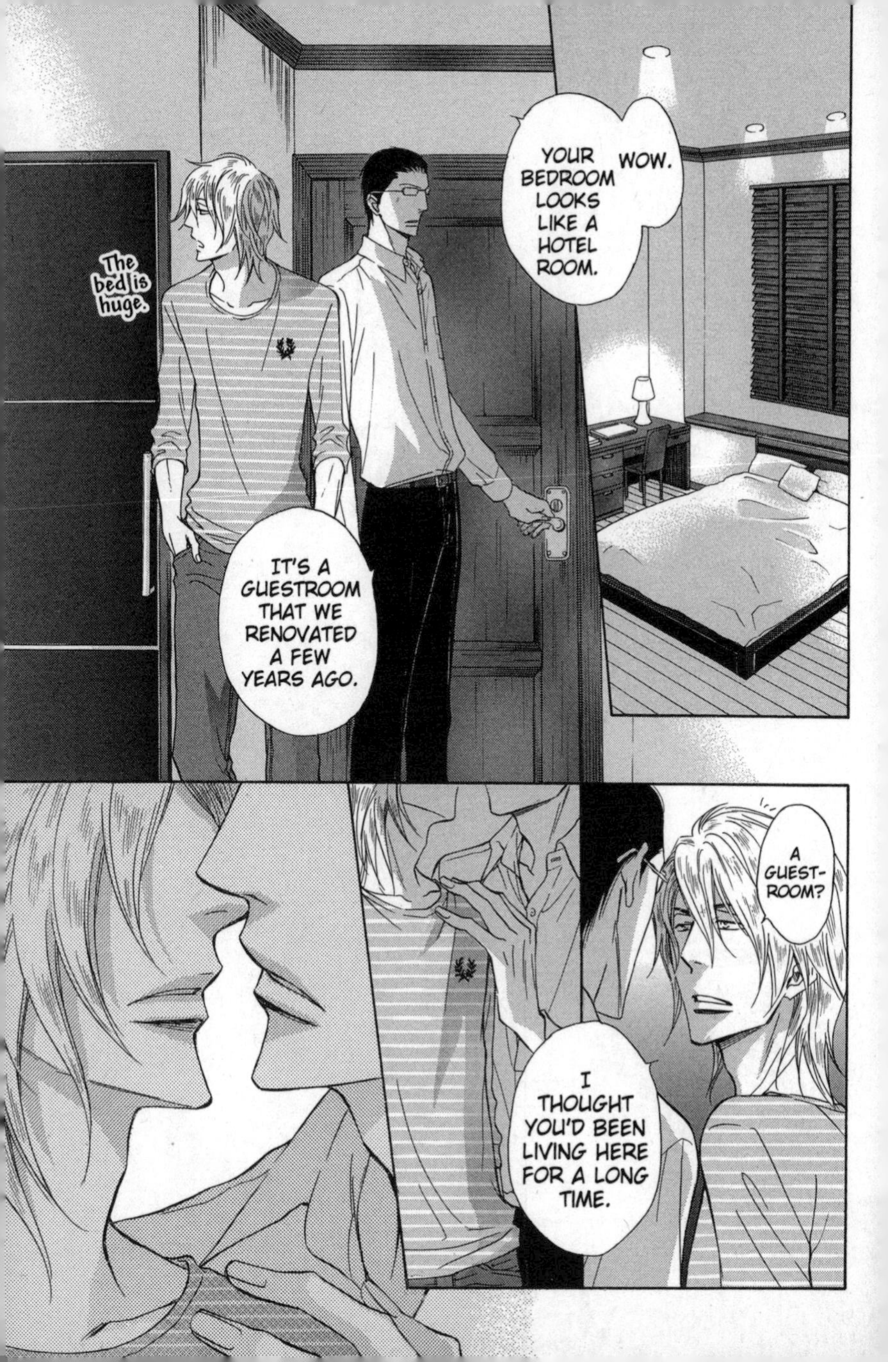
WOW.
YOUR BEDROOM LOOKS LIKE A HOTEL ROOM.
The bed is huge.
IT'S A GUESTROOM THAT WE RENOVATED A FEW YEARS AGO.
A GUEST-ROOM?
I THOUGHT YOU'D BEEN LIVING HERE FOR A LONG TIME.

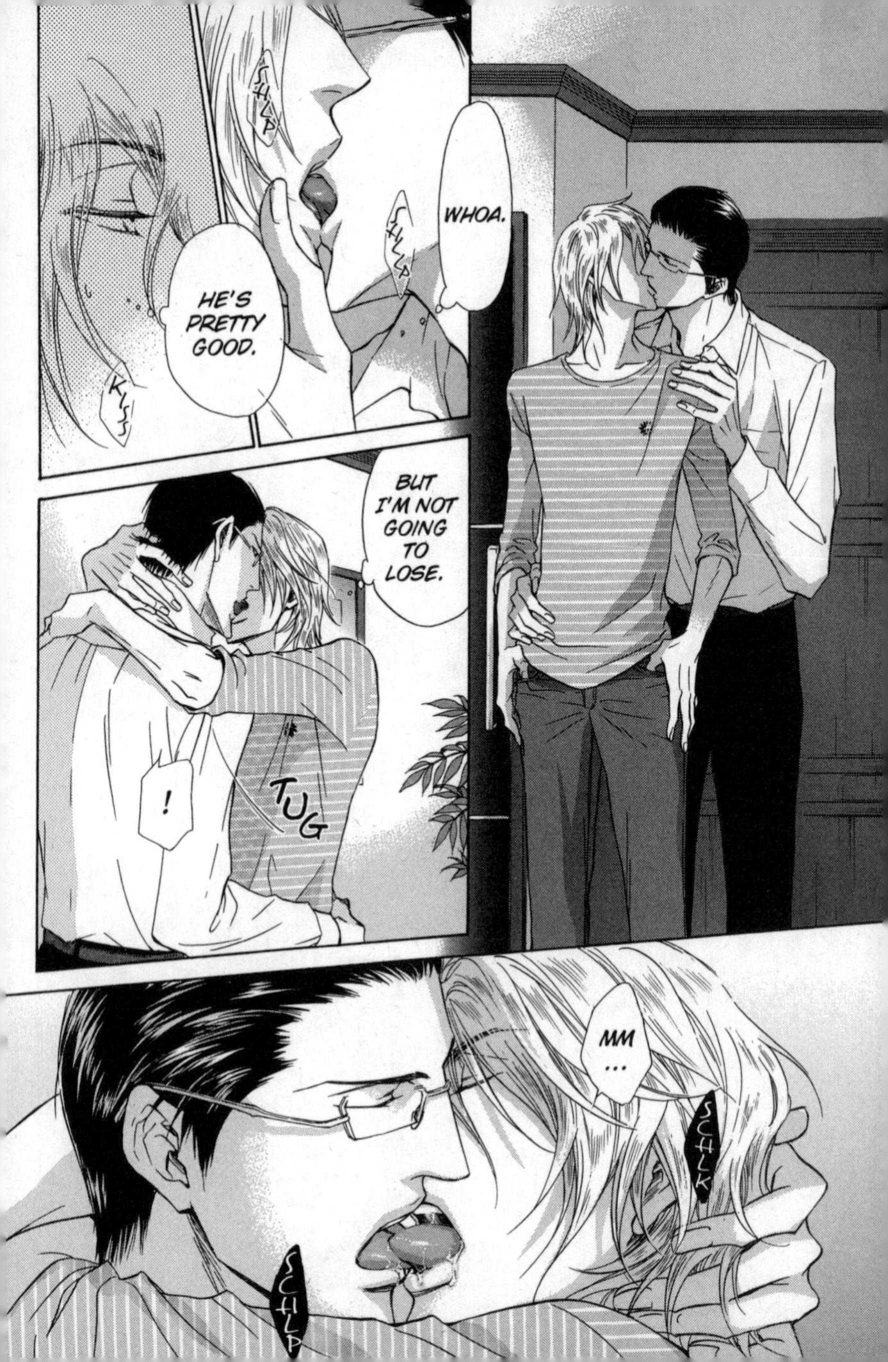
WHOA.
SCHLP
SCHLP
HE'S PRETTY GOOD.
KISS
BUT I'M NOT GOING TO LOSE.
!
TUG
MM...
SCHLK
SCHLP

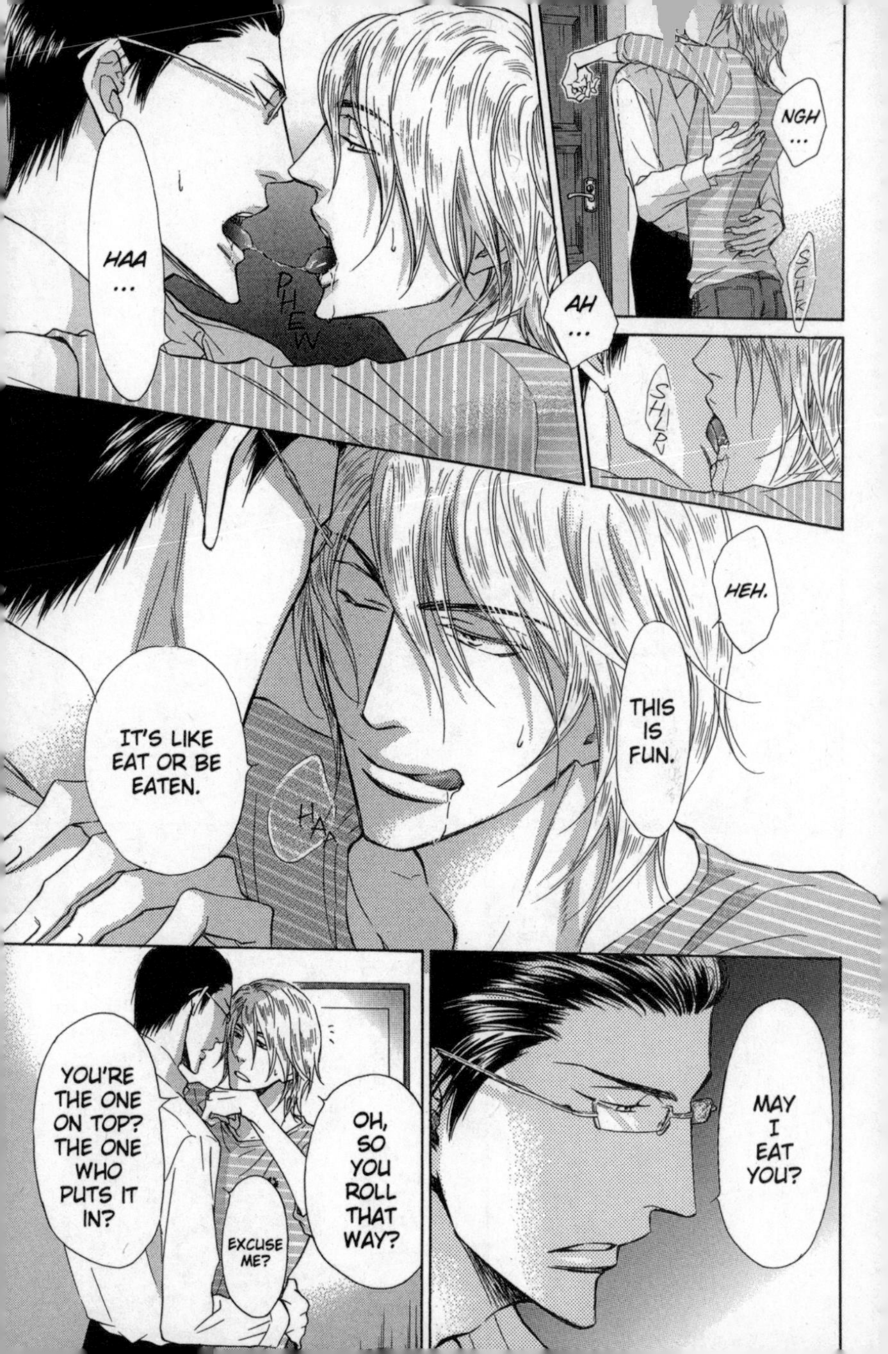
NGH ...
SCHK
SHLR
AH ...
HAA ...
PHEW
HEH.
THIS IS FUN.
HA
IT'S LIKE EAT OR BE EATEN.
MAY I EAT YOU?
OH, SO YOU ROLL THAT WAY?
EXCUSE ME?
YOU'RE THE ONE ON TOP? THE ONE WHO PUTS IT IN?

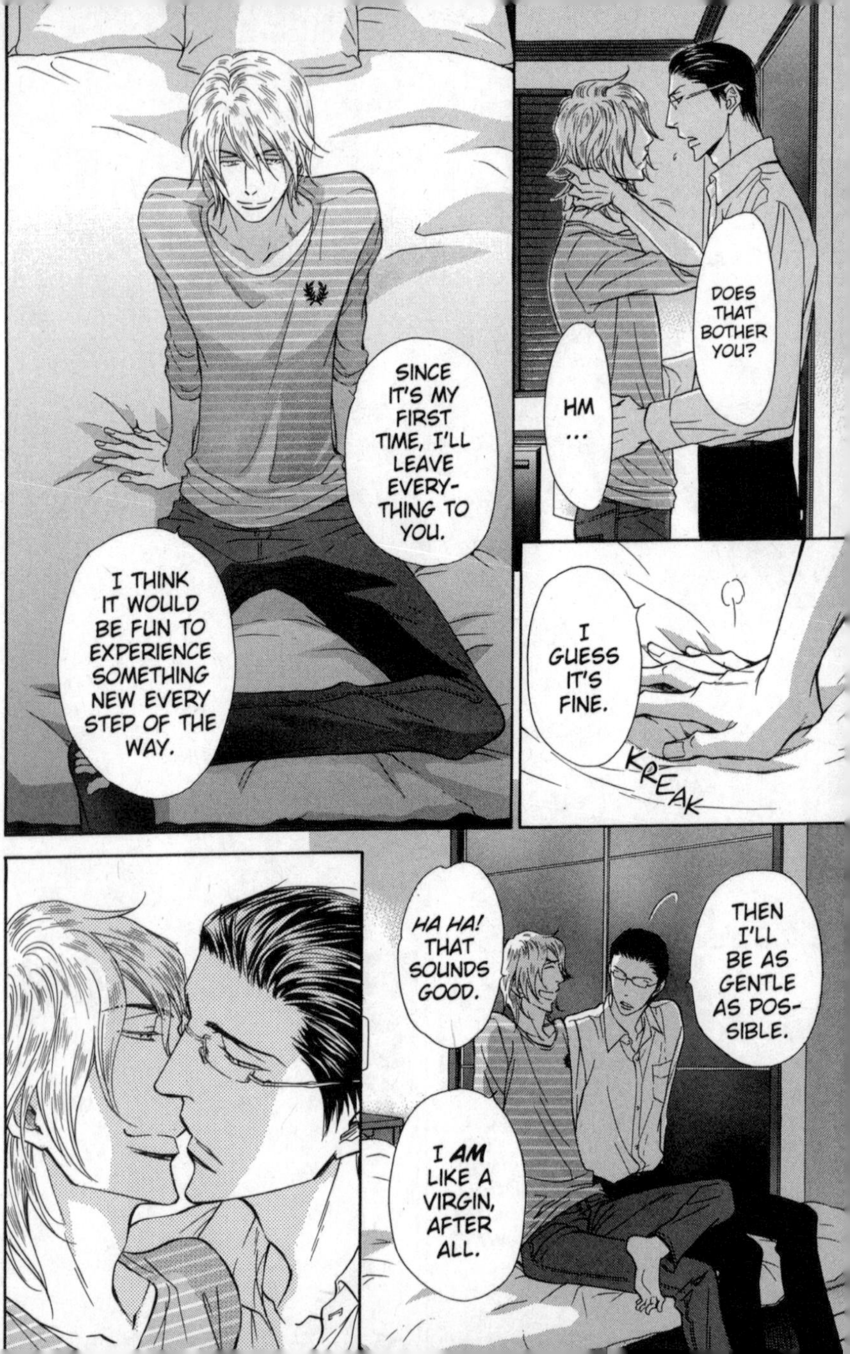
DOES THAT BOTHER YOU?
HM ...
I GUESS IT'S FINE.
KREAK
SINCE IT'S MY FIRST TIME, I'LL LEAVE EVERY-THING TO YOU.
I THINK IT WOULD BE FUN TO EXPERIENCE SOMETHING NEW EVERY STEP OF THE WAY.
THEN I'LL BE AS GENTLE AS POS-SIBLE.
HA HA! THAT SOUNDS GOOD.
I *AM* LIKE A VIRGIN, AFTER ALL.

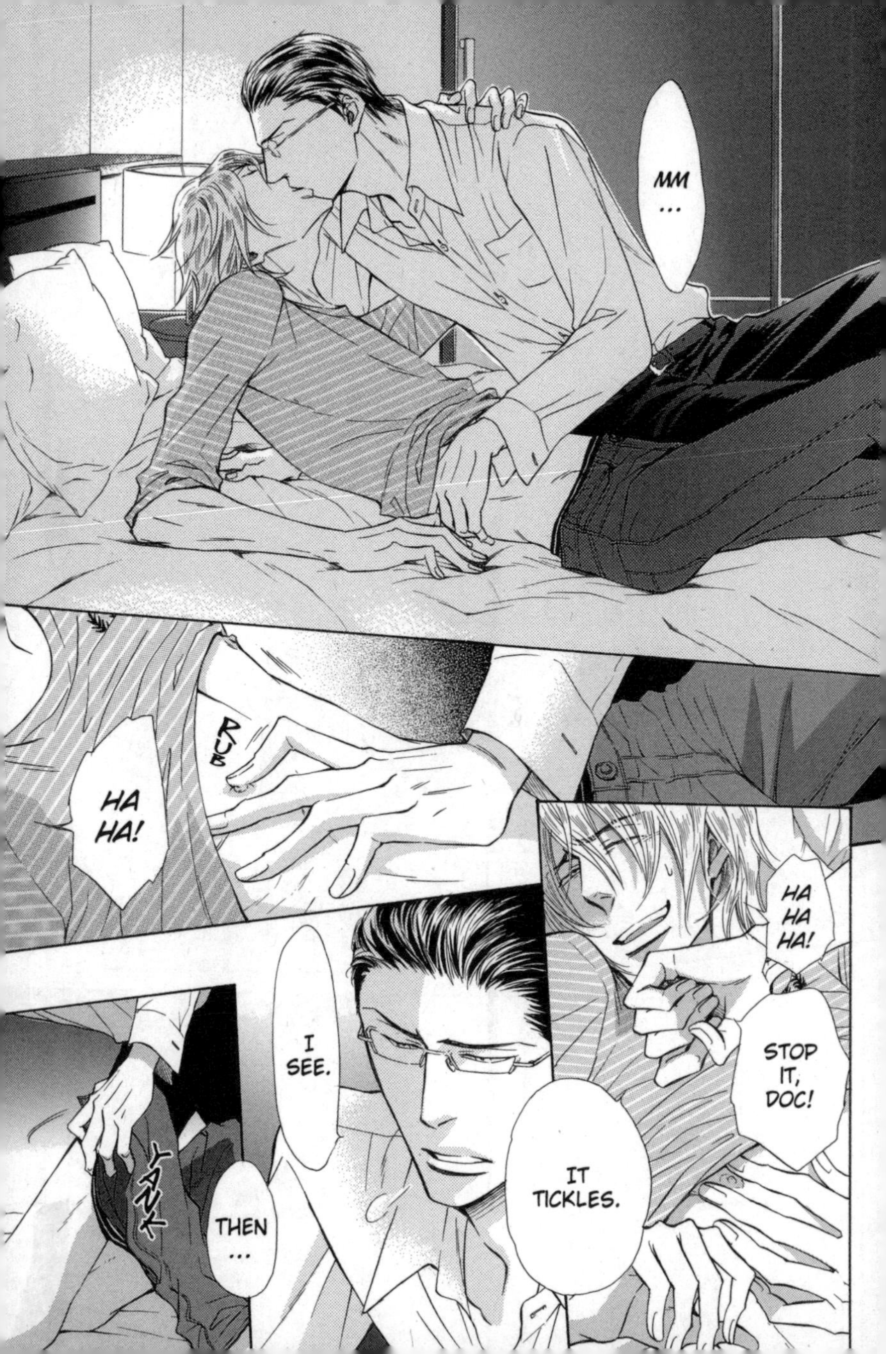
MM ...
RUB
HA HA!
HA HA HA!
STOP IT, DOC!
IT TICKLES.
I SEE.
THEN ...
YANK

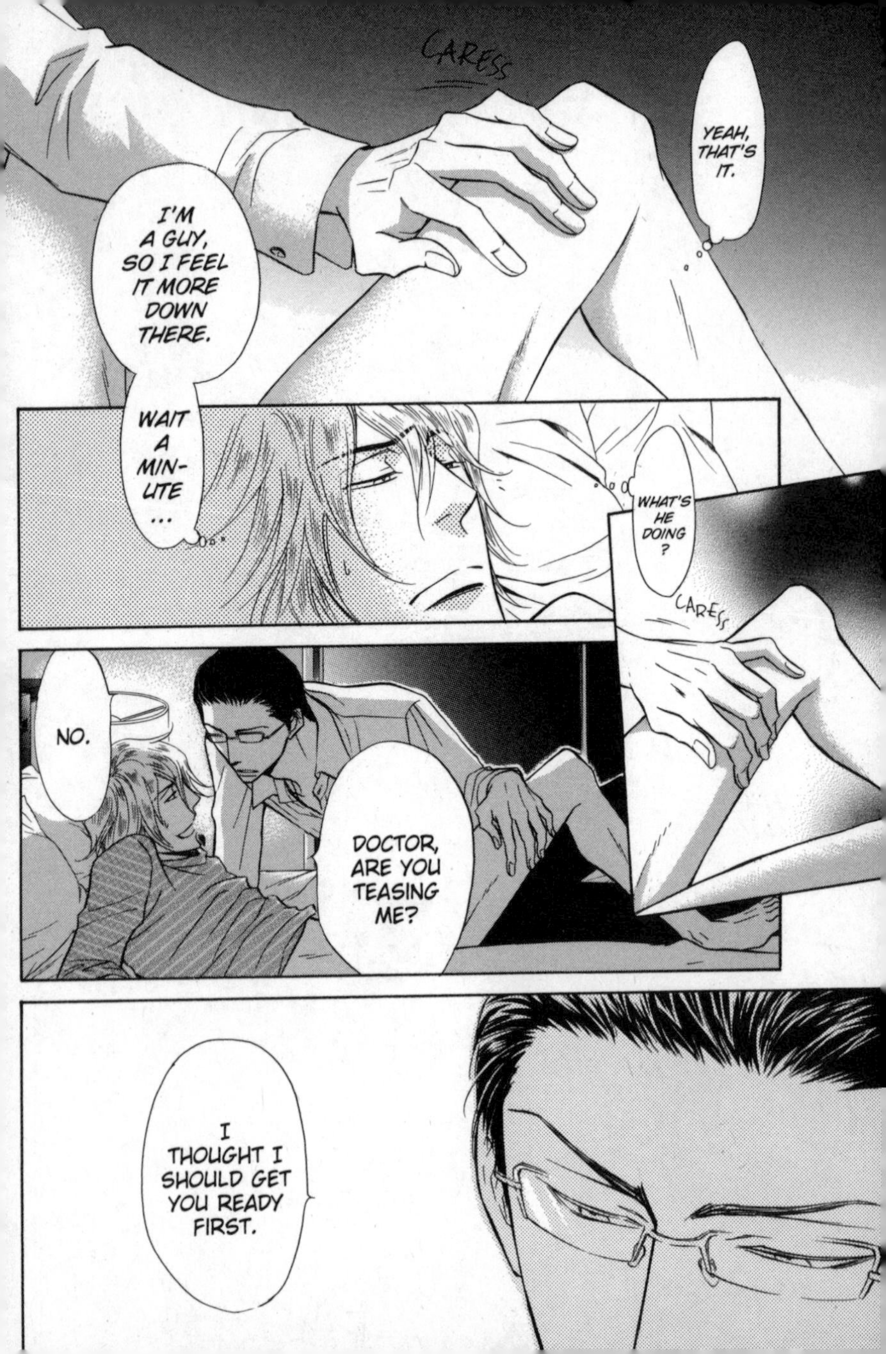
CARESS
YEAH, THAT'S IT.
I'M A GUY, SO I FEEL IT MORE DOWN THERE.
WHAT'S HE DOING?
WAIT A MIN-UTE...
CARESS
DOCTOR, ARE YOU TEASING ME?
NO.
I THOUGHT I SHOULD GET YOU READY FIRST.

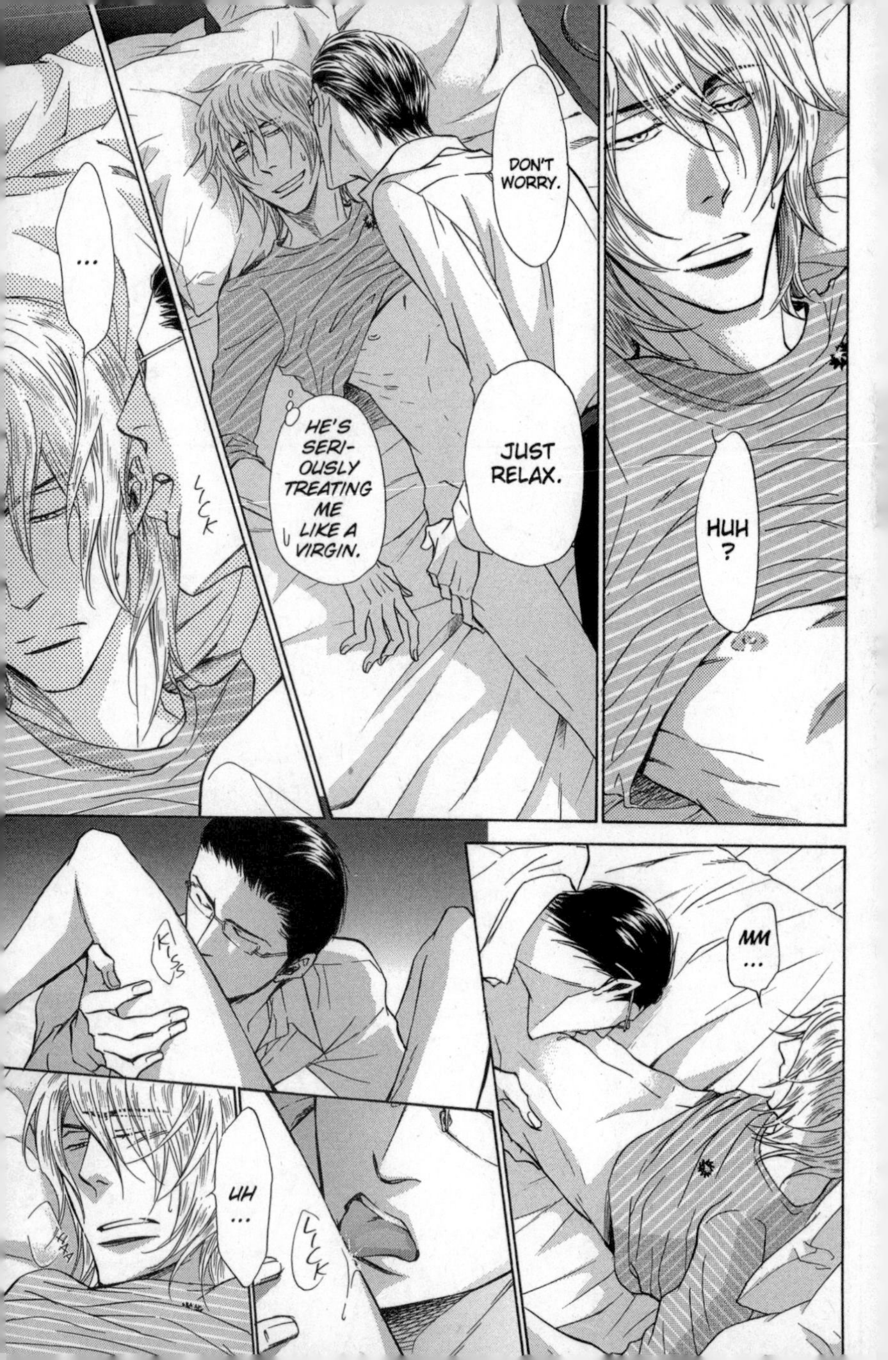
HUH?
DON'T WORRY.
JUST RELAX.
HE'S SERI-OUSLY TREATING ME LIKE A VIRGIN.
...
LICK
MM...
KISS
UH...
LICK
HAA

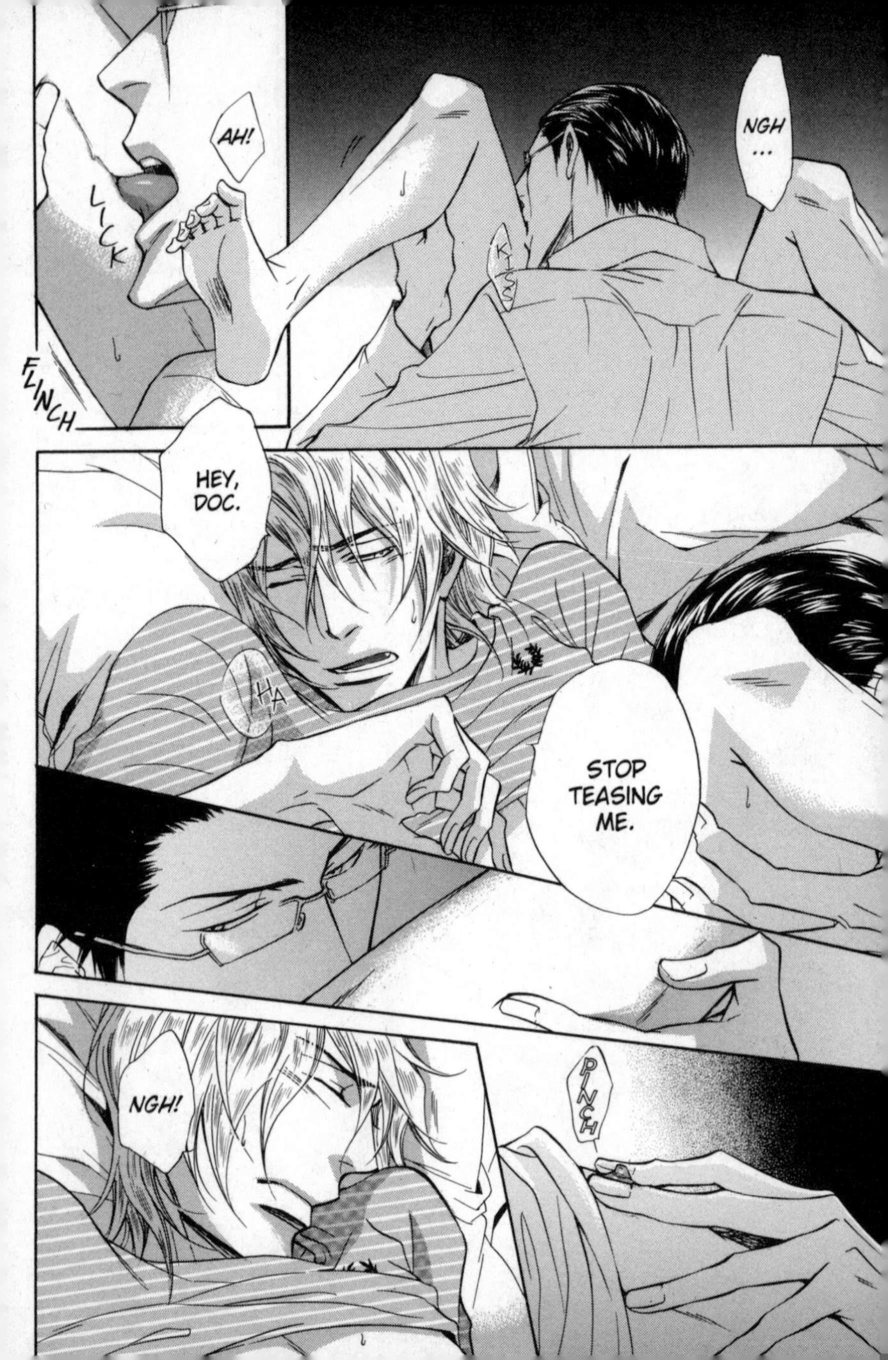
NGH ...
KISS
AH!
LICK
FLINCH
HEY, DOC.
HA
STOP TEASING ME.
PINCH
NGH!

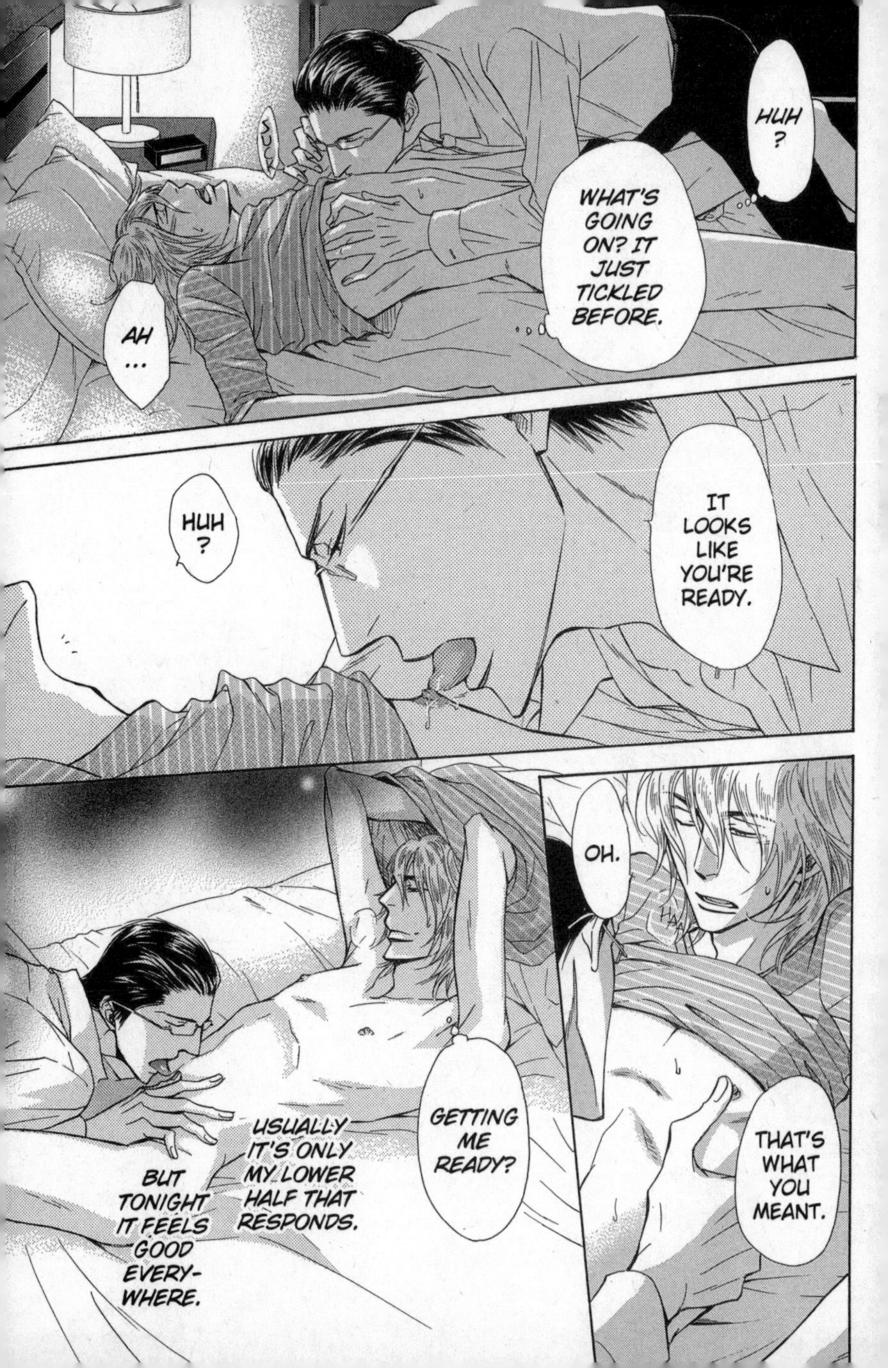
HUH ?
WHAT'S GOING ON? IT JUST TICKLED BEFORE.
SUK
AH ...
IT LOOKS LIKE YOU'RE READY.
HUH ?
OH.
THAT'S WHAT YOU MEANT.
GETTING ME READY?
USUALLY IT'S ONLY MY LOWER HALF THAT RESPONDS.
BUT TONIGHT IT FEELS GOOD EVERYWHERE.

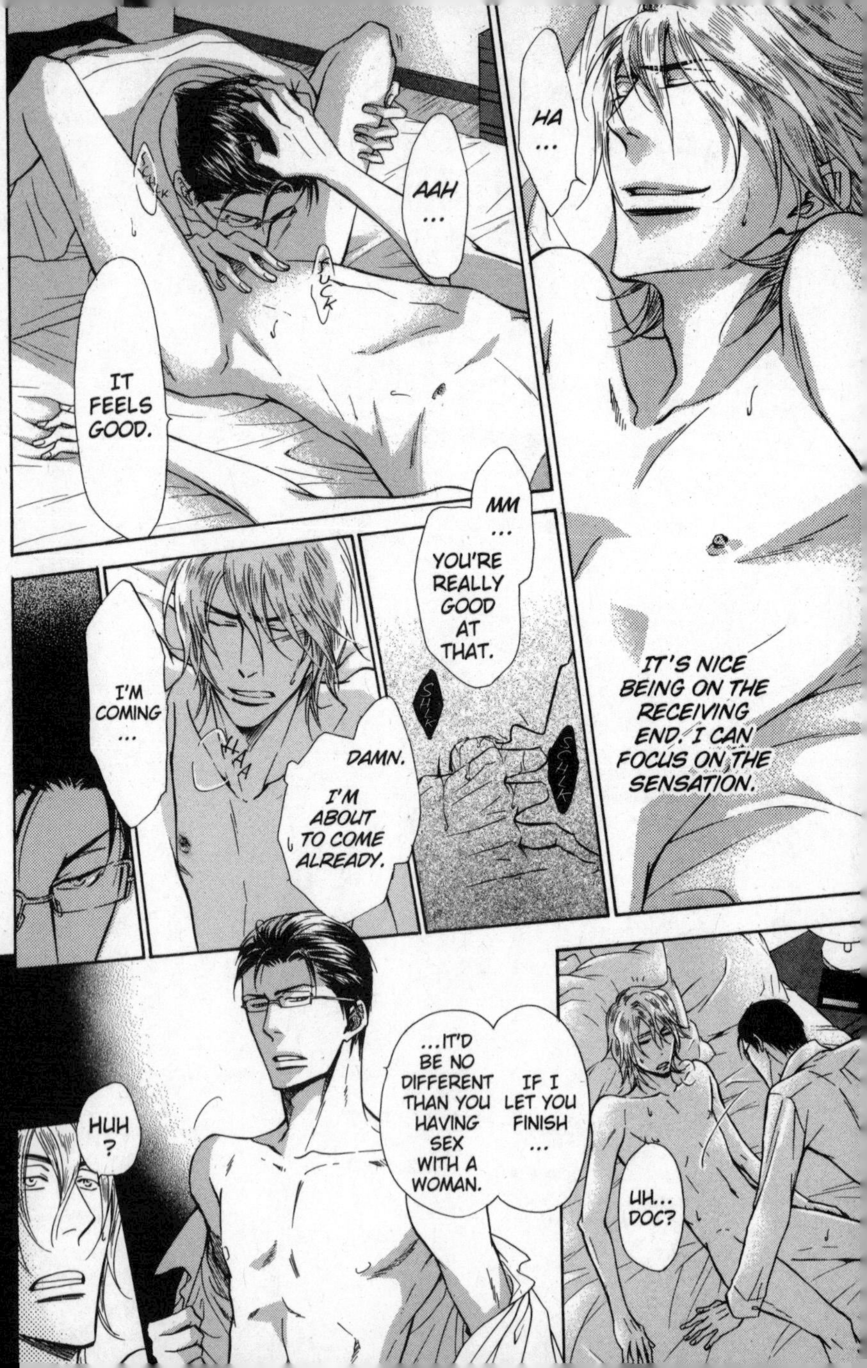
HA ...
IT'S NICE BEING ON THE RECEIVING END. I CAN FOCUS ON THE SENSATION.
AAH ...
SUCK
SCHLK
IT FEELS GOOD.
MM ... YOU'RE REALLY GOOD AT THAT.
SCHLK
SHLK
DAMN.
I'M ABOUT TO COME ALREADY.
HAA
I'M COMING ...
UH... DOC?
IF I LET YOU FINISH ...
...IT'D BE NO DIFFERENT THAN YOU HAVING SEX WITH A WOMAN.
HUH?

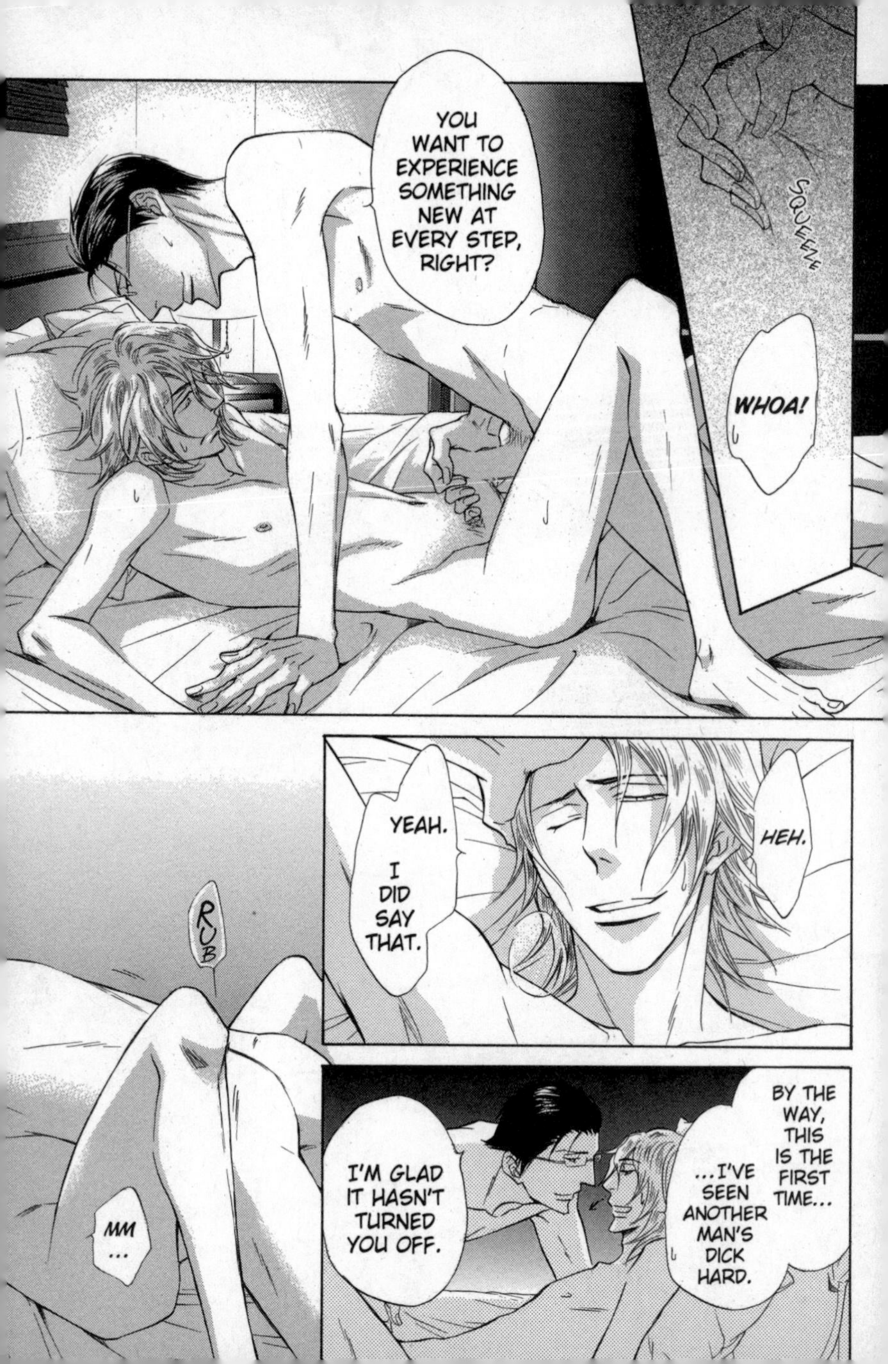
SQUEEZE
WHOA!
YOU WANT TO EXPERIENCE SOMETHING NEW AT EVERY STEP, RIGHT?
HEH.
YEAH.
I DID SAY THAT.
BY THE WAY, THIS IS THE FIRST TIME...
...I'VE SEEN ANOTHER MAN'S DICK HARD.
I'M GLAD IT HASN'T TURNED YOU OFF.
RUB
MM...

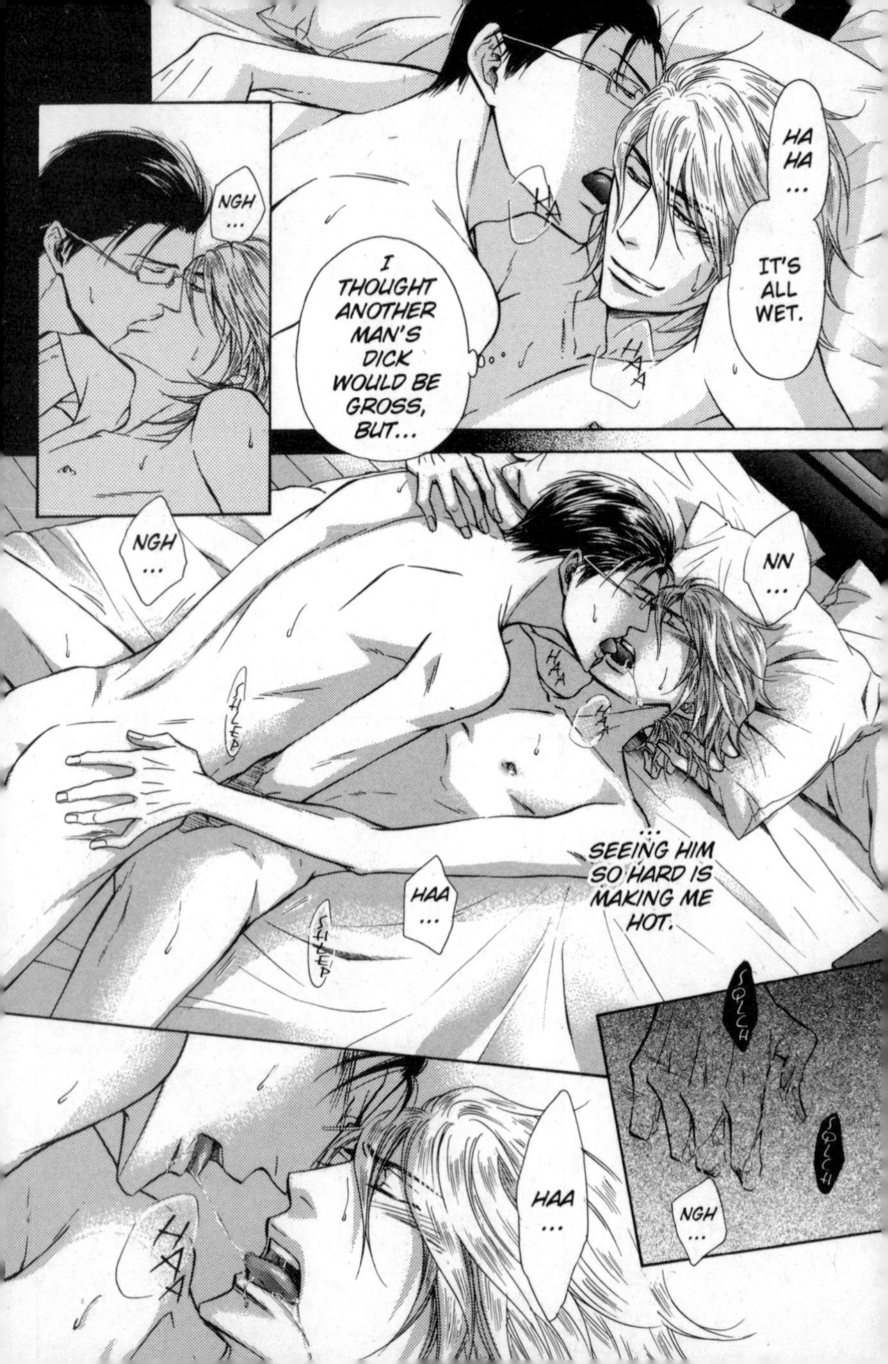
HA HA ...
IT'S ALL WET.
HAA
I THOUGHT ANOTHER MAN'S DICK WOULD BE GROSS, BUT...
NGH ...
NN ...
NGH ...
SHLEP
... SEEING HIM SO HARD IS MAKING ME HOT.
HAA ...
SHLEP
SQLCH
SQLCH
NGH ...
HAA ...
HAA

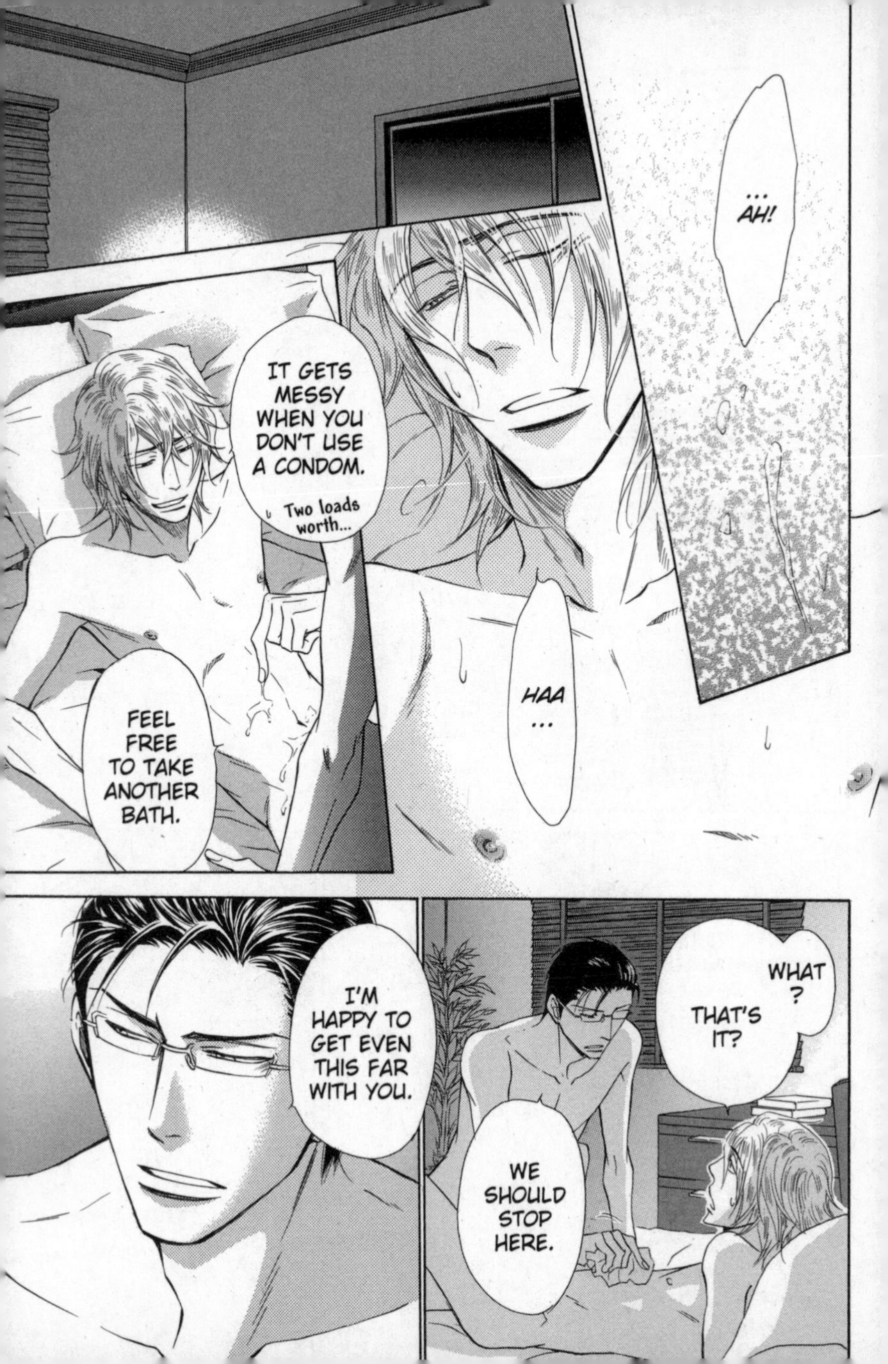
...AH!
HAA...
IT GETS MESSY WHEN YOU DON'T USE A CONDOM.
Two loads worth...
FEEL FREE TO TAKE ANOTHER BATH.
WHAT?
THAT'S IT?
WE SHOULD STOP HERE.
I'M HAPPY TO GET EVEN THIS FAR WITH YOU.

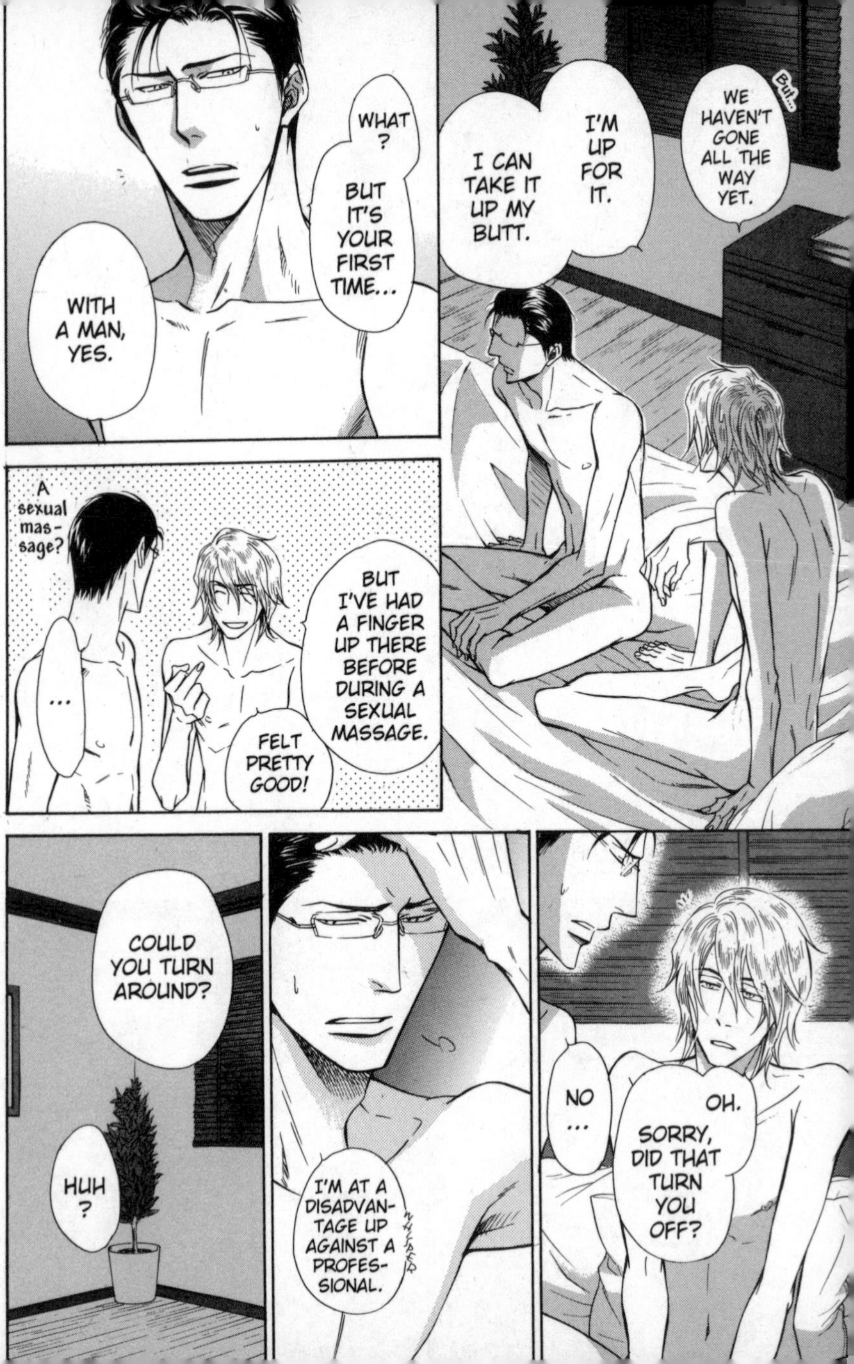
But...
WE HAVEN'T GONE ALL THE WAY YET.
I'M UP FOR IT.
I CAN TAKE IT UP MY BUTT.
WHAT? BUT IT'S YOUR FIRST TIME...
WITH A MAN, YES.
BUT I'VE HAD A FINGER UP THERE BEFORE DURING A SEXUAL MASSAGE.
FELT PRETTY GOOD!
A sexual mas-sage?
...
OH. SORRY, DID THAT TURN YOU OFF?
NO...
I'M AT A DISADVAN-TAGE UP AGAINST A PROFES-SIONAL.
WHISPER
COULD YOU TURN AROUND?
HUH?

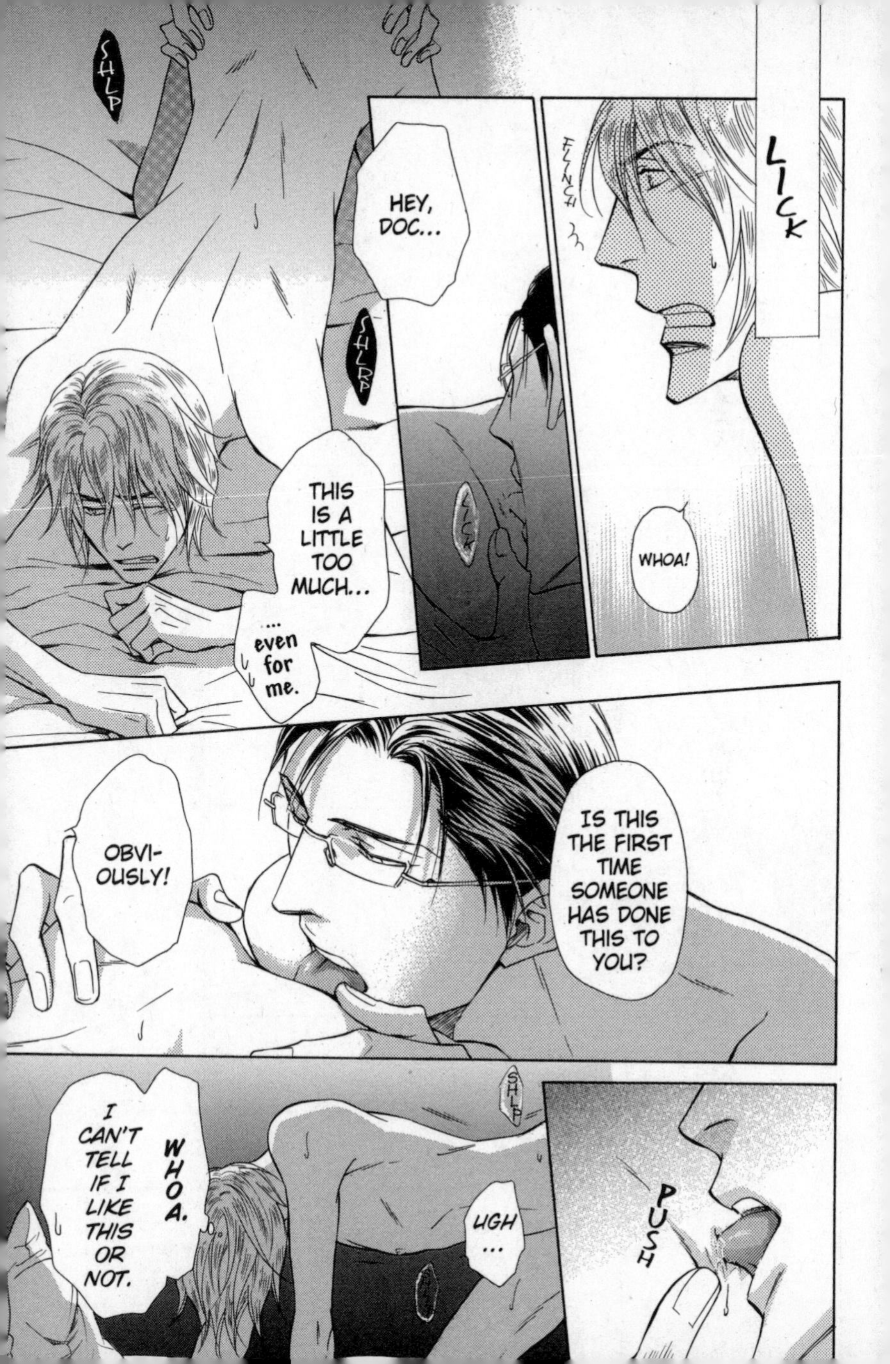
LICK
FLINCH
WHOA!
HEY, DOC...
SHLRP
LICK
SHLP
THIS IS A LITTLE TOO MUCH...
... even for me.
IS THIS THE FIRST TIME SOMEONE HAS DONE THIS TO YOU?
OBVI-OUSLY!
PUSH
SHLP
UGH ...
WHOA.
I CAN'T TELL IF I LIKE THIS OR NOT.

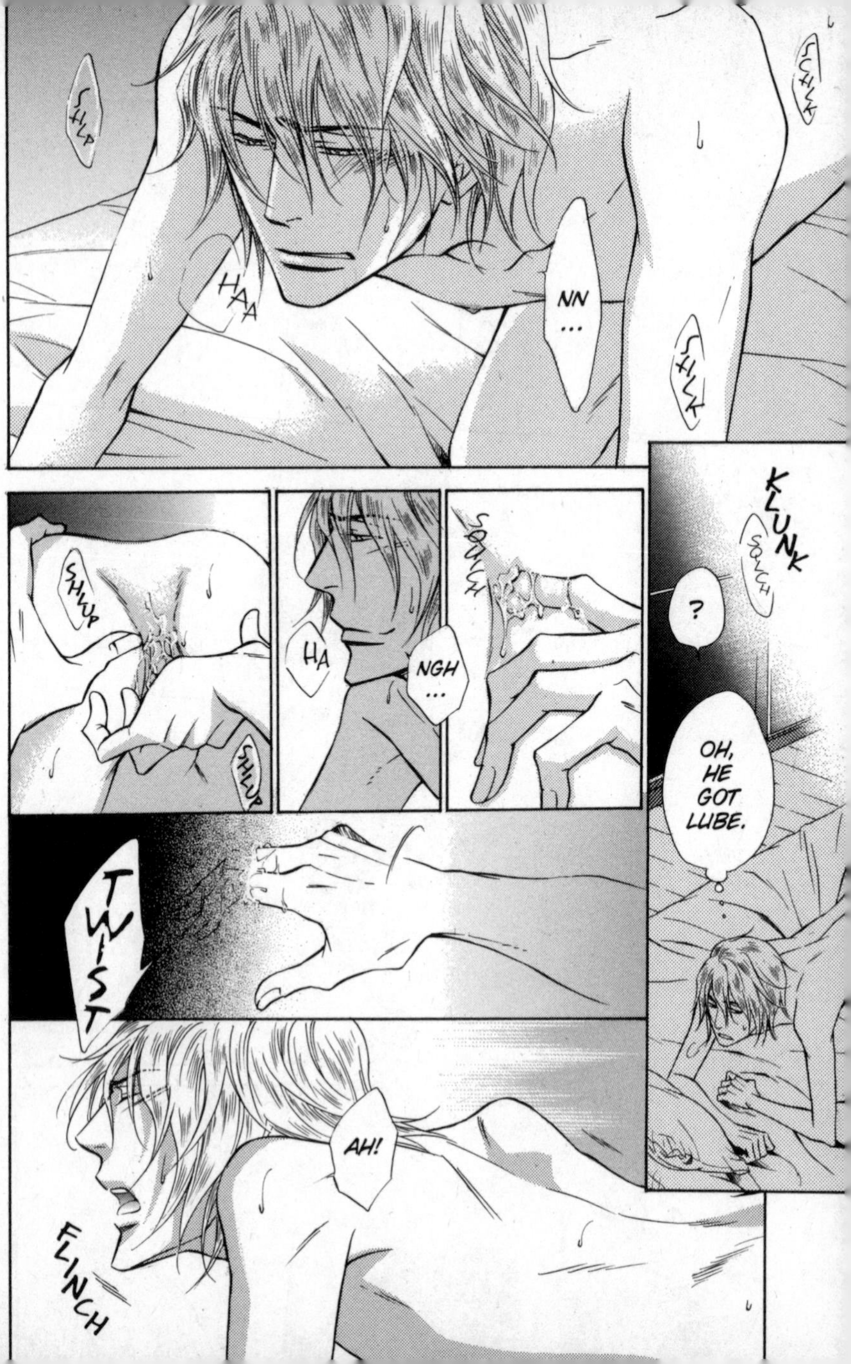
SHLK
SHLK
NN...
HAA
SHLP
KLUNK
SQUCH
?
OH, HE GOT LUBE.
SQUCH
NGH...
HA
SHLUP
SHLUP
TWIST
AH!
FLINCH

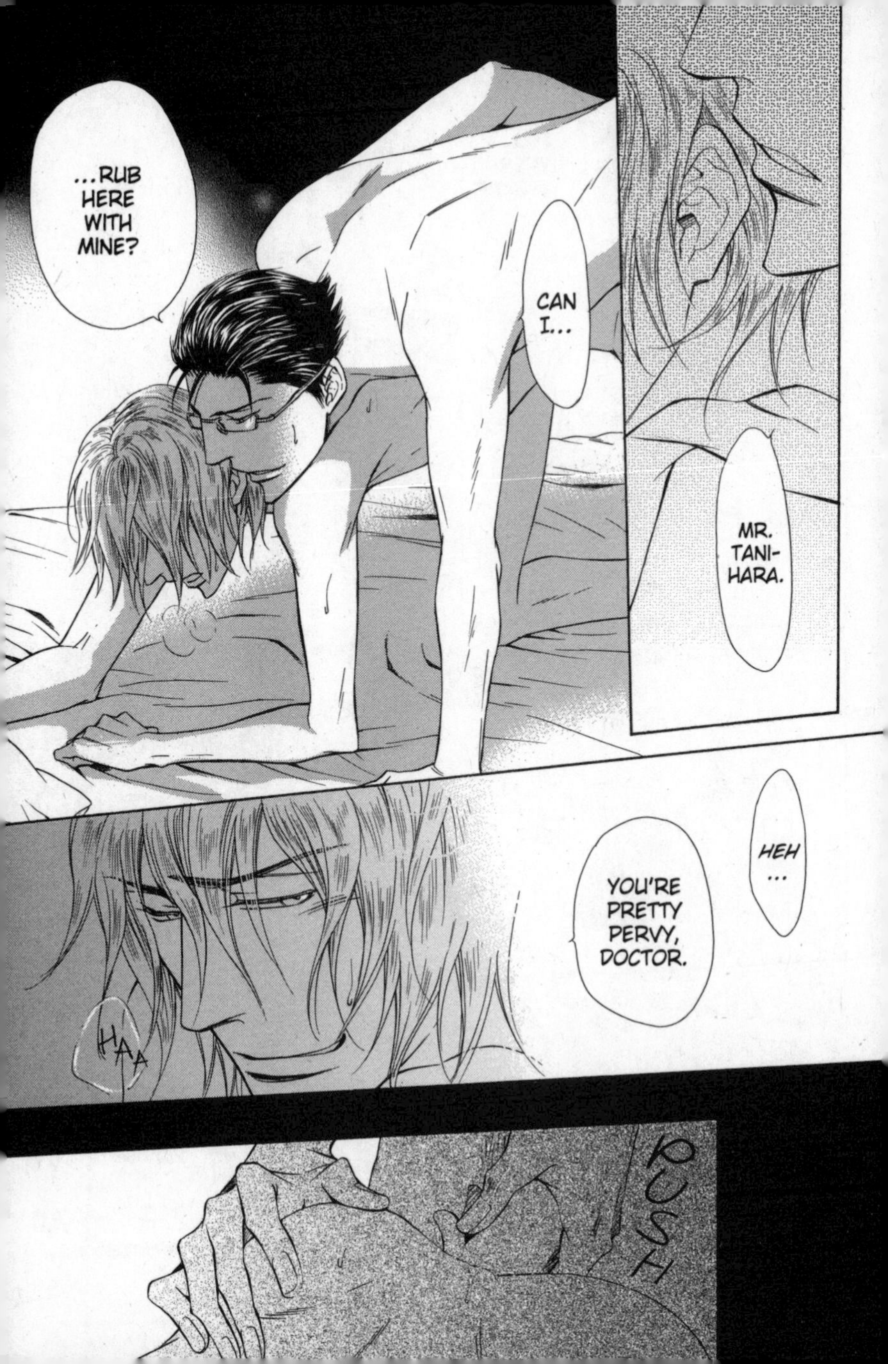
MR. TANI-HARA.
CAN I...
...RUB HERE WITH MINE?
HEH ...
YOU'RE PRETTY PERVY, DOCTOR.
HAA
RUSH

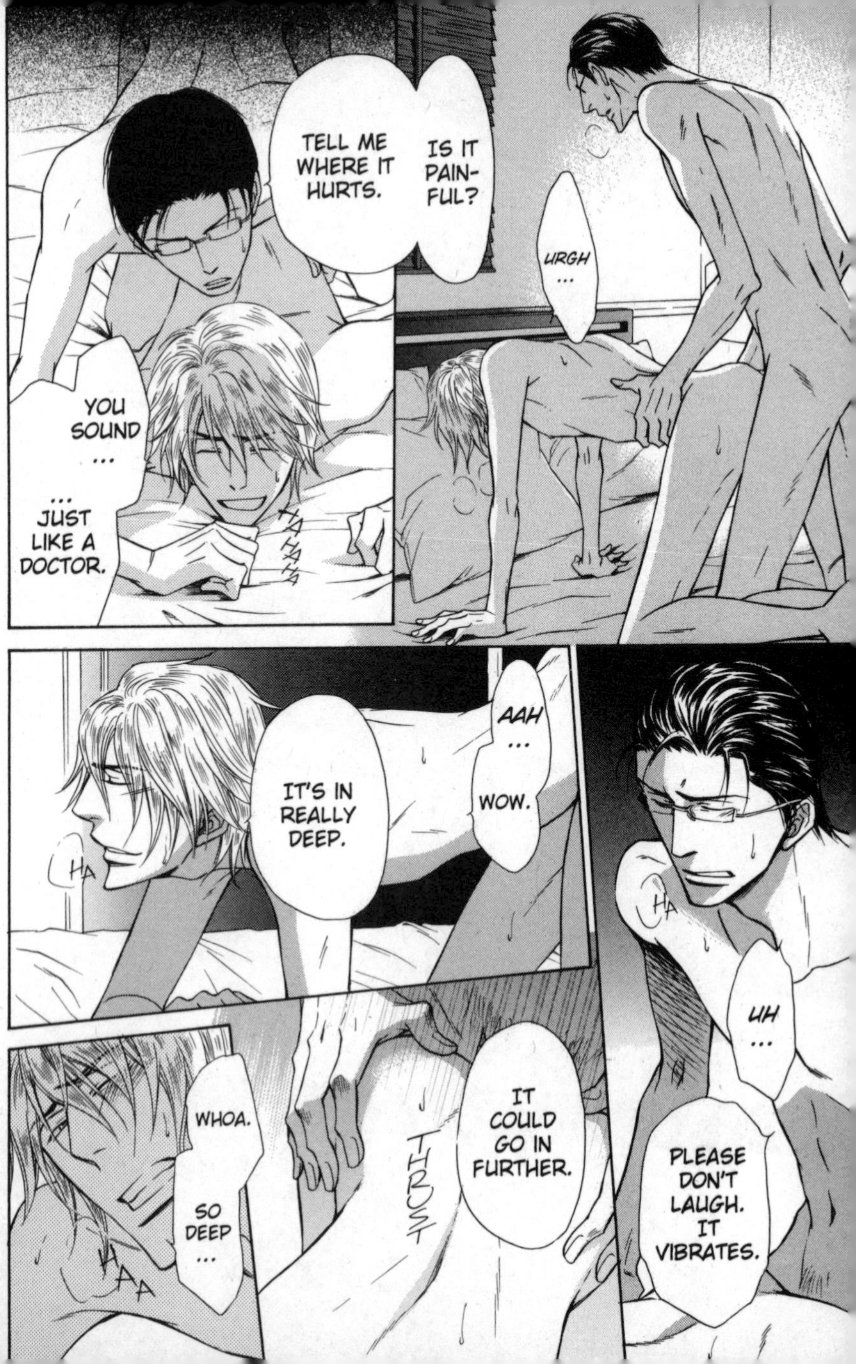
URGH ...
IS IT PAINFUL?
TELL ME WHERE IT HURTS.
YOU SOUND ...
... JUST LIKE A DOCTOR.
HAHAHA
HA
UH ...
PLEASE DON'T LAUGH. IT VIBRATES.
AAH ... WOW.
IT'S IN REALLY DEEP.
HA
IT COULD GO IN FURTHER.
THRUST
WHOA.
SO DEEP ...
HAA

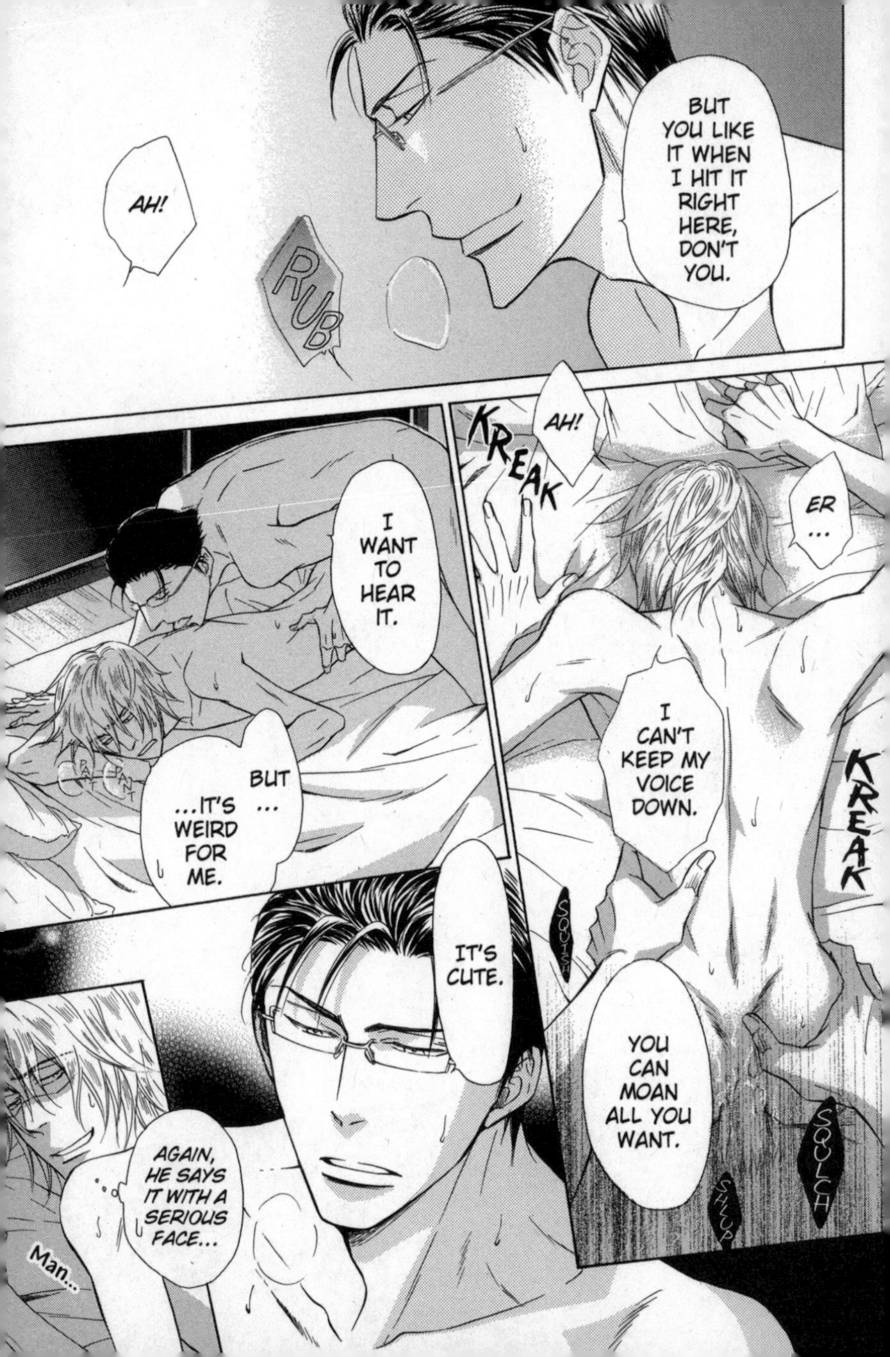
BUT YOU LIKE IT WHEN I HIT IT RIGHT HERE, DON'T YOU.
RUB
AH!
AH!
KREAK
ER...
I CAN'T KEEP MY VOICE DOWN.
KREAK
SQUISH
YOU CAN MOAN ALL YOU WANT.
SQUELCH
SHLUP
I WANT TO HEAR IT.
BUT...
...IT'S WEIRD FOR ME.
PANT PANT
IT'S CUTE.
AGAIN, HE SAYS IT WITH A SERIOUS FACE...
Man...

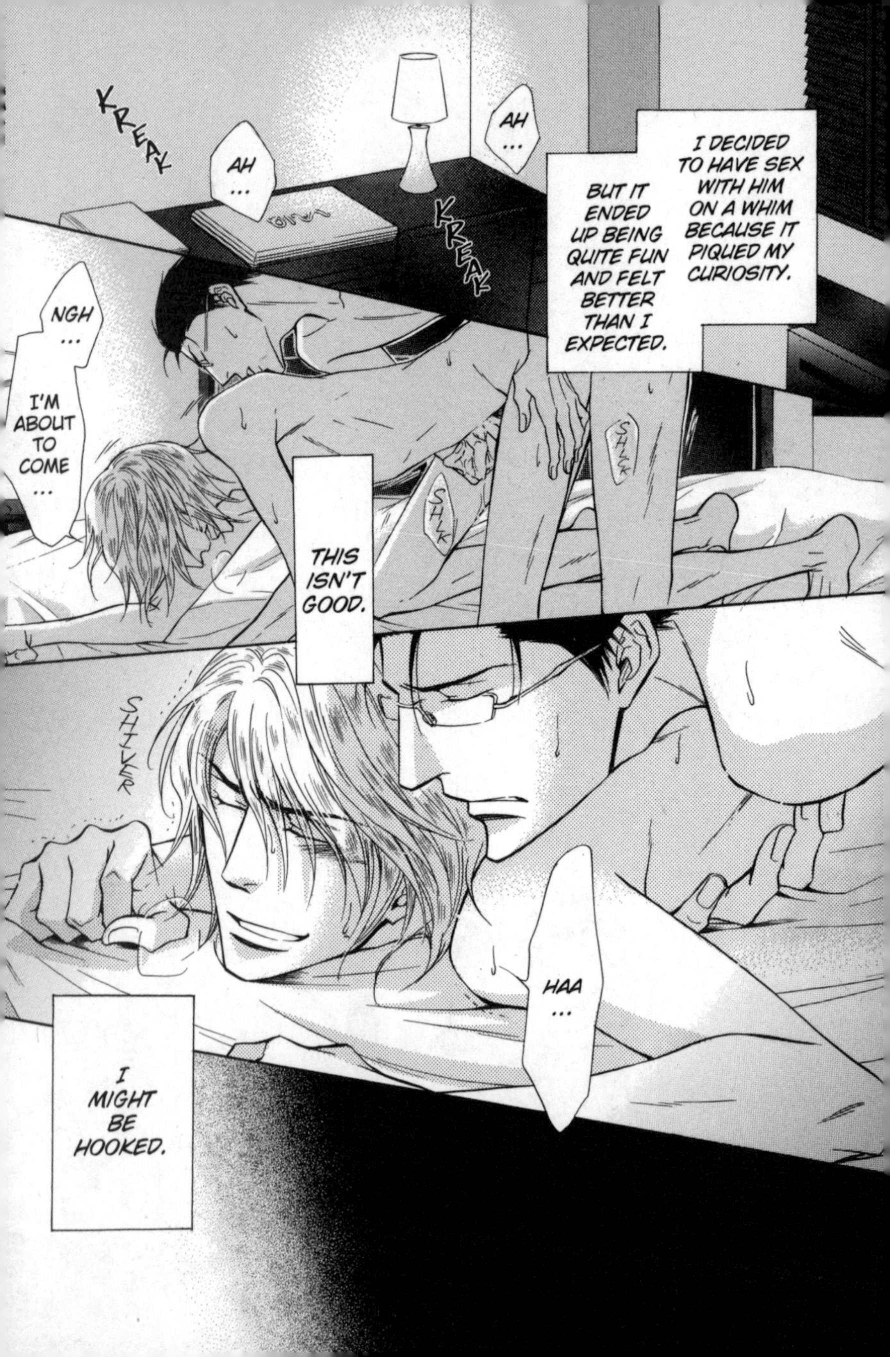
I DECIDED TO HAVE SEX WITH HIM ON A WHIM BECAUSE IT PIQUED MY CURIOSITY.
BUT IT ENDED UP BEING QUITE FUN AND FELT BETTER THAN I EXPECTED.
AH...
KREAK
AH...
KREAK
SHLK
SHLK
THIS ISN'T GOOD.
NGH...
I'M ABOUT TO COME...
HAA...
SHIVER
I MIGHT BE HOOKED.

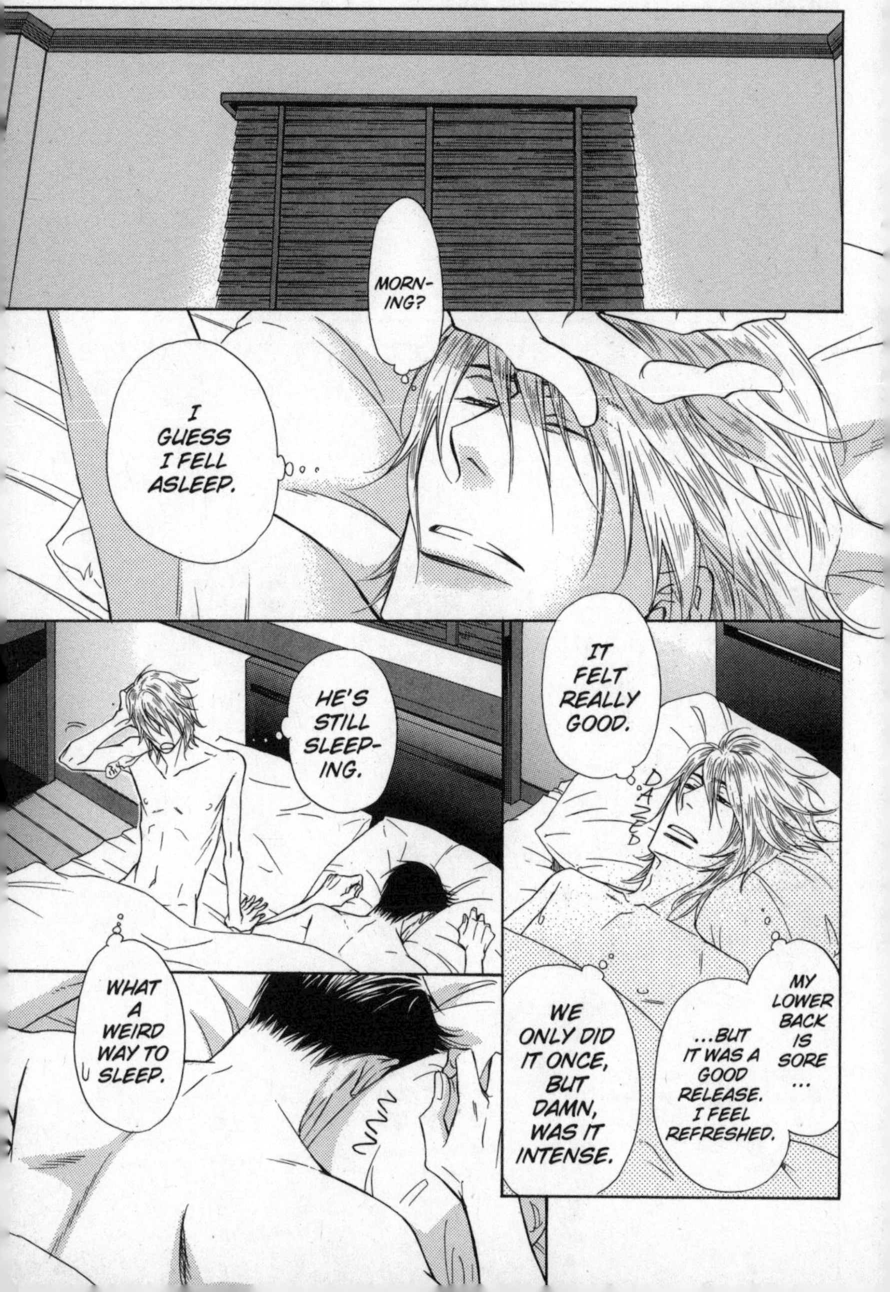
MORNING?
I GUESS I FELL ASLEEP.
IT FELT REALLY GOOD.
DAZED
MY LOWER BACK IS SORE...
...BUT IT WAS A GOOD RELEASE. I FEEL REFRESHED.
WE ONLY DID IT ONCE, BUT DAMN, WAS IT INTENSE.
HE'S STILL SLEEPING.
WHAT A WEIRD WAY TO SLEEP.
NNN

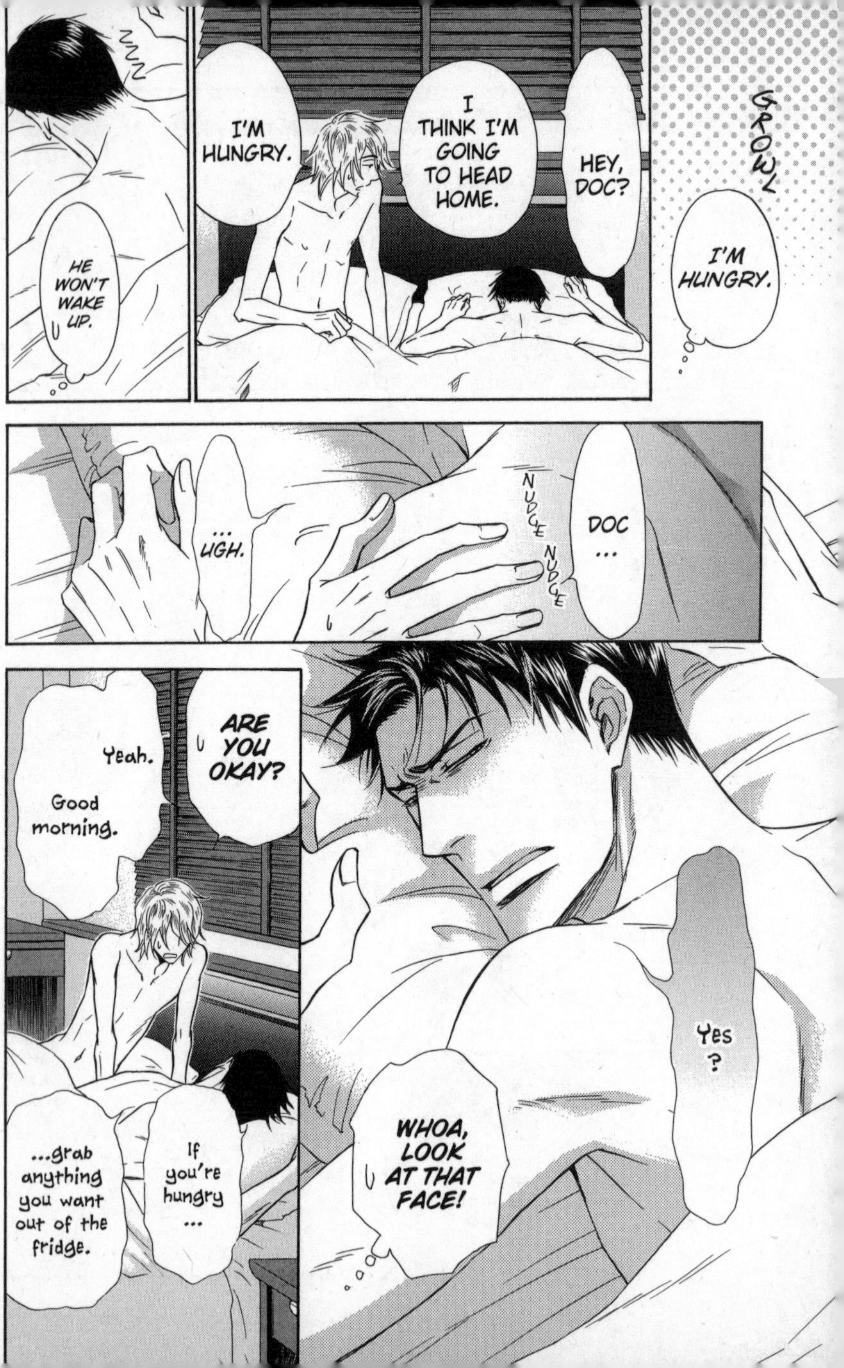
GROWL
I'M HUNGRY.
HEY, DOC?
I THINK I'M GOING TO HEAD HOME.
I'M HUNGRY.
ZZZ
HE WON'T WAKE UP.
DOC...
NUDGE NUDGE
...UGH.
Yes?
WHOA, LOOK AT THAT FACE!
ARE YOU OKAY?
Yeah.
Good morning.
If you're hungry...
...grab anything you want out of the fridge.

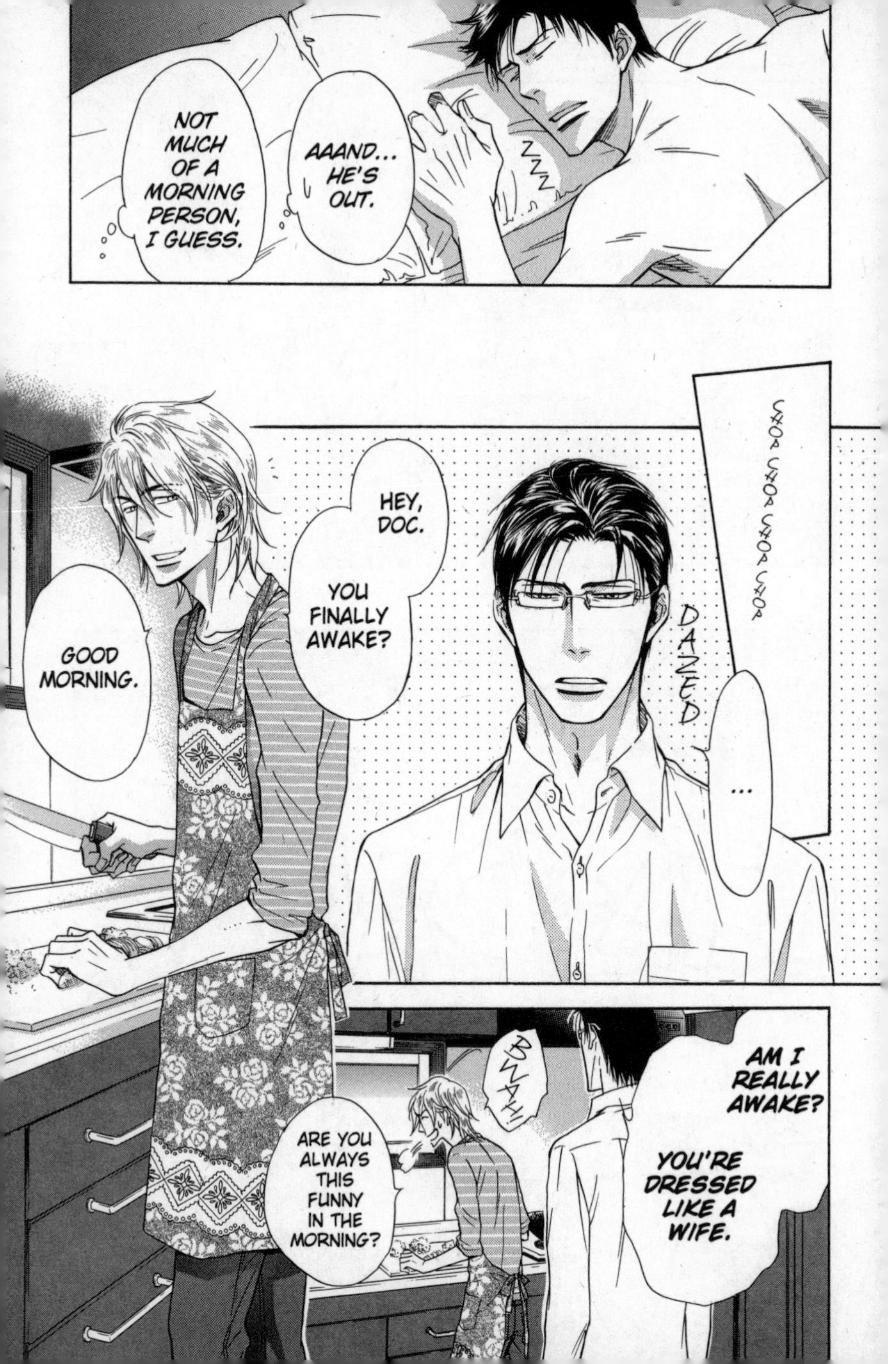
AAAND... HE'S OUT.
ZZZ
NOT MUCH OF A MORNING PERSON, I GUESS.
CHOP CHOP CHOP CHOP CHOP
DAZED
...
HEY, DOC.
YOU FINALLY AWAKE?
GOOD MORNING.
AM I REALLY AWAKE?
YOU'RE DRESSED LIKE A WIFE.
BWAH!
ARE YOU ALWAYS THIS FUNNY IN THE MORNING?

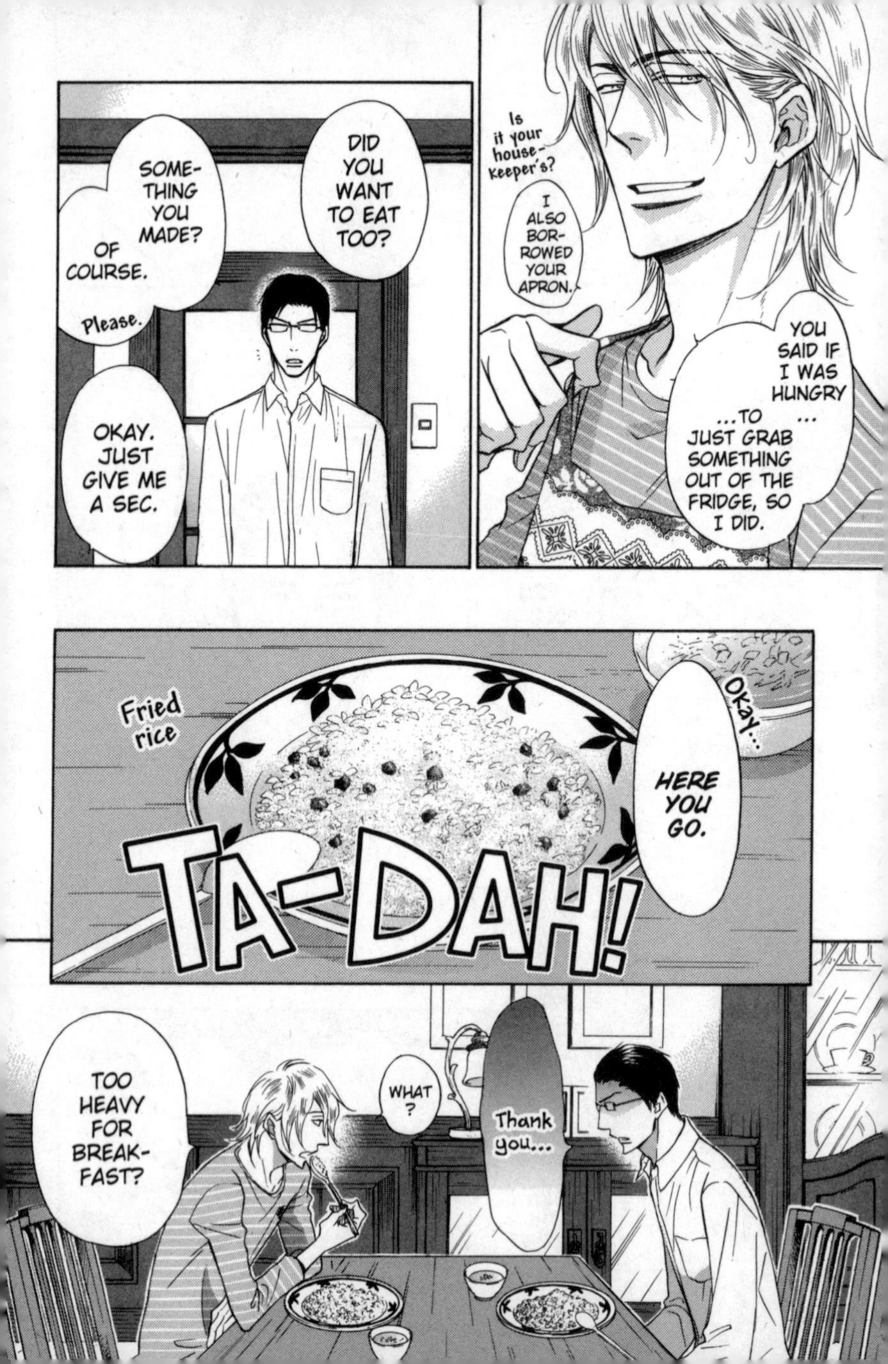
YOU SAID IF I WAS HUNGRY ... ...TO JUST GRAB SOMETHING OUT OF THE FRIDGE, SO I DID.
Is it your house-keeper's?
I ALSO BOR-ROWED YOUR APRON.
DID YOU WANT TO EAT TOO?
SOME-THING YOU MADE? OF COURSE.
Please.
OKAY. JUST GIVE ME A SEC.
Okay...
HERE YOU GO.
Fried rice
TA-DAH!
Thank you...
WHAT?
TOO HEAVY FOR BREAK-FAST?

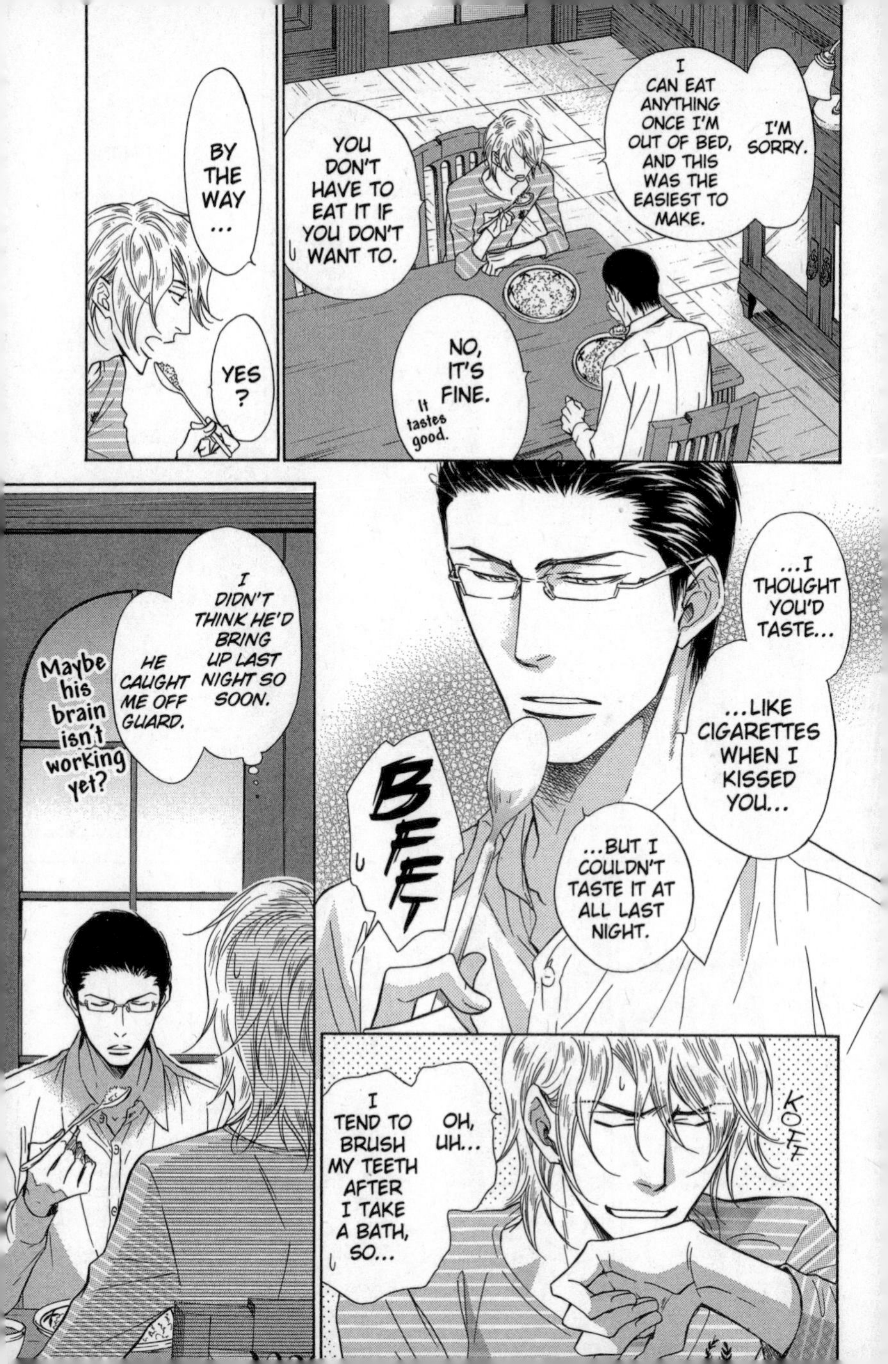
I'M SORRY.
I CAN EAT ANYTHING ONCE I'M OUT OF BED, AND THIS WAS THE EASIEST TO MAKE.
YOU DON'T HAVE TO EAT IT IF YOU DON'T WANT TO.
NO, IT'S FINE.
It tastes good.
BY THE WAY...
YES?
...I THOUGHT YOU'D TASTE...
...LIKE CIGARETTES WHEN I KISSED YOU...
...BUT I COULDN'T TASTE IT AT ALL LAST NIGHT.
BFFT
KOFF
OH, UH...
I TEND TO BRUSH MY TEETH AFTER I TAKE A BATH, SO...
I DIDN'T THINK HE'D BRING UP LAST NIGHT SO SOON.
HE CAUGHT ME OFF GUARD.
Maybe his brain isn't working yet?

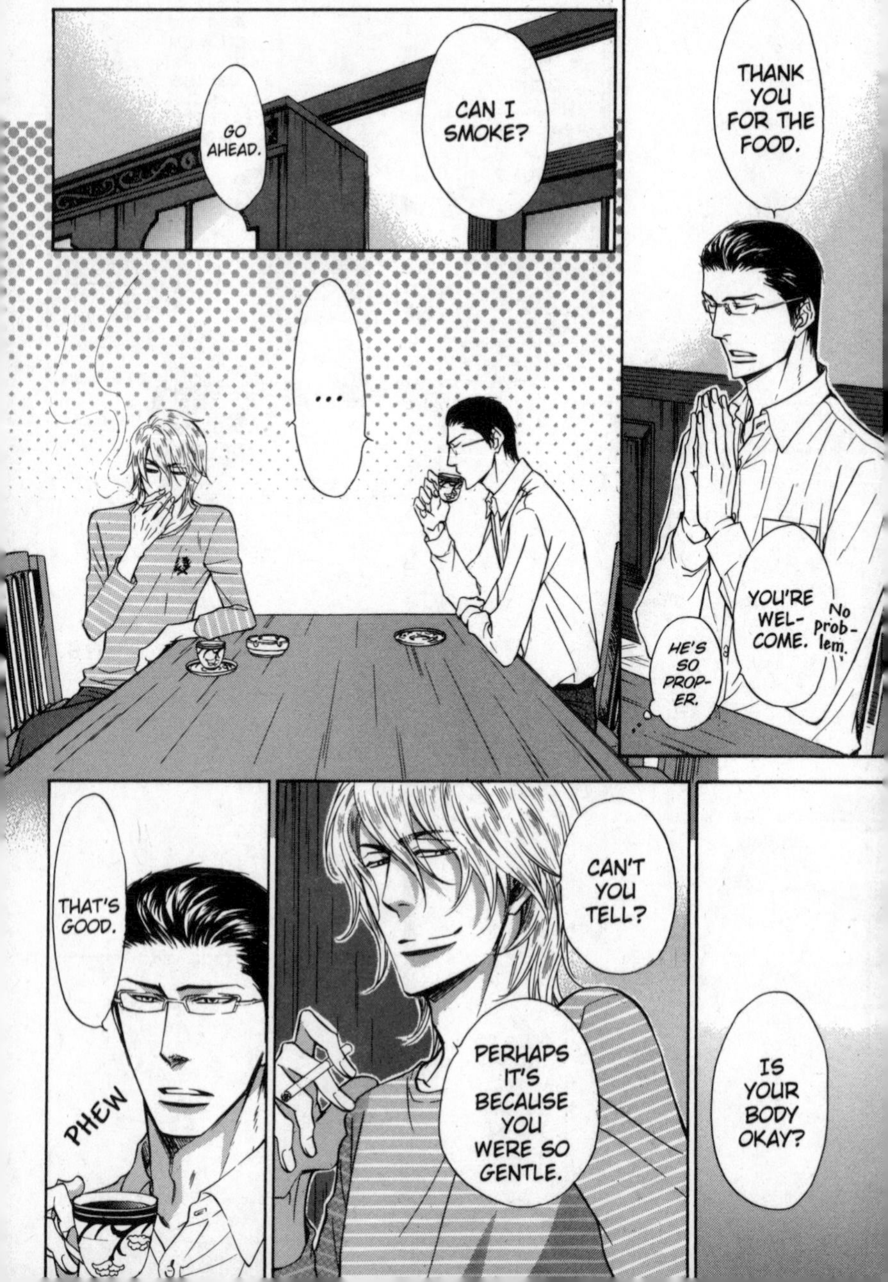
THANK YOU FOR THE FOOD.
YOU'RE WELCOME.
No problem.
HE'S SO PROPER.
CAN I SMOKE?
GO AHEAD.
...
IS YOUR BODY OKAY?
CAN'T YOU TELL?
PERHAPS IT'S BECAUSE YOU WERE SO GENTLE.
THAT'S GOOD.
PHEW

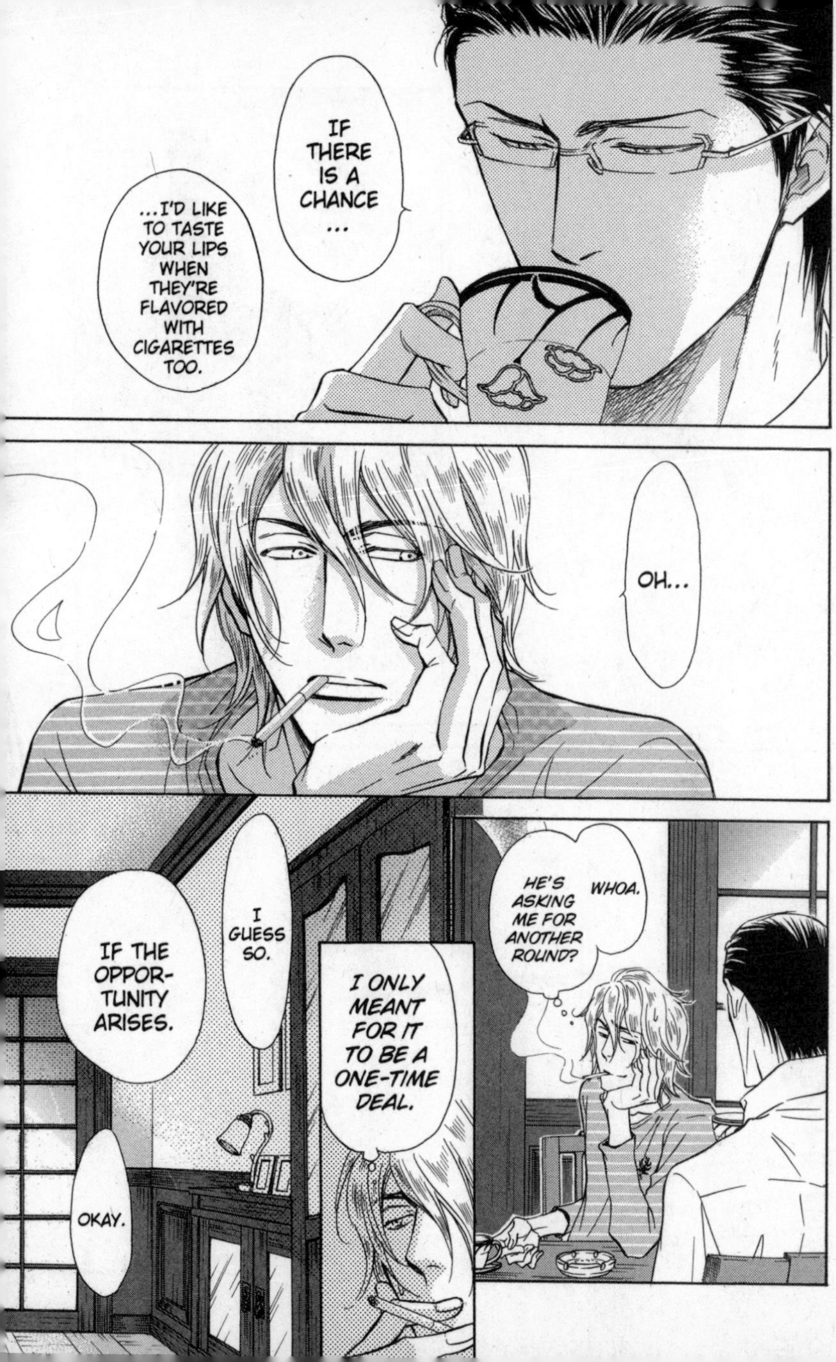
IF THERE IS A CHANCE ...
...I'D LIKE TO TASTE YOUR LIPS WHEN THEY'RE FLAVORED WITH CIGARETTES TOO.
OH...
WHOA.
HE'S ASKING ME FOR ANOTHER ROUND?
I ONLY MEANT FOR IT TO BE A ONE-TIME DEAL.
I GUESS SO.
IF THE OPPOR-TUNITY ARISES.
OKAY.

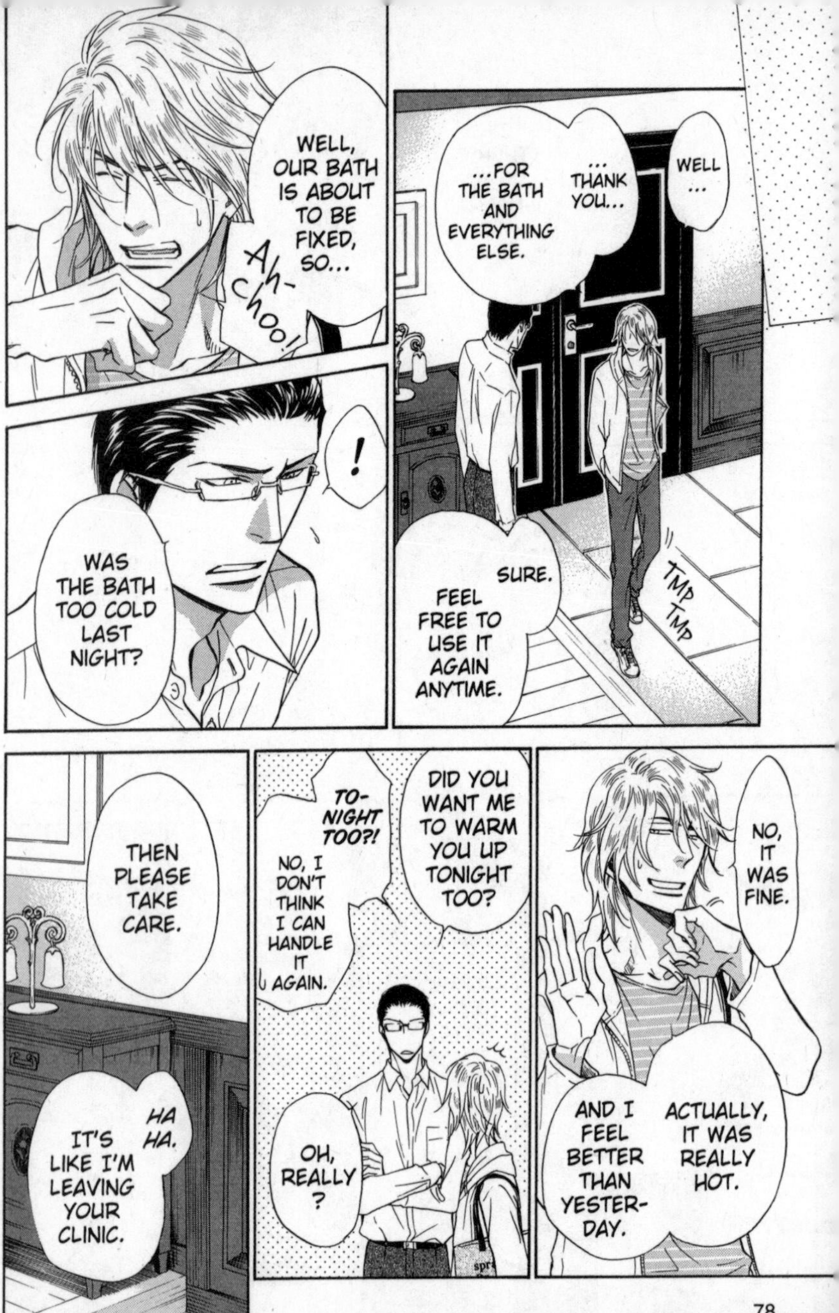
WELL...
...THANK YOU...
...FOR THE BATH AND EVERYTHING ELSE.
SURE.
FEEL FREE TO USE IT AGAIN ANYTIME.
TMP TMP
WELL, OUR BATH IS ABOUT TO BE FIXED, SO...
Ah-choo!
!
WAS THE BATH TOO COLD LAST NIGHT?
NO, IT WAS FINE.
ACTUALLY, IT WAS REALLY HOT.
AND I FEEL BETTER THAN YESTER-DAY.
DID YOU WANT ME TO WARM YOU UP TONIGHT TOO?
TO-NIGHT TOO?!
NO, I DON'T THINK I CAN HANDLE IT AGAIN.
OH, REALLY?
THEN PLEASE TAKE CARE.
HA HA.
IT'S LIKE I'M LEAVING YOUR CLINIC.

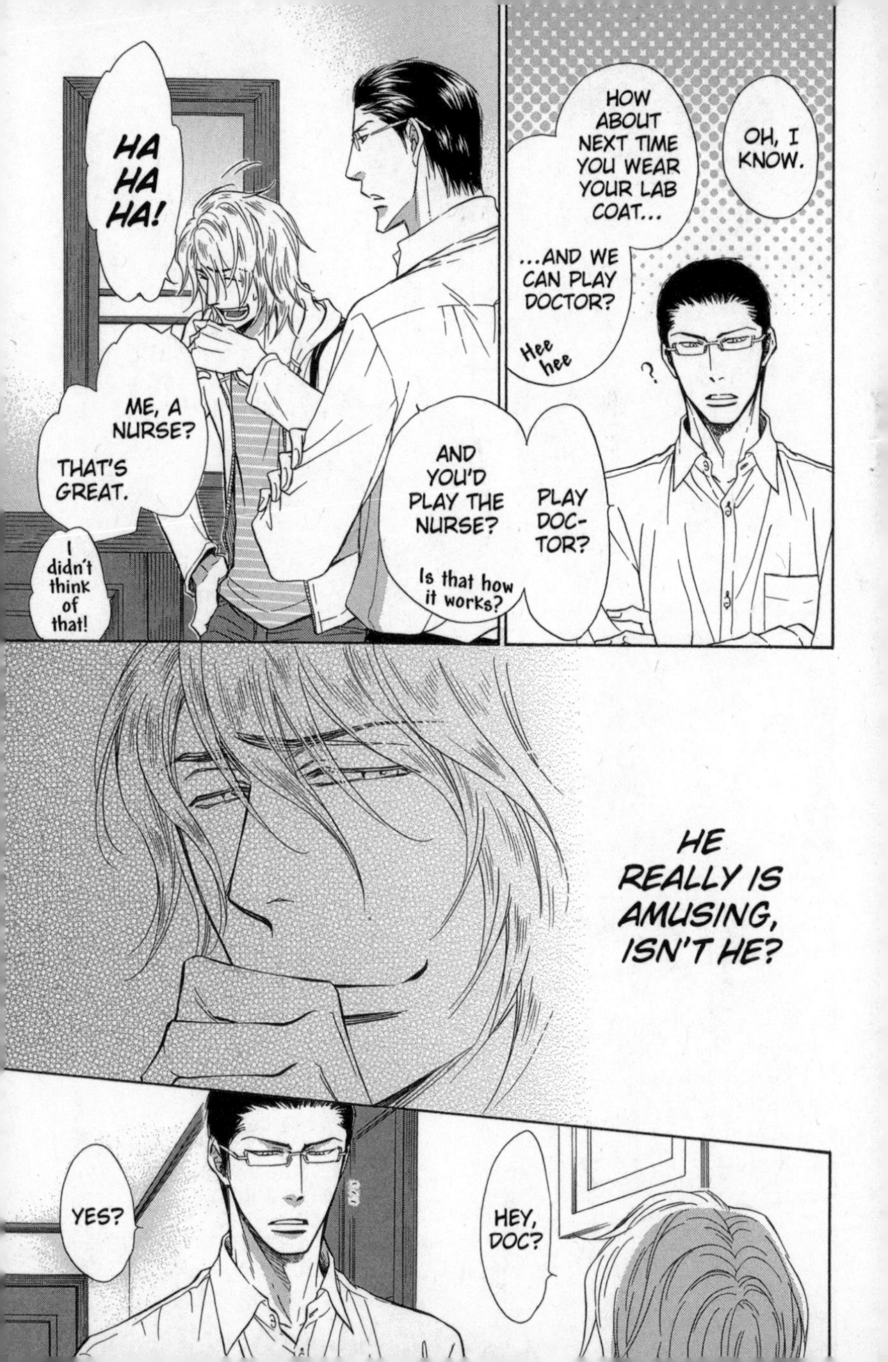
OH, I KNOW.
HOW ABOUT NEXT TIME YOU WEAR YOUR LAB COAT...
...AND WE CAN PLAY DOCTOR?
Hee hee
?
PLAY DOC-TOR?
AND YOU'D PLAY THE NURSE?
Is that how it works?
HA HA HA!
ME, A NURSE?
THAT'S GREAT.
I didn't think of that!
HE REALLY IS AMUSING, ISN'T HE?
HEY, DOC?
YES?

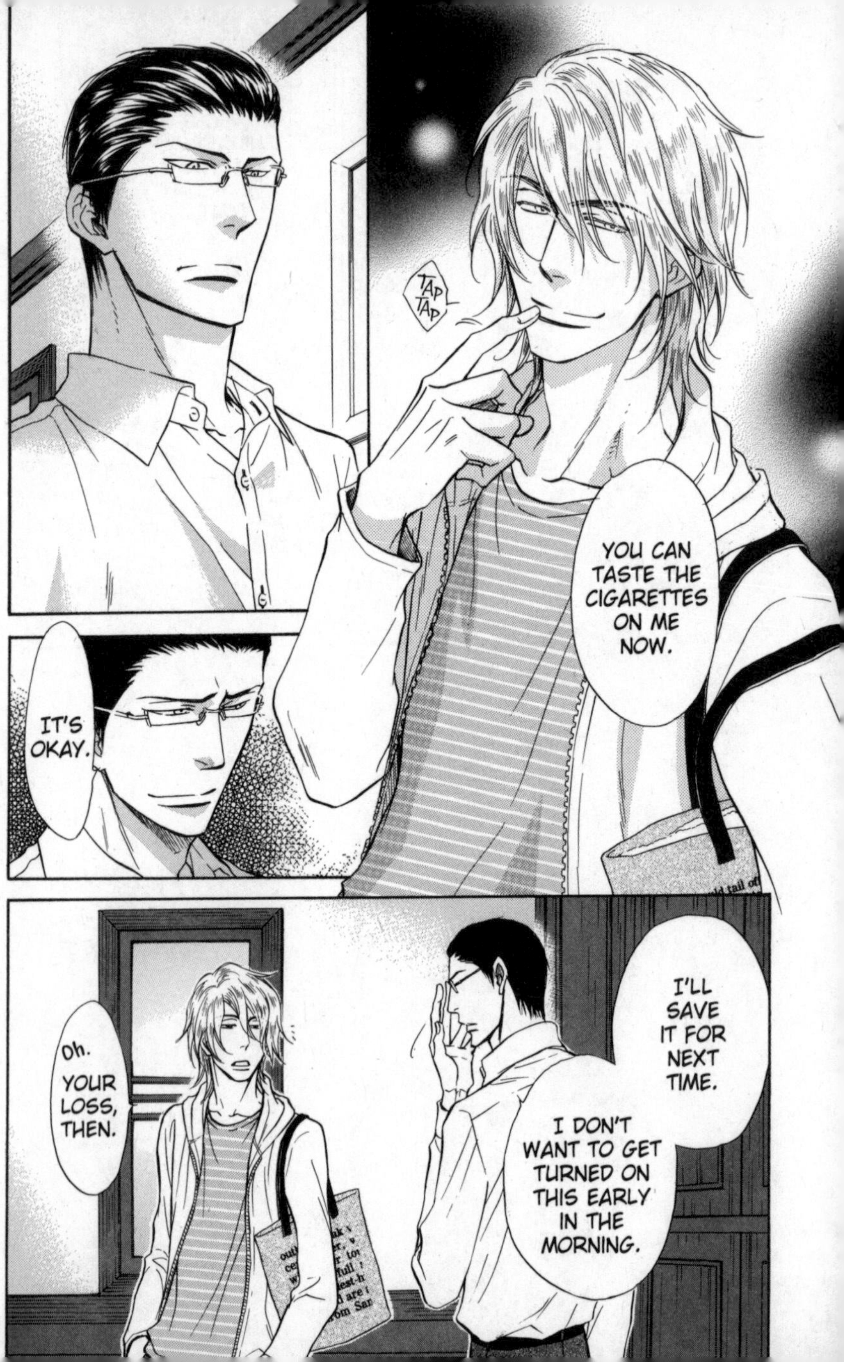
TAP TAP
YOU CAN TASTE THE CIGARETTES ON ME NOW.
IT'S OKAY.
I'LL SAVE IT FOR NEXT TIME.
I DON'T WANT TO GET TURNED ON THIS EARLY IN THE MORNING.
Oh. YOUR LOSS, THEN.

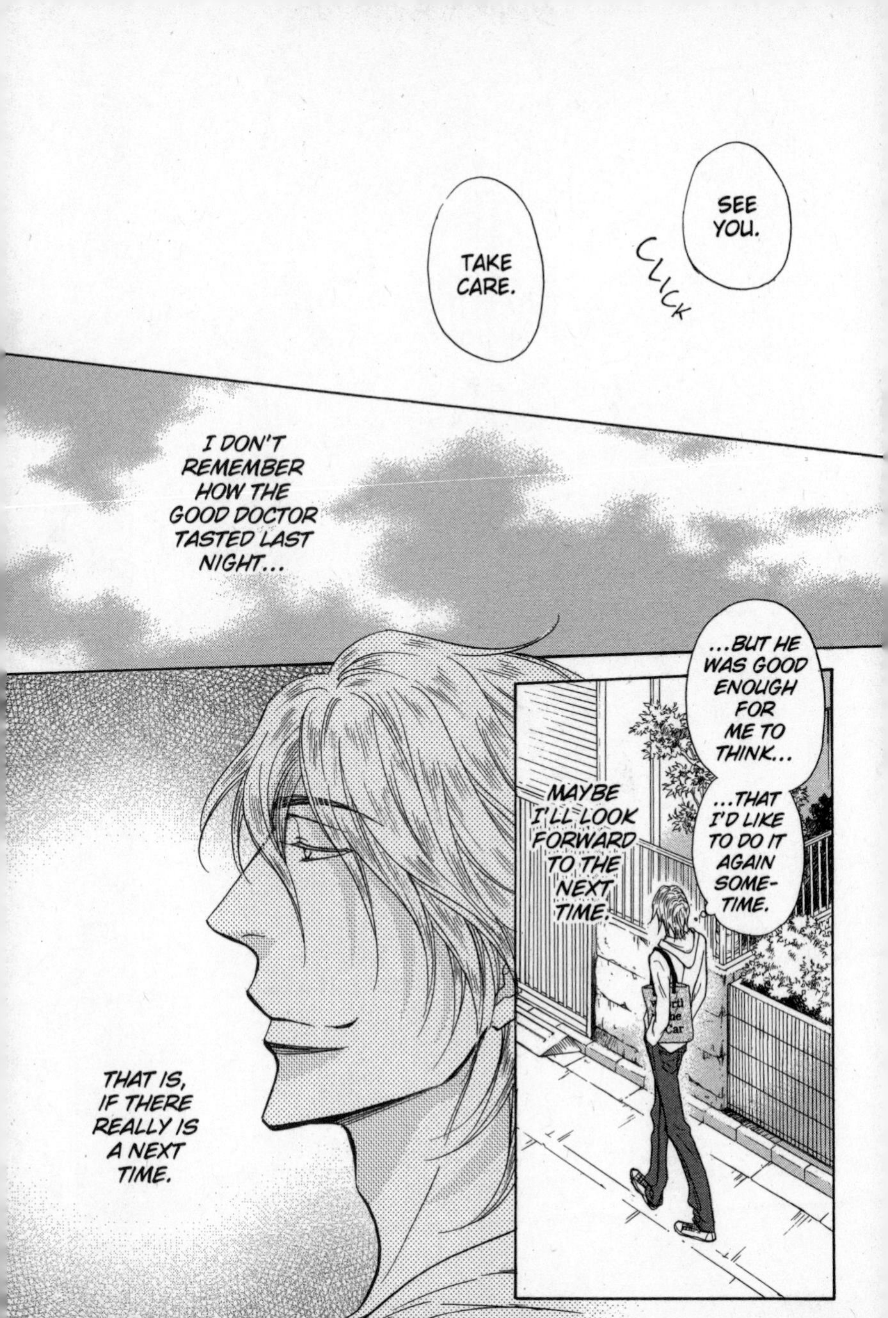
SEE YOU.
CLICK
TAKE CARE.
I DON'T REMEMBER HOW THE GOOD DOCTOR TASTED LAST NIGHT...
...BUT HE WAS GOOD ENOUGH FOR ME TO THINK...
...THAT I'D LIKE TO DO IT AGAIN SOME-TIME.
MAYBE I'LL LOOK FORWARD TO THE NEXT TIME.
THAT IS, IF THERE REALLY IS A NEXT TIME.

act.2 end

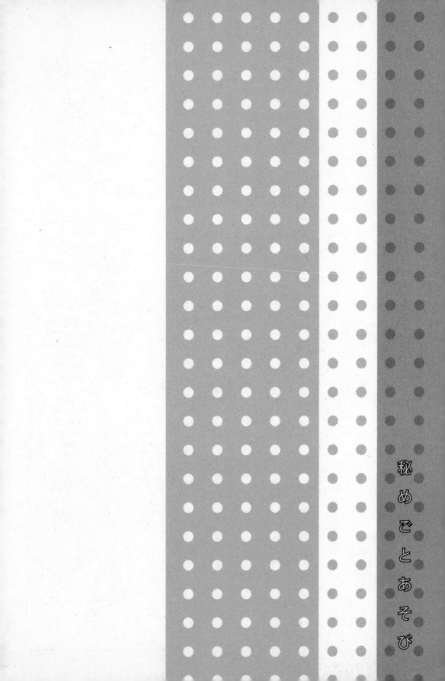

秘めごとあそび

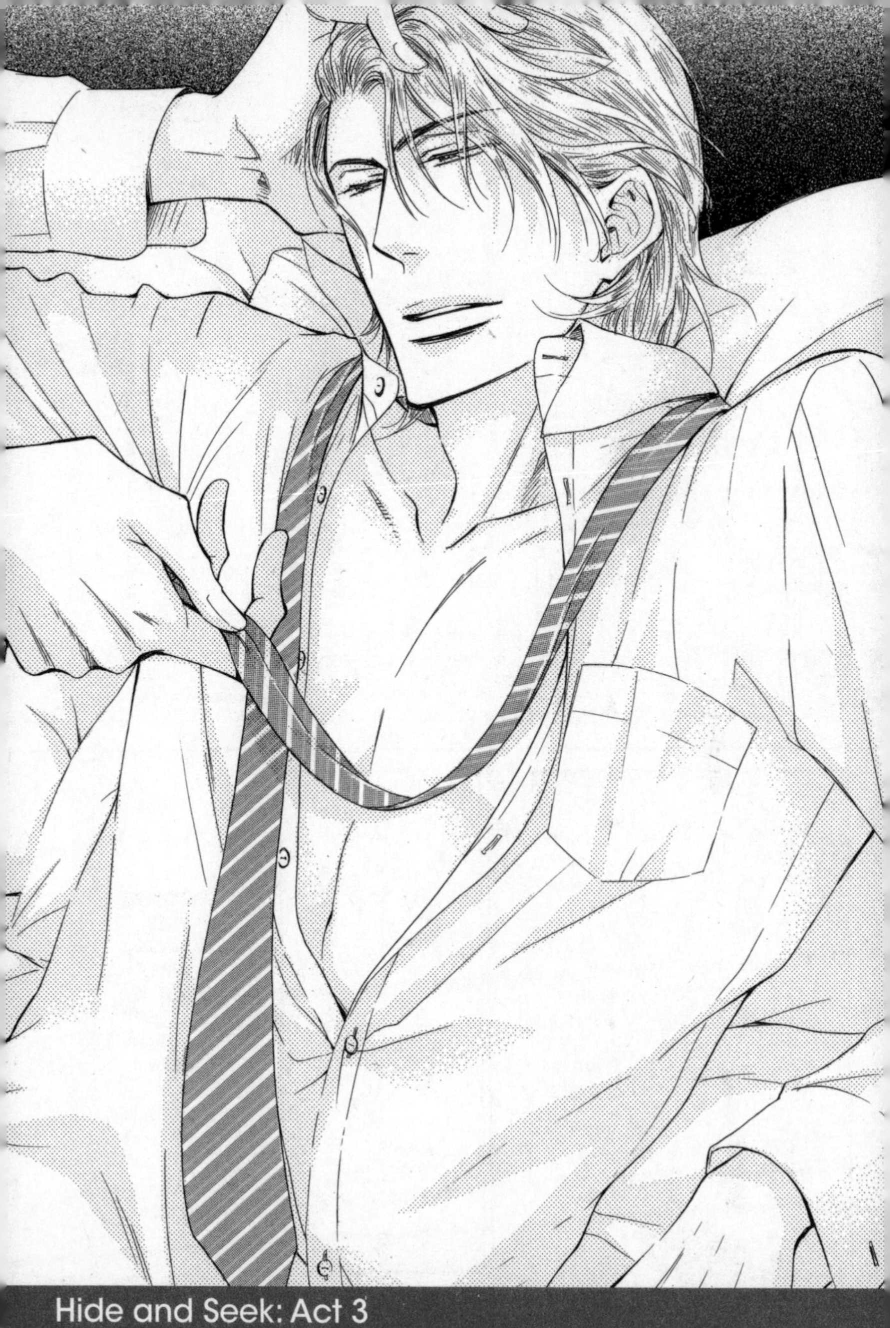

Hide and Seek: Act 3

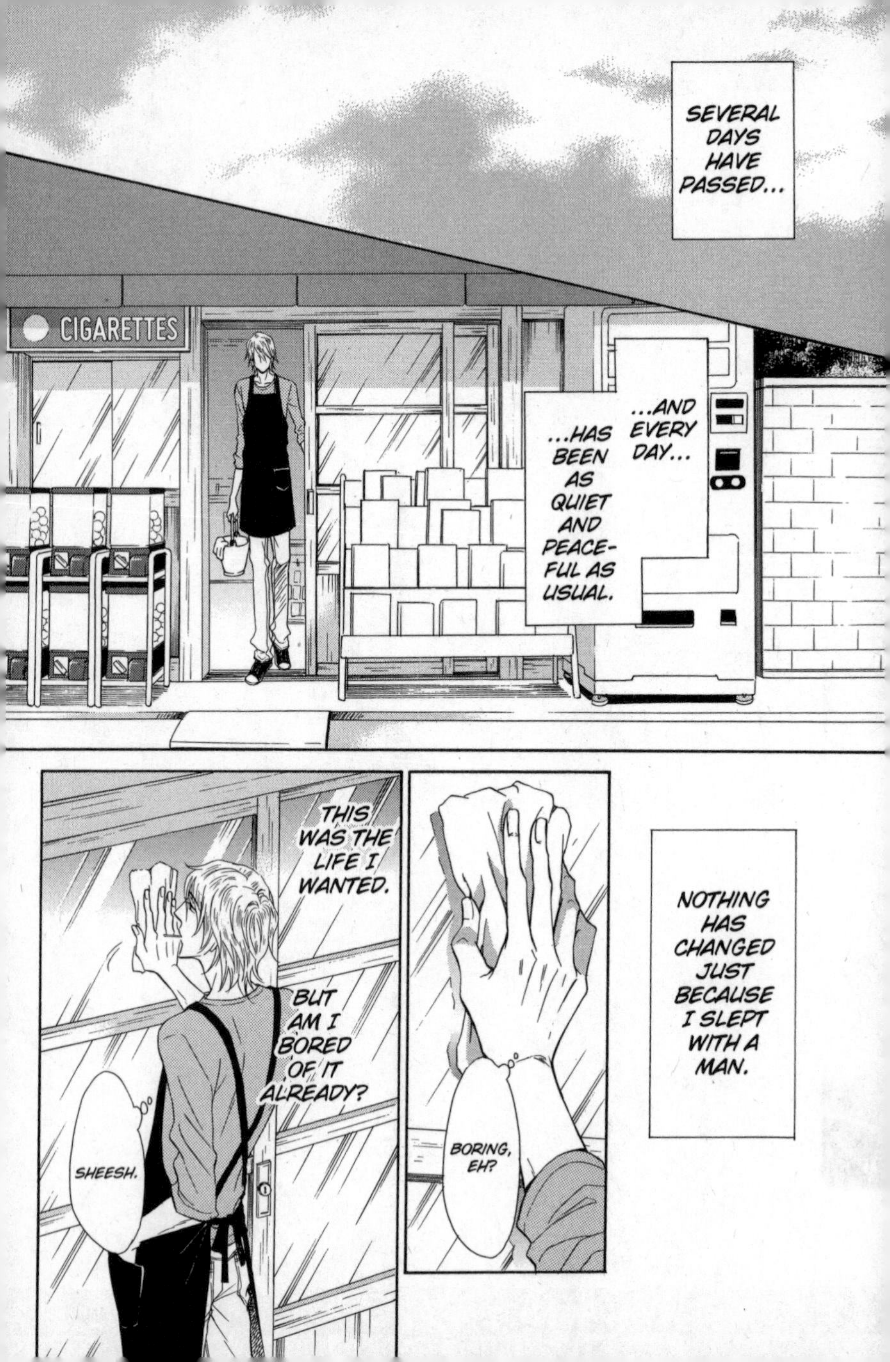
SEVERAL DAYS HAVE PASSED...
CIGARETTES
...AND EVERY DAY...
...HAS BEEN AS QUIET AND PEACE-FUL AS USUAL.
NOTHING HAS CHANGED JUST BECAUSE I SLEPT WITH A MAN.
BORING, EH?
THIS WAS THE LIFE I WANTED.
BUT AM I BORED OF IT ALREADY?
SHEESH.

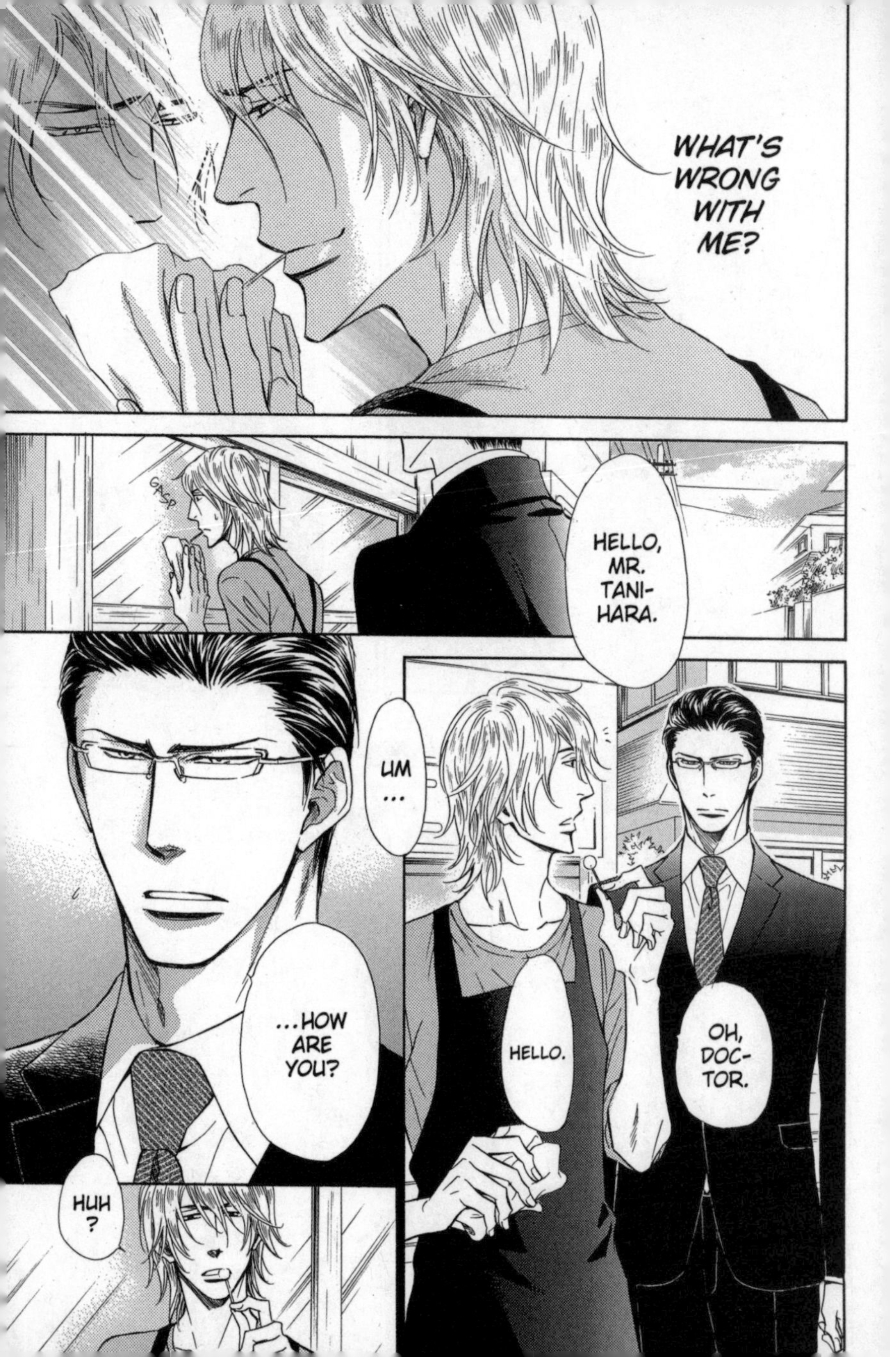
WHAT'S WRONG WITH ME?
GASP
HELLO, MR. TANI-HARA.
OH, DOC-TOR.
HELLO.
UM ...
...HOW ARE YOU?
HUH?

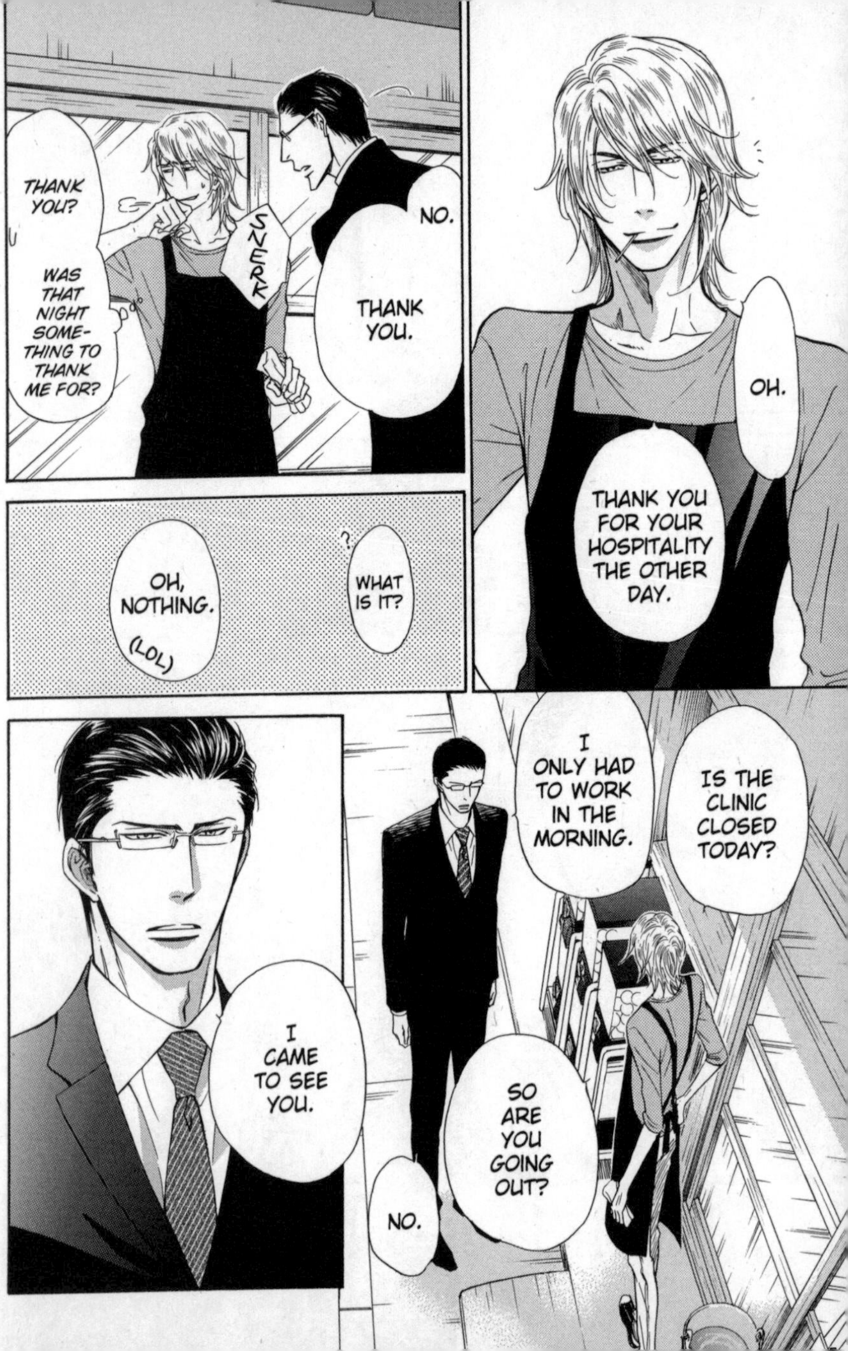
OH.
THANK YOU FOR YOUR HOSPITALITY THE OTHER DAY.
NO.
THANK YOU.
SNERK
THANK YOU?
WAS THAT NIGHT SOMETHING TO THANK ME FOR?
WHAT IS IT?
OH, NOTHING.
(LOL)
IS THE CLINIC CLOSED TODAY?
I ONLY HAD TO WORK IN THE MORNING.
SO ARE YOU GOING OUT?
NO.
I CAME TO SEE YOU.

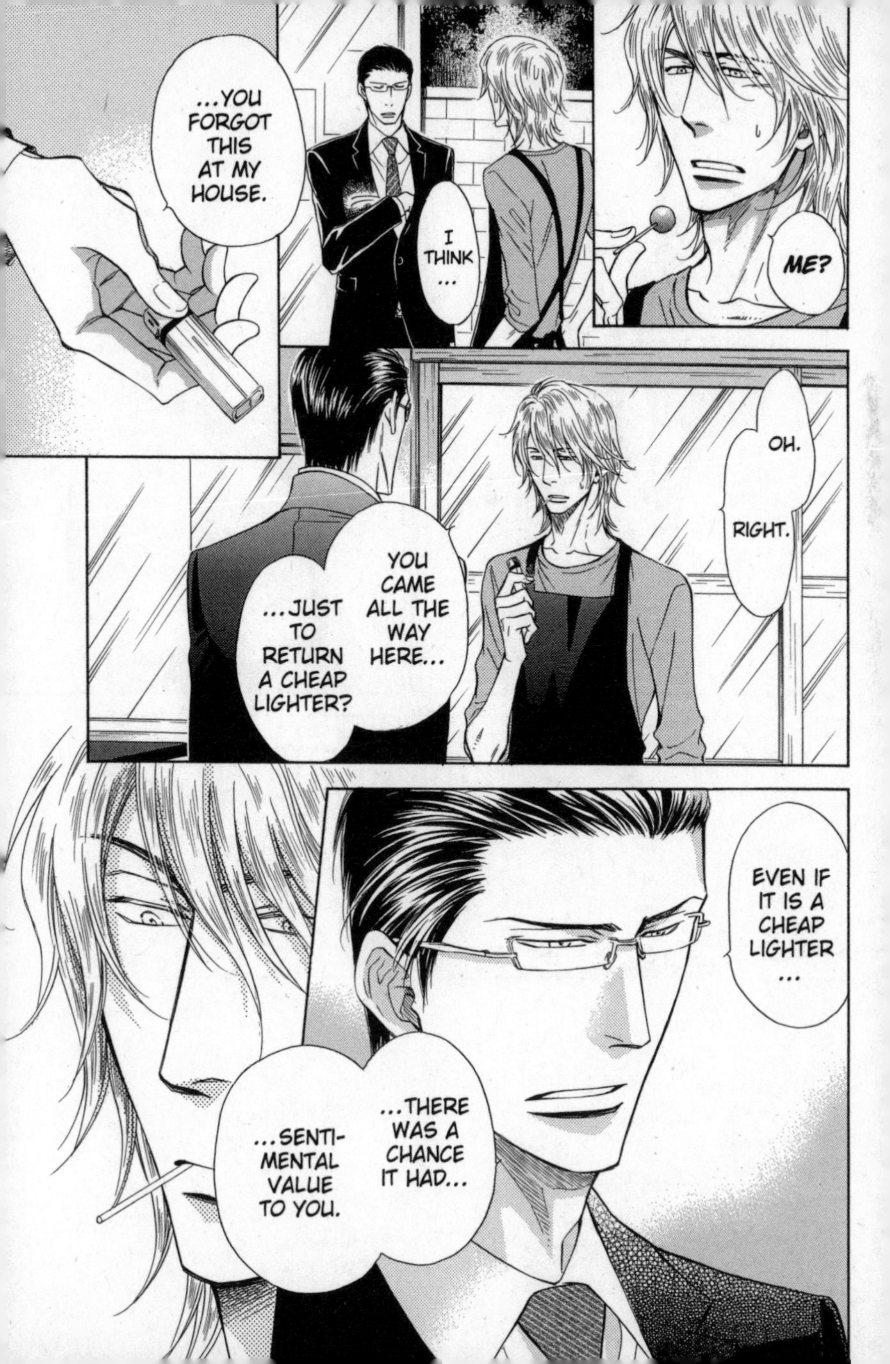
ME?
I THINK ...
...YOU FORGOT THIS AT MY HOUSE.
OH. RIGHT.
YOU CAME ALL THE WAY HERE...
...JUST TO RETURN A CHEAP LIGHTER?
EVEN IF IT IS A CHEAP LIGHTER ...
...THERE WAS A CHANCE IT HAD...
...SENTI-MENTAL VALUE TO YOU.

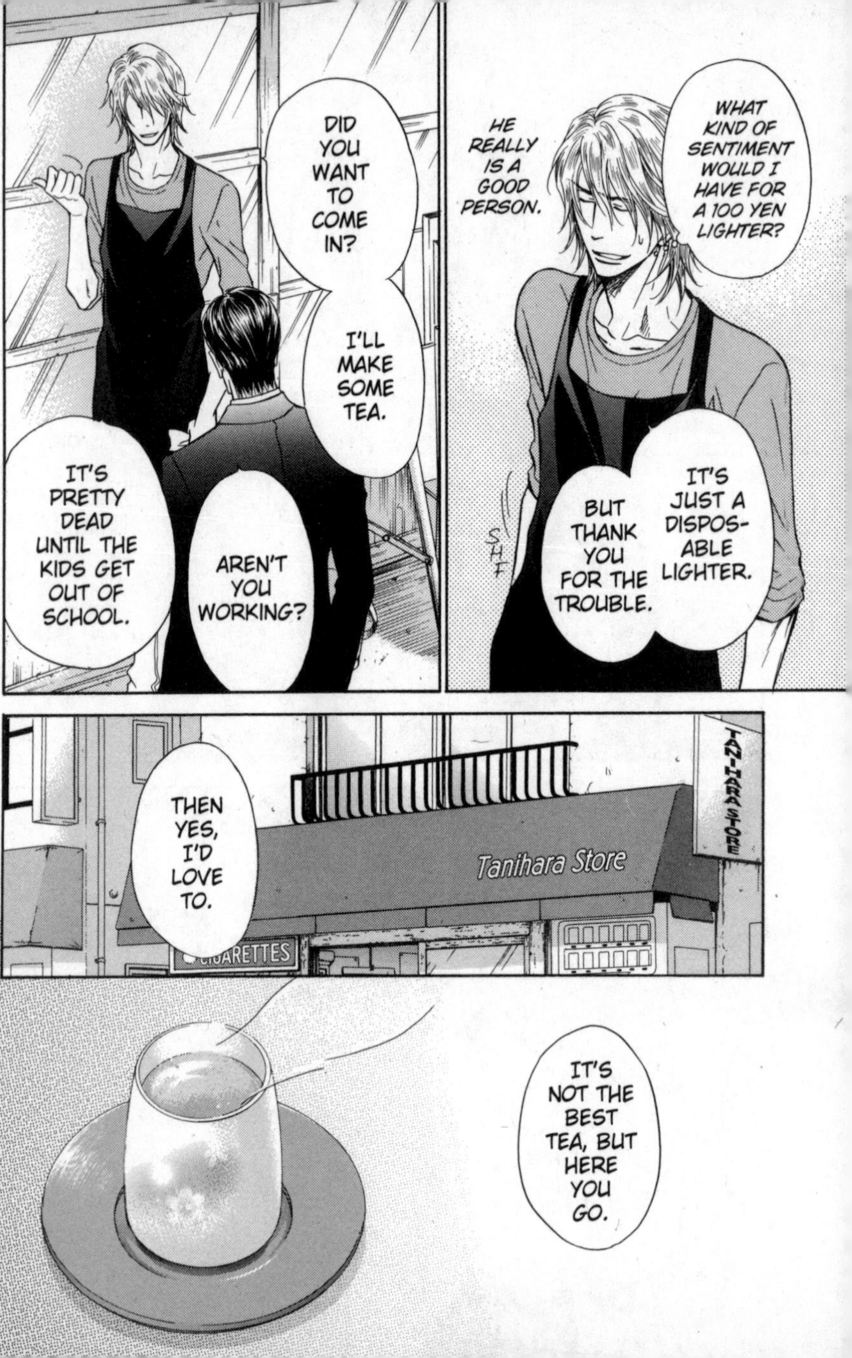
WHAT KIND OF SENTIMENT WOULD I HAVE FOR A 100 YEN LIGHTER?
HE REALLY IS A GOOD PERSON.
IT'S JUST A DISPOS-ABLE LIGHTER.
BUT THANK YOU FOR THE TROUBLE.
SHF
DID YOU WANT TO COME IN?
I'LL MAKE SOME TEA.
AREN'T YOU WORKING?
IT'S PRETTY DEAD UNTIL THE KIDS GET OUT OF SCHOOL.
TANIHARA STORE
Tanihara Store
THEN YES, I'D LOVE TO.
CIGARETTES
IT'S NOT THE BEST TEA, BUT HERE YOU GO.

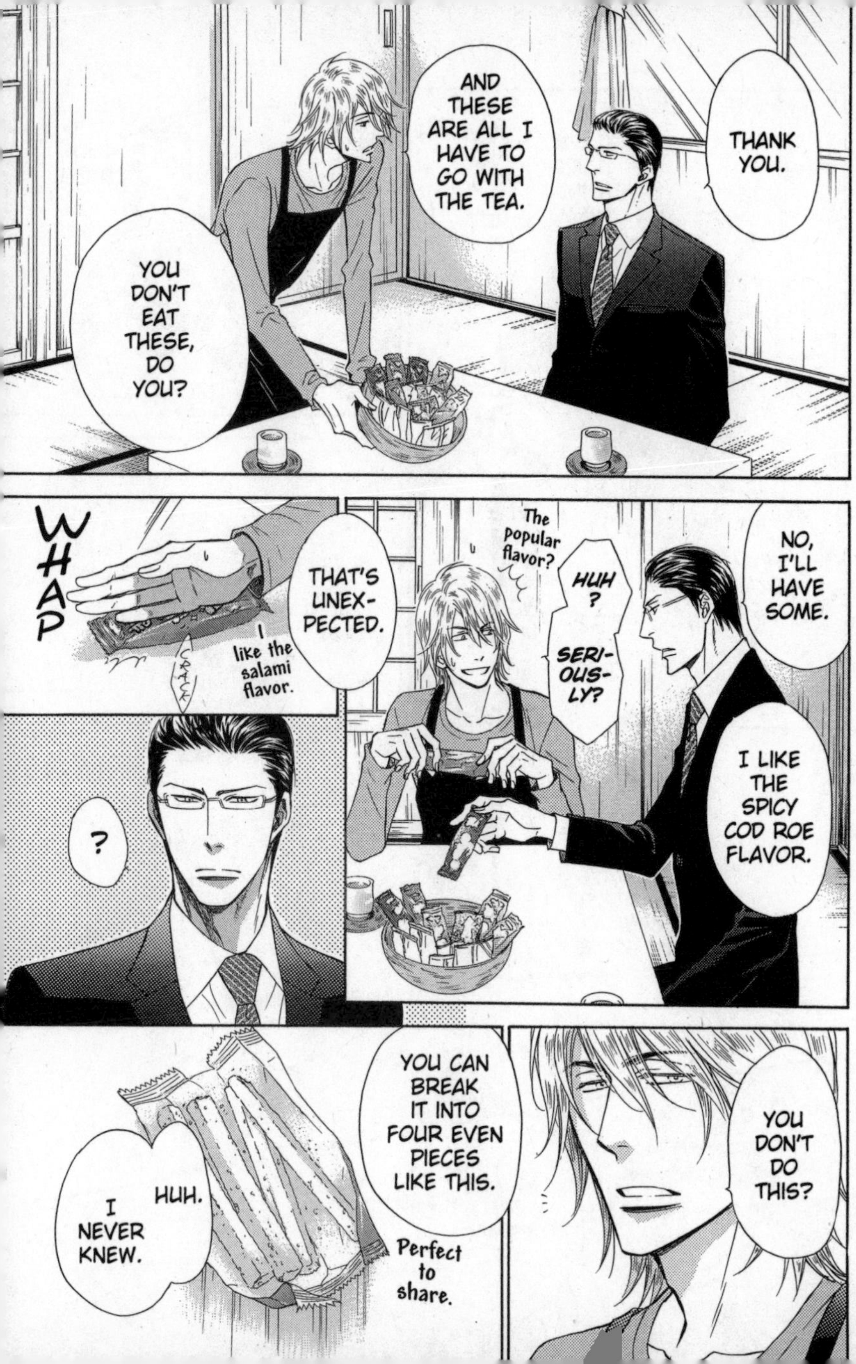

THANK YOU.
AND THESE ARE ALL I HAVE TO GO WITH THE TEA.
YOU DON'T EAT THESE, DO YOU?
NO, I'LL HAVE SOME.
HUH? SERI-OUS-LY?
The popular flavor?
THAT'S UNEX-PECTED.
I LIKE THE SPICY COD ROE FLAVOR.
WHAP
I like the salami flavor.
CRACK
?
YOU DON'T DO THIS?
YOU CAN BREAK IT INTO FOUR EVEN PIECES LIKE THIS.
Perfect to share.
HUH.
I NEVER KNEW.

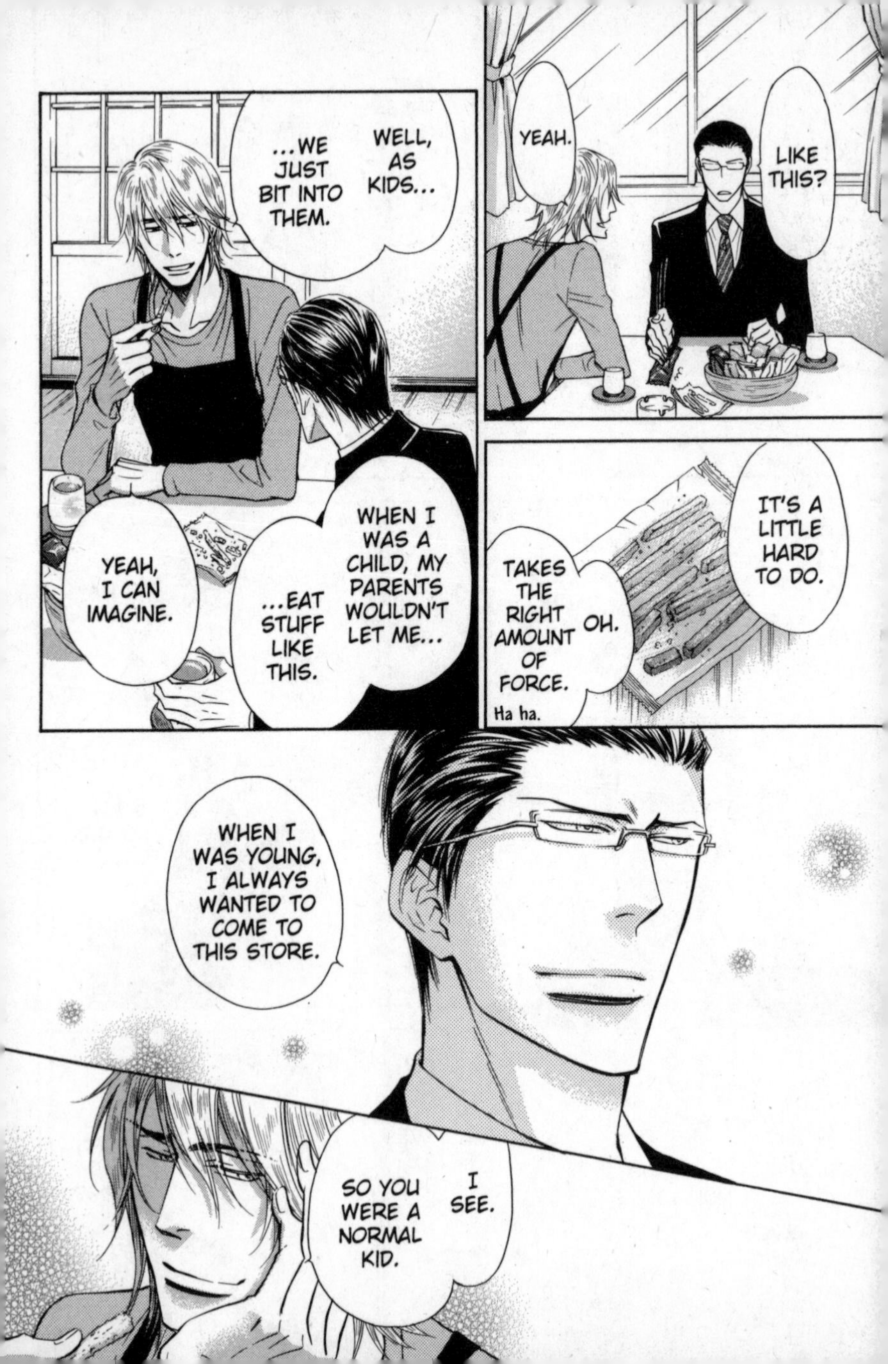
LIKE THIS?
YEAH.
IT'S A LITTLE HARD TO DO.
OH. TAKES THE RIGHT AMOUNT OF FORCE.
Ha ha.
WELL, AS KIDS... ...WE JUST BIT INTO THEM.
WHEN I WAS A CHILD, MY PARENTS WOULDN'T LET ME... ...EAT STUFF LIKE THIS.
YEAH, I CAN IMAGINE.
WHEN I WAS YOUNG, I ALWAYS WANTED TO COME TO THIS STORE.
I SEE. SO YOU WERE A NORMAL KID.

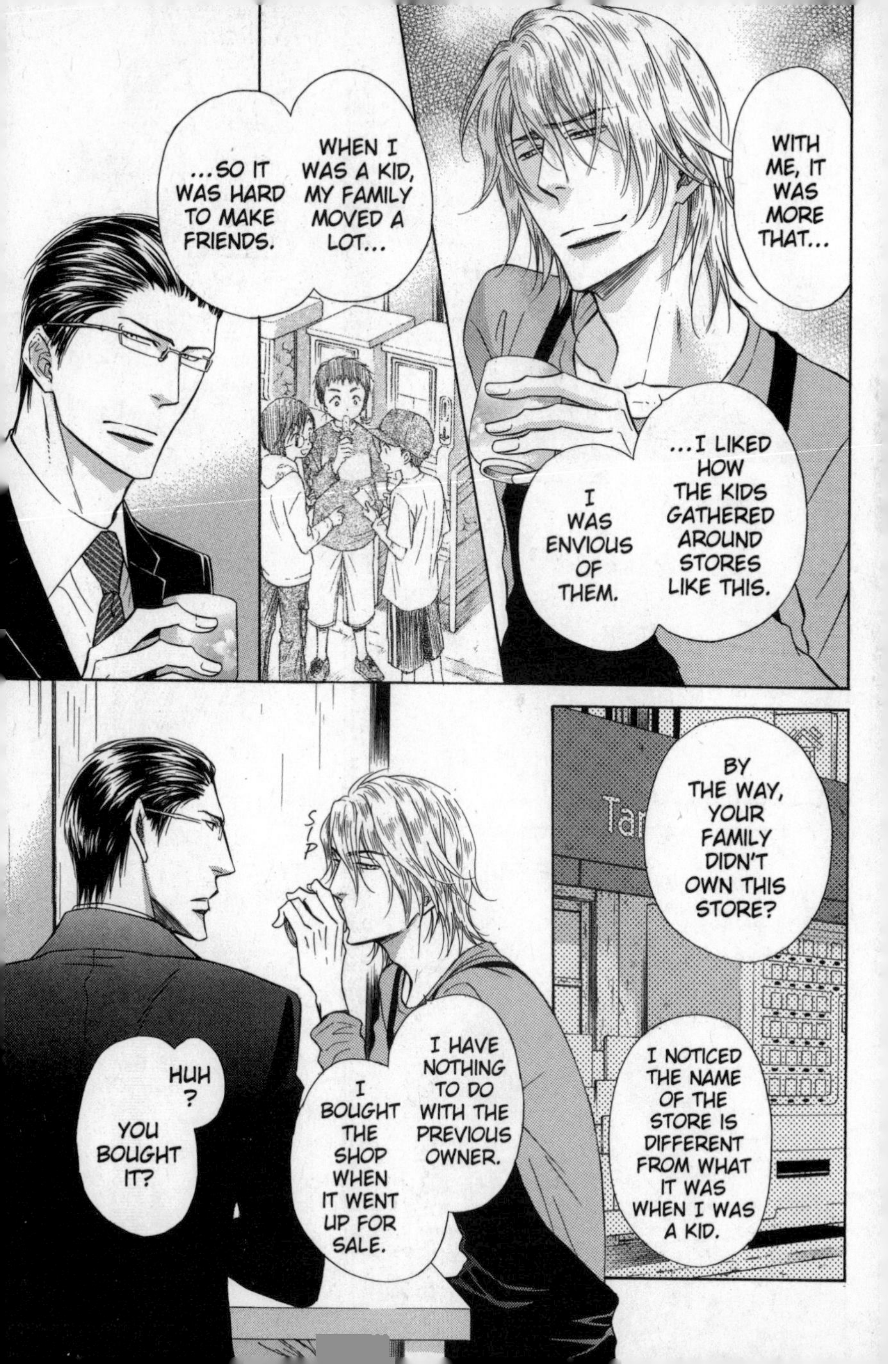
WITH ME, IT WAS MORE THAT...
...I LIKED HOW THE KIDS GATHERED AROUND STORES LIKE THIS.
I WAS ENVIOUS OF THEM.
WHEN I WAS A KID, MY FAMILY MOVED A LOT...
...SO IT WAS HARD TO MAKE FRIENDS.
BY THE WAY, YOUR FAMILY DIDN'T OWN THIS STORE?
I NOTICED THE NAME OF THE STORE IS DIFFERENT FROM WHAT IT WAS WHEN I WAS A KID.
SIP
I HAVE NOTHING TO DO WITH THE PREVIOUS OWNER.
I BOUGHT THE SHOP WHEN IT WENT UP FOR SALE.
HUH? YOU BOUGHT IT?

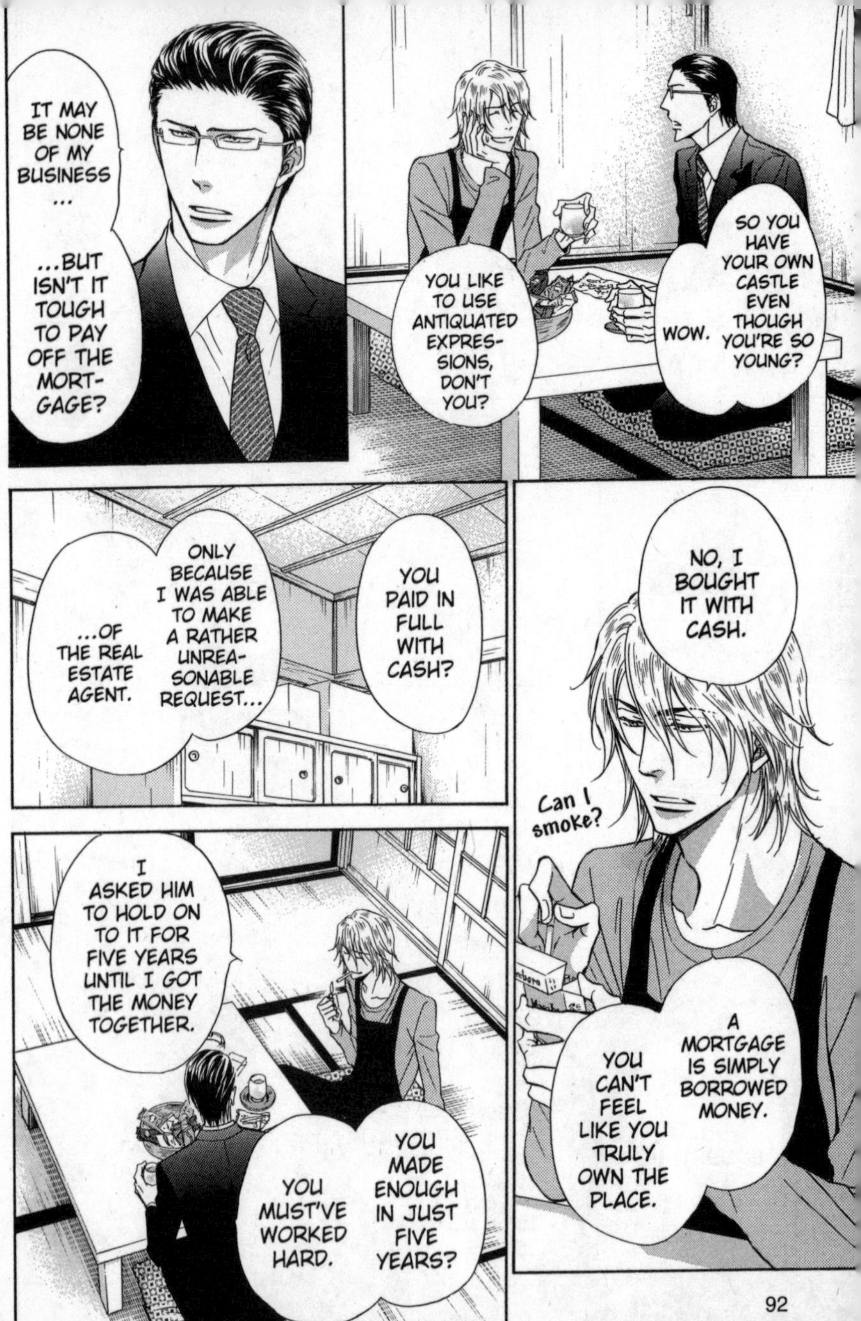
SO YOU HAVE YOUR OWN CASTLE EVEN THOUGH YOU'RE SO YOUNG?
WOW.
YOU LIKE TO USE ANTIQUATED EXPRES-SIONS, DON'T YOU?
IT MAY BE NONE OF MY BUSINESS ...
...BUT ISN'T IT TOUGH TO PAY OFF THE MORT-GAGE?
NO, I BOUGHT IT WITH CASH.
Can I smoke?
A MORTGAGE IS SIMPLY BORROWED MONEY.
YOU CAN'T FEEL LIKE YOU TRULY OWN THE PLACE.
YOU PAID IN FULL WITH CASH?
ONLY BECAUSE I WAS ABLE TO MAKE A RATHER UNREA-SONABLE REQUEST...
...OF THE REAL ESTATE AGENT.
I ASKED HIM TO HOLD ON TO IT FOR FIVE YEARS UNTIL I GOT THE MONEY TOGETHER.
YOU MADE ENOUGH IN JUST FIVE YEARS?
YOU MUST'VE WORKED HARD.

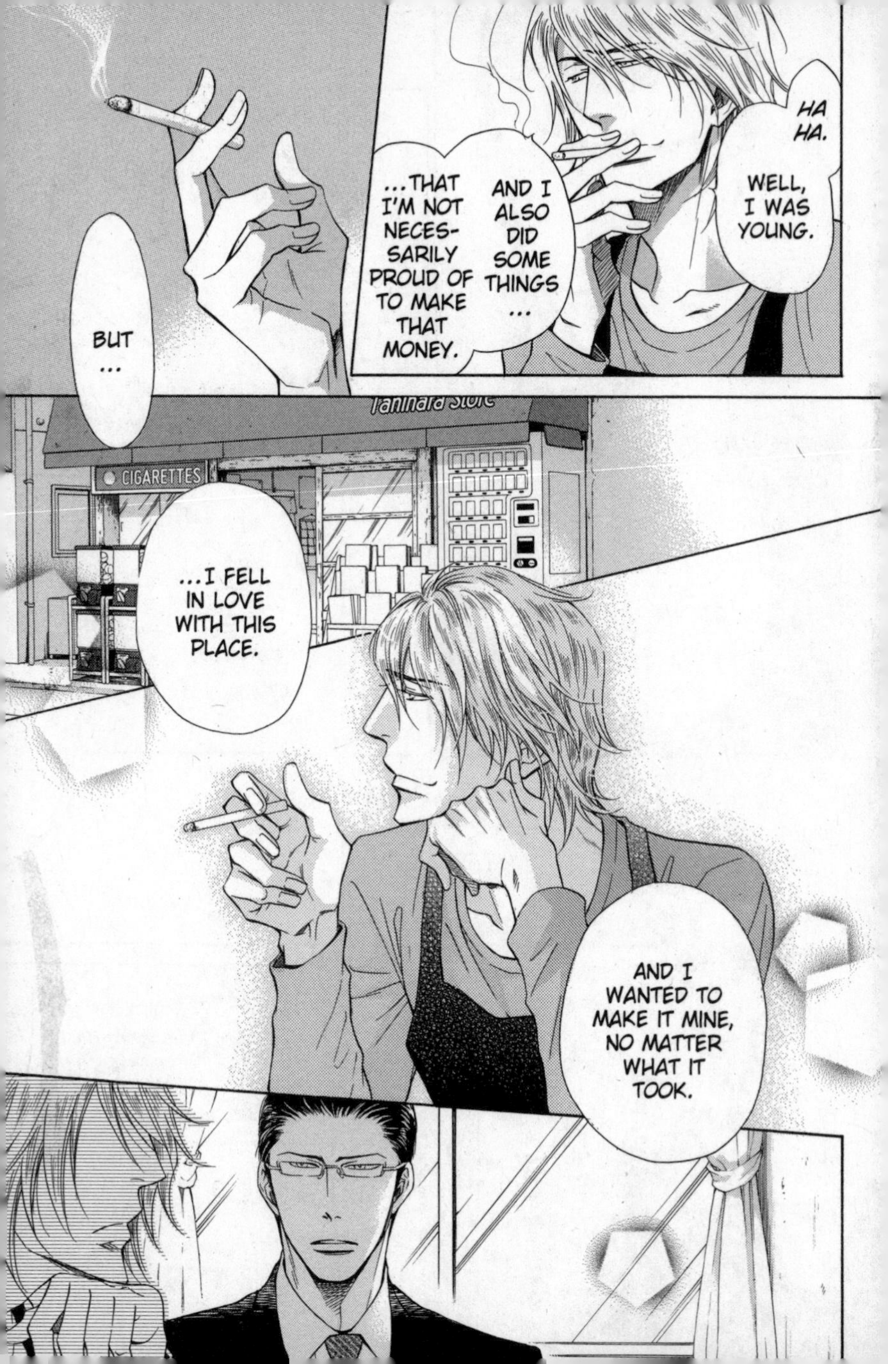
HA HA.
WELL, I WAS YOUNG.
AND I ALSO DID SOME THINGS...
...THAT I'M NOT NECES-SARILY PROUD OF TO MAKE THAT MONEY.
BUT...
CIGARETTES
...I FELL IN LOVE WITH THIS PLACE.
AND I WANTED TO MAKE IT MINE, NO MATTER WHAT IT TOOK.

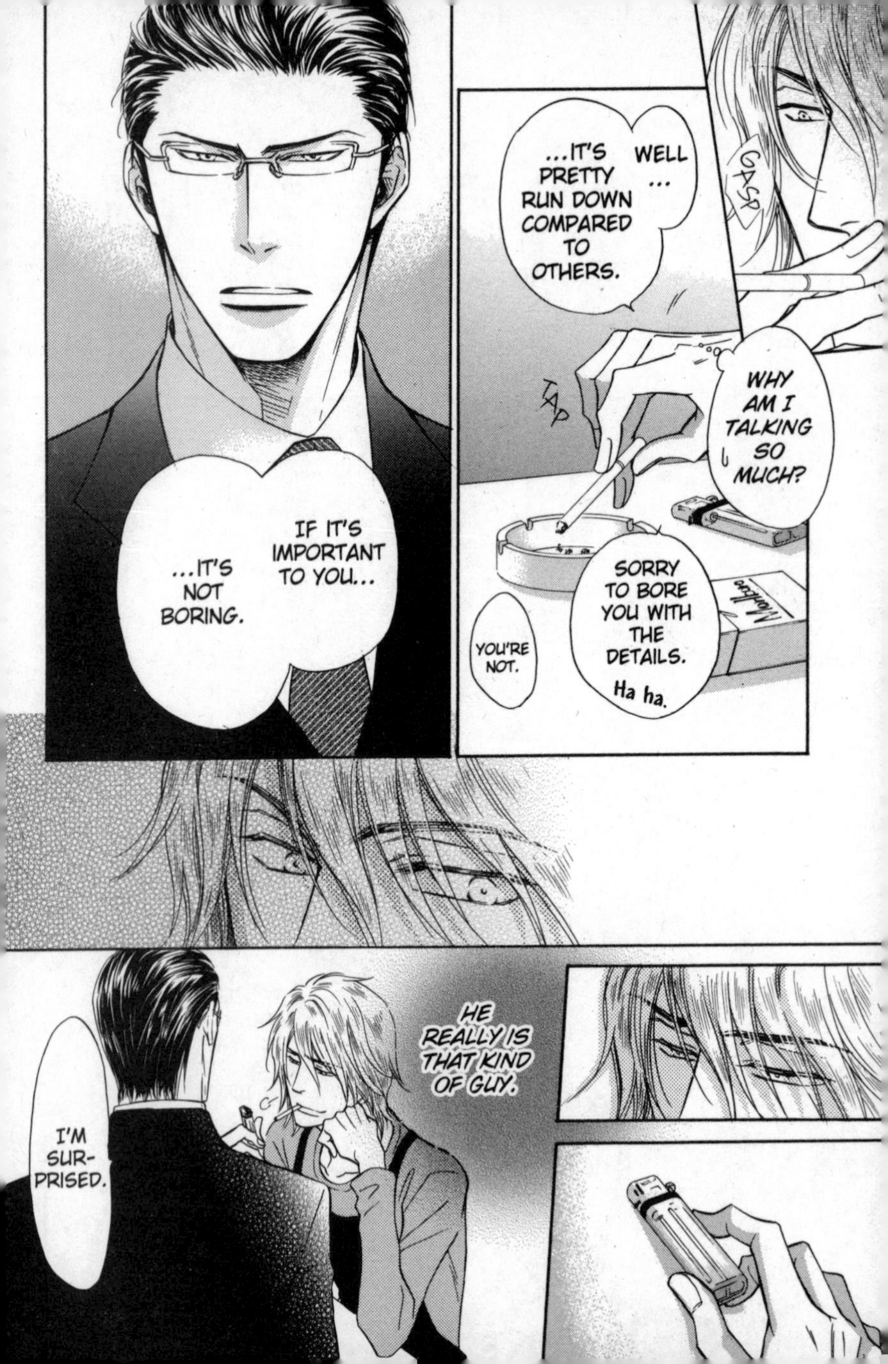
WELL ...
...IT'S PRETTY RUN DOWN COMPARED TO OTHERS.
GASP
WHY AM I TALKING SO MUCH?
TAP
SORRY TO BORE YOU WITH THE DETAILS.
Ha ha.
YOU'RE NOT.
IF IT'S IMPORTANT TO YOU...
...IT'S NOT BORING.
HE REALLY IS THAT KIND OF GUY.
I'M SUR-PRISED.

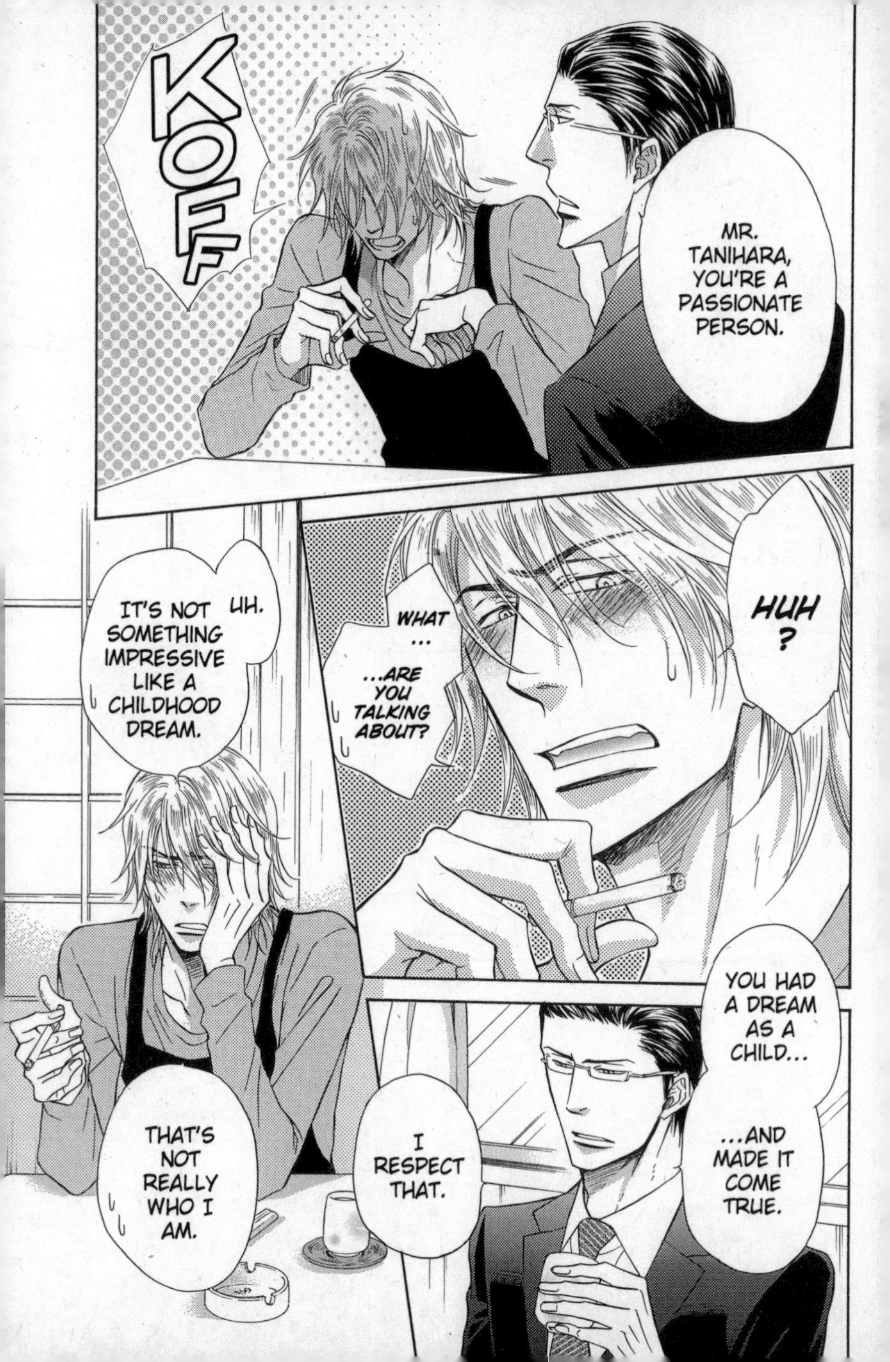
MR. TANIHARA, YOU'RE A PASSIONATE PERSON.
KOFF
HUH?
WHAT... ...ARE YOU TALKING ABOUT?
YOU HAD A DREAM AS A CHILD...
...AND MADE IT COME TRUE.
I RESPECT THAT.
UH.
IT'S NOT SOMETHING IMPRESSIVE LIKE A CHILDHOOD DREAM.
THAT'S NOT REALLY WHO I AM.

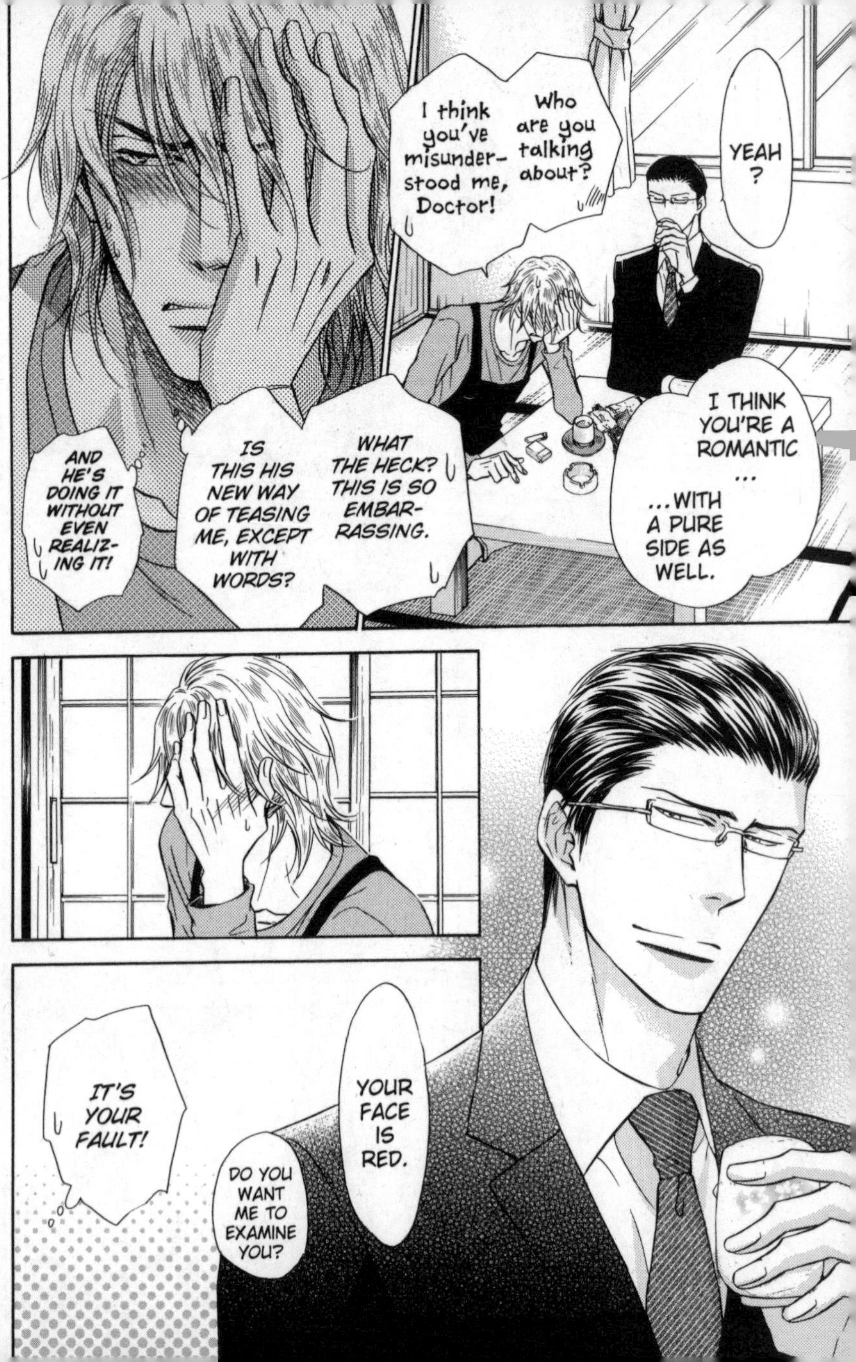
YEAH ?
Who are you talking about?
I think you've misunder-stood me, Doctor!
I THINK YOU'RE A ROMANTIC ...
...WITH A PURE SIDE AS WELL.
WHAT THE HECK? THIS IS SO EMBAR-RASSING.
IS THIS HIS NEW WAY OF TEASING ME, EXCEPT WITH WORDS?
AND HE'S DOING IT WITHOUT EVEN REALIZ-ING IT!
YOUR FACE IS RED.
DO YOU WANT ME TO EXAMINE YOU?
IT'S YOUR FAULT!

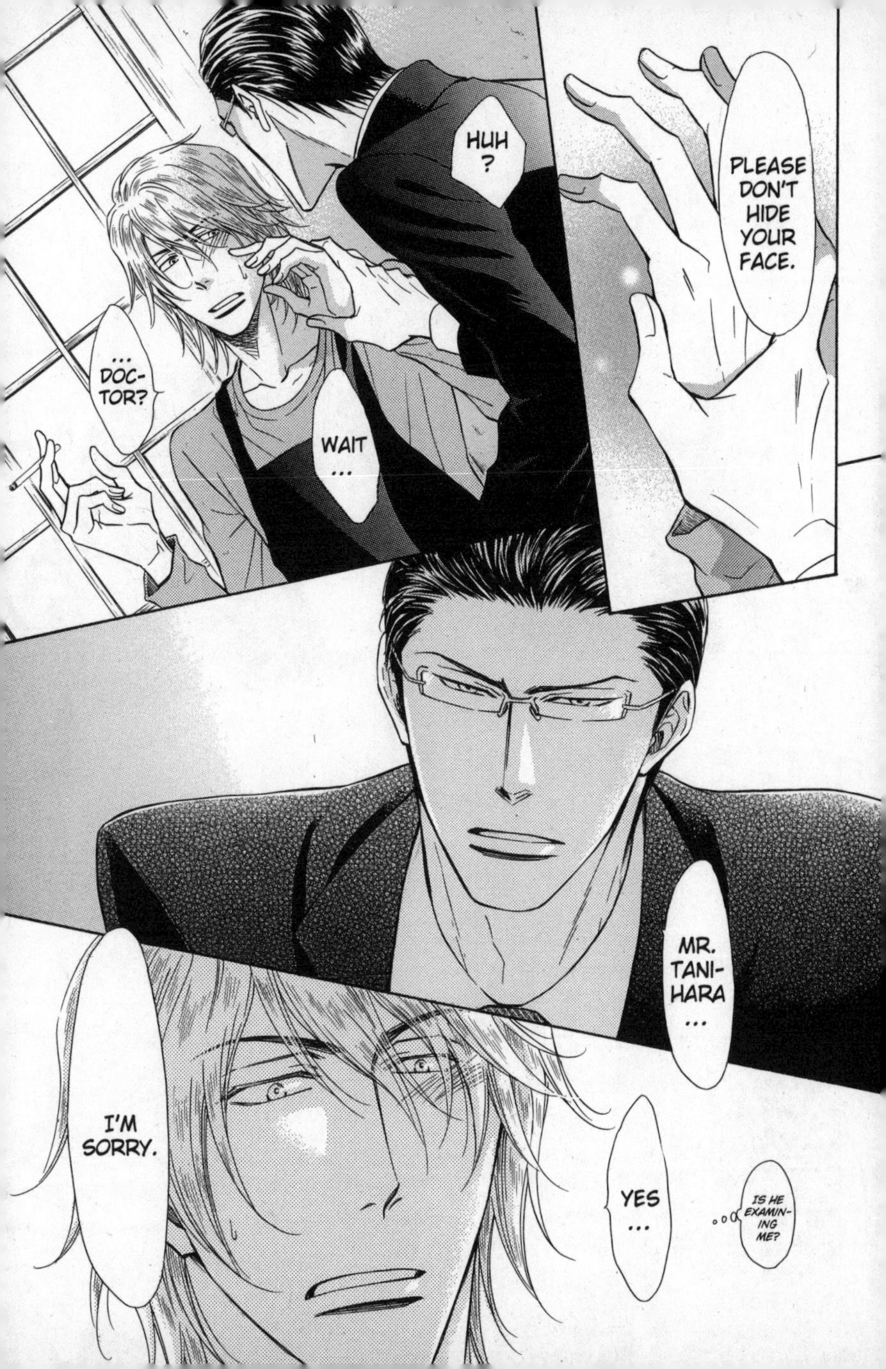
PLEASE DON'T HIDE YOUR FACE.
HUH?
WAIT...
...DOCTOR?
MR. TANIHARA...
YES...
IS HE EXAMINING ME?
I'M SORRY.

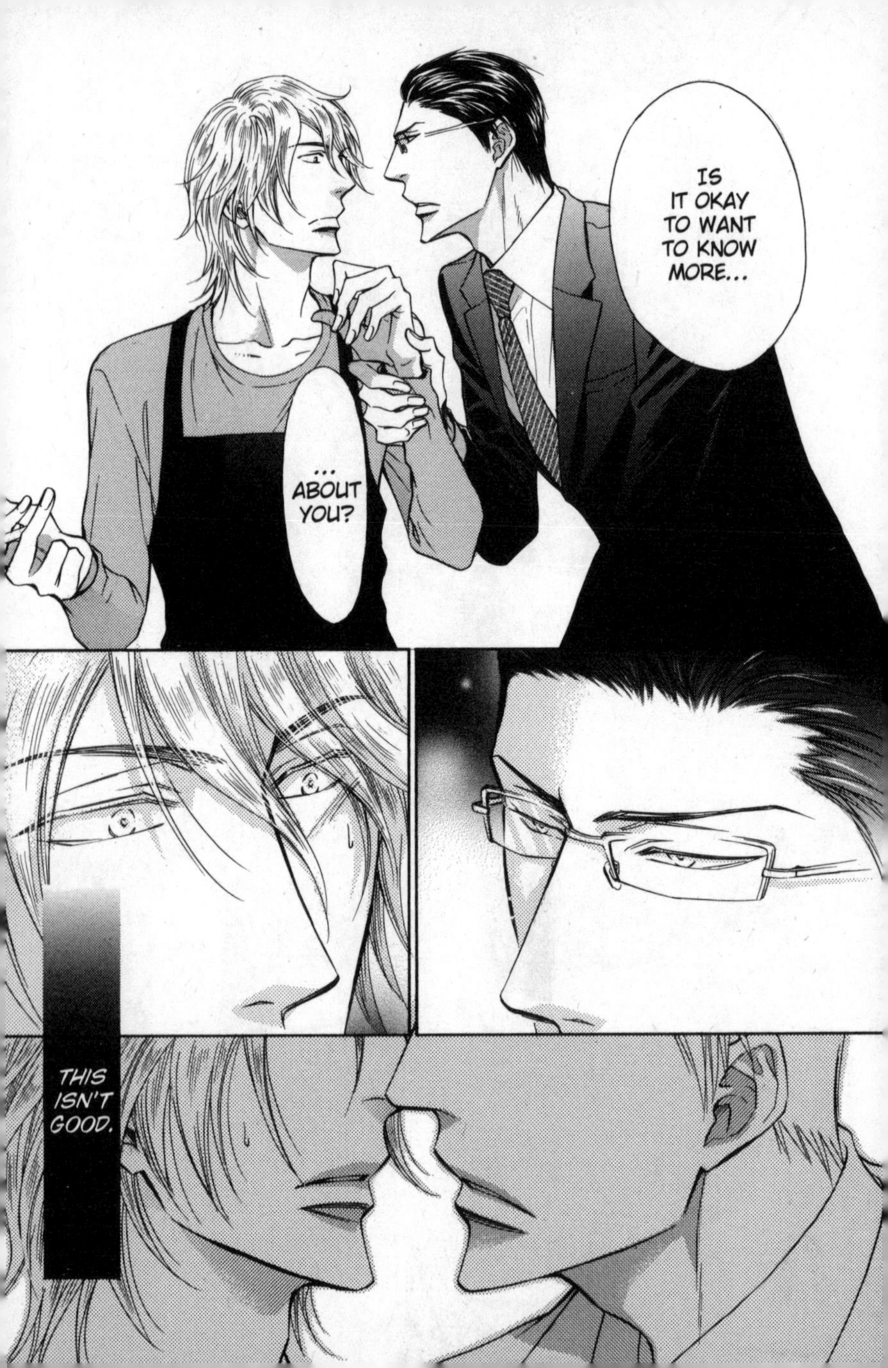
IS IT OKAY TO WANT TO KNOW MORE...
...ABOUT YOU?
THIS ISN'T GOOD.

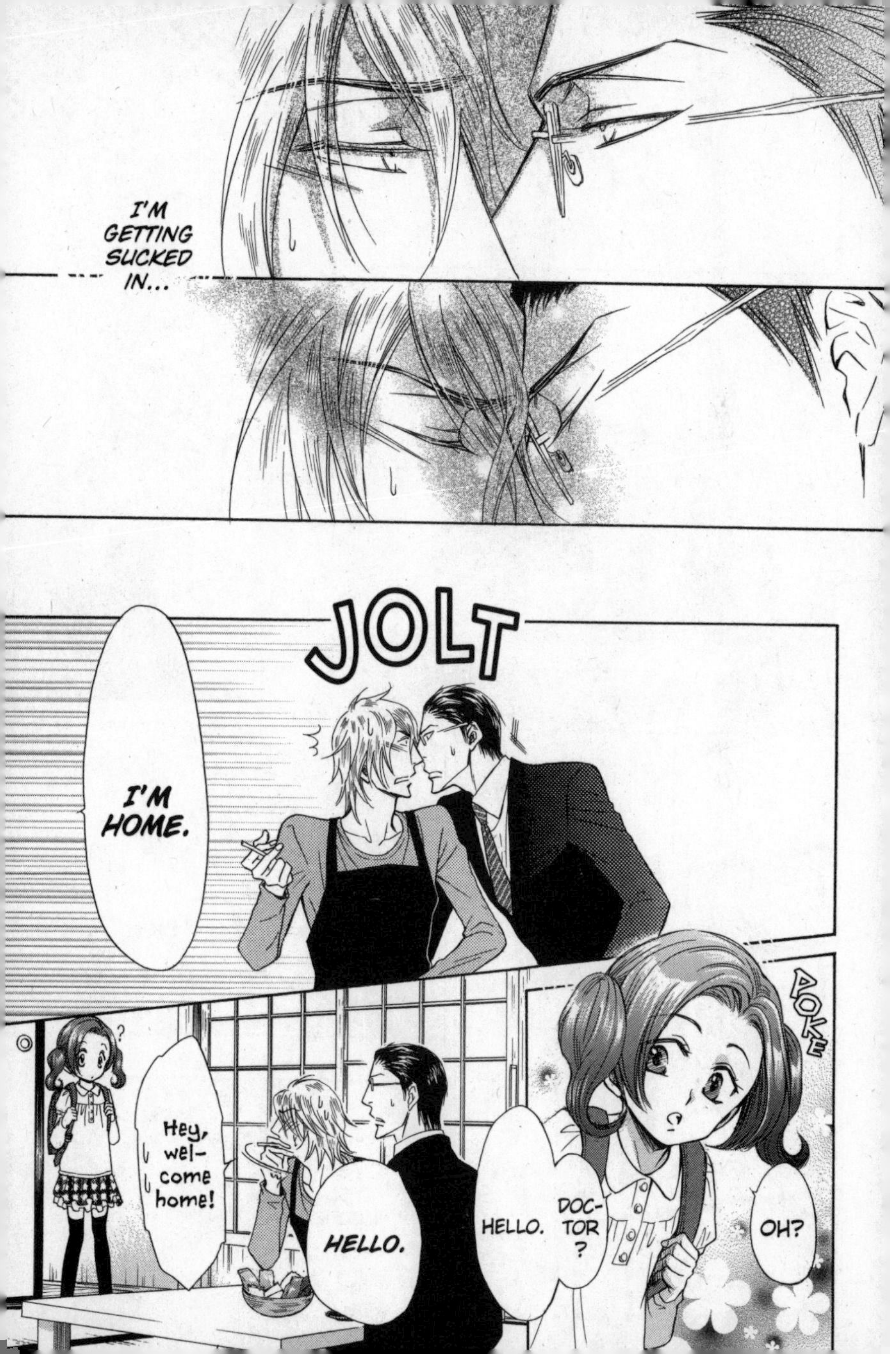
I'M GETTING SUCKED IN...
JOLT
I'M HOME.
POKE
OH?
DOC-TOR?
HELLO.
HELLO.
Hey, wel-come home!

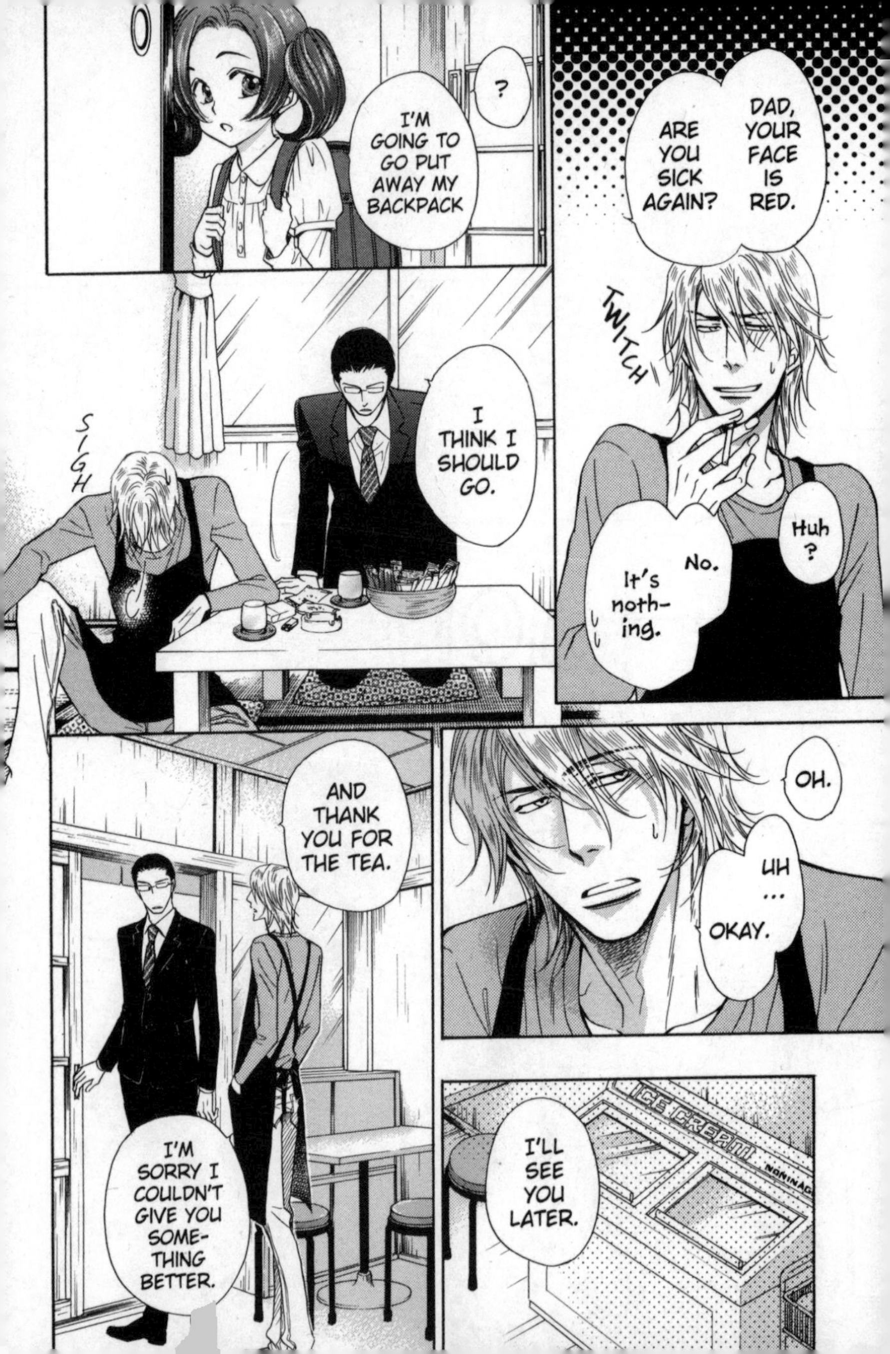
DAD, YOUR FACE IS RED.
ARE YOU SICK AGAIN?
TWITCH
Huh?
No.
It's nothing.
?
I'M GOING TO GO PUT AWAY MY BACKPACK
I THINK I SHOULD GO.
SIGH
OH.
UH... OKAY.
ICE CREAM
I'LL SEE YOU LATER.
AND THANK YOU FOR THE TEA.
I'M SORRY I COULDN'T GIVE YOU SOME-THING BETTER.

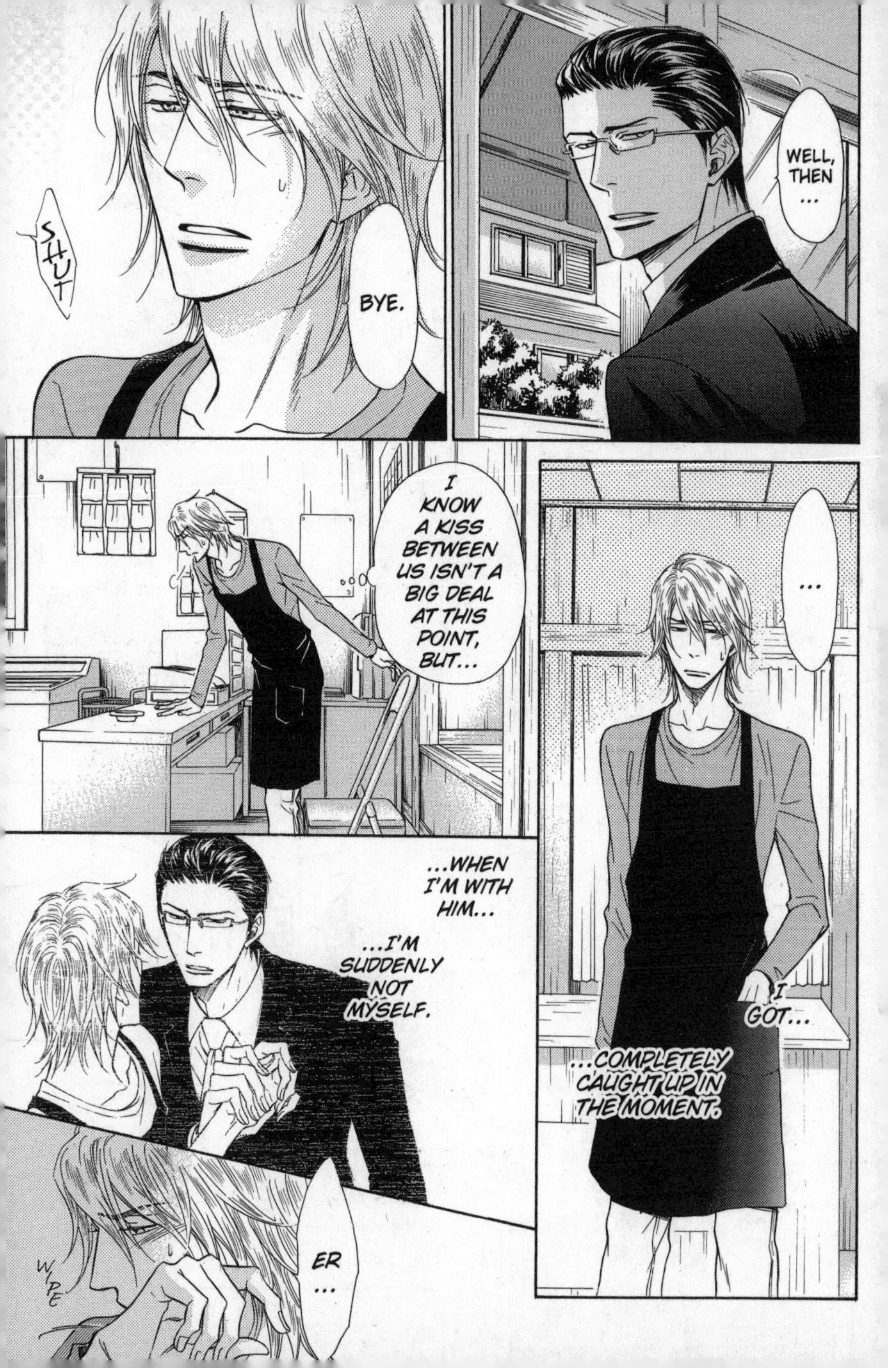

WELL, THEN ...
BYE.
SHUT
...
I GOT...
...COMPLETELY CAUGHT UP IN THE MOMENT.
I KNOW A KISS BETWEEN US ISN'T A BIG DEAL AT THIS POINT, BUT...
...WHEN I'M WITH HIM...
...I'M SUDDENLY NOT MYSELF.
ER ...
WIPE

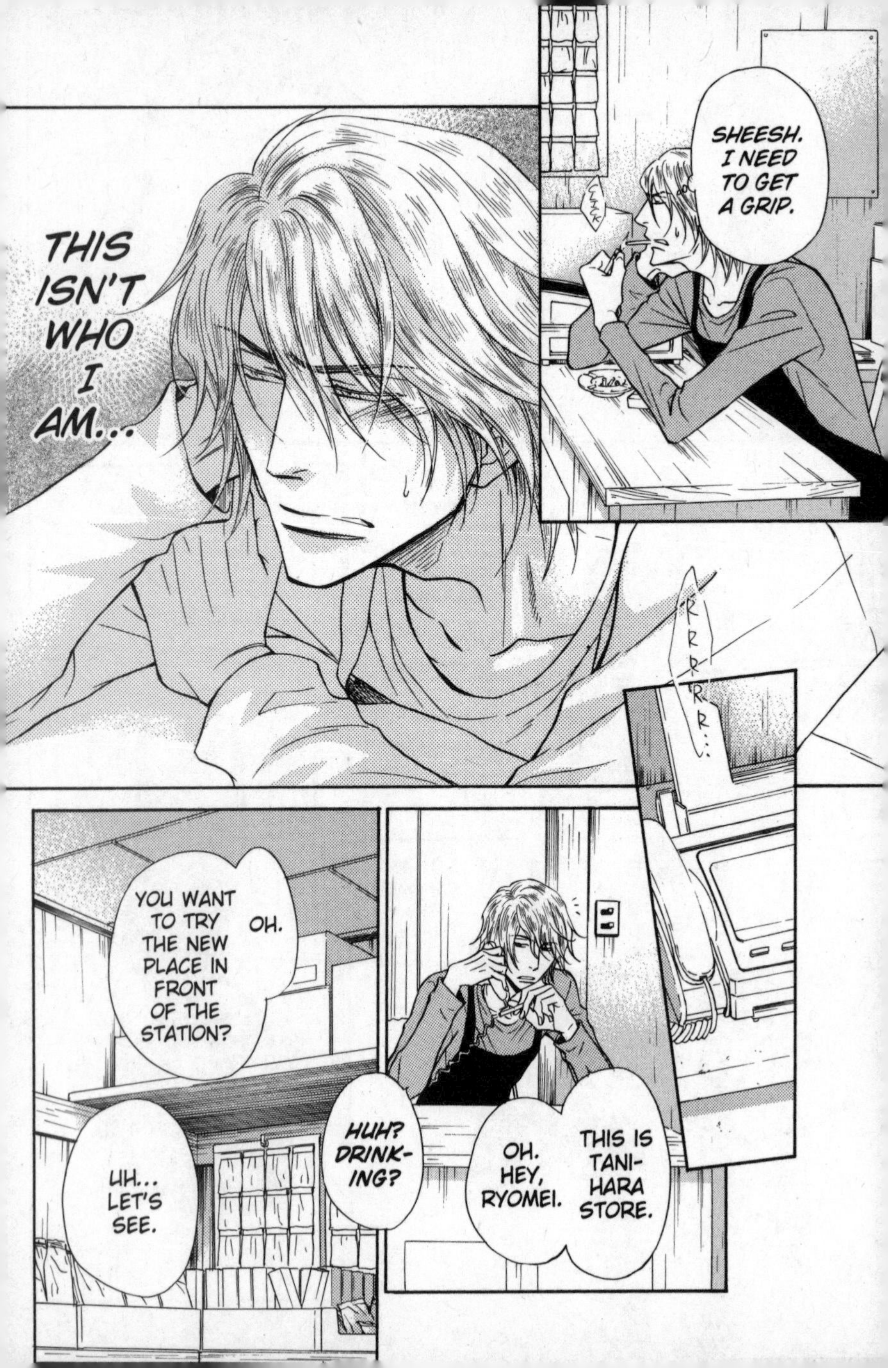
CLICK
SHEESH. I NEED TO GET A GRIP.
THIS ISN'T WHO I AM...
RRRRR...
THIS IS TANI-HARA STORE.
OH. HEY, RYOMEI.
HUH? DRINK-ING?
OH.
YOU WANT TO TRY THE NEW PLACE IN FRONT OF THE STATION?
UH... LET'S SEE.

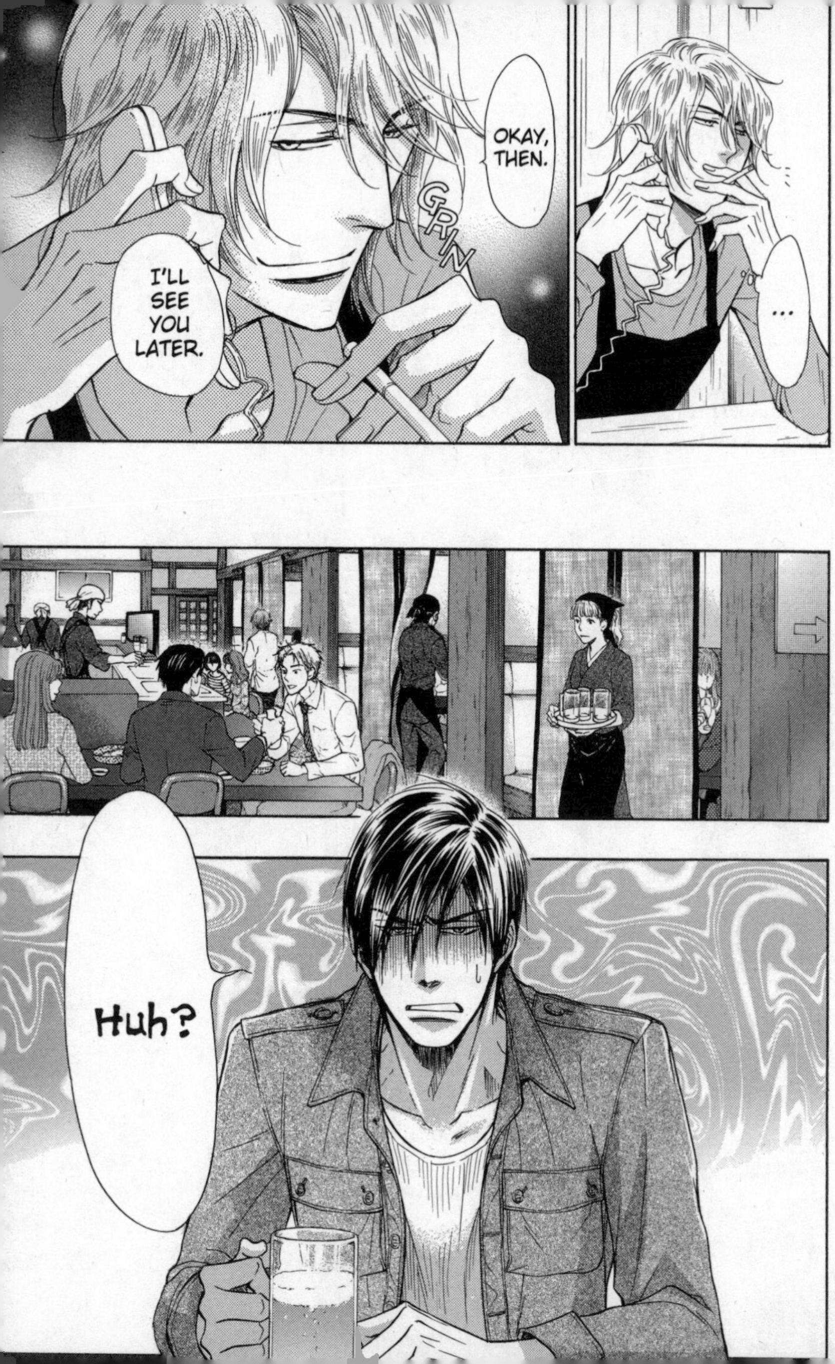
...
OKAY, THEN.
GRIN
I'LL SEE YOU LATER.
Huh?

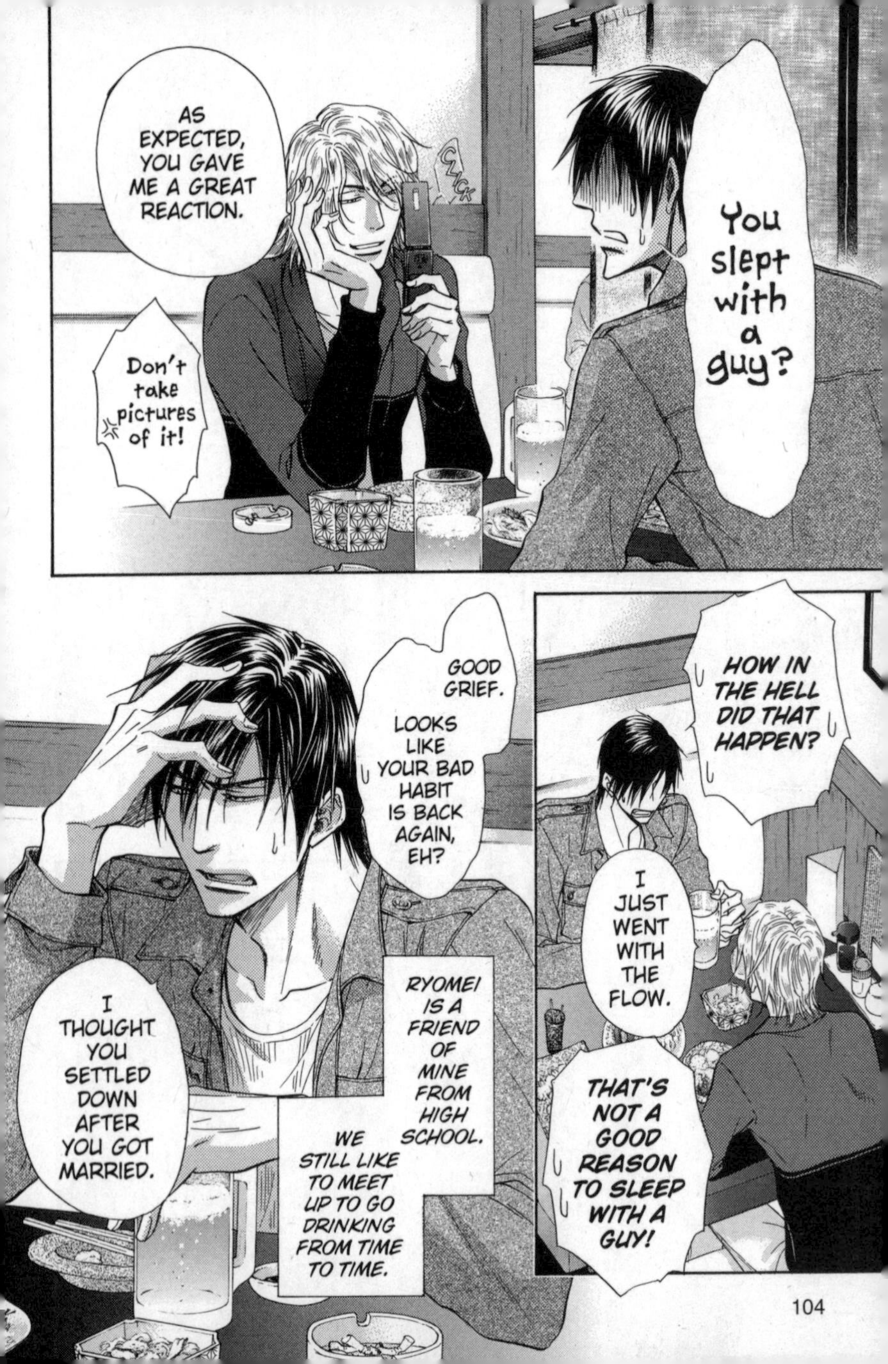
You slept with a guy?
AS EXPECTED, YOU GAVE ME A GREAT REACTION.
CLICK
Don't take pictures of it!
HOW IN THE HELL DID THAT HAPPEN?
I JUST WENT WITH THE FLOW.
THAT'S NOT A GOOD REASON TO SLEEP WITH A GUY!
GOOD GRIEF.
LOOKS LIKE YOUR BAD HABIT IS BACK AGAIN, EH?
RYOMEI IS A FRIEND OF MINE FROM HIGH SCHOOL.
WE STILL LIKE TO MEET UP TO GO DRINKING FROM TIME TO TIME.
I THOUGHT YOU SETTLED DOWN AFTER YOU GOT MARRIED.

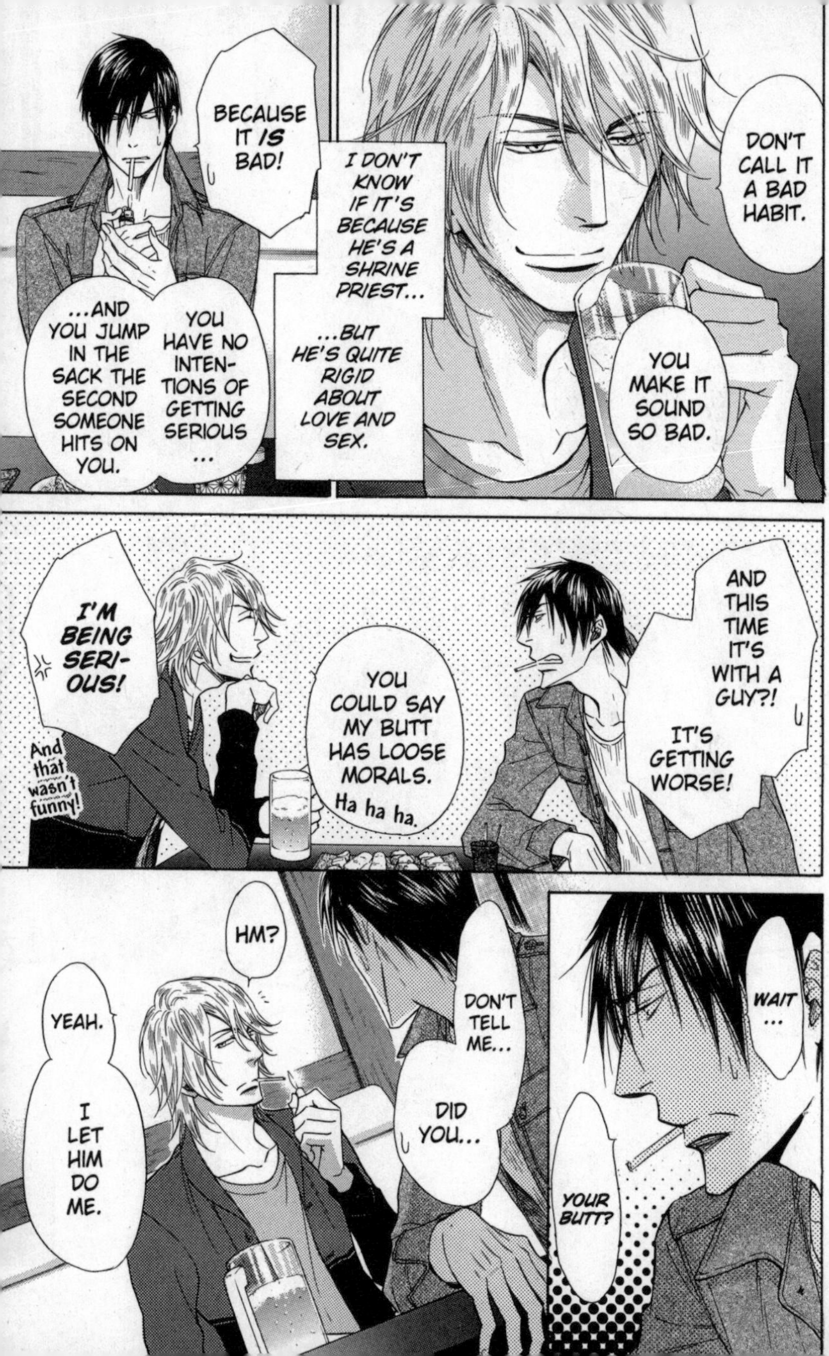

DON'T CALL IT A BAD HABIT.
YOU MAKE IT SOUND SO BAD.
I DON'T KNOW IF IT'S BECAUSE HE'S A SHRINE PRIEST...
...BUT HE'S QUITE RIGID ABOUT LOVE AND SEX.
BECAUSE IT IS BAD!
YOU HAVE NO INTENTIONS OF GETTING SERIOUS...
...AND YOU JUMP IN THE SACK THE SECOND SOMEONE HITS ON YOU.
AND THIS TIME IT'S WITH A GUY?!
IT'S GETTING WORSE!
YOU COULD SAY MY BUTT HAS LOOSE MORALS.
Ha ha ha.
I'M BEING SERIOUS!
And that wasn't funny!
WAIT...
YOUR BUTT?
DON'T TELL ME...
DID YOU...
HM?
YEAH.
I LET HIM DO ME.

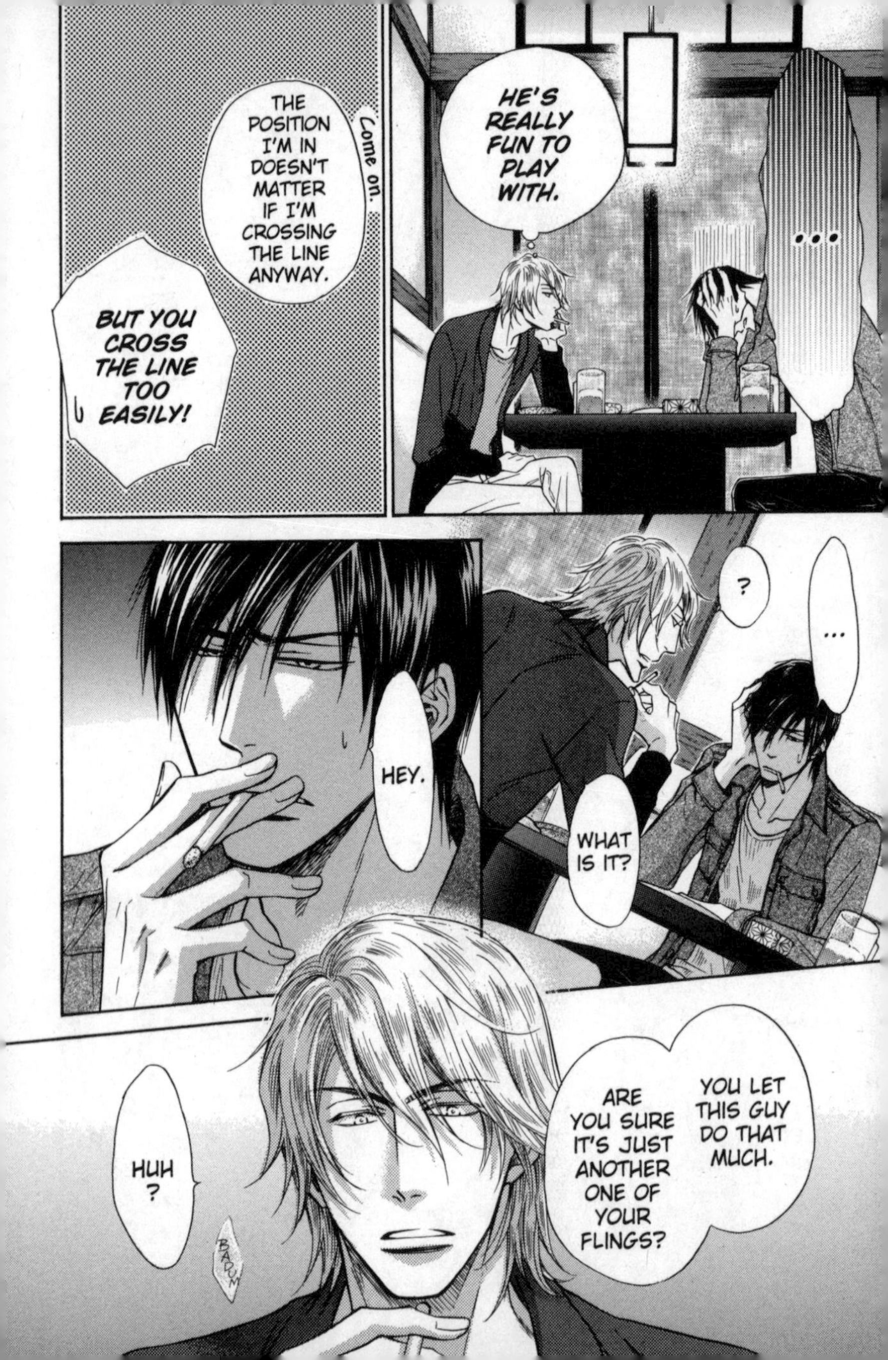
HE'S REALLY FUN TO PLAY WITH.
...
THE POSITION I'M IN DOESN'T MATTER IF I'M CROSSING THE LINE ANYWAY.
Come on.
BUT YOU CROSS THE LINE TOO EASILY!
...
?
WHAT IS IT?
HEY.
YOU LET THIS GUY DO THAT MUCH.
ARE YOU SURE IT'S JUST ANOTHER ONE OF YOUR FLINGS?
HUH?
BADUM

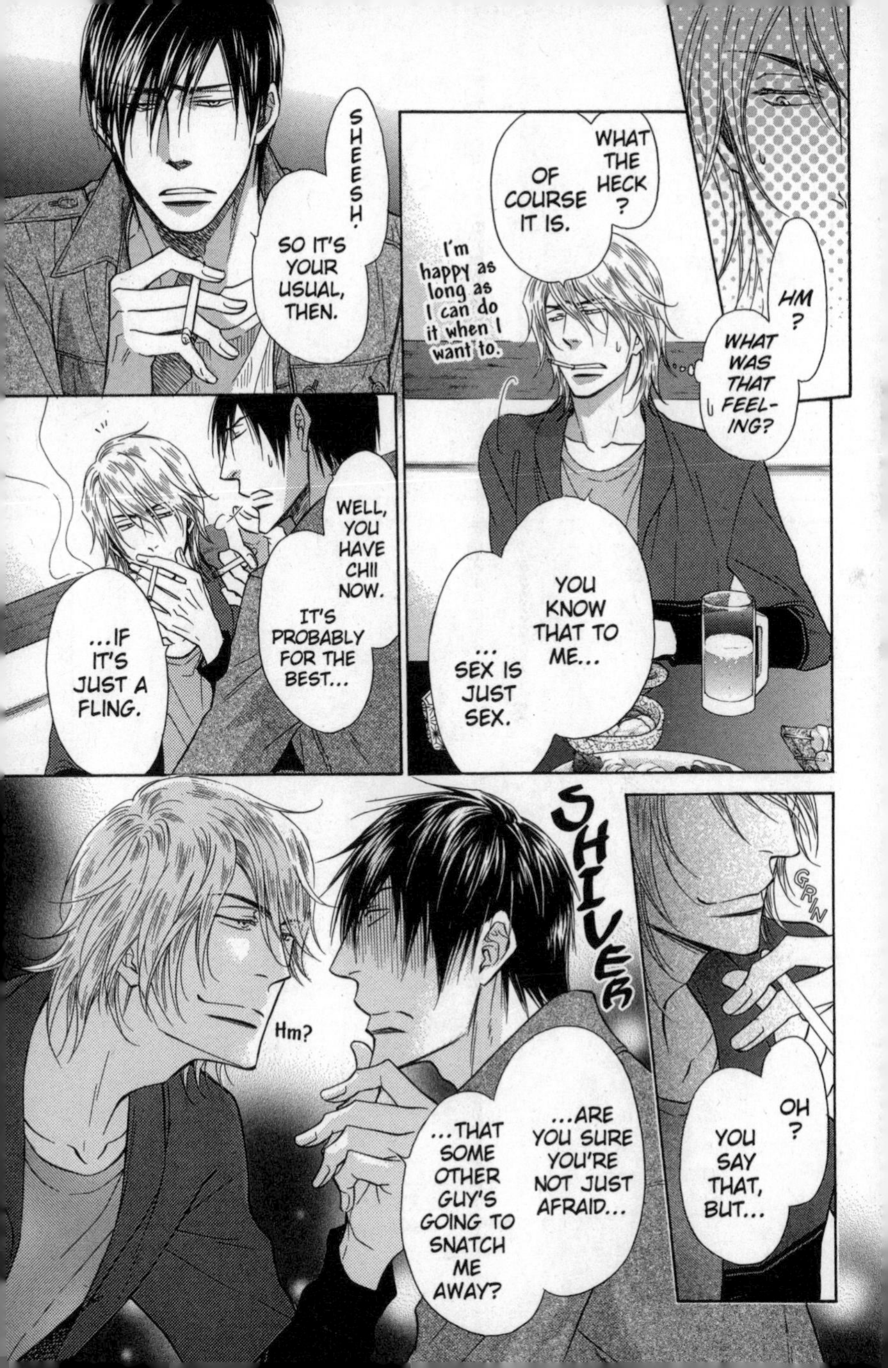
HM? WHAT WAS THAT FEELING?
WHAT THE HECK?
OF COURSE IT IS.
I'm happy as long as I can do it when I want to.
YOU KNOW THAT TO ME...
... SEX IS JUST SEX.
SHEESH.
SO IT'S YOUR USUAL, THEN.
WELL, YOU HAVE CHII NOW.
IT'S PROBABLY FOR THE BEST...
...IF IT'S JUST A FLING.
GRIN
OH? YOU SAY THAT, BUT...
SHIVER
...ARE YOU SURE YOU'RE NOT JUST AFRAID...
...THAT SOME OTHER GUY'S GOING TO SNATCH ME AWAY?
Hm?

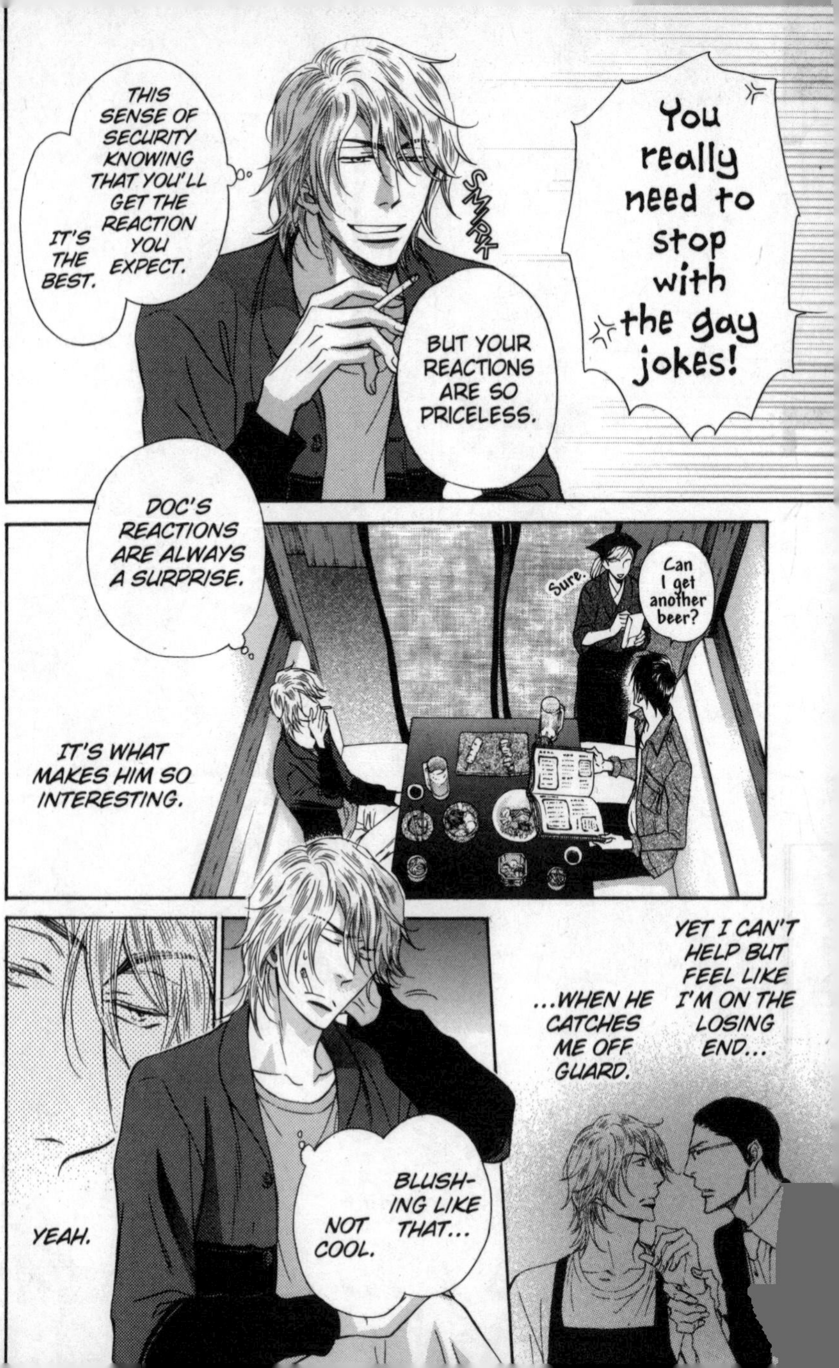
You really need to stop with the gay jokes!
BUT YOUR REACTIONS ARE SO PRICELESS.
SMIRK
THIS SENSE OF SECURITY KNOWING THAT YOU'LL GET THE REACTION YOU EXPECT.
IT'S THE BEST.
Can I get another beer?
Sure.
DOC'S REACTIONS ARE ALWAYS A SURPRISE.
IT'S WHAT MAKES HIM SO INTERESTING.
YET I CAN'T HELP BUT FEEL LIKE I'M ON THE LOSING END...
...WHEN HE CATCHES ME OFF GUARD.
BLUSH-ING LIKE THAT...
NOT COOL.
YEAH.

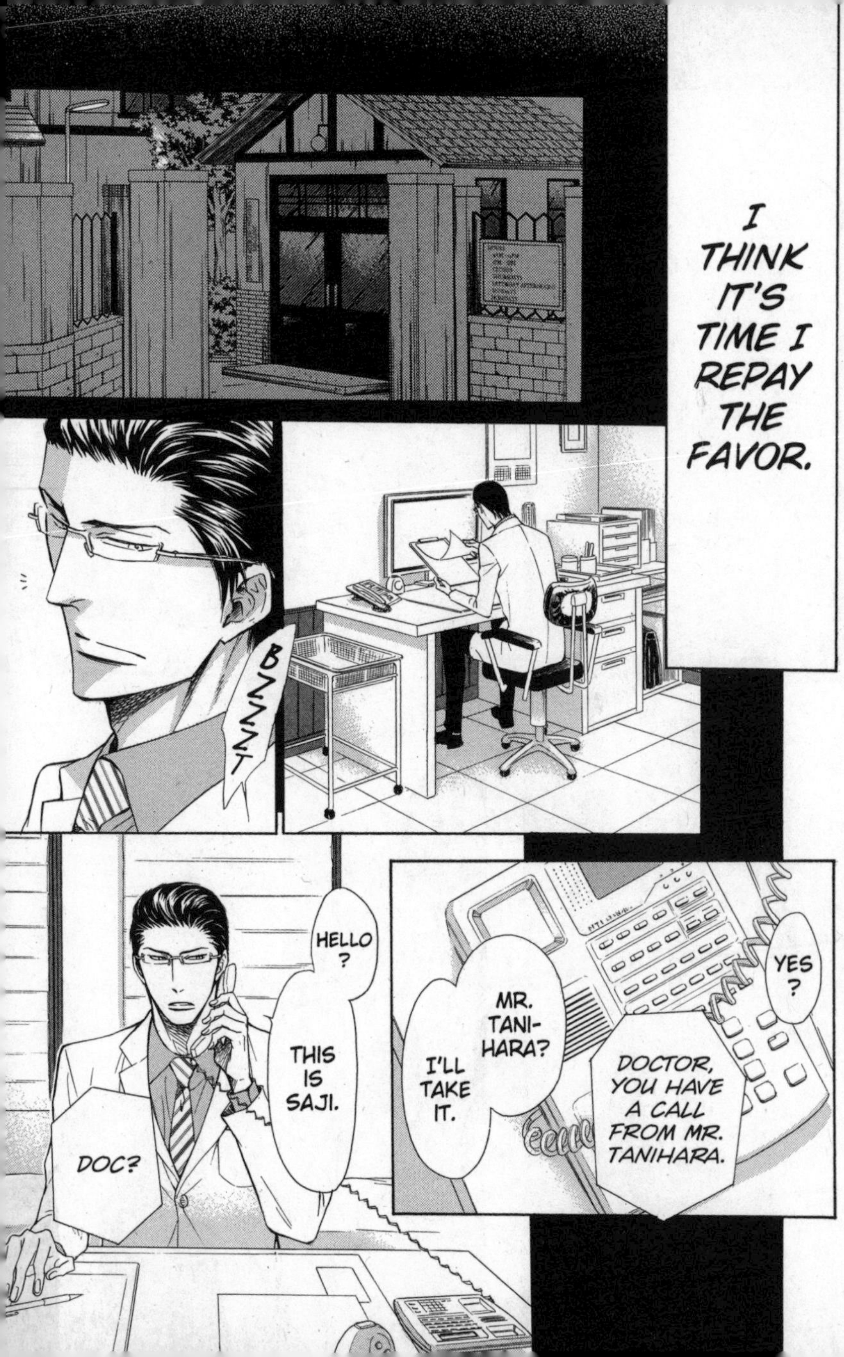
I THINK IT'S TIME I REPAY THE FAVOR.
BZZZZT
YES?
DOCTOR, YOU HAVE A CALL FROM MR. TANIHARA.
MR. TANIHARA?
I'LL TAKE IT.
HELLO?
THIS IS SAJI.
DOC?

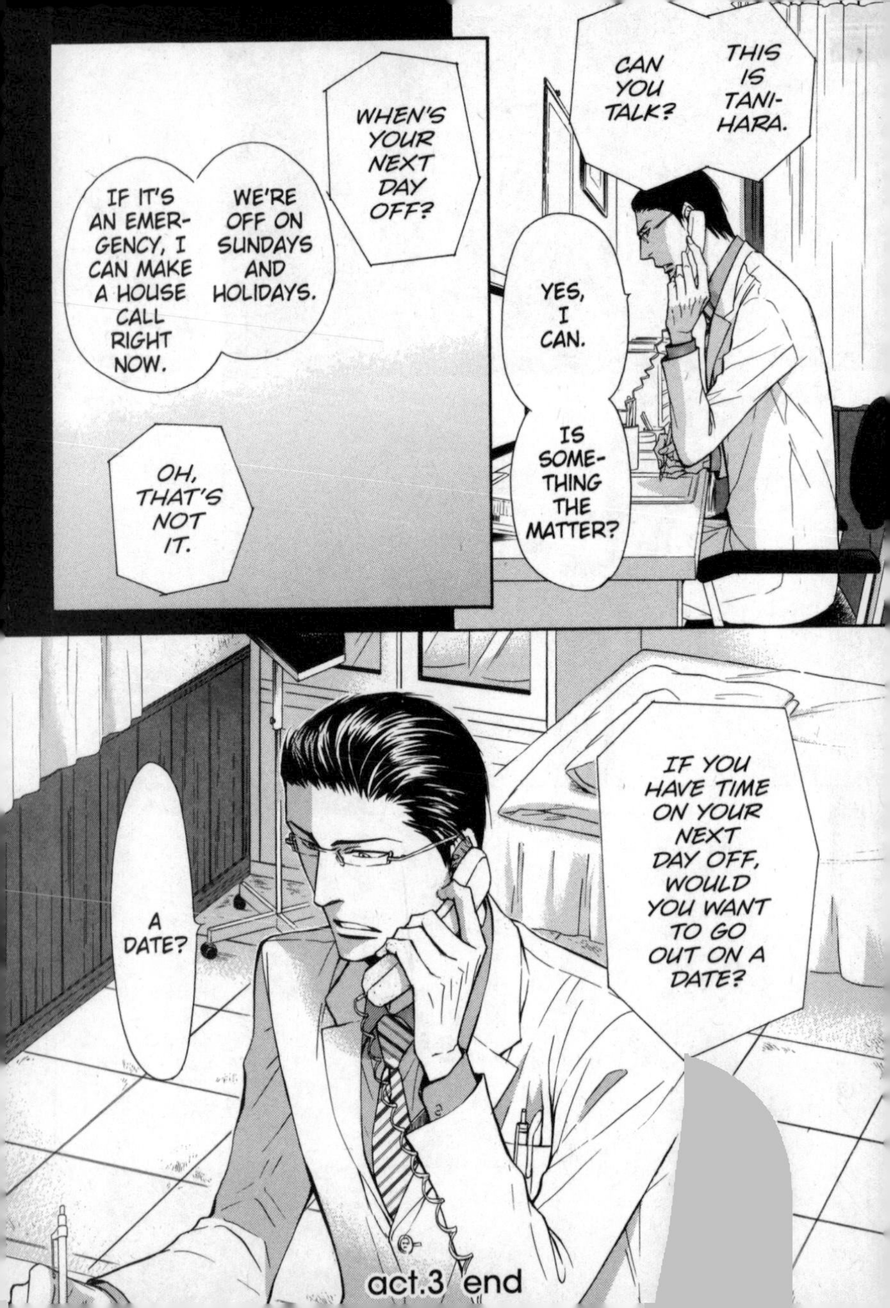
THIS IS TANIHARA.
CAN YOU TALK?
YES, I CAN.
IS SOMETHING THE MATTER?
WHEN'S YOUR NEXT DAY OFF?
WE'RE OFF ON SUNDAYS AND HOLIDAYS.
IF IT'S AN EMERGENCY, I CAN MAKE A HOUSE CALL RIGHT NOW.
OH, THAT'S NOT IT.
IF YOU HAVE TIME ON YOUR NEXT DAY OFF, WOULD YOU WANT TO GO OUT ON A DATE?
A DATE?
act.3 end

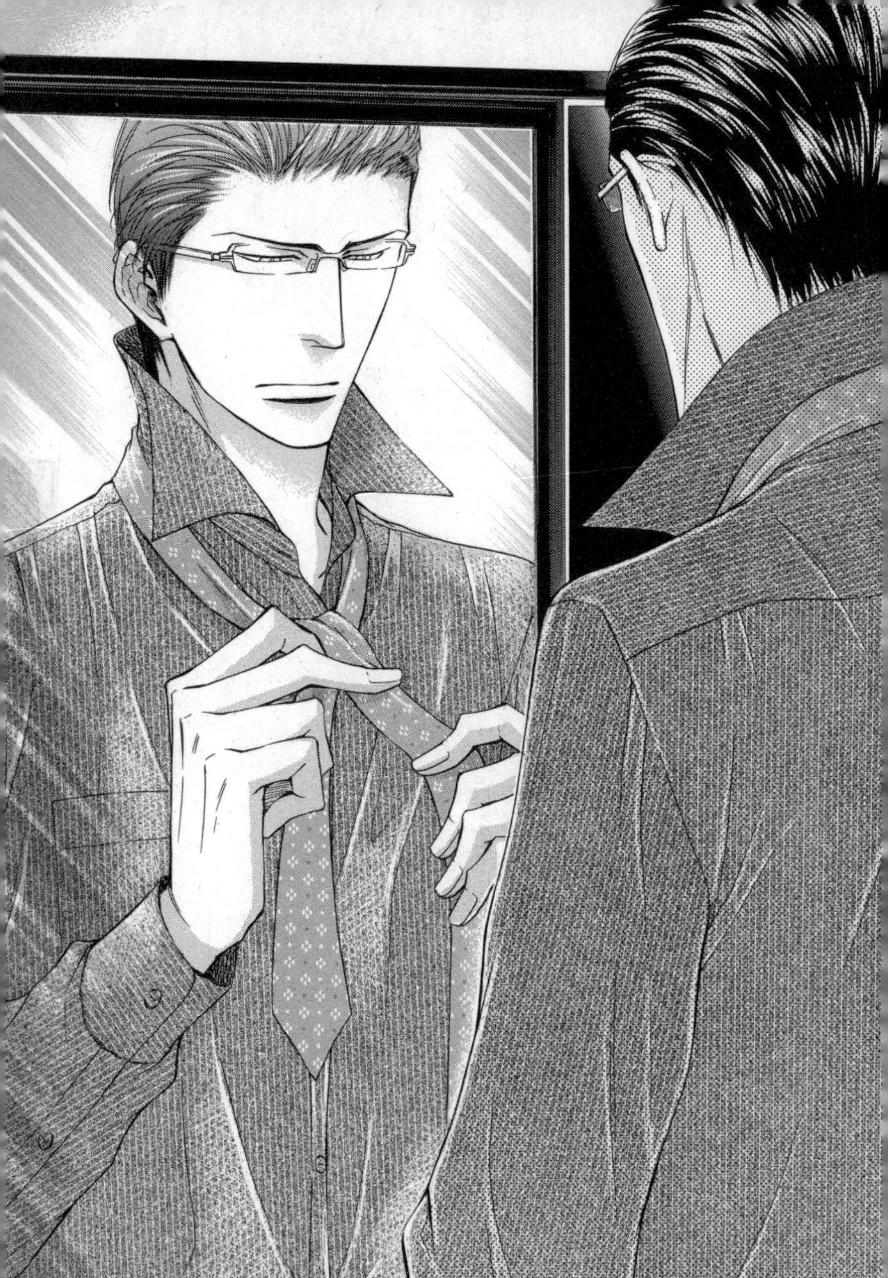

Hide and Seek: Act 4

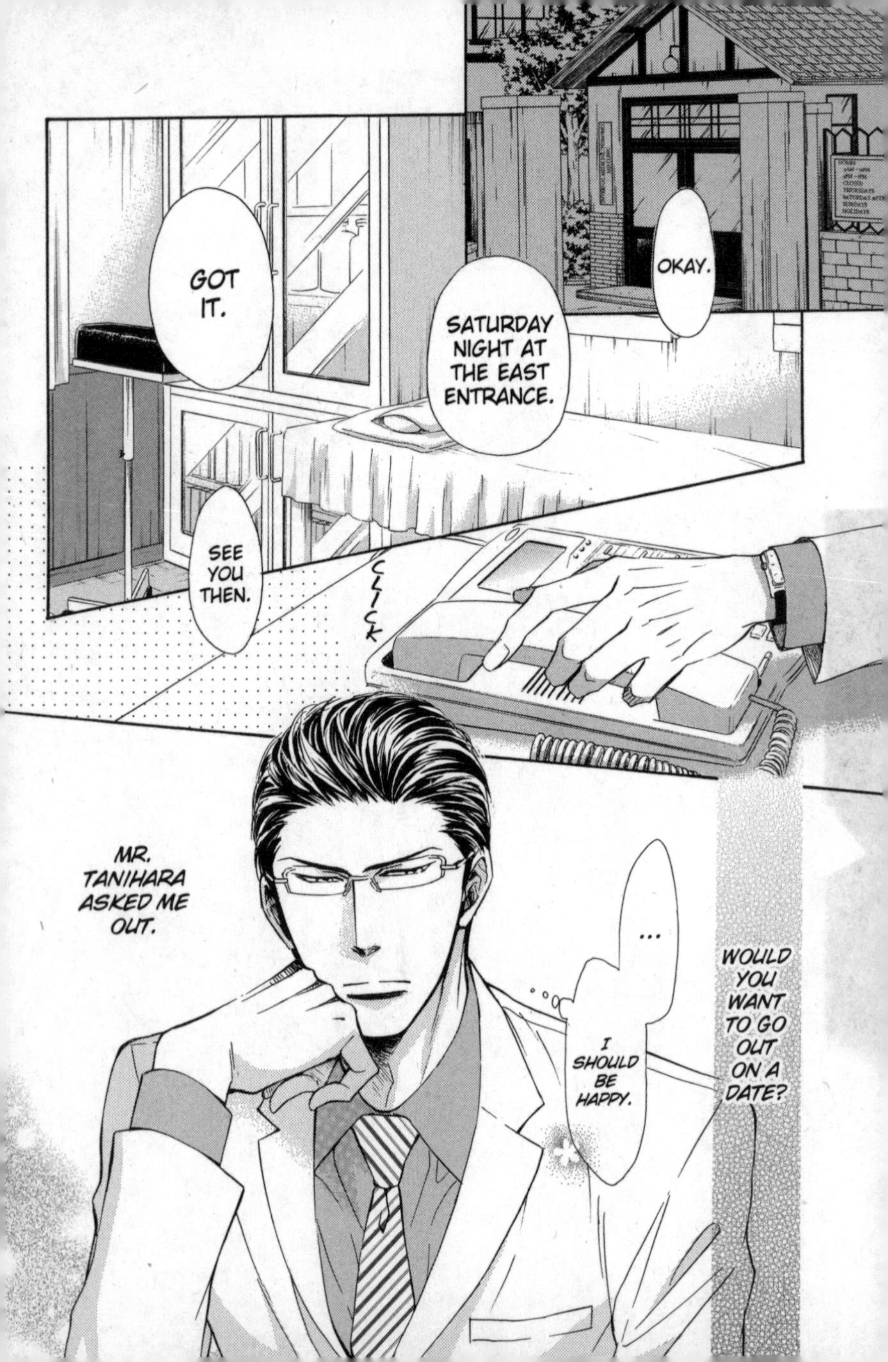
OKAY.
SATURDAY NIGHT AT THE EAST ENTRANCE.
GOT IT.
SEE YOU THEN.
CLICK
WOULD YOU WANT TO GO OUT ON A DATE?
...
I SHOULD BE HAPPY.
MR. TANIHARA ASKED ME OUT.

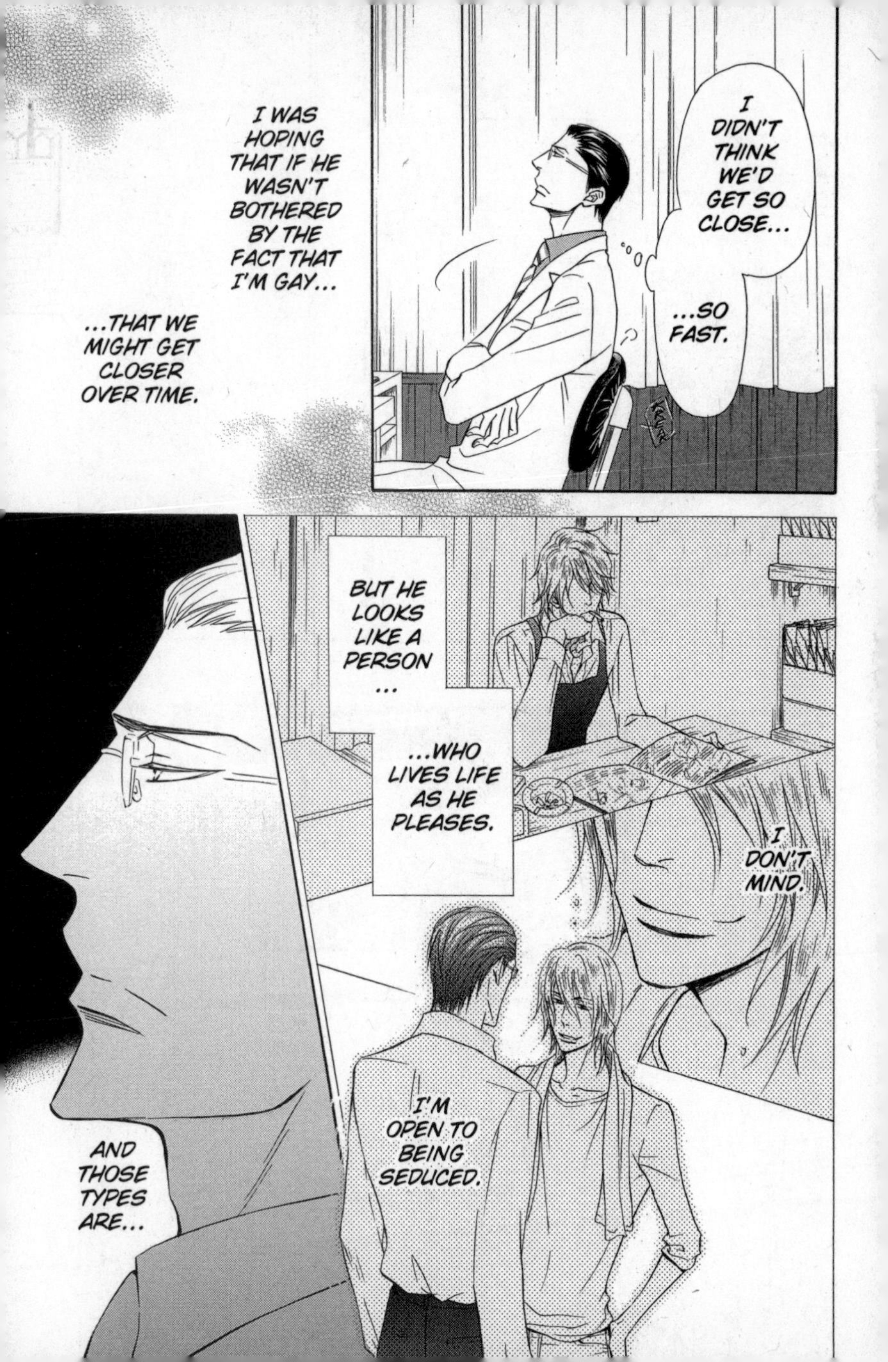
I DIDN'T THINK WE'D GET SO CLOSE...
...SO FAST.
I WAS HOPING THAT IF HE WASN'T BOTHERED BY THE FACT THAT I'M GAY...
...THAT WE MIGHT GET CLOSER OVER TIME.
BUT HE LOOKS LIKE A PERSON...
...WHO LIVES LIFE AS HE PLEASES.
I DON'T MIND.
I'M OPEN TO BEING SEDUCED.
AND THOSE TYPES ARE...

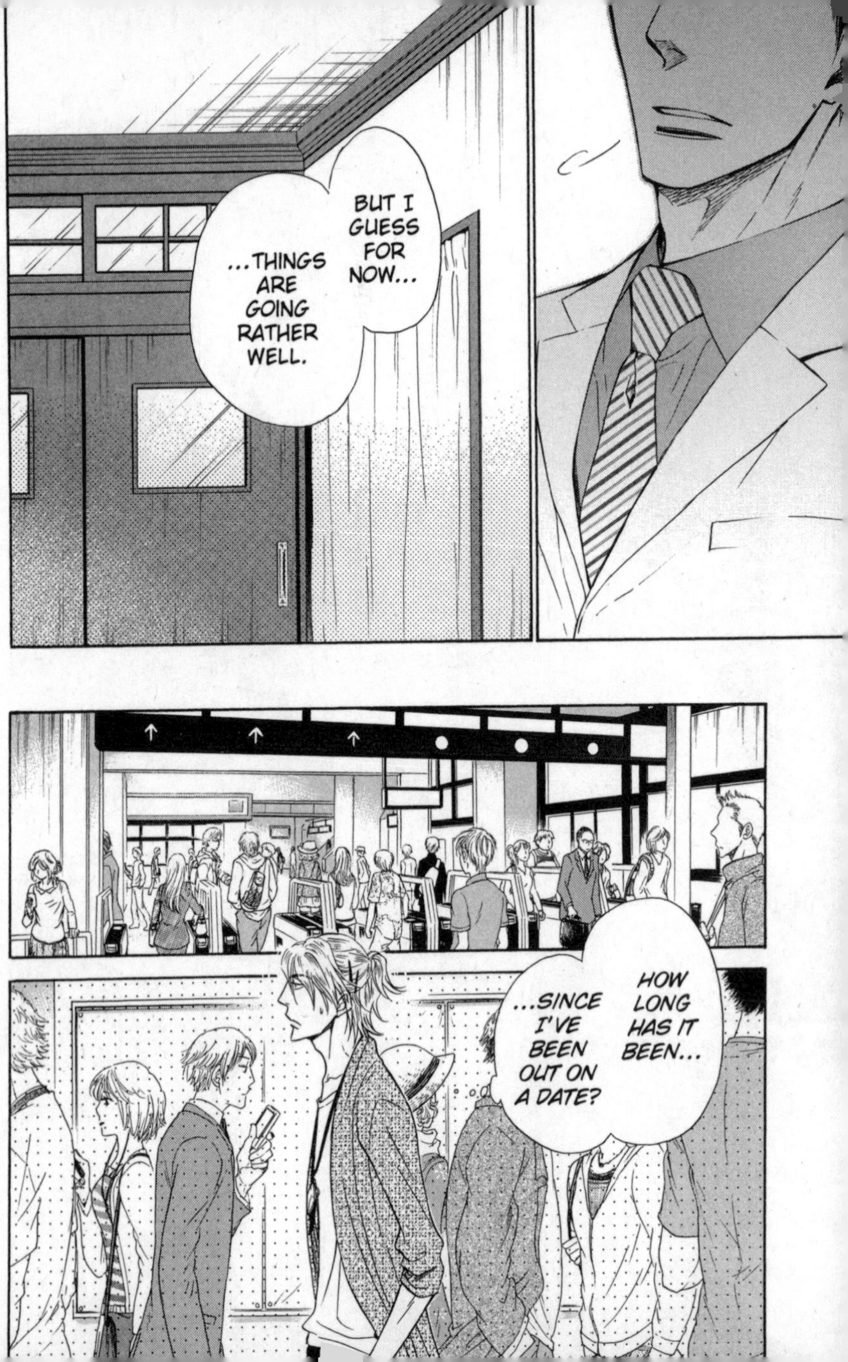
BUT I GUESS FOR NOW...
...THINGS ARE GOING RATHER WELL.
HOW LONG HAS IT BEEN...
...SINCE I'VE BEEN OUT ON A DATE?

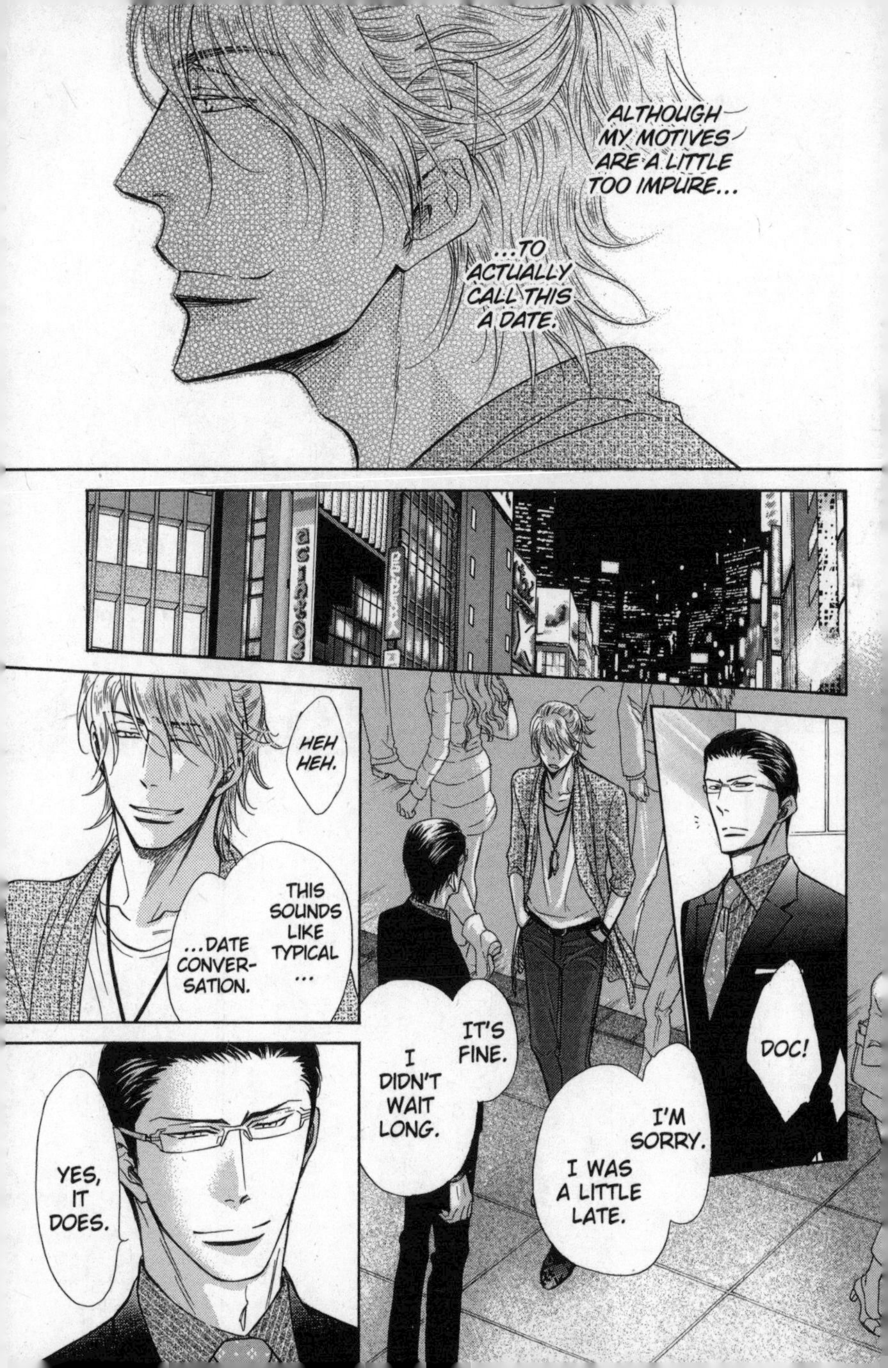
ALTHOUGH MY MOTIVES ARE A LITTLE TOO IMPURE...
...TO ACTUALLY CALL THIS A DATE.
DOC!
I'M SORRY. I WAS A LITTLE LATE.
IT'S FINE. I DIDN'T WAIT LONG.
HEH HEH.
THIS SOUNDS LIKE TYPICAL...
...DATE CONVERSATION.
YES, IT DOES.

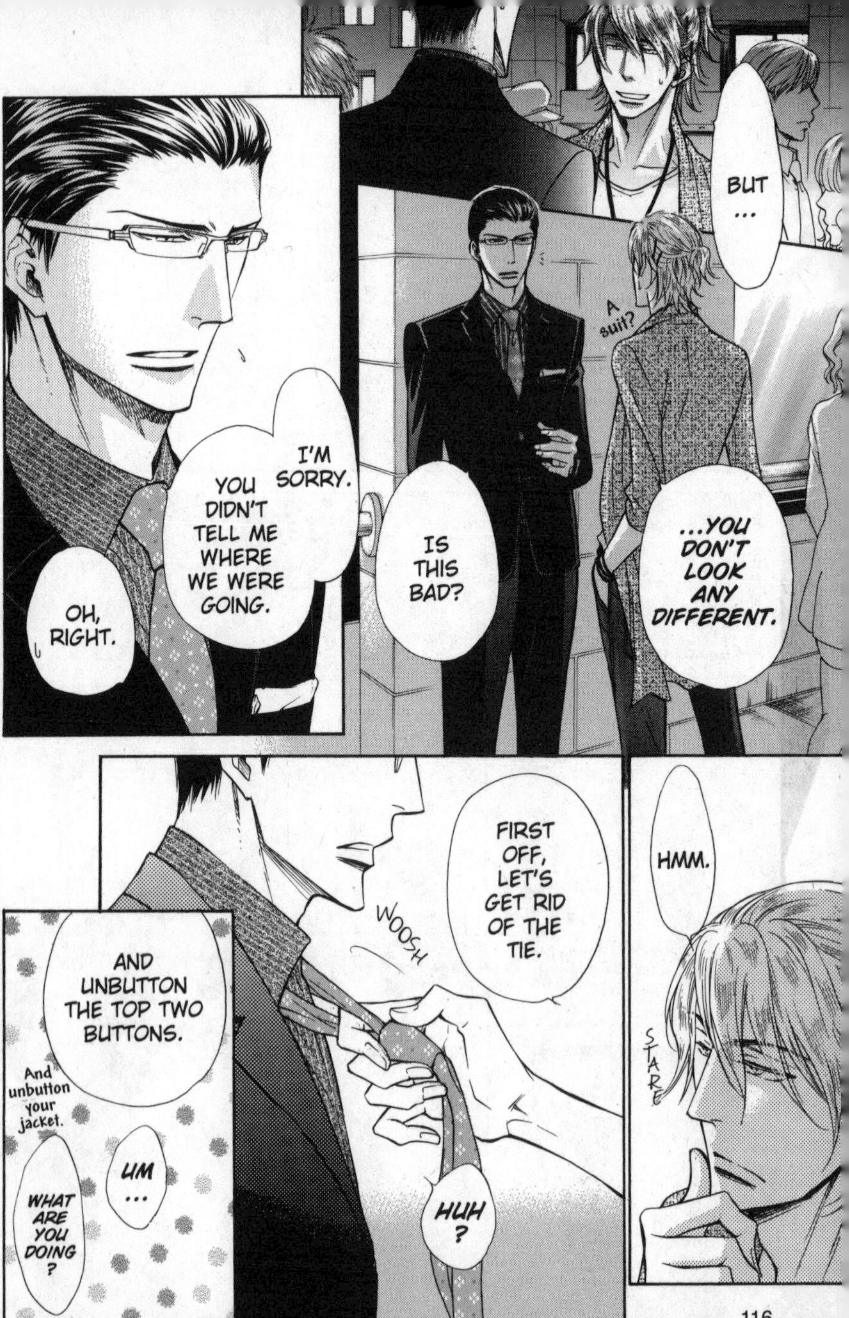
BUT ...
A suit?
...YOU DON'T LOOK ANY DIFFERENT.
IS THIS BAD?
I'M SORRY.
YOU DIDN'T TELL ME WHERE WE WERE GOING.
OH, RIGHT.
HMM.
STARE
FIRST OFF, LET'S GET RID OF THE TIE.
WOOSH
HUH?
AND UNBUTTON THE TOP TWO BUTTONS.
And unbutton your jacket.
UM ...
WHAT ARE YOU DOING?

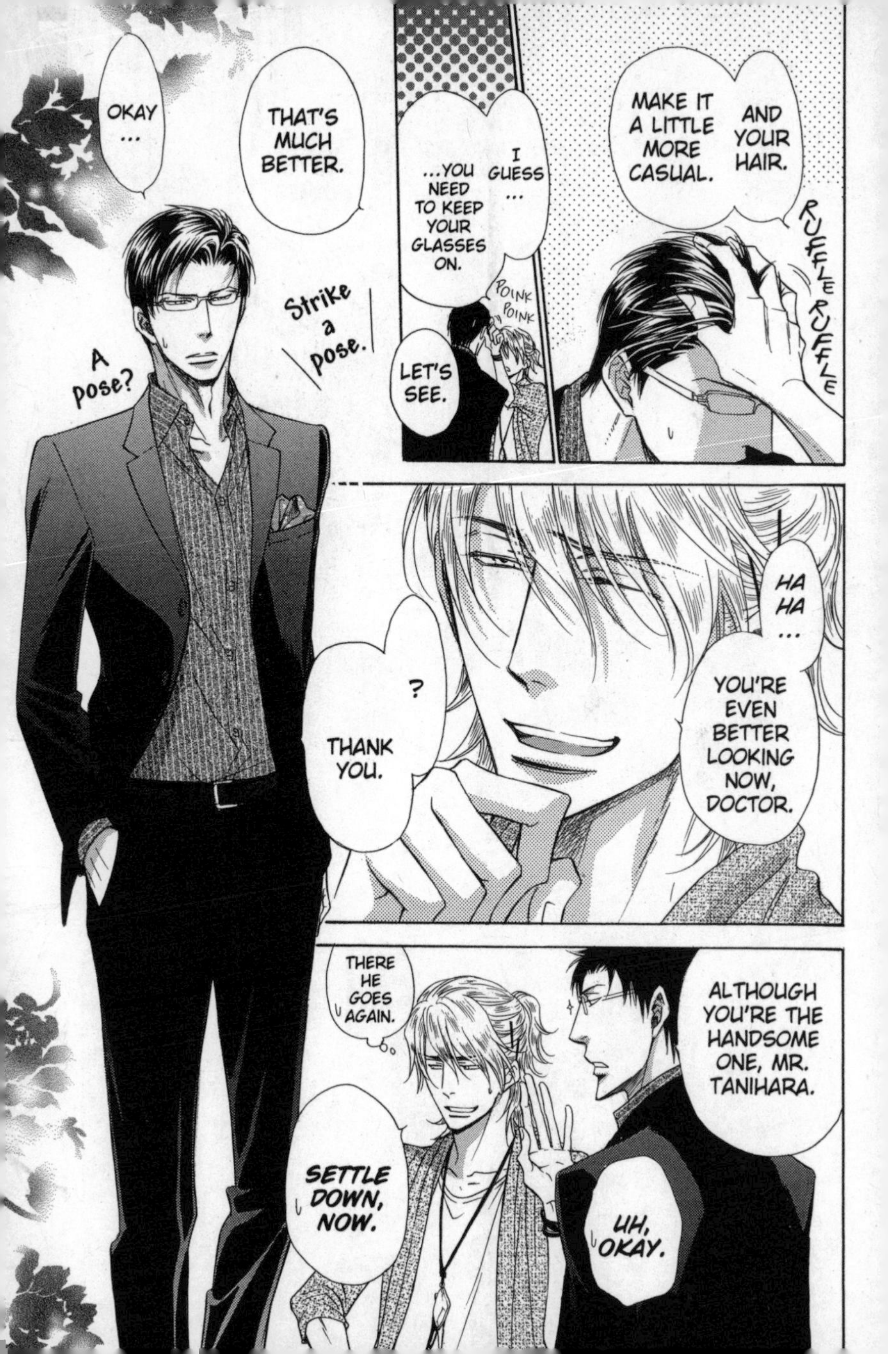
AND YOUR HAIR.
MAKE IT A LITTLE MORE CASUAL.
RUFFLE RUFFLE
I GUESS ...
...YOU NEED TO KEEP YOUR GLASSES ON.
POINK POINK
LET'S SEE.
HA HA ...
YOU'RE EVEN BETTER LOOKING NOW, DOCTOR.
?
THANK YOU.
ALTHOUGH YOU'RE THE HANDSOME ONE, MR. TANIHARA.
THERE HE GOES AGAIN.
UH, OKAY.
SETTLE DOWN, NOW.
THAT'S MUCH BETTER.
OKAY ...
Strike a pose.
A pose?

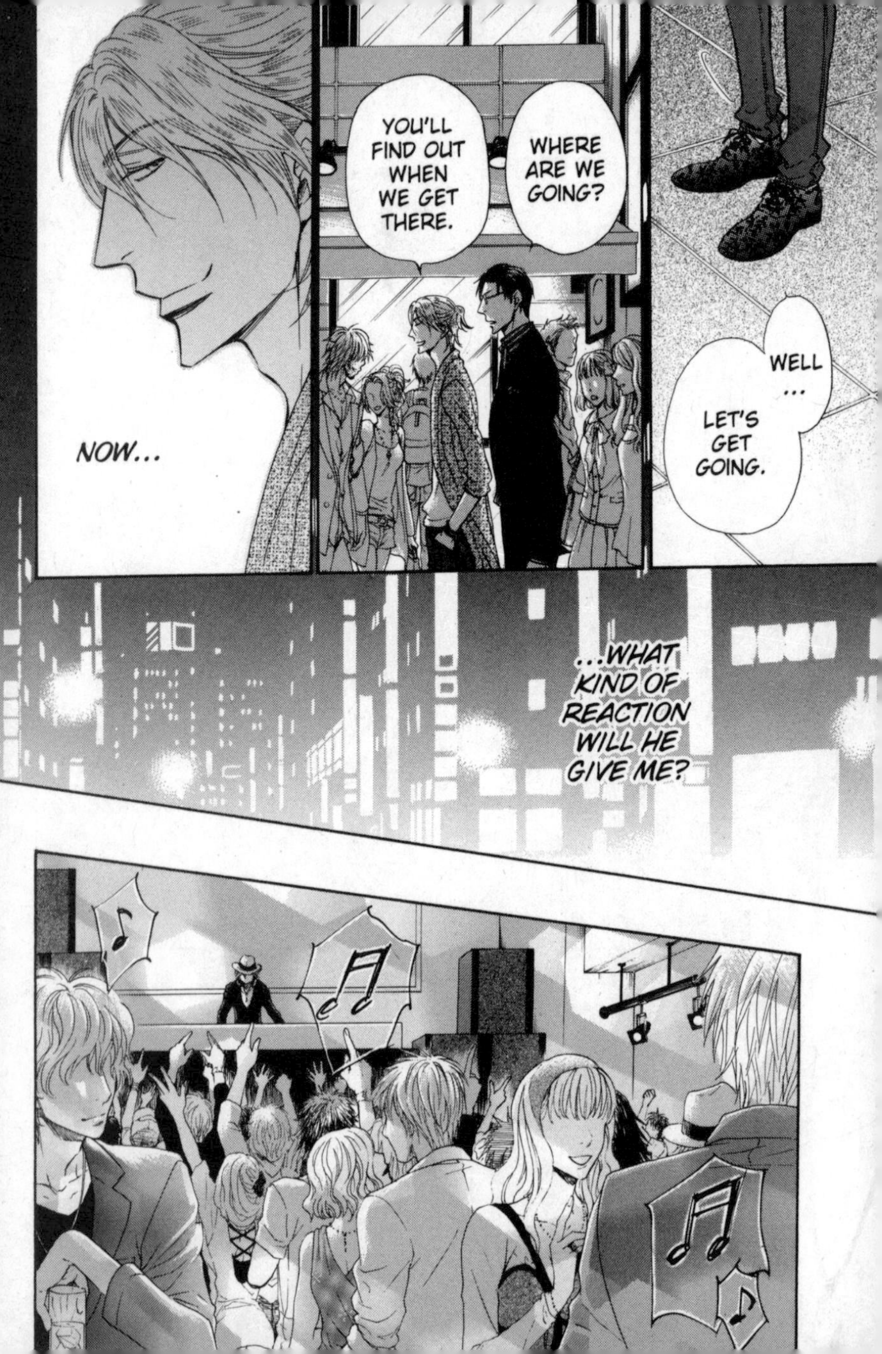
WELL ... LET'S GET GOING.
WHERE ARE WE GOING?
YOU'LL FIND OUT WHEN WE GET THERE.
NOW...
...WHAT KIND OF REACTION WILL HE GIVE ME?

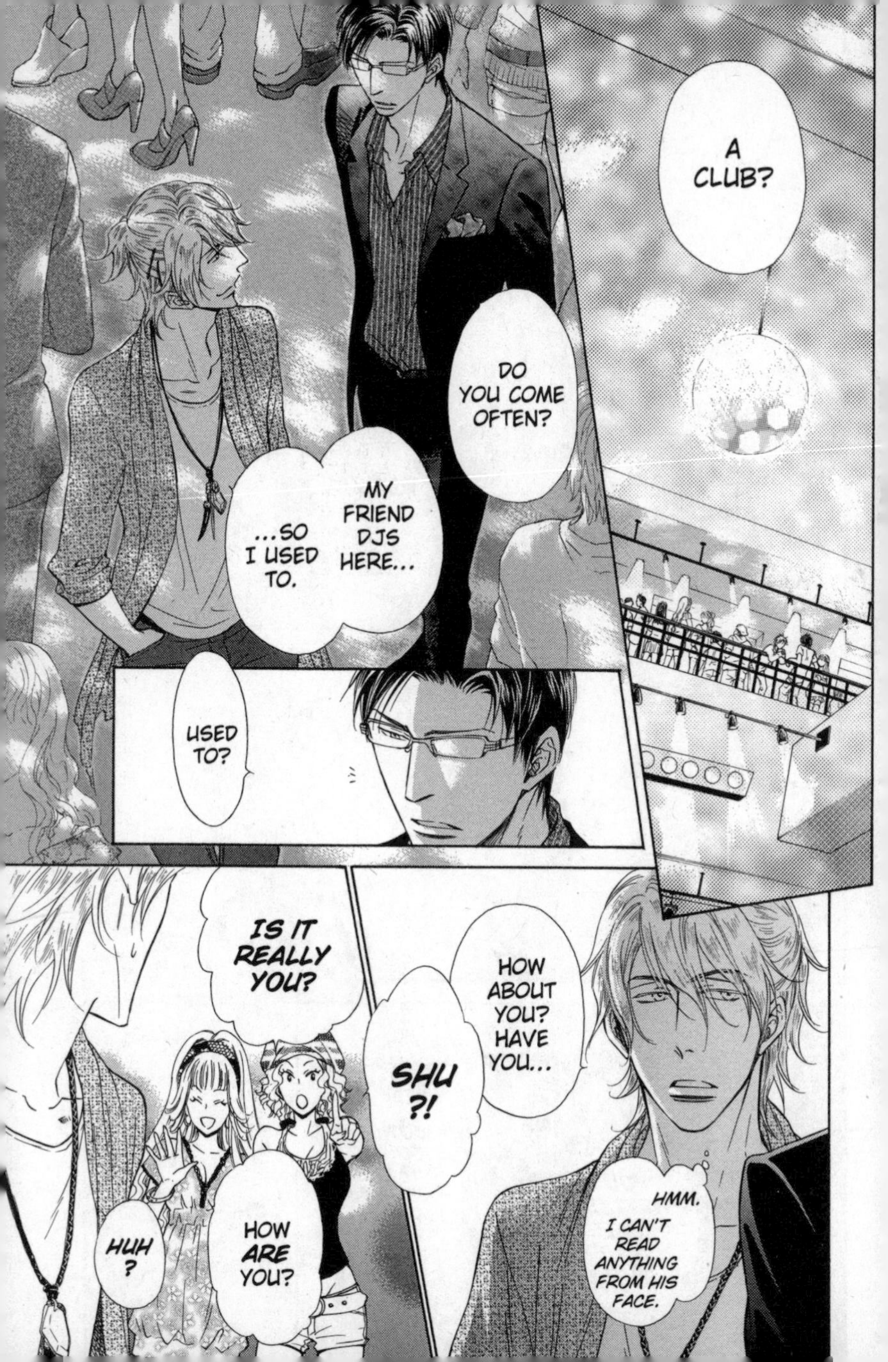
A CLUB?
DO YOU COME OFTEN?
MY FRIEND DJS HERE...
...SO I USED TO.
USED TO?
HOW ABOUT YOU? HAVE YOU...
HMM. I CAN'T READ ANYTHING FROM HIS FACE.
IS IT REALLY YOU?
SHU?!
HOW ARE YOU?
HUH?

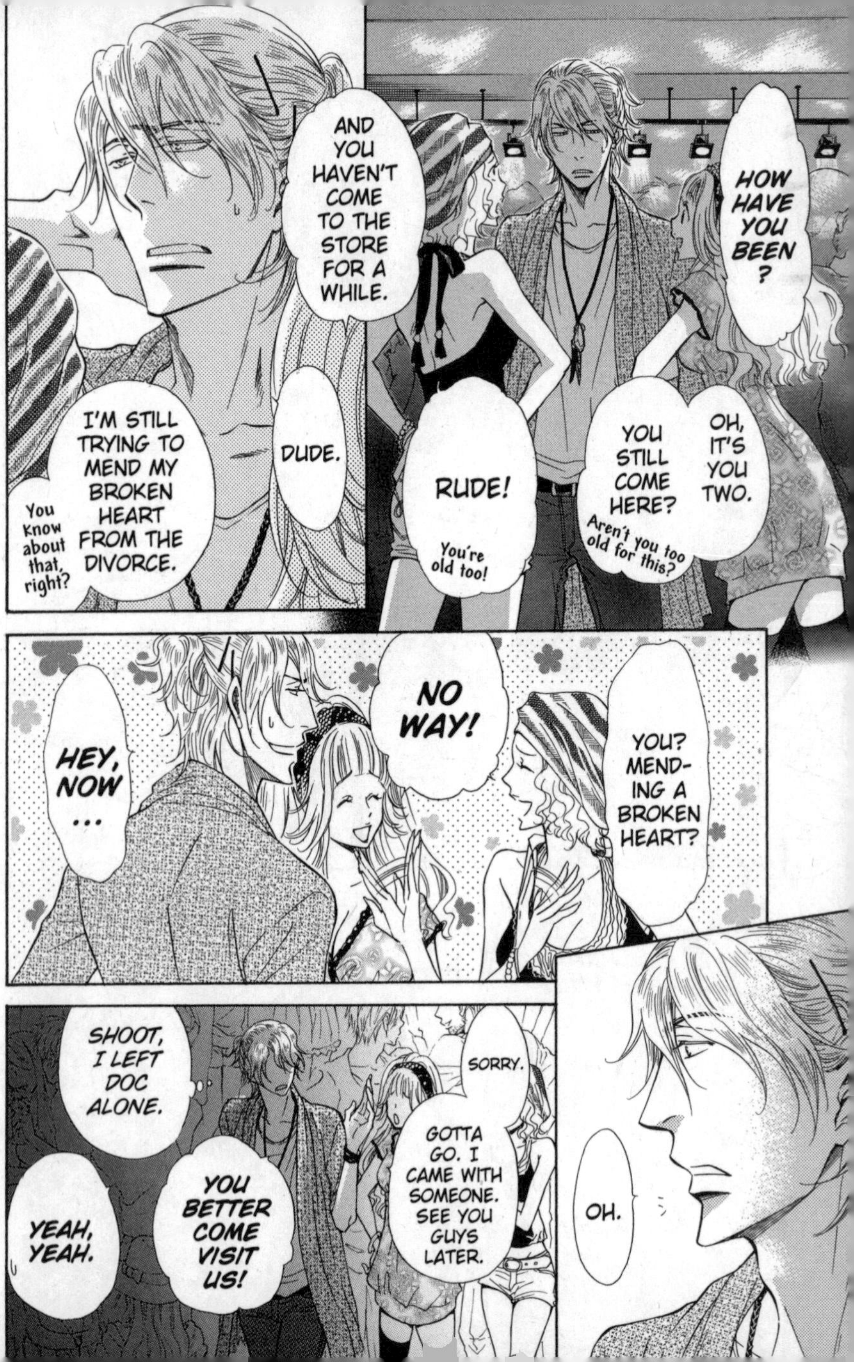
HOW HAVE YOU BEEN?
OH, IT'S YOU TWO.
YOU STILL COME HERE?
Aren't you too old for this?
RUDE!
You're old too!
AND YOU HAVEN'T COME TO THE STORE FOR A WHILE.
DUDE.
I'M STILL TRYING TO MEND MY BROKEN HEART FROM THE DIVORCE.
You know about that, right?
YOU? MEND-ING A BROKEN HEART?
NO WAY!
HEY, NOW...
OH.
SORRY.
GOTTA GO. I CAME WITH SOMEONE. SEE YOU GUYS LATER.
YOU BETTER COME VISIT US!
YEAH, YEAH.
SHOOT, I LEFT DOC ALONE.

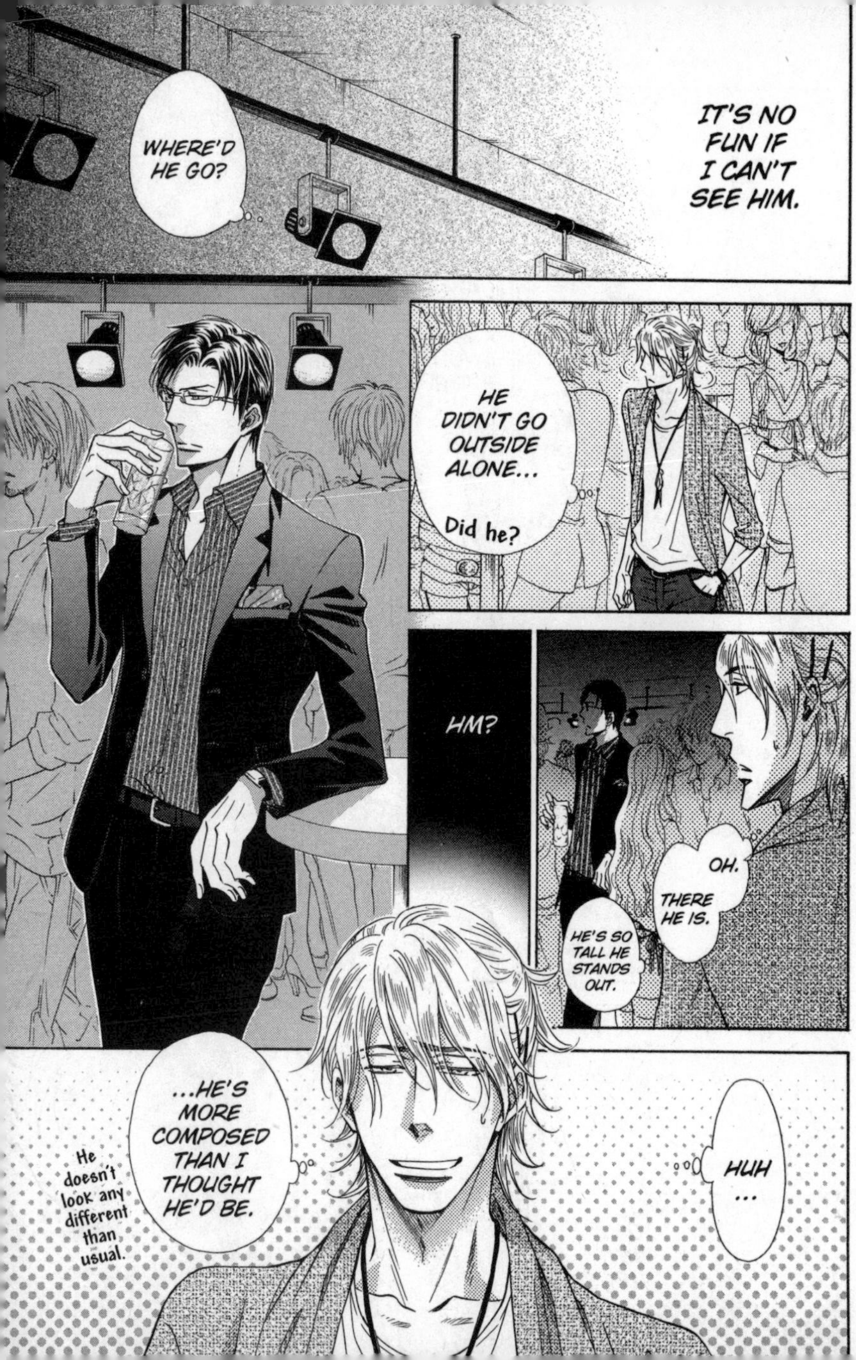
IT'S NO FUN IF I CAN'T SEE HIM.
WHERE'D HE GO?
HE DIDN'T GO OUTSIDE ALONE...
Did he?
OH.
THERE HE IS.
HE'S SO TALL HE STANDS OUT.
HM?
HUH ...
...HE'S MORE COMPOSED THAN I THOUGHT HE'D BE.
He doesn't look any different than usual.

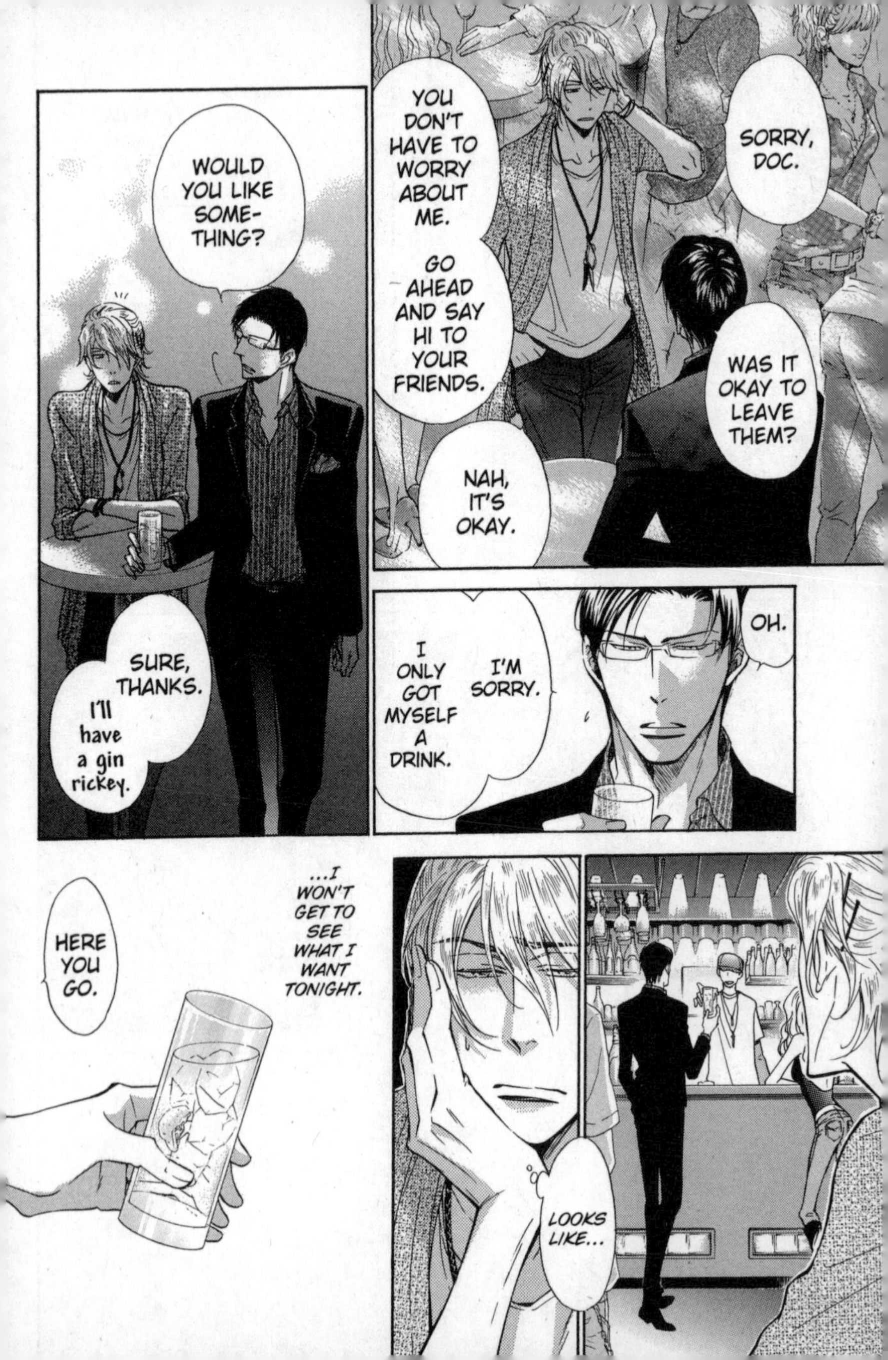
SORRY, DOC.
YOU DON'T HAVE TO WORRY ABOUT ME.
GO AHEAD AND SAY HI TO YOUR FRIENDS.
WAS IT OKAY TO LEAVE THEM?
NAH, IT'S OKAY.
OH.
I'M SORRY.
I ONLY GOT MYSELF A DRINK.
WOULD YOU LIKE SOME-THING?
SURE, THANKS.
I'll have a gin rickey.
LOOKS LIKE...
...I WON'T GET TO SEE WHAT I WANT TONIGHT.
HERE YOU GO.

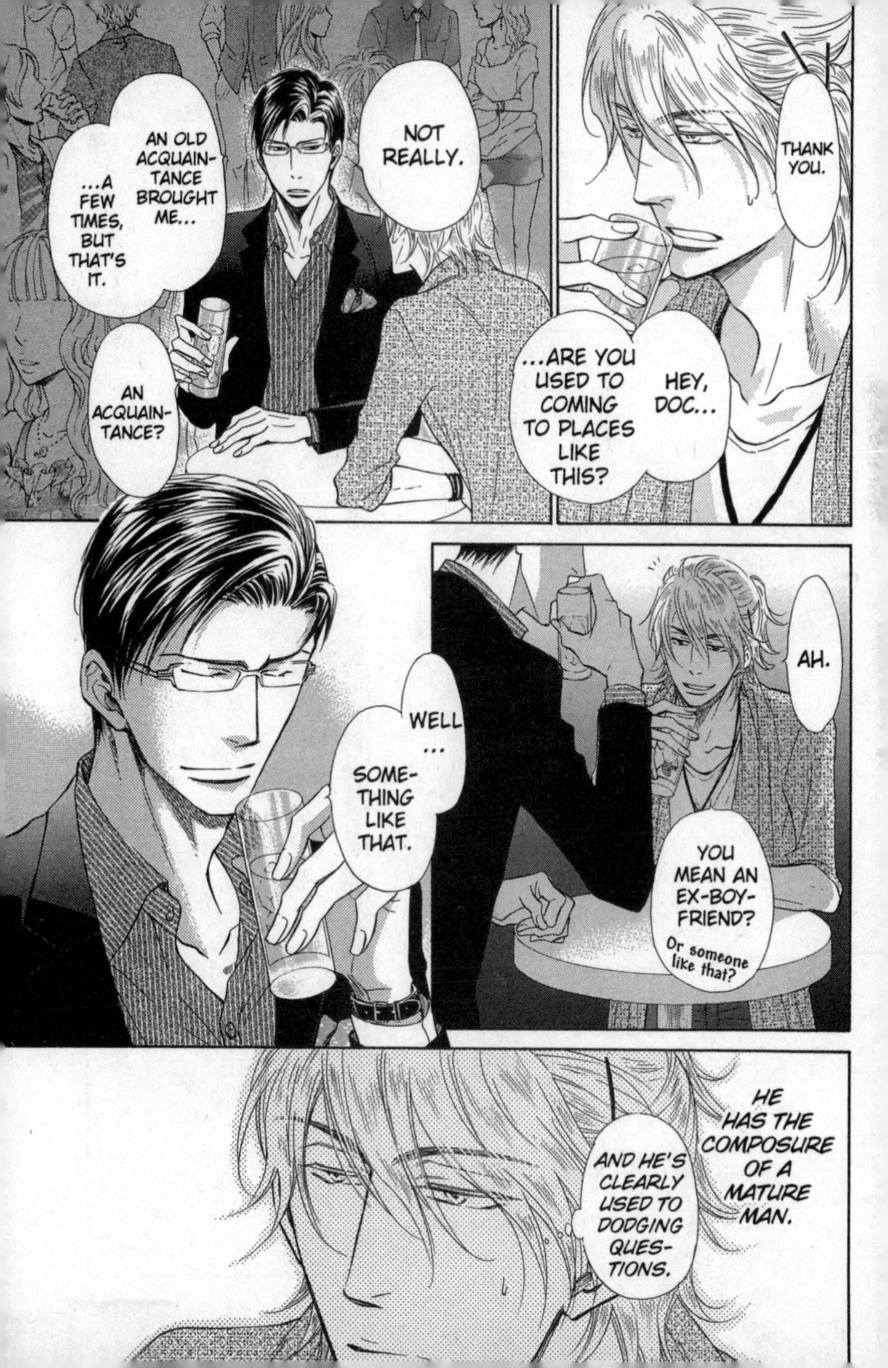
THANK YOU.
HEY, DOC...
...ARE YOU USED TO COMING TO PLACES LIKE THIS?
NOT REALLY.
AN OLD ACQUAINTANCE BROUGHT ME...
...A FEW TIMES, BUT THAT'S IT.
AN ACQUAINTANCE?
AH.
YOU MEAN AN EX-BOYFRIEND?
Or someone like that?
WELL... SOMETHING LIKE THAT.
HE HAS THE COMPOSURE OF A MATURE MAN.
AND HE'S CLEARLY USED TO DODGING QUESTIONS.

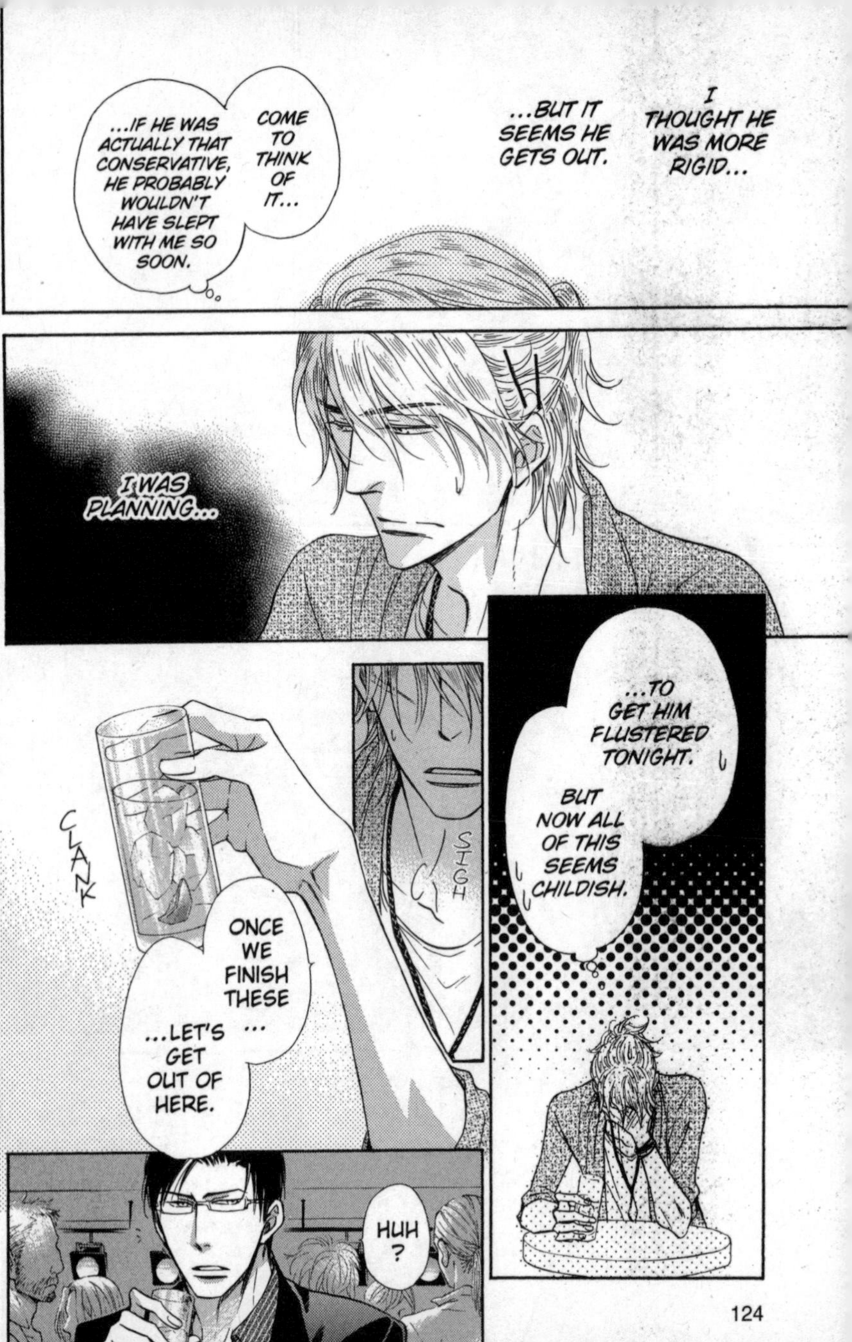
I THOUGHT HE WAS MORE RIGID...
...BUT IT SEEMS HE GETS OUT.
COME TO THINK OF IT...
...IF HE WAS ACTUALLY THAT CONSERVATIVE, HE PROBABLY WOULDN'T HAVE SLEPT WITH ME SO SOON.
I WAS PLANNING...
...TO GET HIM FLUSTERED TONIGHT.
BUT NOW ALL OF THIS SEEMS CHILDISH.
SIGH
CLANK
ONCE WE FINISH THESE...
...LET'S GET OUT OF HERE.
HUH?

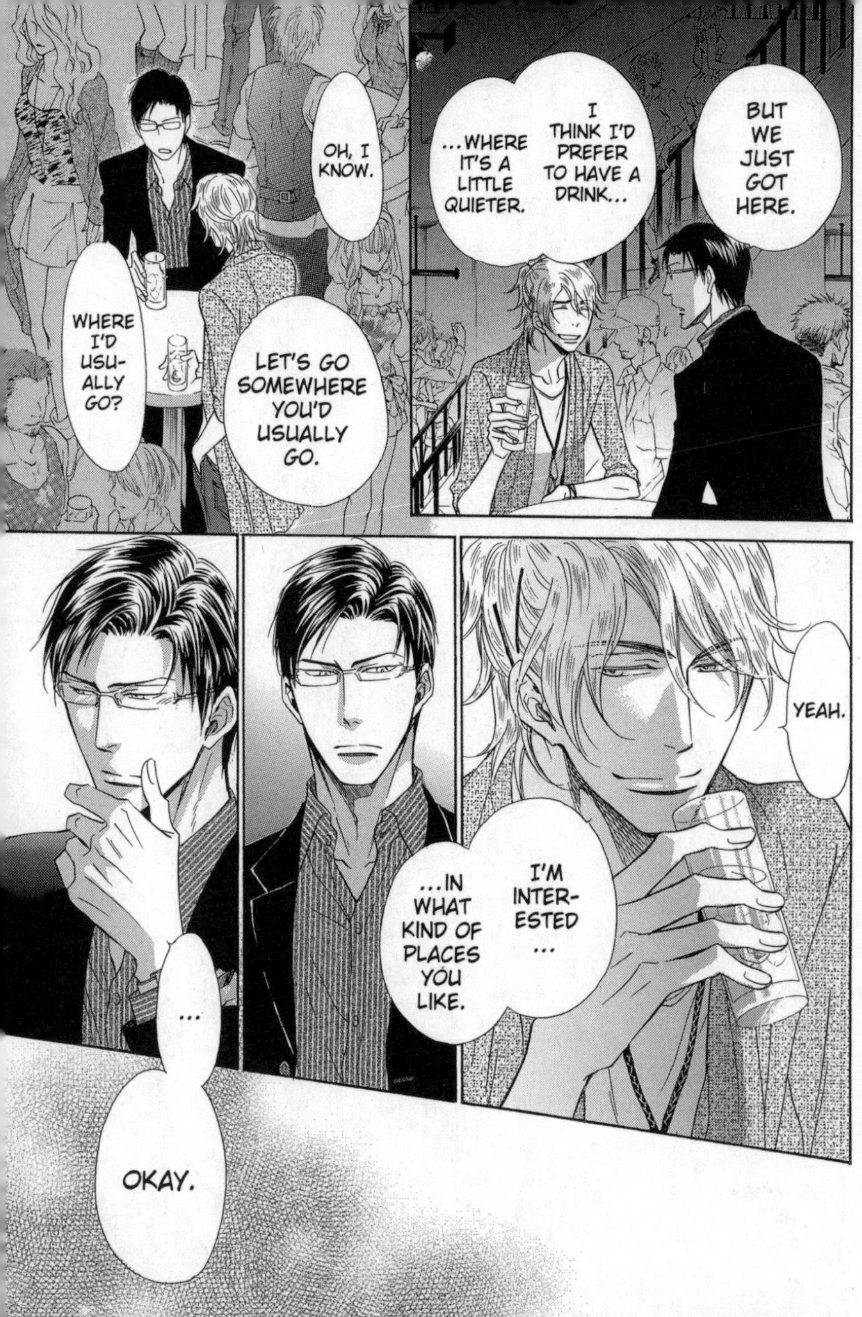
BUT WE JUST GOT HERE.
I THINK I'D PREFER TO HAVE A DRINK...
...WHERE IT'S A LITTLE QUIETER.
OH, I KNOW.
LET'S GO SOMEWHERE YOU'D USUALLY GO.
WHERE I'D USU-ALLY GO?
YEAH.
I'M INTER-ESTED...
...IN WHAT KIND OF PLACES YOU LIKE.
...
OKAY.

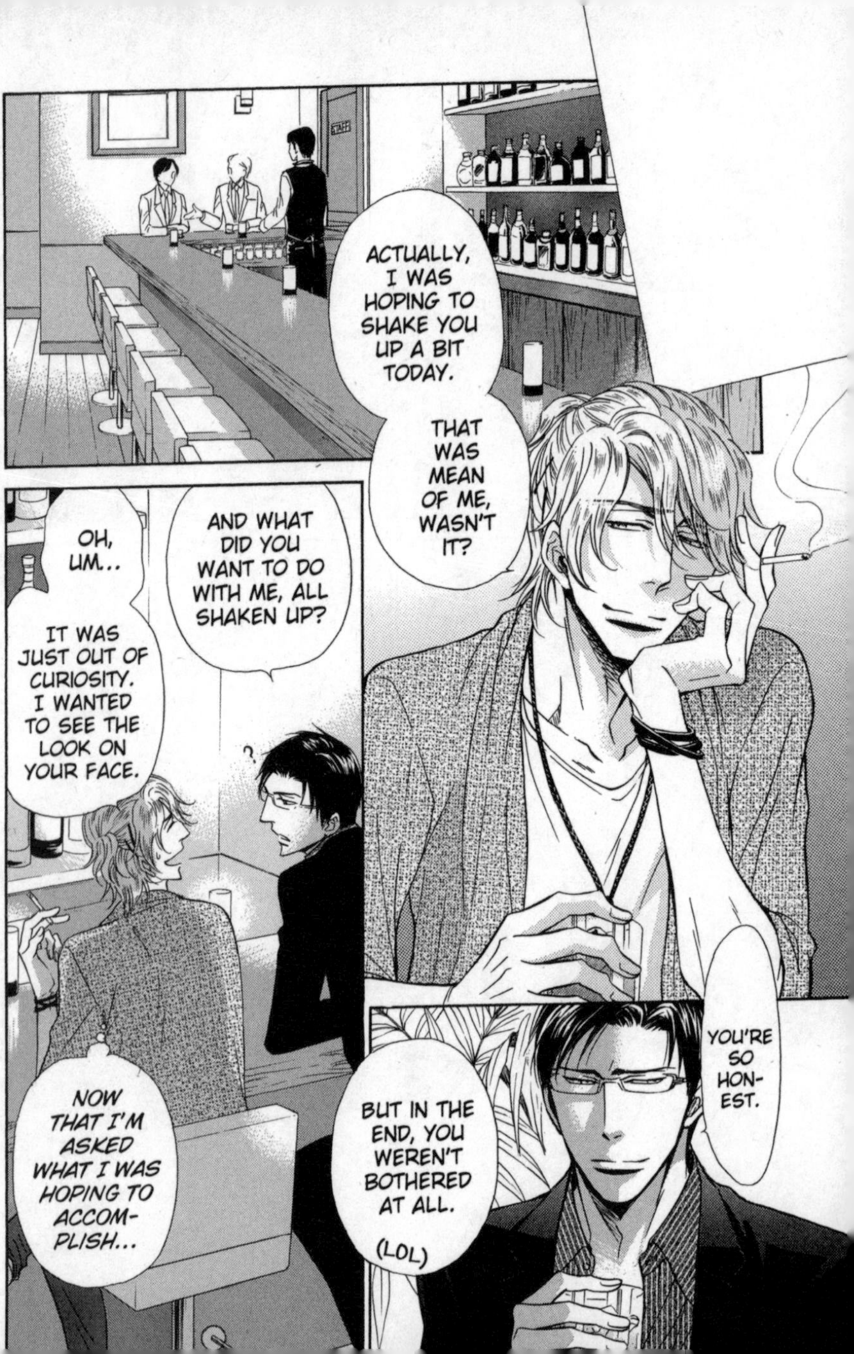

ACTUALLY, I WAS HOPING TO SHAKE YOU UP A BIT TODAY.
THAT WAS MEAN OF ME, WASN'T IT?
AND WHAT DID YOU WANT TO DO WITH ME, ALL SHAKEN UP?
OH, UM...
IT WAS JUST OUT OF CURIOSITY. I WANTED TO SEE THE LOOK ON YOUR FACE.
NOW THAT I'M ASKED WHAT I WAS HOPING TO ACCOMPLISH...
YOU'RE SO HON-EST.
BUT IN THE END, YOU WEREN'T BOTHERED AT ALL.
(LOL)

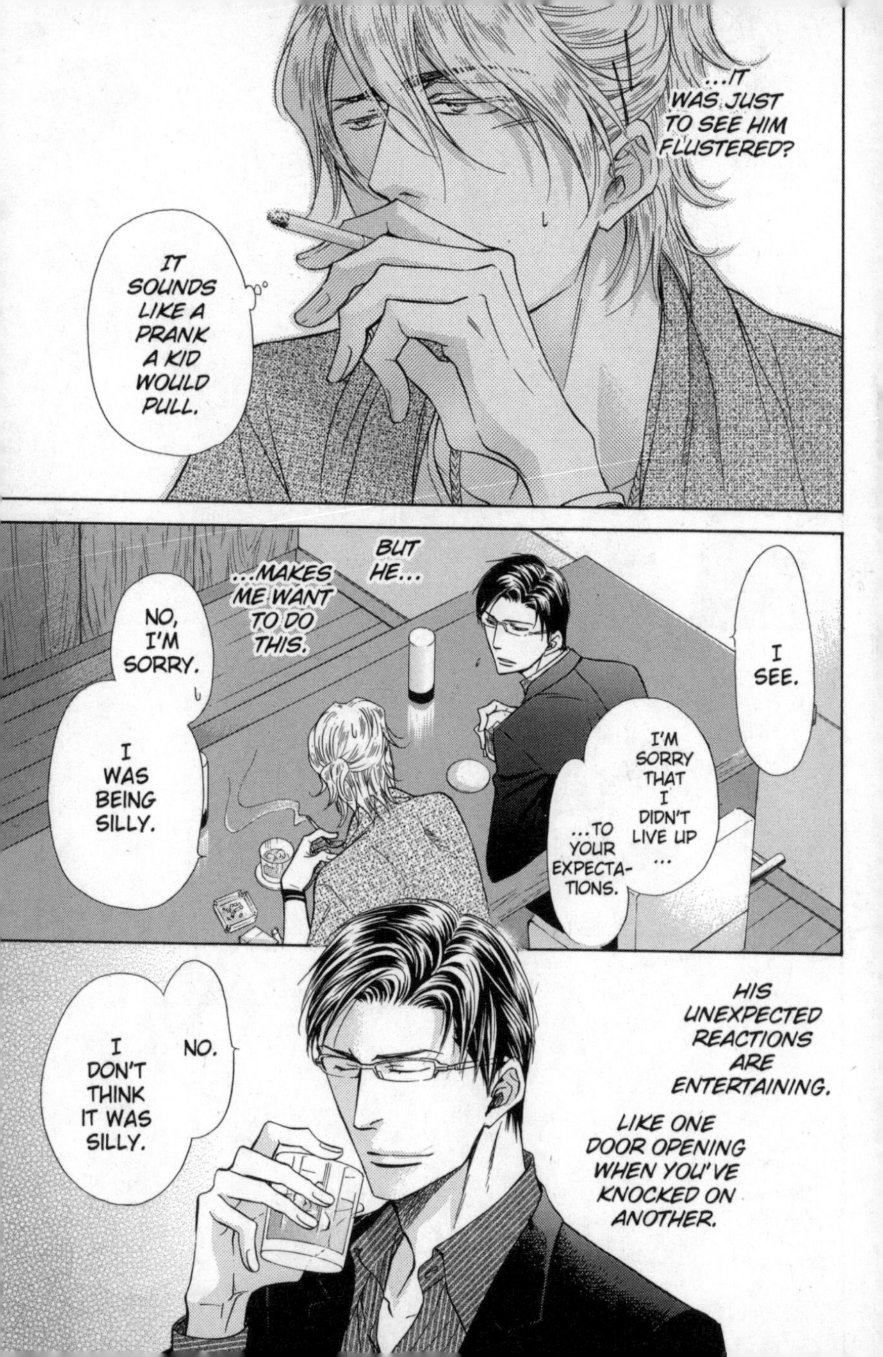
...IT WAS JUST TO SEE HIM FLUSTERED?
IT SOUNDS LIKE A PRANK A KID WOULD PULL.
I SEE.
I'M SORRY THAT I DIDN'T LIVE UP ...
...TO YOUR EXPECTATIONS.
BUT HE...
...MAKES ME WANT TO DO THIS.
NO, I'M SORRY.
I WAS BEING SILLY.
HIS UNEXPECTED REACTIONS ARE ENTERTAINING.
LIKE ONE DOOR OPENING WHEN YOU'VE KNOCKED ON ANOTHER.
NO.
I DON'T THINK IT WAS SILLY.

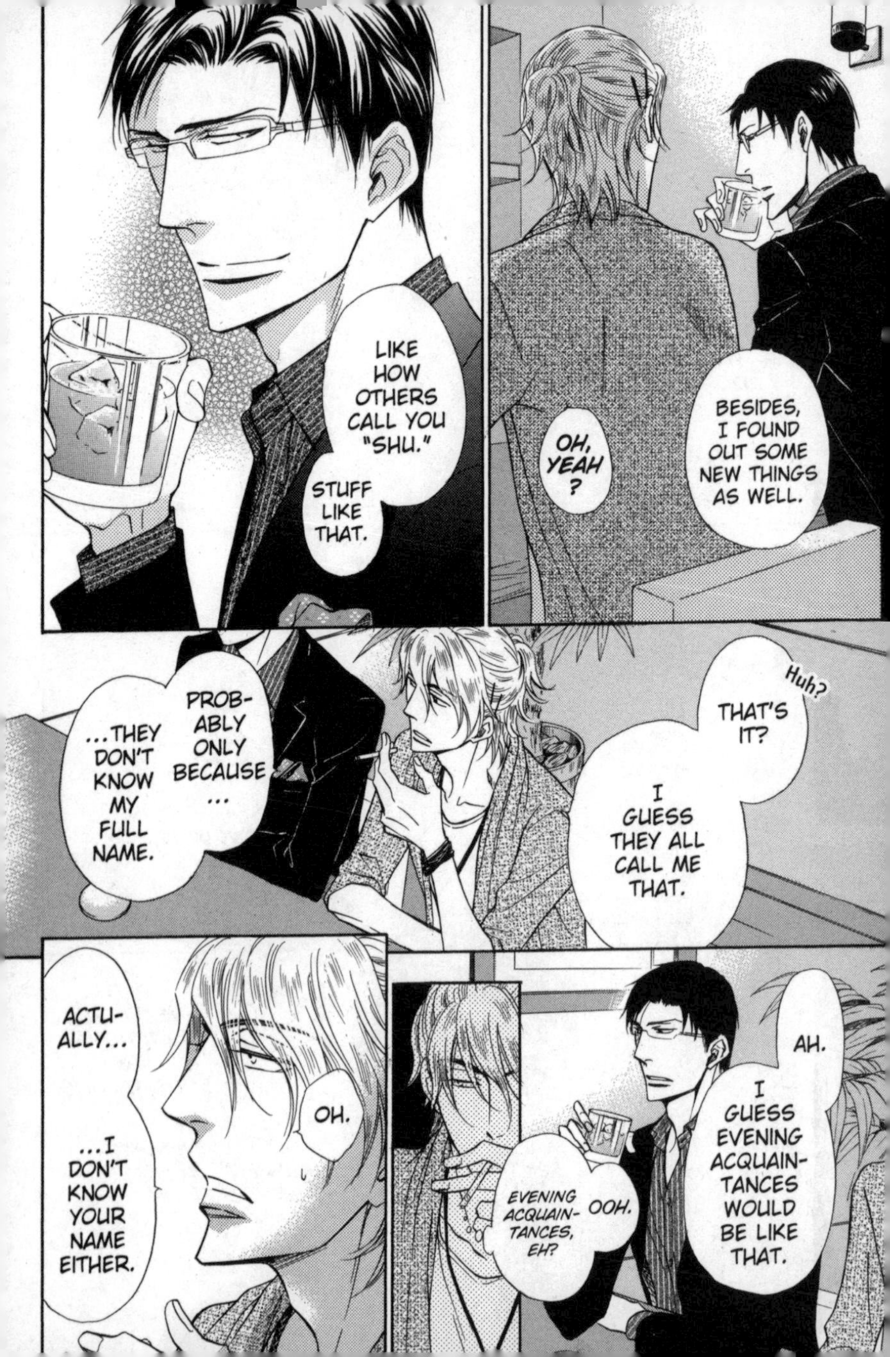
BESIDES, I FOUND OUT SOME NEW THINGS AS WELL.
OH, YEAH?
LIKE HOW OTHERS CALL YOU "SHU."
STUFF LIKE THAT.
Huh?
THAT'S IT?
I GUESS THEY ALL CALL ME THAT.
PROBABLY ONLY BECAUSE...
...THEY DON'T KNOW MY FULL NAME.
AH.
I GUESS EVENING ACQUAINTANCES WOULD BE LIKE THAT.
OOH.
EVENING ACQUAINTANCES, EH?
OH.
ACTUALLY...
...I DON'T KNOW YOUR NAME EITHER.

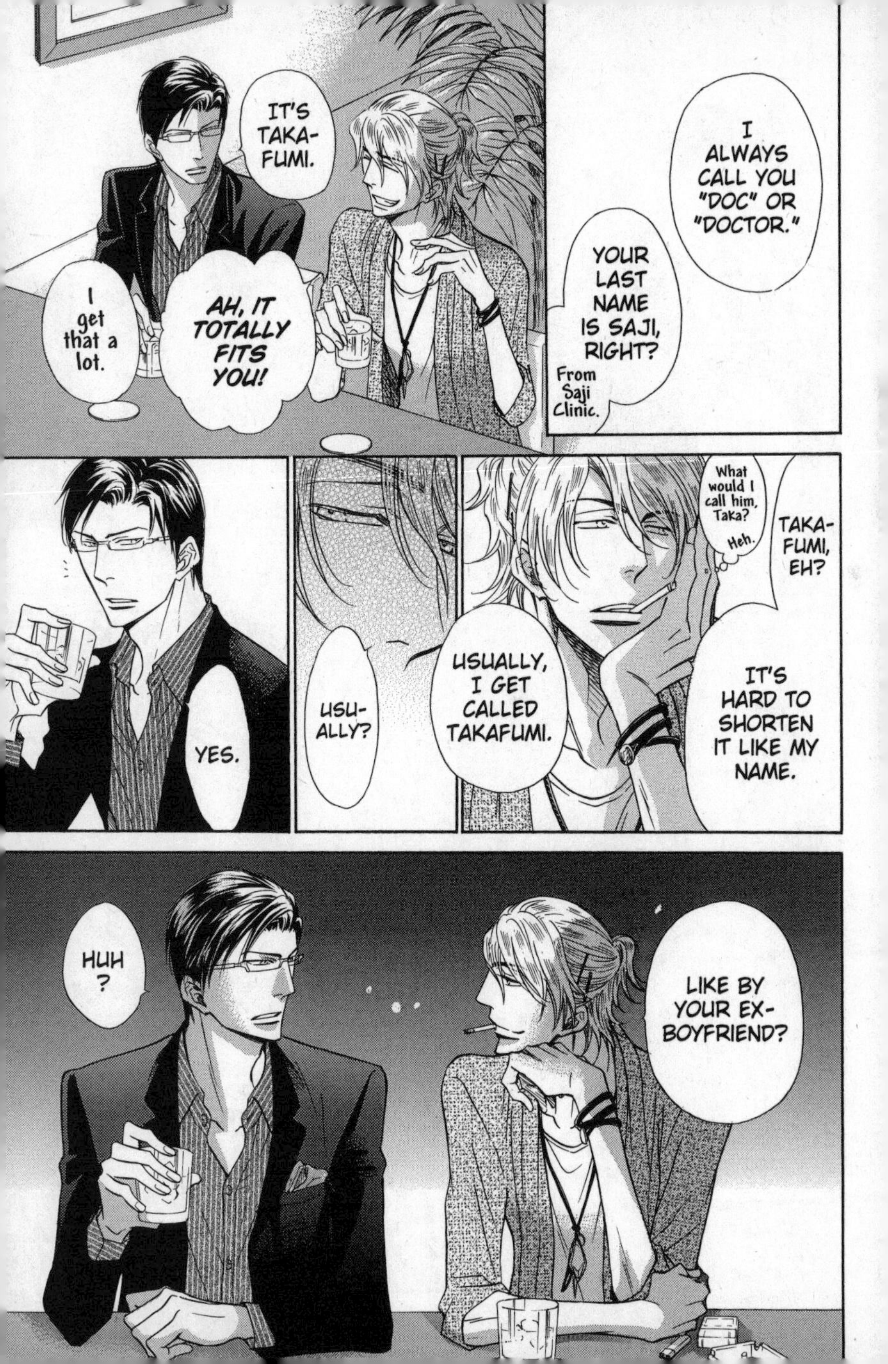
I ALWAYS CALL YOU "DOC" OR "DOCTOR."
YOUR LAST NAME IS SAJI, RIGHT?
From Saji Clinic.
IT'S TAKA-FUMI.
AH, IT TOTALLY FITS YOU!
I get that a lot.
TAKA-FUMI, EH?
What would I call him, Taka? Heh.
IT'S HARD TO SHORTEN IT LIKE MY NAME.
USUALLY, I GET CALLED TAKAFUMI.
USU-ALLY?
YES.
LIKE BY YOUR EX-BOYFRIEND?
HUH?

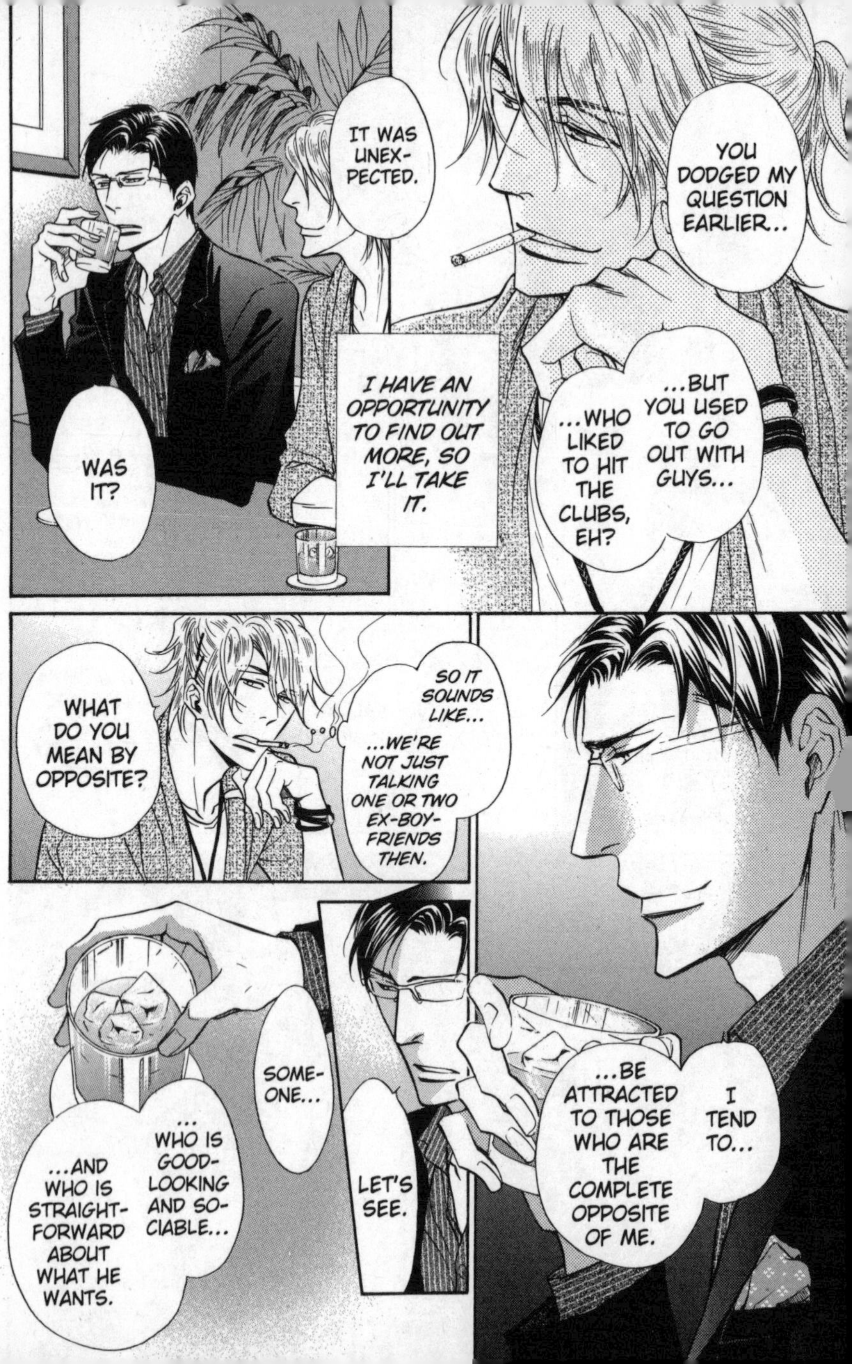
YOU DODGED MY QUESTION EARLIER...
...BUT YOU USED TO GO OUT WITH GUYS...
...WHO LIKED TO HIT THE CLUBS, EH?
IT WAS UNEXPECTED.
I HAVE AN OPPORTUNITY TO FIND OUT MORE, SO I'LL TAKE IT.
WAS IT?
I TEND TO...
...BE ATTRACTED TO THOSE WHO ARE THE COMPLETE OPPOSITE OF ME.
SO IT SOUNDS LIKE...
...WE'RE NOT JUST TALKING ONE OR TWO EX-BOY-FRIENDS THEN.
WHAT DO YOU MEAN BY OPPOSITE?
LET'S SEE.
SOME-ONE...
... WHO IS GOOD-LOOKING AND SO-CIABLE...
...AND WHO IS STRAIGHT-FORWARD ABOUT WHAT HE WANTS.

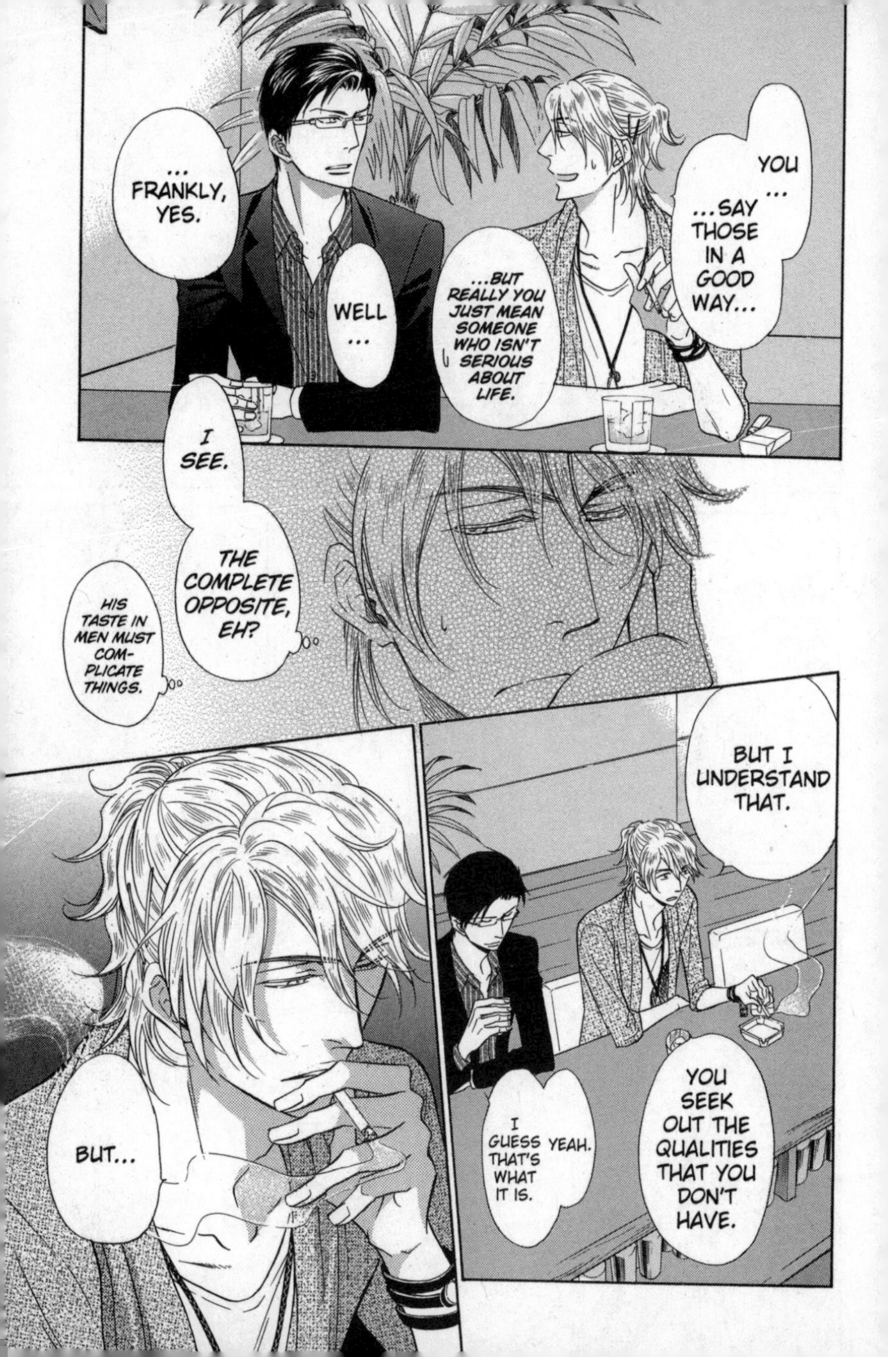
YOU ... ...SAY THOSE IN A GOOD WAY...
...BUT REALLY YOU JUST MEAN SOMEONE WHO ISN'T SERIOUS ABOUT LIFE.
WELL ...
... FRANKLY, YES.
I SEE.
THE COMPLETE OPPOSITE, EH?
HIS TASTE IN MEN MUST COM-PLICATE THINGS.
BUT I UNDERSTAND THAT.
YOU SEEK OUT THE QUALITIES THAT YOU DON'T HAVE.
YEAH.
I GUESS THAT'S WHAT IT IS.
BUT...

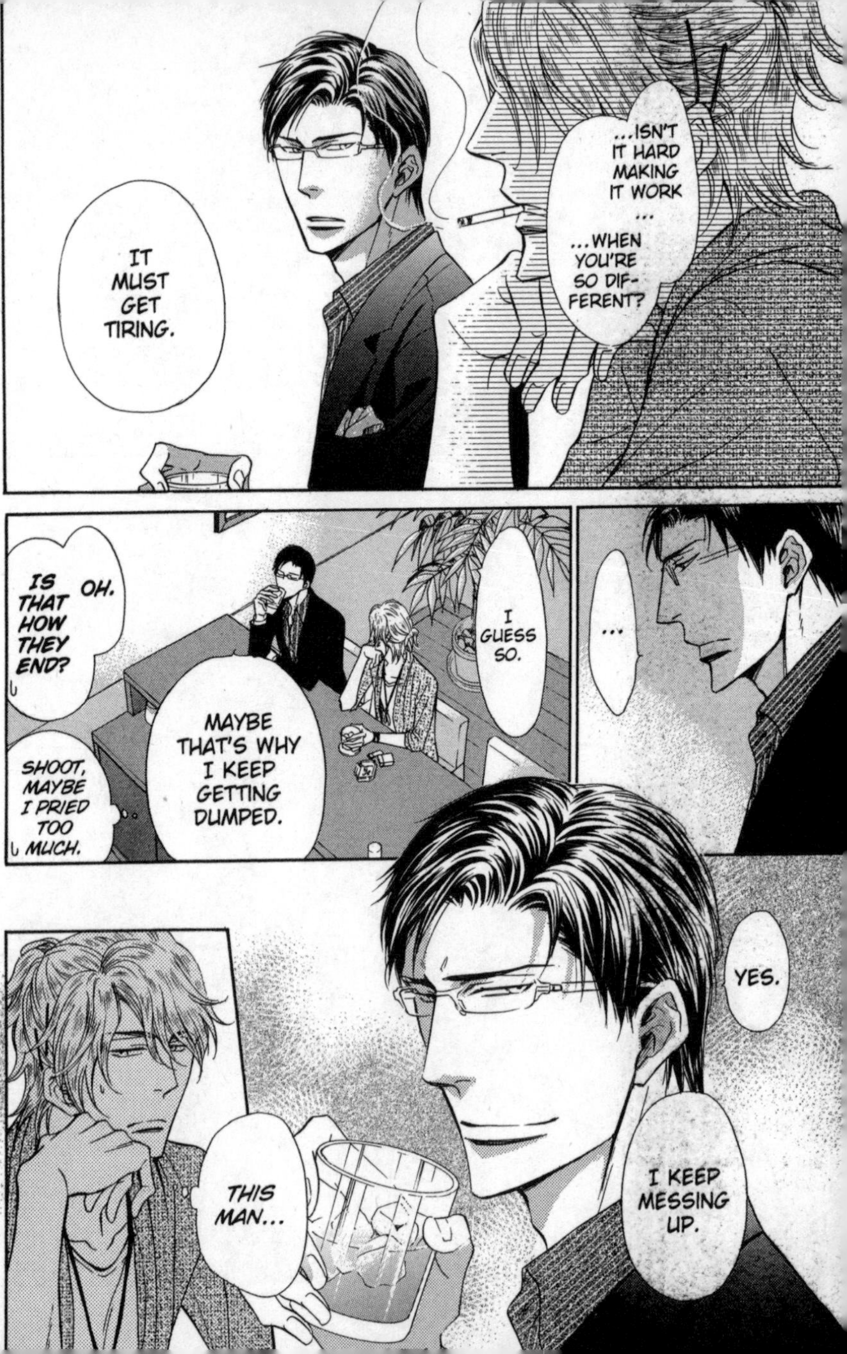
...ISN'T IT HARD MAKING IT WORK ...
...WHEN YOU'RE SO DIF-FERENT?
IT MUST GET TIRING.
...
I GUESS SO.
MAYBE THAT'S WHY I KEEP GETTING DUMPED.
OH.
IS THAT HOW THEY END?
SHOOT, MAYBE I PRIED TOO MUCH.
YES.
I KEEP MESSING UP.
THIS MAN...

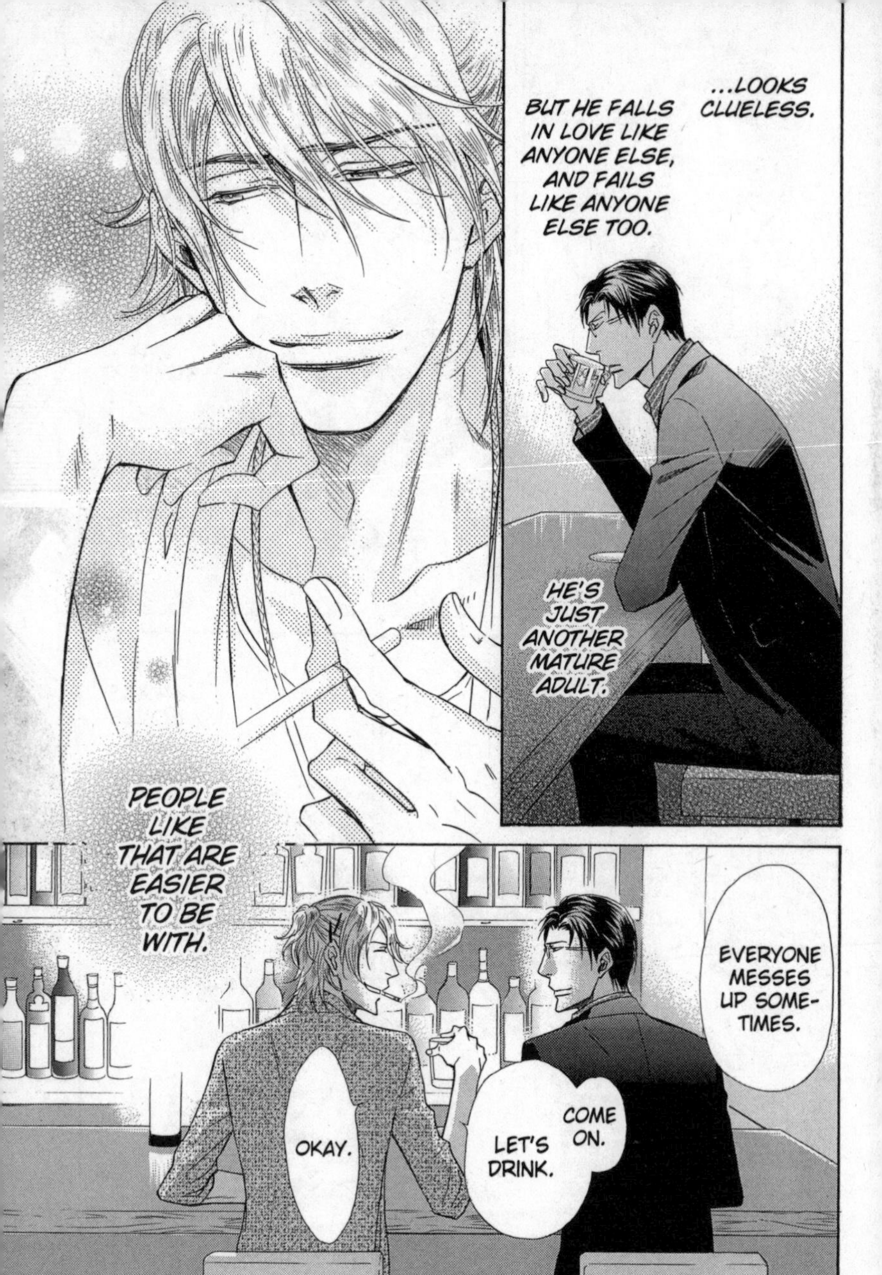
...LOOKS CLUELESS.
BUT HE FALLS IN LOVE LIKE ANYONE ELSE, AND FAILS LIKE ANYONE ELSE TOO.
HE'S JUST ANOTHER MATURE ADULT.
PEOPLE LIKE THAT ARE EASIER TO BE WITH.
EVERYONE MESSES UP SOME-TIMES.
COME ON.
LET'S DRINK.
OKAY.

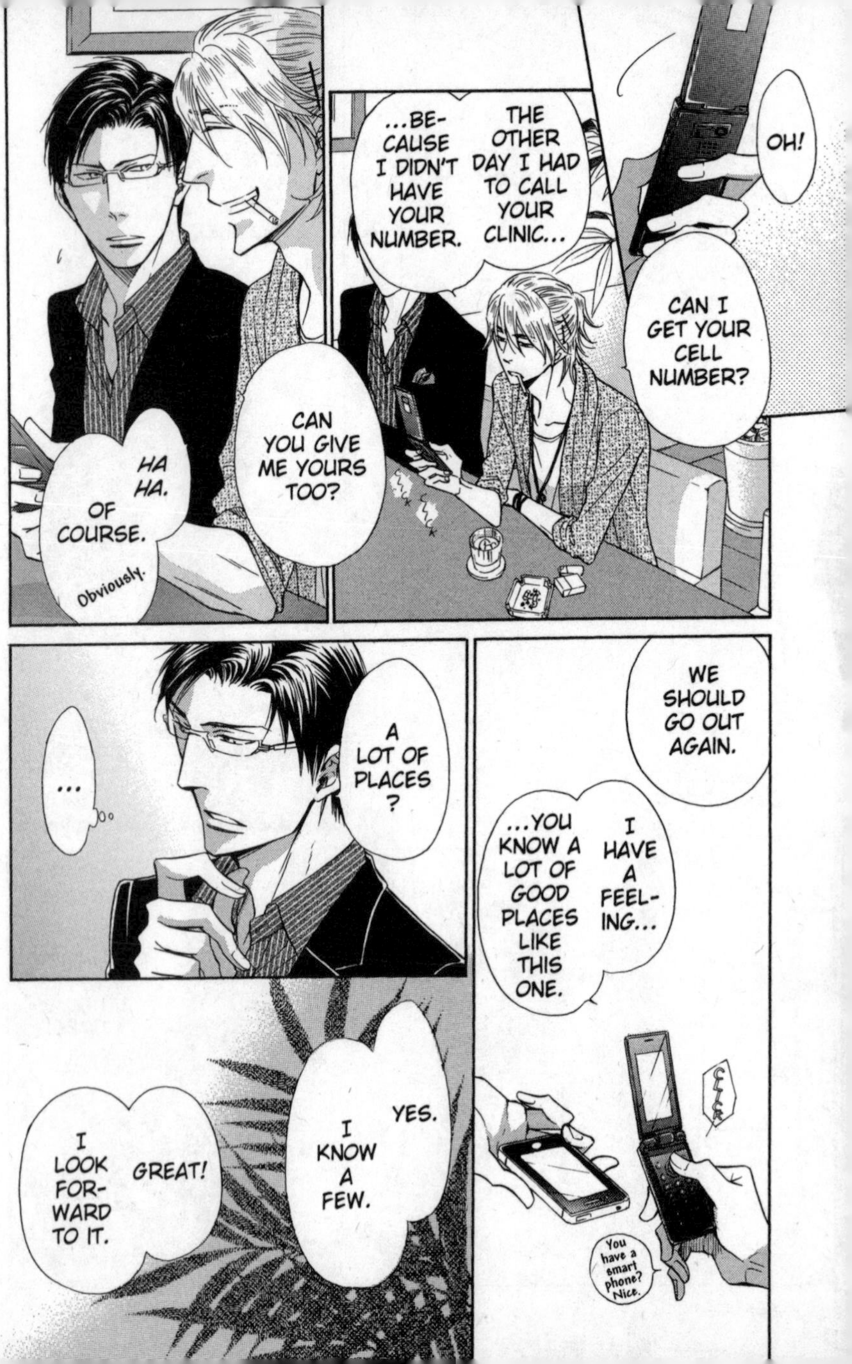
OH!
CAN I GET YOUR CELL NUMBER?
THE OTHER DAY I HAD TO CALL YOUR CLINIC...
...BECAUSE I DIDN'T HAVE YOUR NUMBER.
CAN YOU GIVE ME YOURS TOO?
HA HA.
OF COURSE.
Obviously.
WE SHOULD GO OUT AGAIN.
I HAVE A FEELING...
...YOU KNOW A LOT OF GOOD PLACES LIKE THIS ONE.
A LOT OF PLACES?
...
CLICK
You have a smart phone? Nice.
YES.
I KNOW A FEW.
GREAT!
I LOOK FORWARD TO IT.

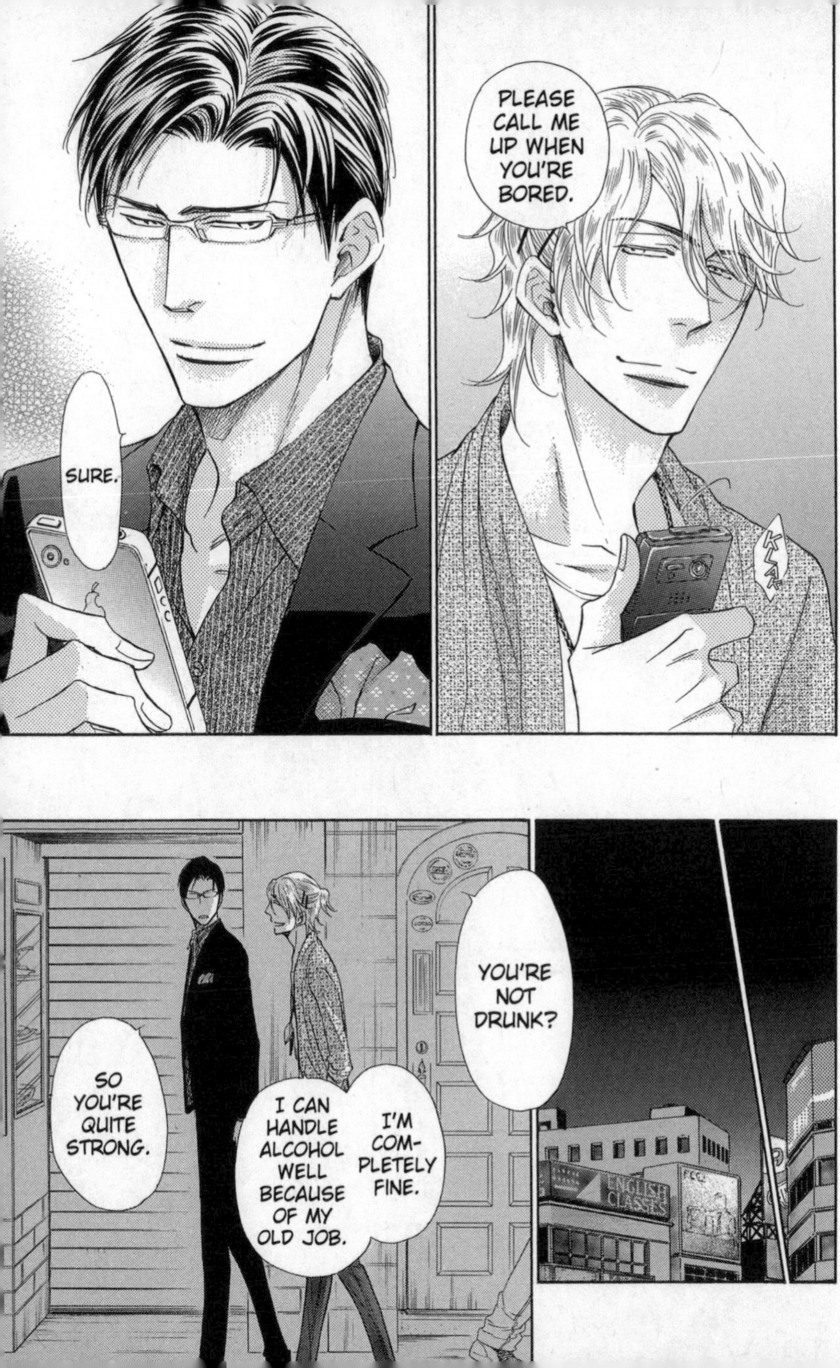
PLEASE CALL ME UP WHEN YOU'RE BORED.
KLAK
SURE.
YOU'RE NOT DRUNK?
ENGLISH CLASSES
I'M COM-PLETELY FINE.
I CAN HANDLE ALCOHOL WELL BECAUSE OF MY OLD JOB.
SO YOU'RE QUITE STRONG.

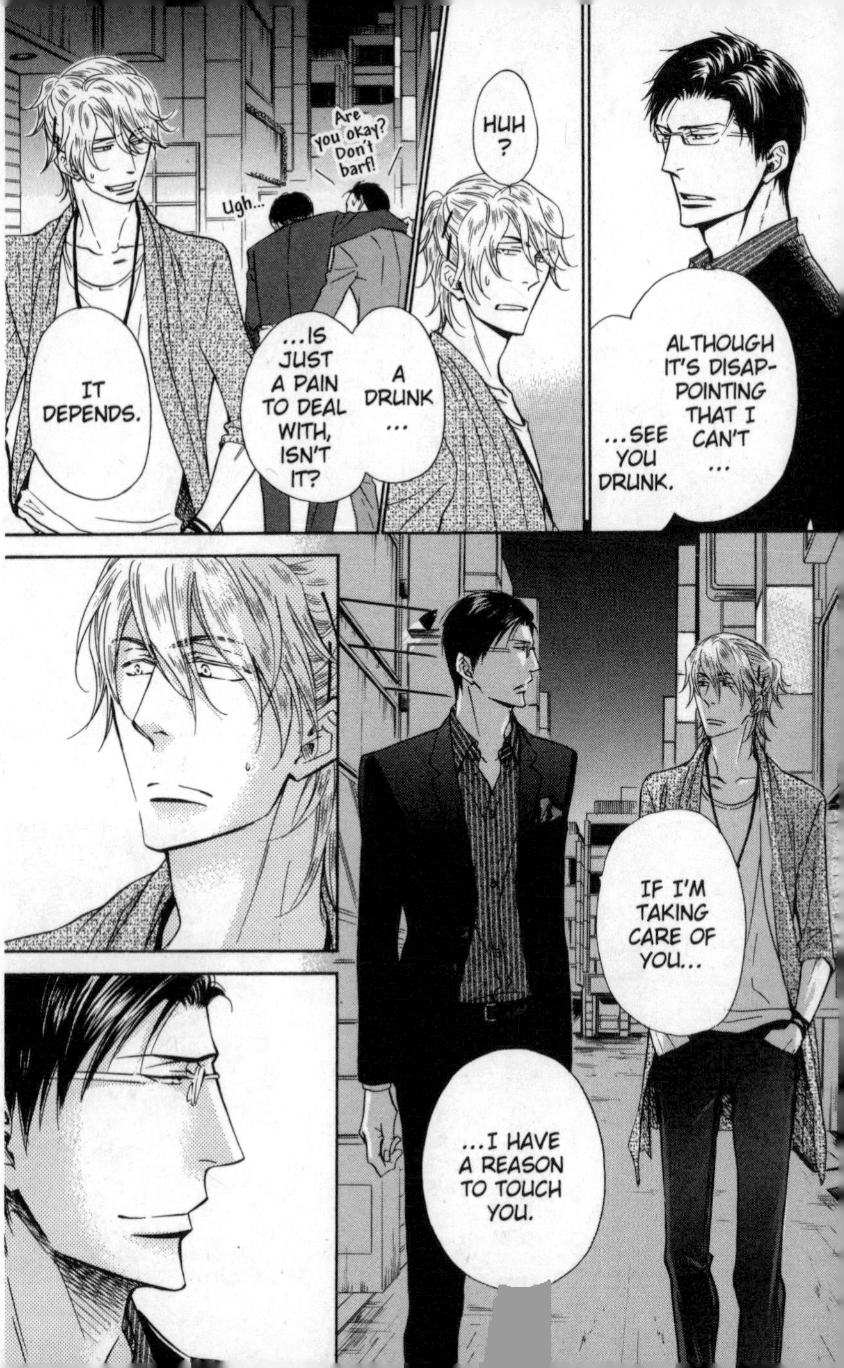
ALTHOUGH IT'S DISAPPOINTING THAT I CAN'T...
...SEE YOU DRUNK.
HUH?
A DRUNK...
...IS JUST A PAIN TO DEAL WITH, ISN'T IT?
Are you okay? Don't barf!
Ugh...
IT DEPENDS.
IF I'M TAKING CARE OF YOU...
...I HAVE A REASON TO TOUCH YOU.

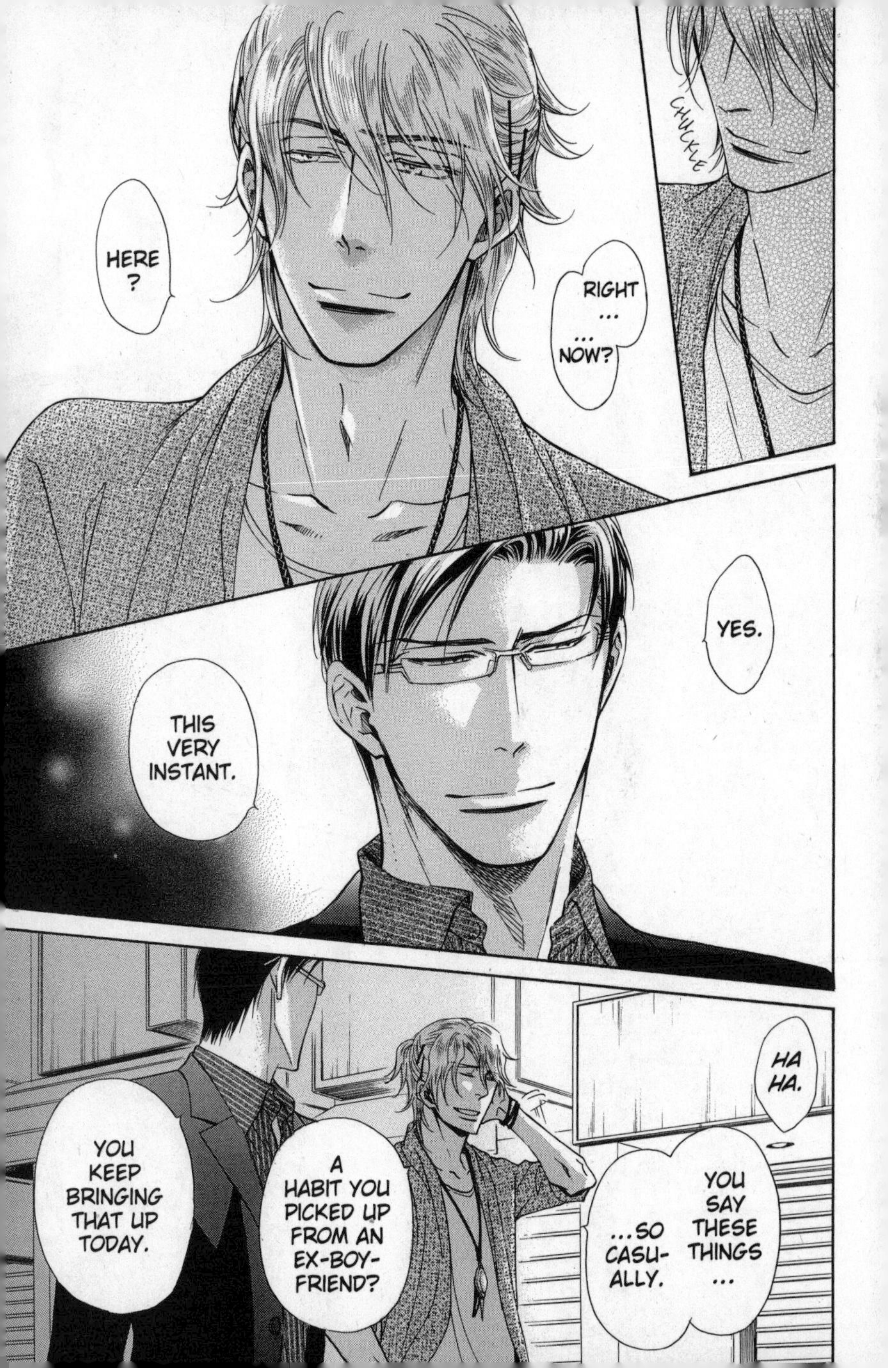
CHUCKLE
RIGHT ... ... NOW?
HERE ?
YES.
THIS VERY INSTANT.
HA HA.
YOU SAY THESE THINGS ...
...SO CASU-ALLY.
A HABIT YOU PICKED UP FROM AN EX-BOY-FRIEND?
YOU KEEP BRINGING THAT UP TODAY.

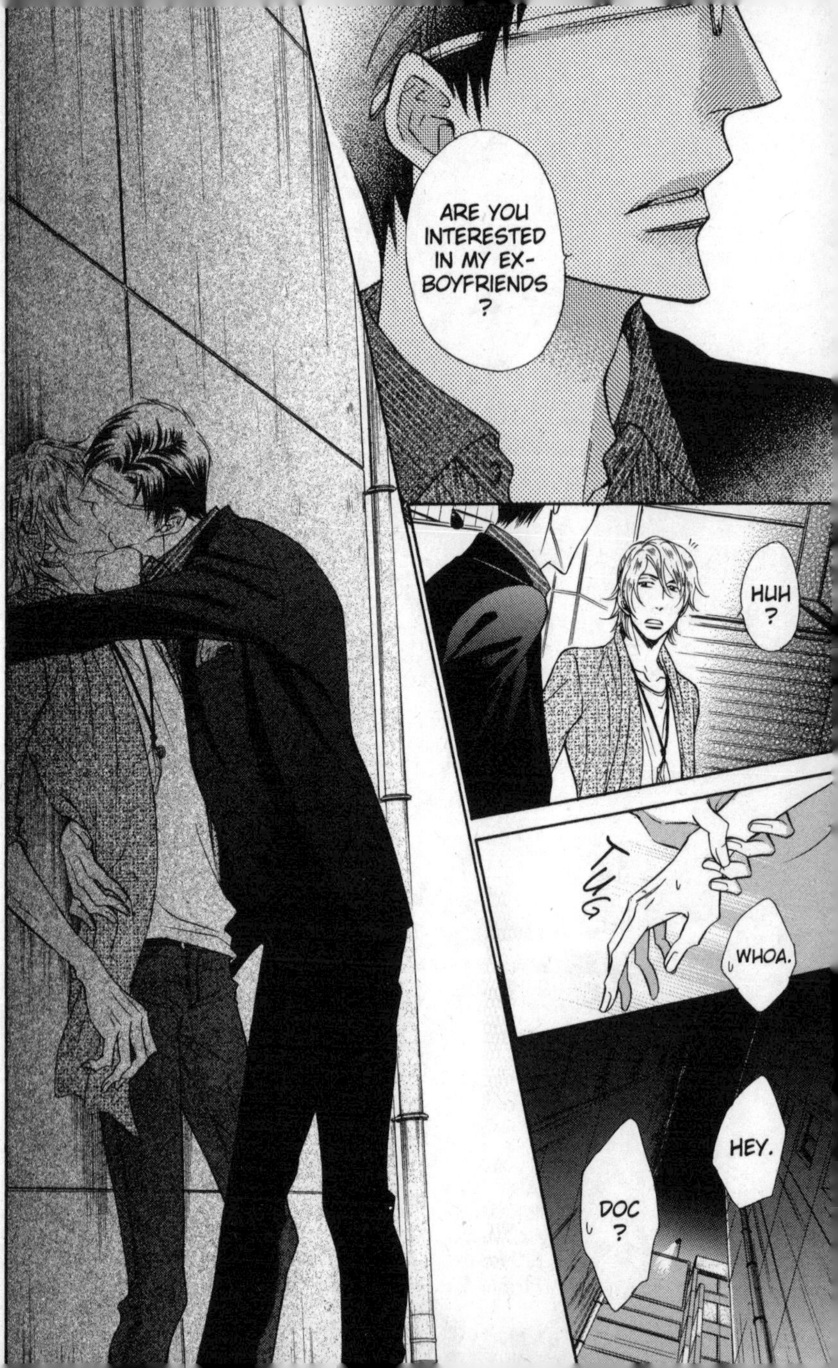
ARE YOU INTERESTED IN MY EX-BOYFRIENDS?
HUH?
TUG
WHOA.
HEY.
DOC?

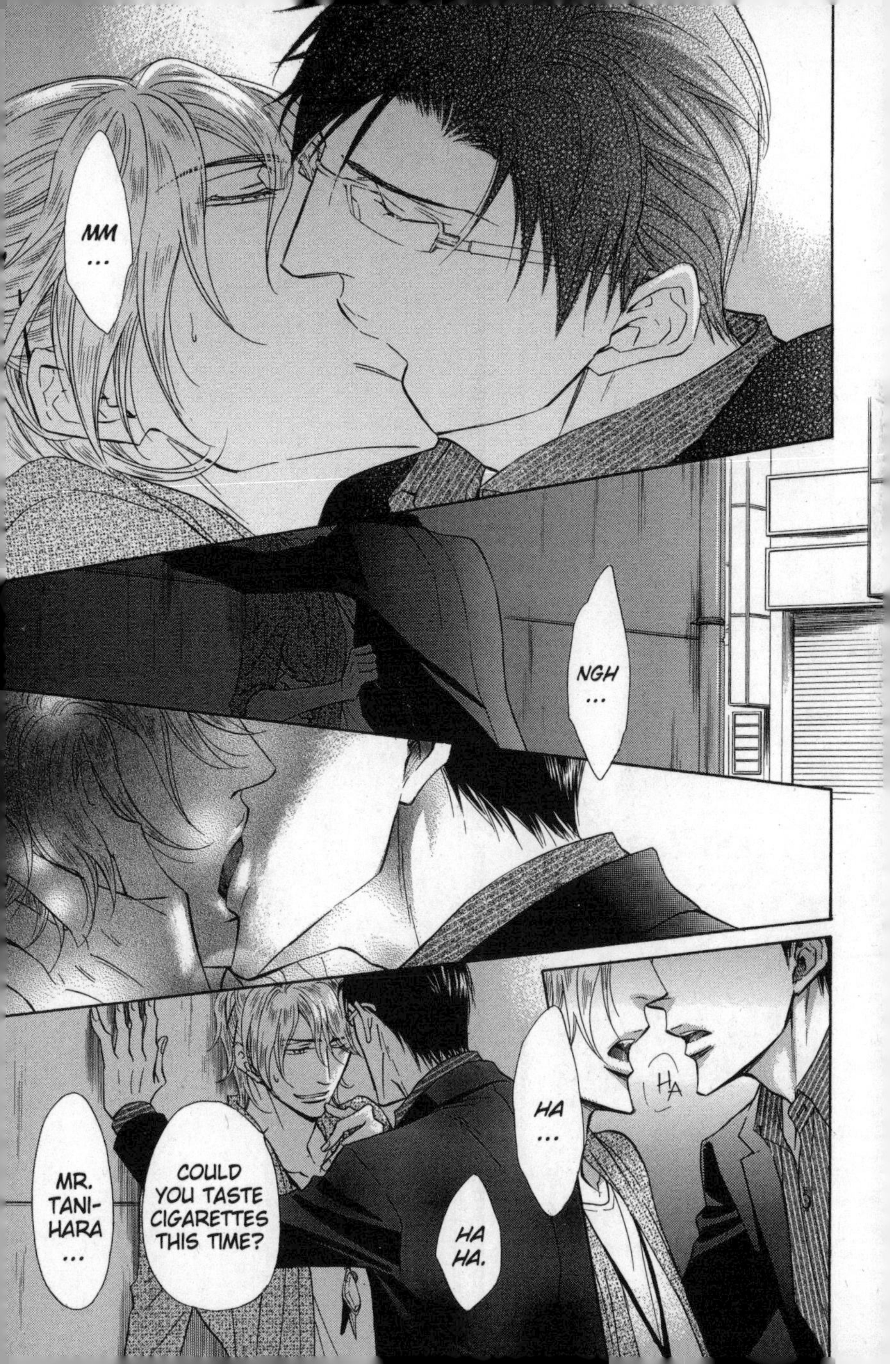
MM ...
NGH ...
HA
HA ...
HA HA.
COULD YOU TASTE CIGARETTES THIS TIME?
MR. TANI-HARA ...

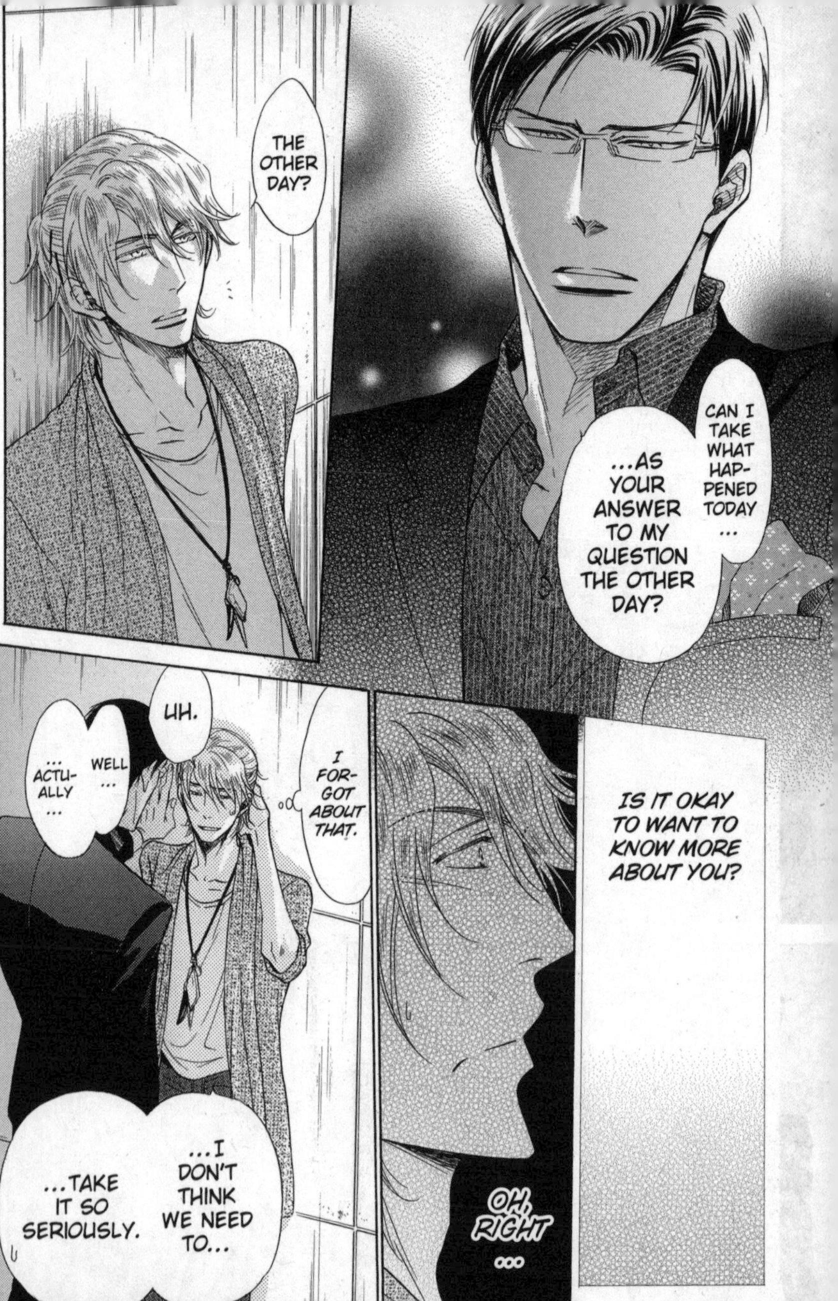
CAN I TAKE WHAT HAP-PENED TODAY...
...AS YOUR ANSWER TO MY QUESTION THE OTHER DAY?
THE OTHER DAY?
IS IT OKAY TO WANT TO KNOW MORE ABOUT YOU?
OH, RIGHT...
I FOR-GOT ABOUT THAT.
UH.
WELL...
...ACTU-ALLY...
...I DON'T THINK WE NEED TO...
...TAKE IT SO SERIOUSLY.

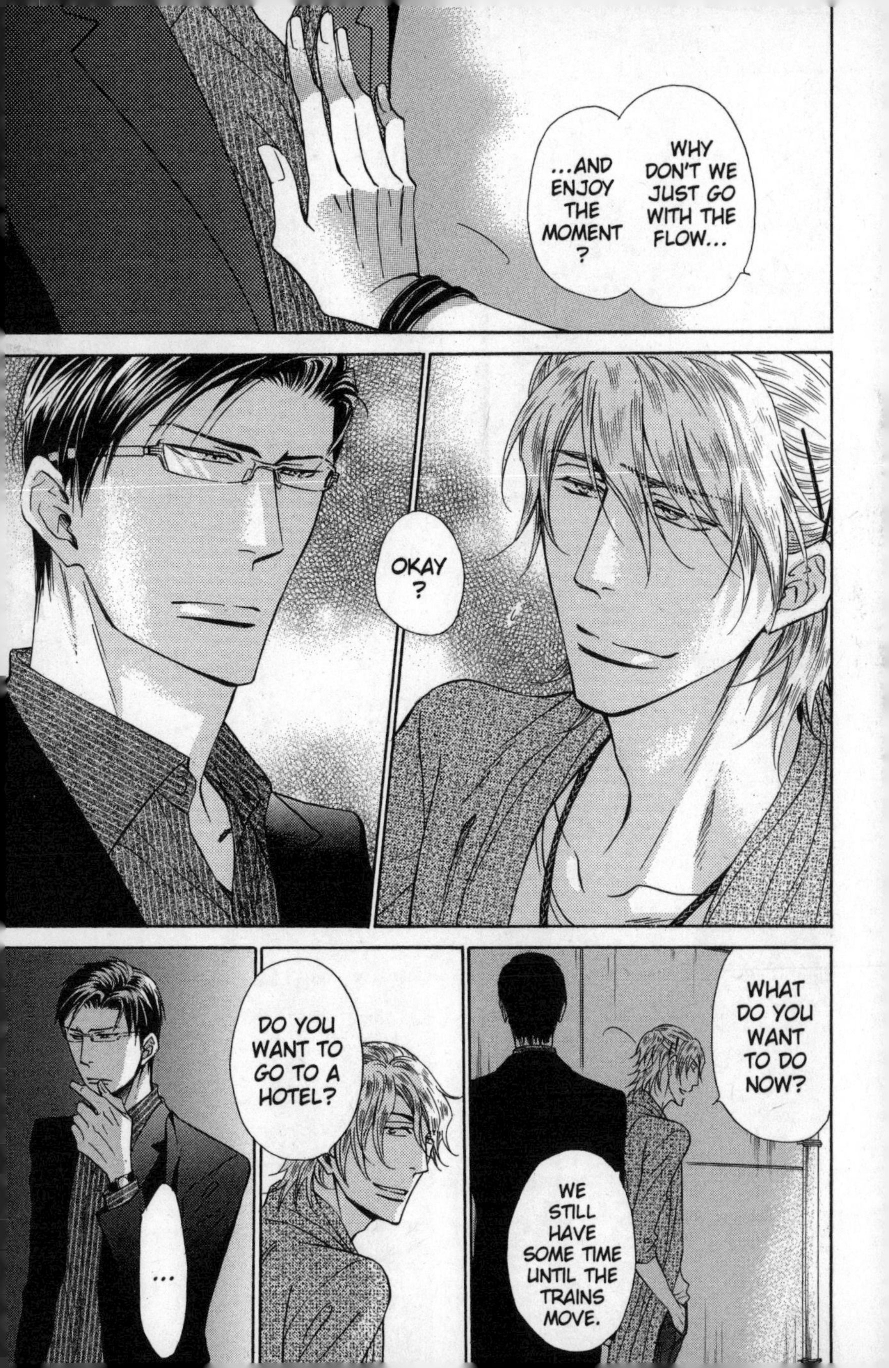
WHY DON'T WE JUST GO WITH THE FLOW...
...AND ENJOY THE MOMENT?
OKAY?
WHAT DO YOU WANT TO DO NOW?
WE STILL HAVE SOME TIME UNTIL THE TRAINS MOVE.
DO YOU WANT TO GO TO A HOTEL?
...

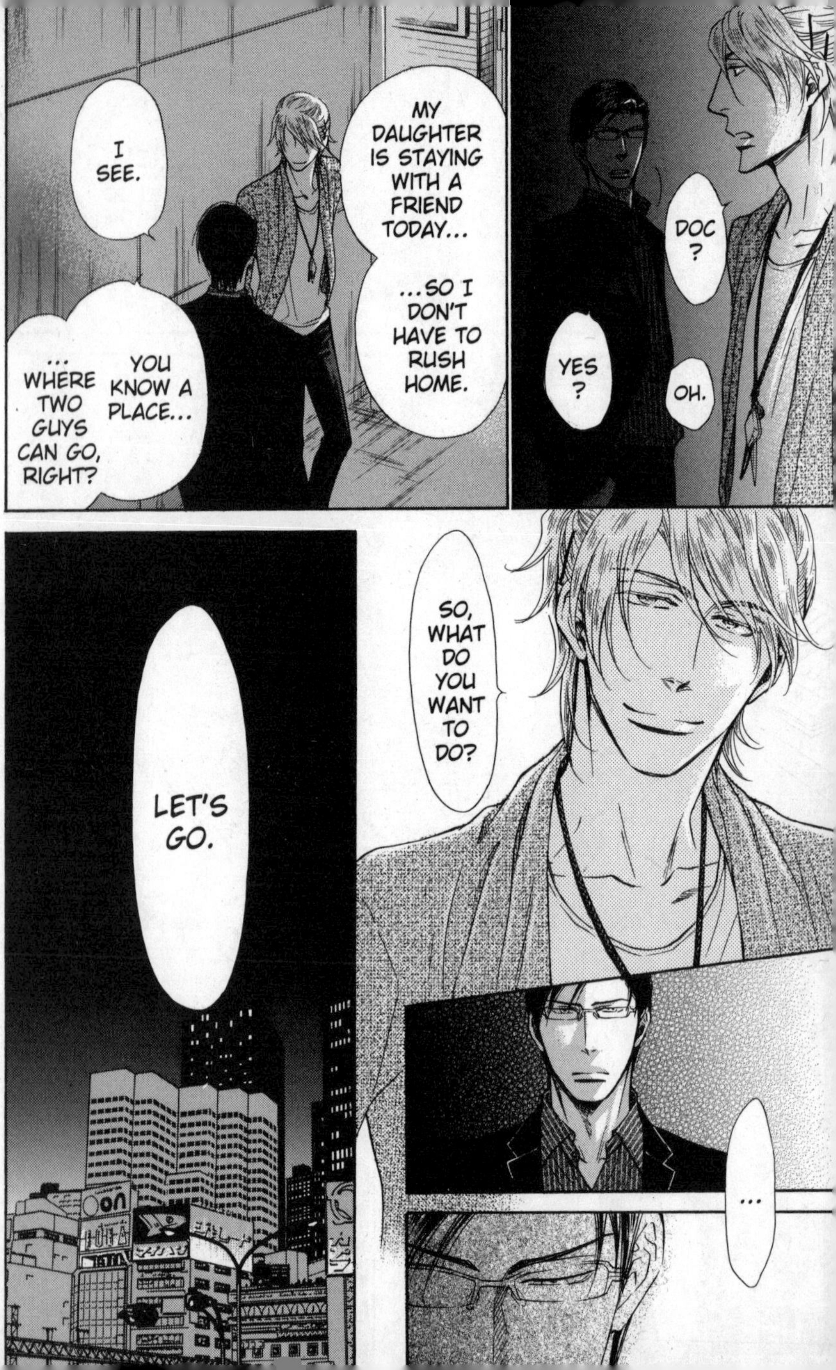
DOC?
YES?
OH.
MY DAUGHTER IS STAYING WITH A FRIEND TODAY...
...SO I DON'T HAVE TO RUSH HOME.
I SEE.
YOU KNOW A PLACE... ...WHERE TWO GUYS CAN GO, RIGHT?
SO, WHAT DO YOU WANT TO DO?
...
LET'S GO.

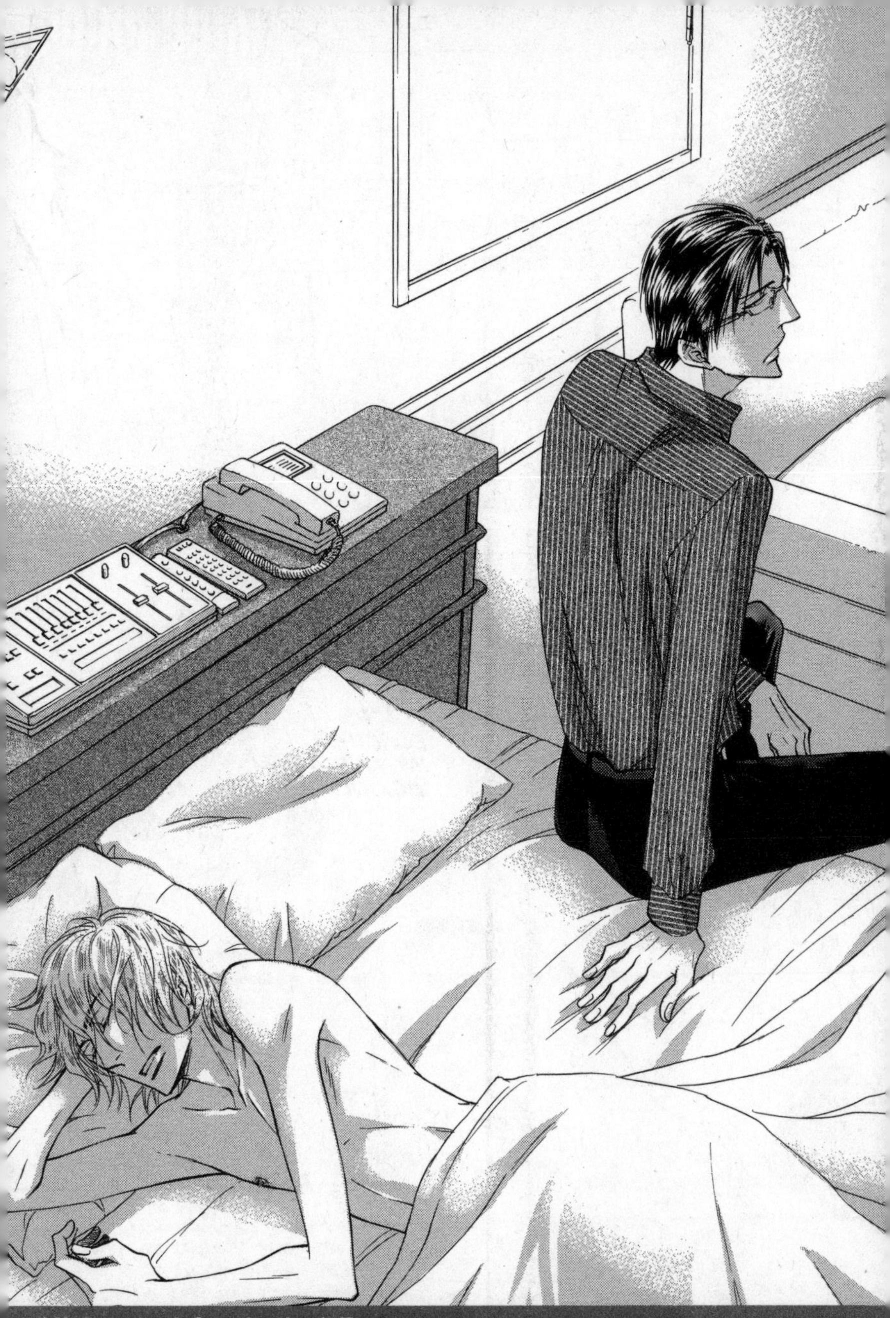

Hide and Seek: Act 5

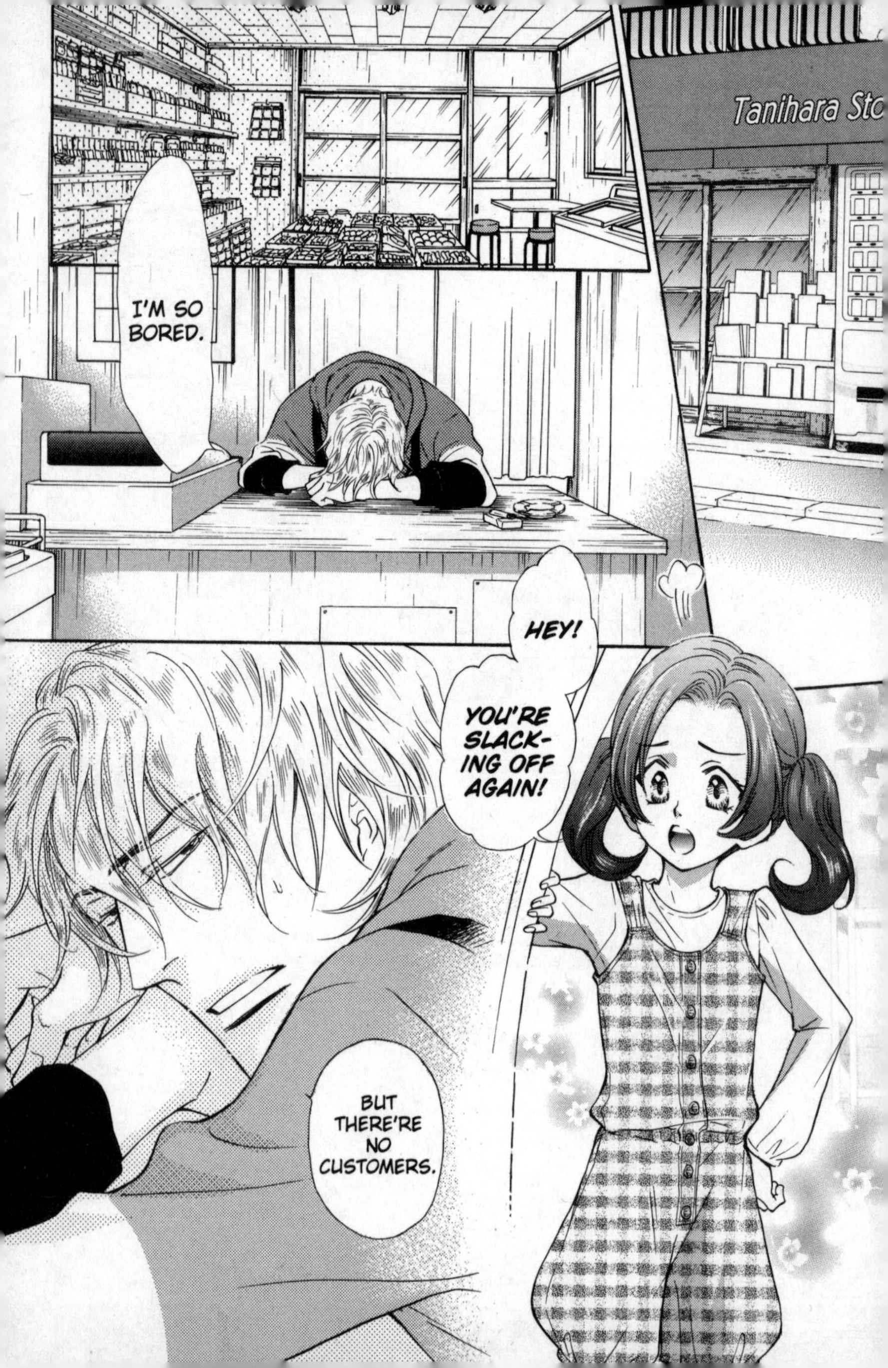
Tanihara Sto
I'M SO BORED.
HEY!
YOU'RE SLACK-ING OFF AGAIN!
BUT THERE'RE NO CUSTOMERS.

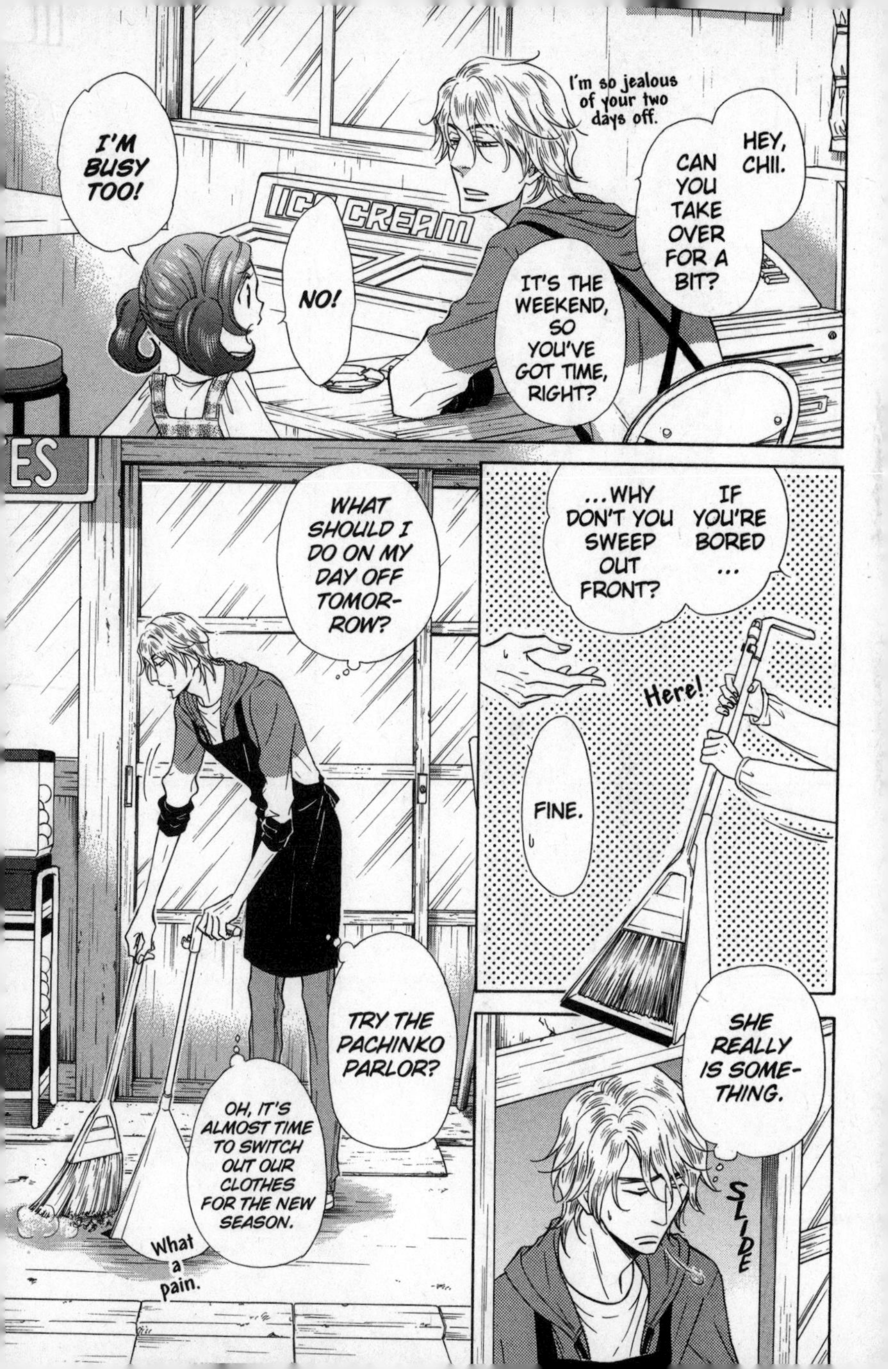
I'm so jealous of your two days off.
HEY, CHII. CAN YOU TAKE OVER FOR A BIT?
IT'S THE WEEKEND, SO YOU'VE GOT TIME, RIGHT?
NO!
I'M BUSY TOO!
IF YOU'RE BORED ... ...WHY DON'T YOU SWEEP OUT FRONT?
Here!
FINE.
SHE REALLY IS SOME-THING.
SLIDE
WHAT SHOULD I DO ON MY DAY OFF TOMOR-ROW?
TRY THE PACHINKO PARLOR?
OH, IT'S ALMOST TIME TO SWITCH OUT OUR CLOTHES FOR THE NEW SEASON.
What a pain.

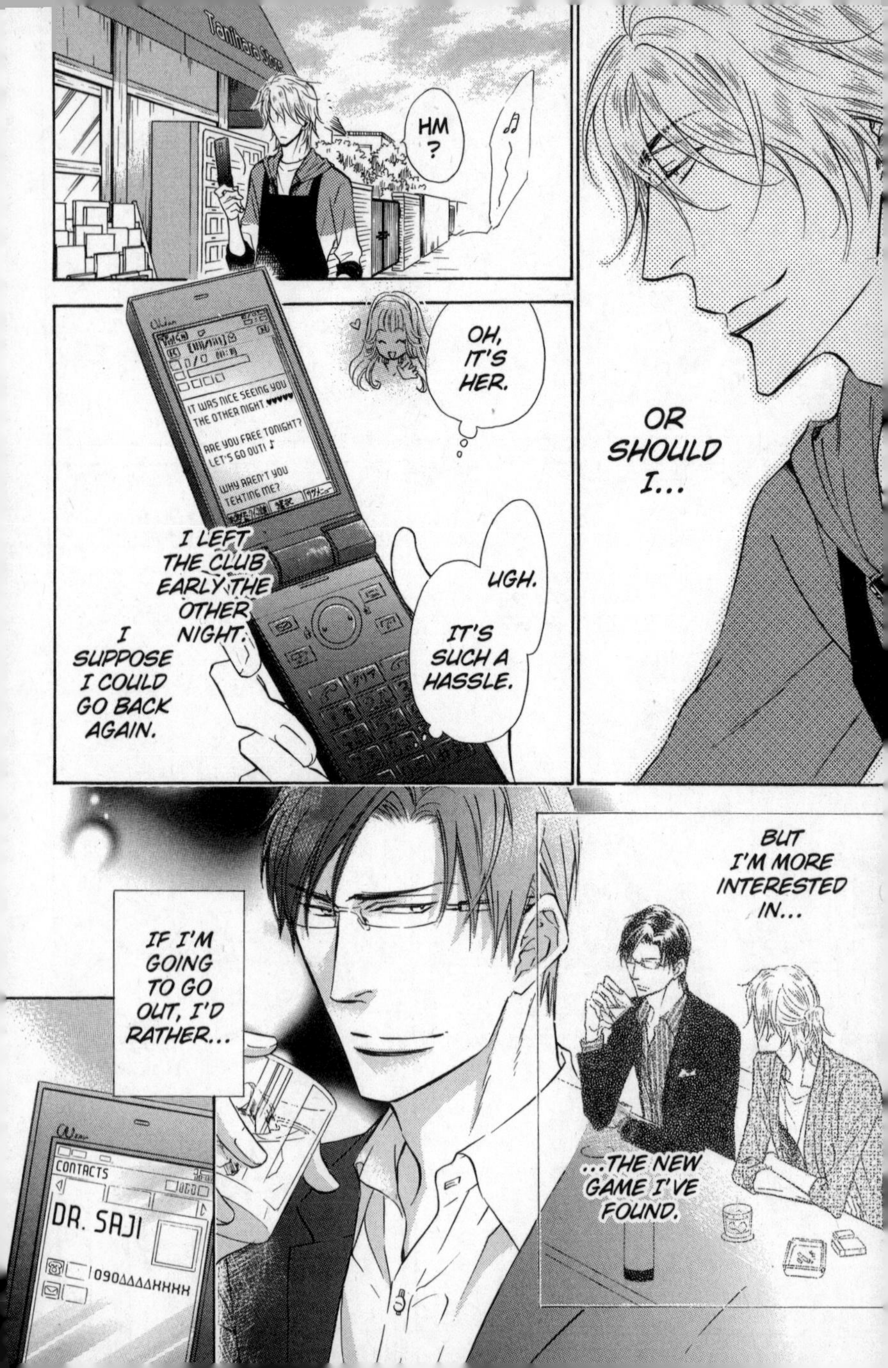
OR SHOULD I...
Tanihara Store
HM?
♪
IT WAS NICE SEEING YOU THE OTHER NIGHT ♥♥♥
ARE YOU FREE TONIGHT? LET'S GO OUT! ♪
WHY AREN'T YOU TEXTING ME?
OH, IT'S HER.
UGH.
IT'S SUCH A HASSLE.
I LEFT THE CLUB EARLY THE OTHER NIGHT.
I SUPPOSE I COULD GO BACK AGAIN.
BUT I'M MORE INTERESTED IN...
...THE NEW GAME I'VE FOUND.
IF I'M GOING TO GO OUT, I'D RATHER...
CONTACTS
DR. SAJI
090△△△△XXXX

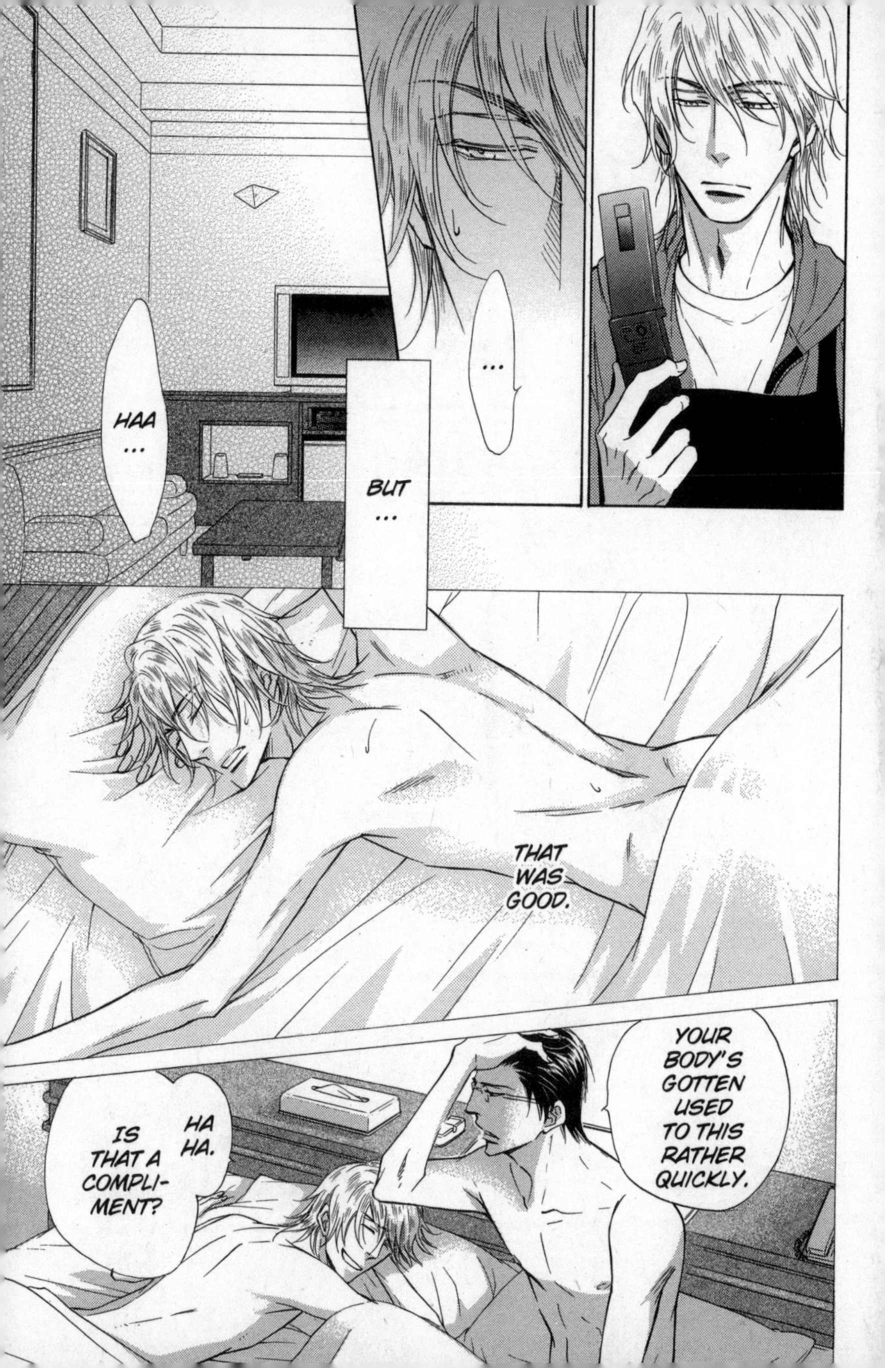
...
BUT ...
HAA ...
THAT WAS GOOD.
YOUR BODY'S GOTTEN USED TO THIS RATHER QUICKLY.
HA HA.
IS THAT A COMPLI-MENT?

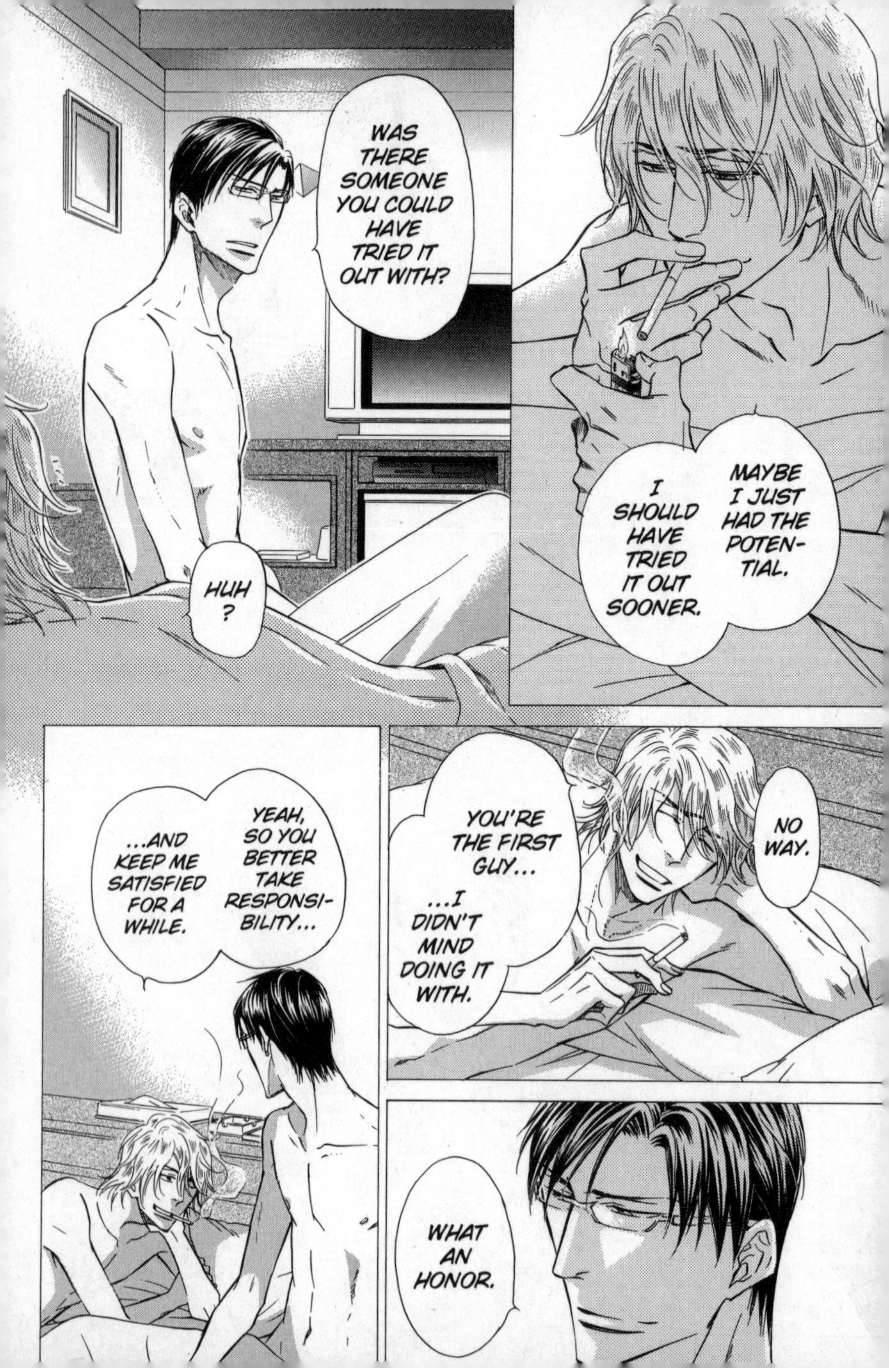
MAYBE I JUST HAD THE POTEN-TIAL.
I SHOULD HAVE TRIED IT OUT SOONER.
WAS THERE SOMEONE YOU COULD HAVE TRIED IT OUT WITH?
HUH?
NO WAY.
YOU'RE THE FIRST GUY...
...I DIDN'T MIND DOING IT WITH.
WHAT AN HONOR.
YEAH, SO YOU BETTER TAKE RESPONSI-BILITY...
...AND KEEP ME SATISFIED FOR A WHILE.

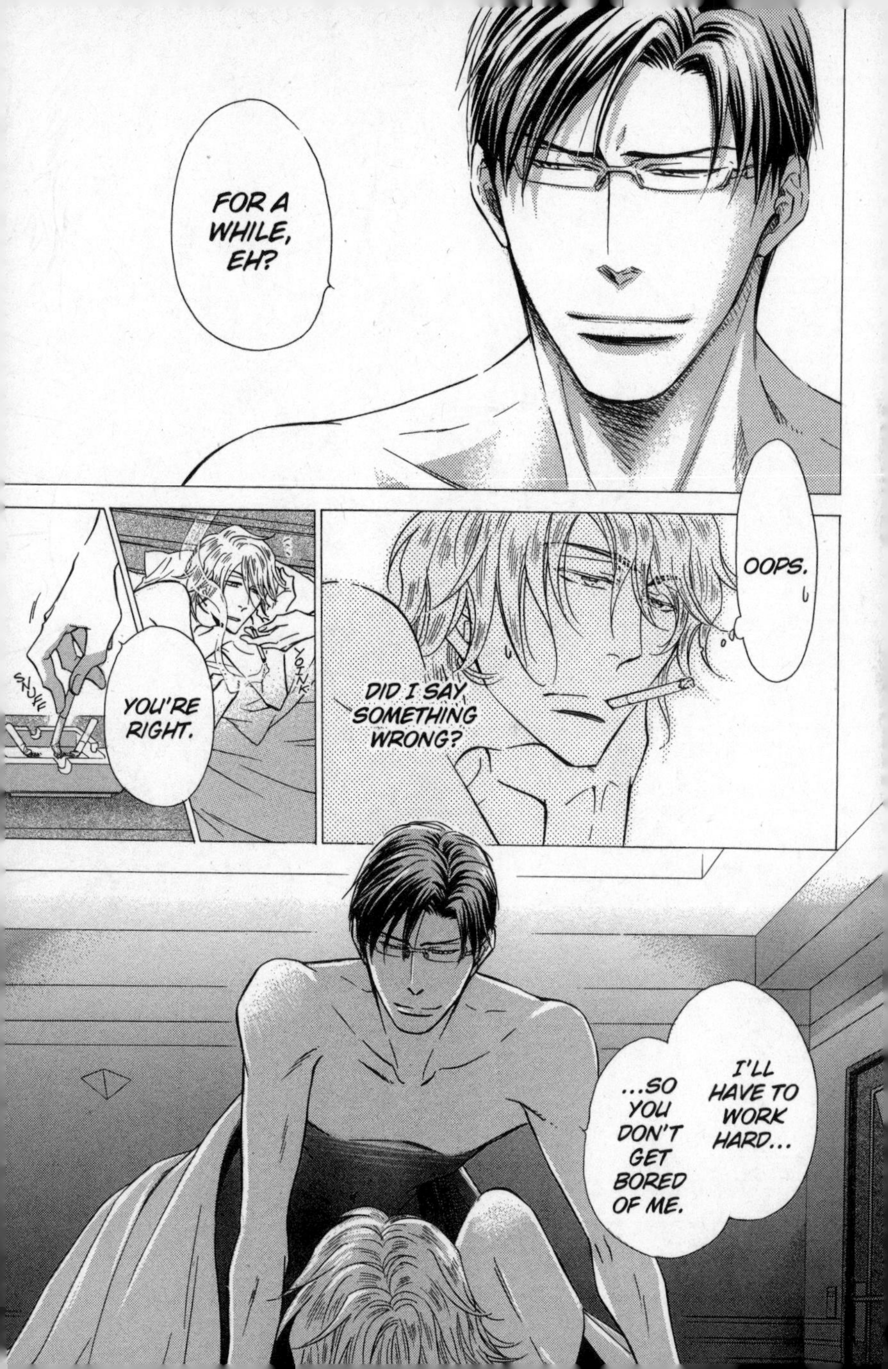
FOR A WHILE, EH?
OOPS.
DID I SAY SOMETHING WRONG?
YOINK
YOU'RE RIGHT.
SNUFF
I'LL HAVE TO WORK HARD...
...SO YOU DON'T GET BORED OF ME.

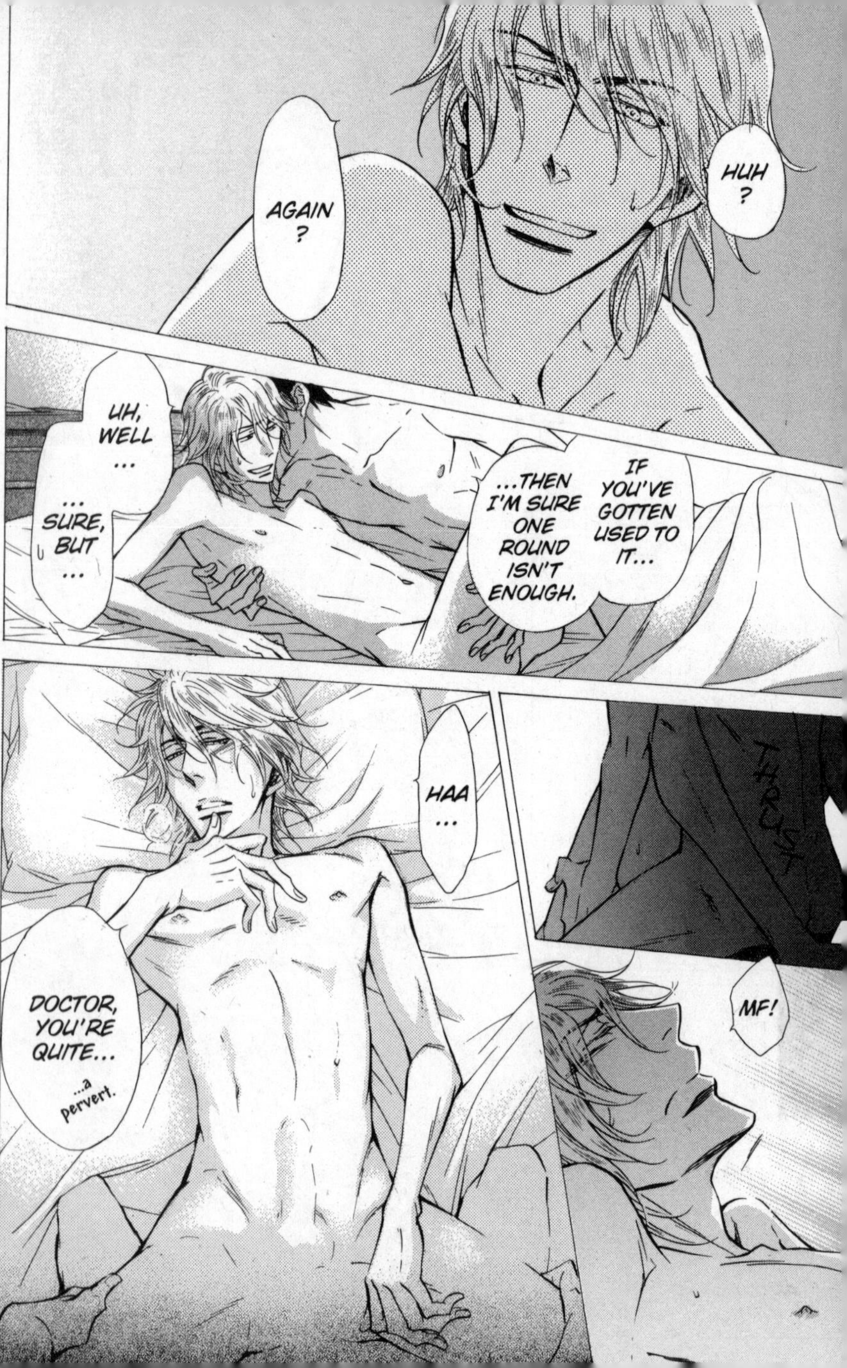
HUH?
AGAIN?
IF YOU'VE GOTTEN USED TO IT...
...THEN I'M SURE ONE ROUND ISN'T ENOUGH.
UH, WELL...
...SURE, BUT...
THRUST
MF!
HAA...
DOCTOR, YOU'RE QUITE...
...a pervert.

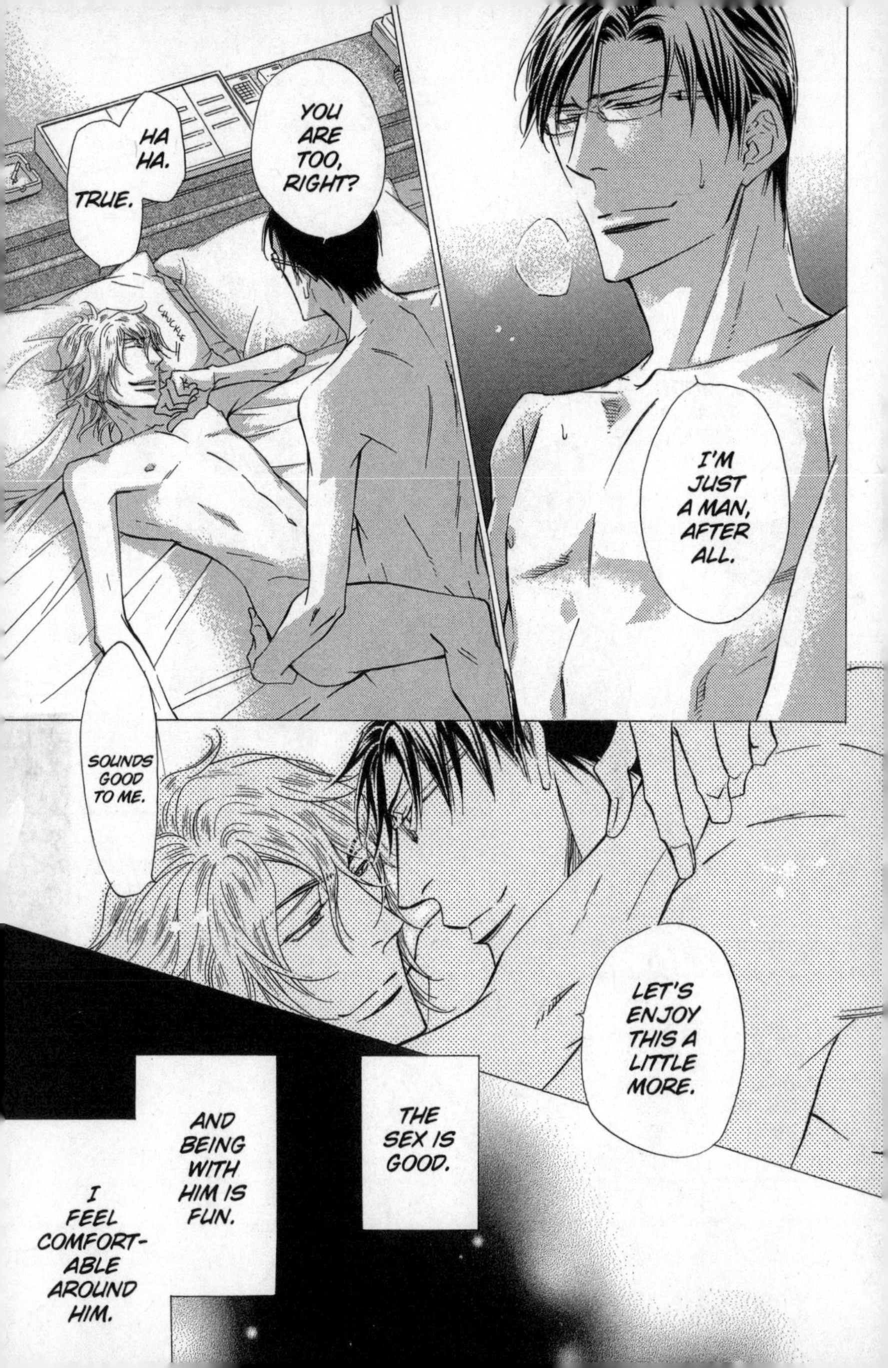
I'M JUST A MAN, AFTER ALL.
YOU ARE TOO, RIGHT?
HA HA.
TRUE.
CHUCKLE
LET'S ENJOY THIS A LITTLE MORE.
SOUNDS GOOD TO ME.
THE SEX IS GOOD.
AND BEING WITH HIM IS FUN.
I FEEL COMFORT-ABLE AROUND HIM.

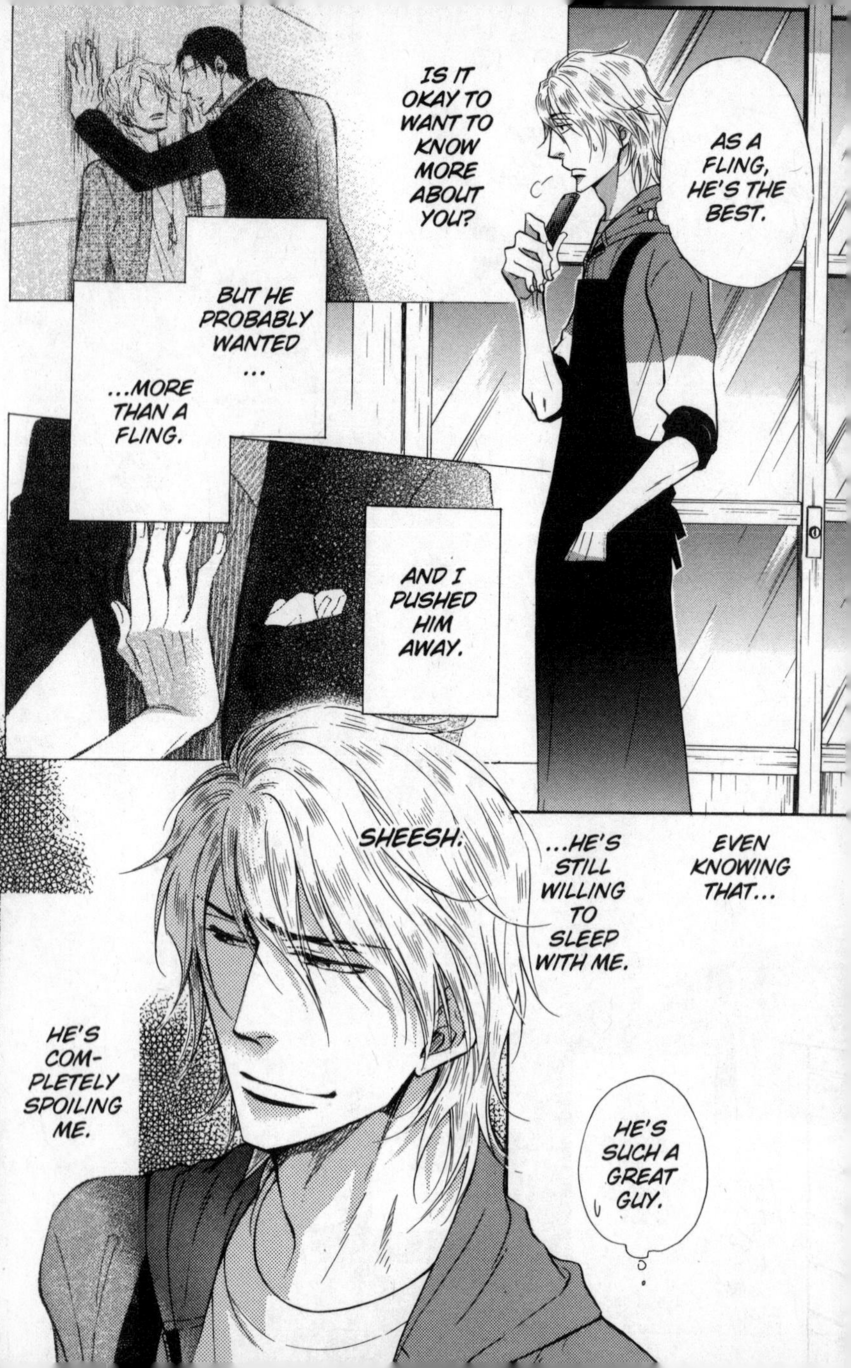
AS A FLING, HE'S THE BEST.
IS IT OKAY TO WANT TO KNOW MORE ABOUT YOU?
BUT HE PROBABLY WANTED ... ...MORE THAN A FLING.
AND I PUSHED HIM AWAY.
EVEN KNOWING THAT...
...HE'S STILL WILLING TO SLEEP WITH ME.
SHEESH.
HE'S SUCH A GREAT GUY.
HE'S COM-PLETELY SPOILING ME.

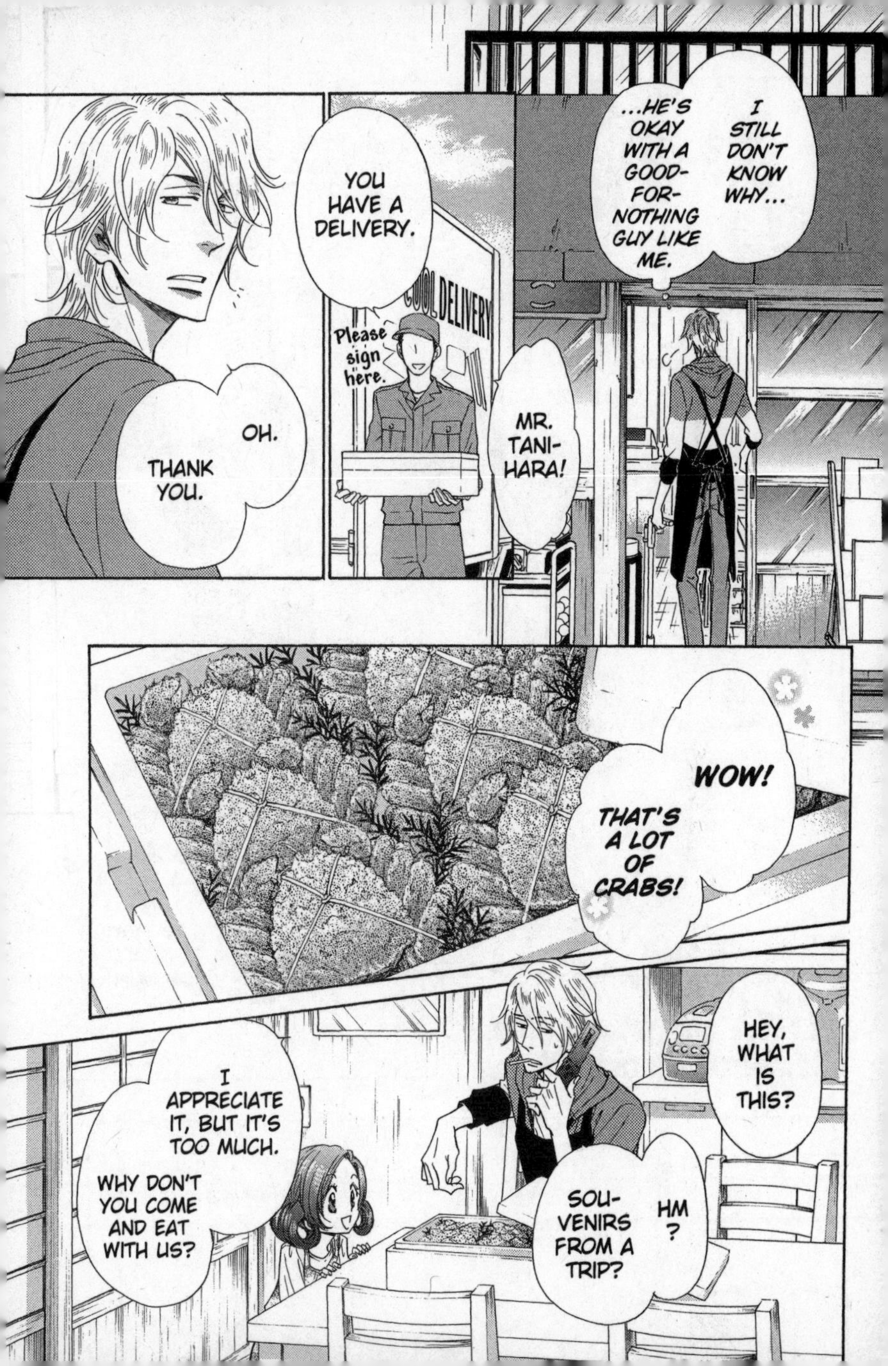
I STILL DON'T KNOW WHY...
...HE'S OKAY WITH A GOOD-FOR-NOTHING GUY LIKE ME.
MR. TANI-HARA!
YOU HAVE A DELIVERY.
COOL DELIVERY
Please sign here.
OH.
THANK YOU.
WOW!
THAT'S A LOT OF CRABS!
HEY, WHAT IS THIS?
HM?
SOU-VENIRS FROM A TRIP?
I APPRECIATE IT, BUT IT'S TOO MUCH.
WHY DON'T YOU COME AND EAT WITH US?

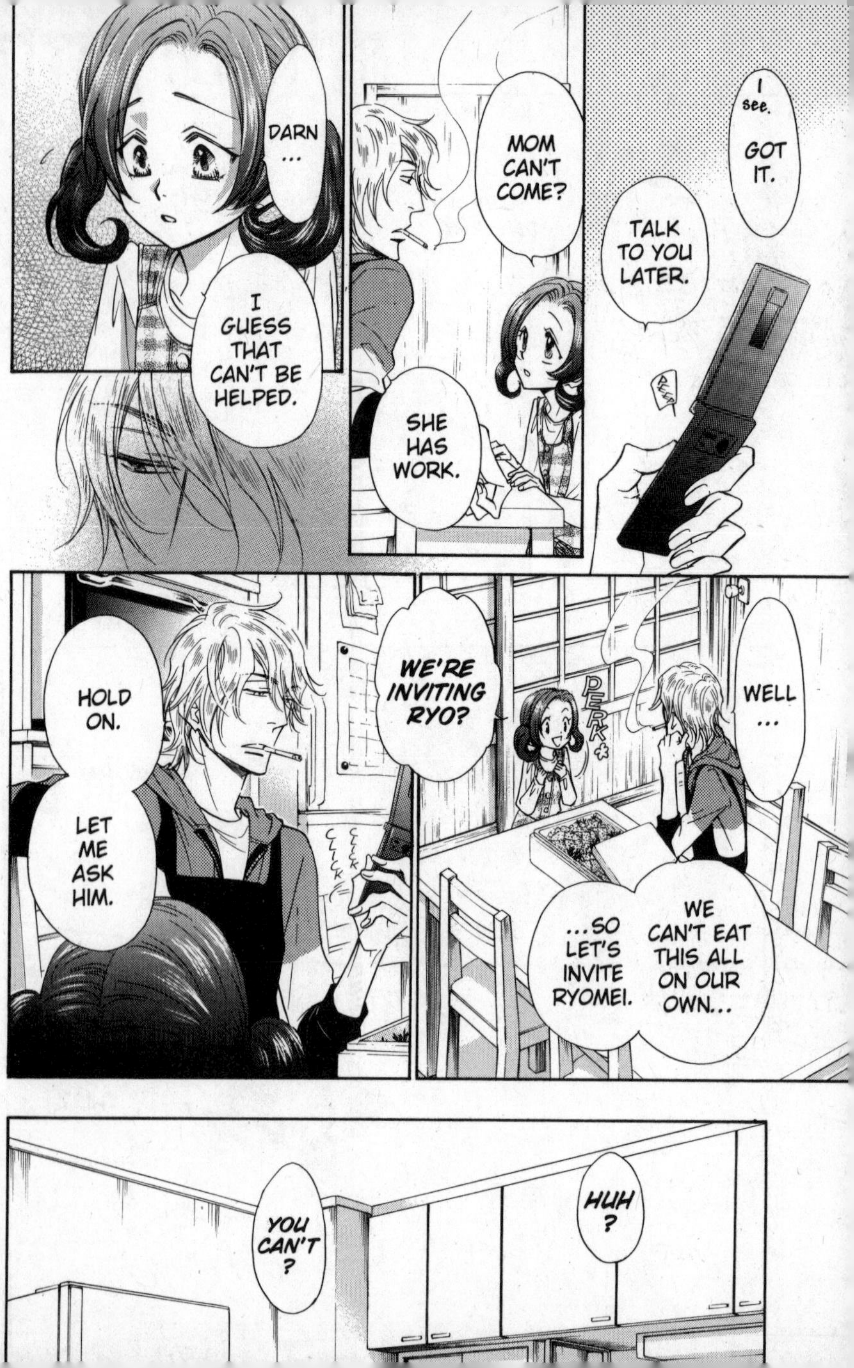
I see.
GOT IT.
TALK TO YOU LATER.
BEEP
MOM CAN'T COME?
SHE HAS WORK.
DARN...
I GUESS THAT CAN'T BE HELPED.
WELL...
PERK
WE CAN'T EAT THIS ALL ON OUR OWN...
...SO LET'S INVITE RYOMEI.
WE'RE INVITING RYO?
HOLD ON.
LET ME ASK HIM.
CLICK CLICK
HUH?
YOU CAN'T?

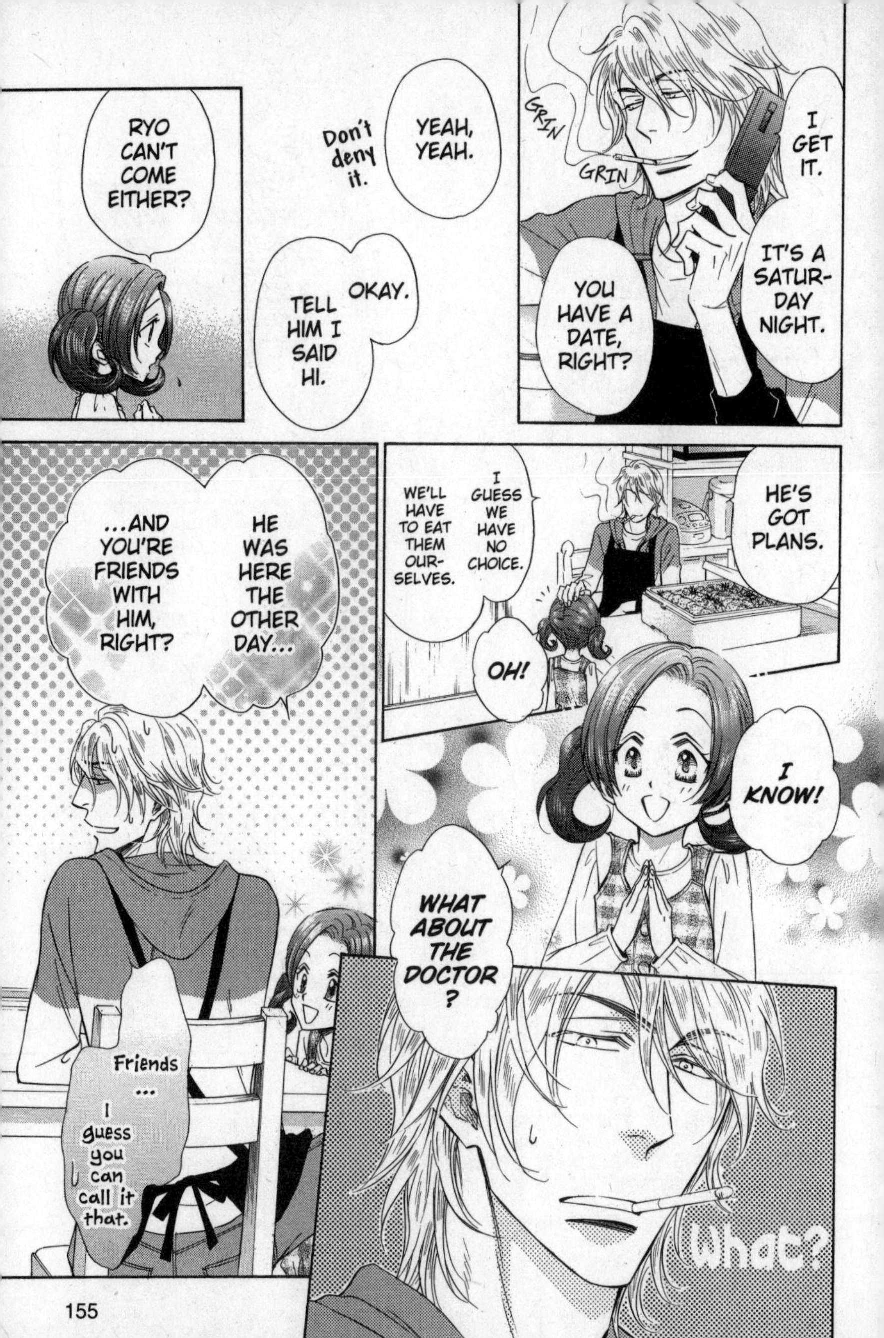
GRIN
GRIN
I GET IT.
IT'S A SATURDAY NIGHT.
YOU HAVE A DATE, RIGHT?
YEAH, YEAH.
Don't deny it.
OKAY.
TELL HIM I SAID HI.
RYO CAN'T COME EITHER?
HE'S GOT PLANS.
I GUESS WE HAVE NO CHOICE.
WE'LL HAVE TO EAT THEM OURSELVES.
OH!
I KNOW!
WHAT ABOUT THE DOCTOR?
What?
HE WAS HERE THE OTHER DAY...
...AND YOU'RE FRIENDS WITH HIM, RIGHT?
Friends... I guess you can call it that.

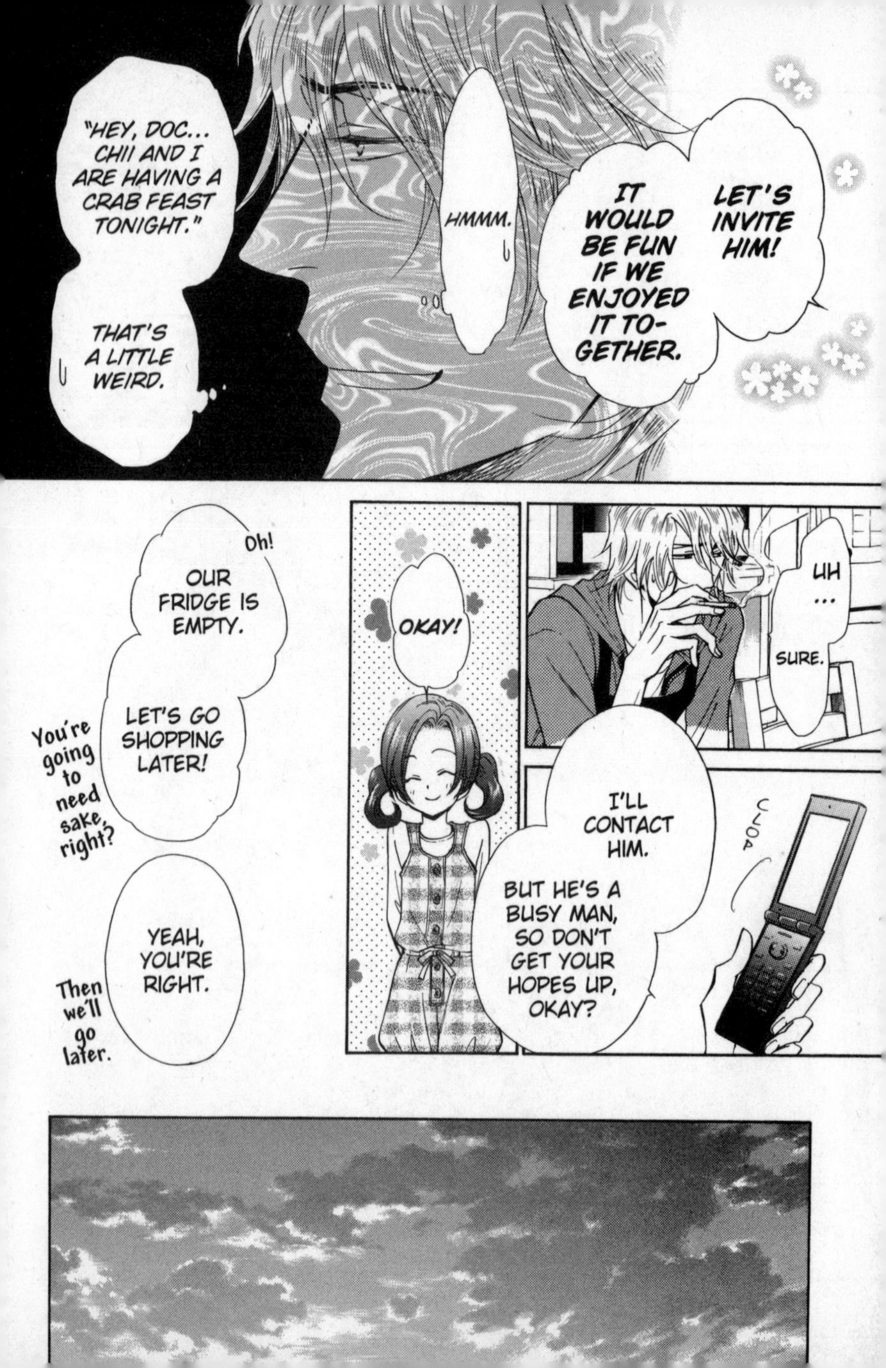
LET'S INVITE HIM!
IT WOULD BE FUN IF WE ENJOYED IT TO-GETHER.
HMMM.
"HEY, DOC... CHII AND I ARE HAVING A CRAB FEAST TONIGHT."
THAT'S A LITTLE WEIRD.
UH ... SURE.
I'LL CONTACT HIM.
BUT HE'S A BUSY MAN, SO DON'T GET YOUR HOPES UP, OKAY?
CLOP
OKAY!
Oh!
OUR FRIDGE IS EMPTY.
LET'S GO SHOPPING LATER!
You're going to need sake, right?
YEAH, YOU'RE RIGHT.
Then we'll go later.

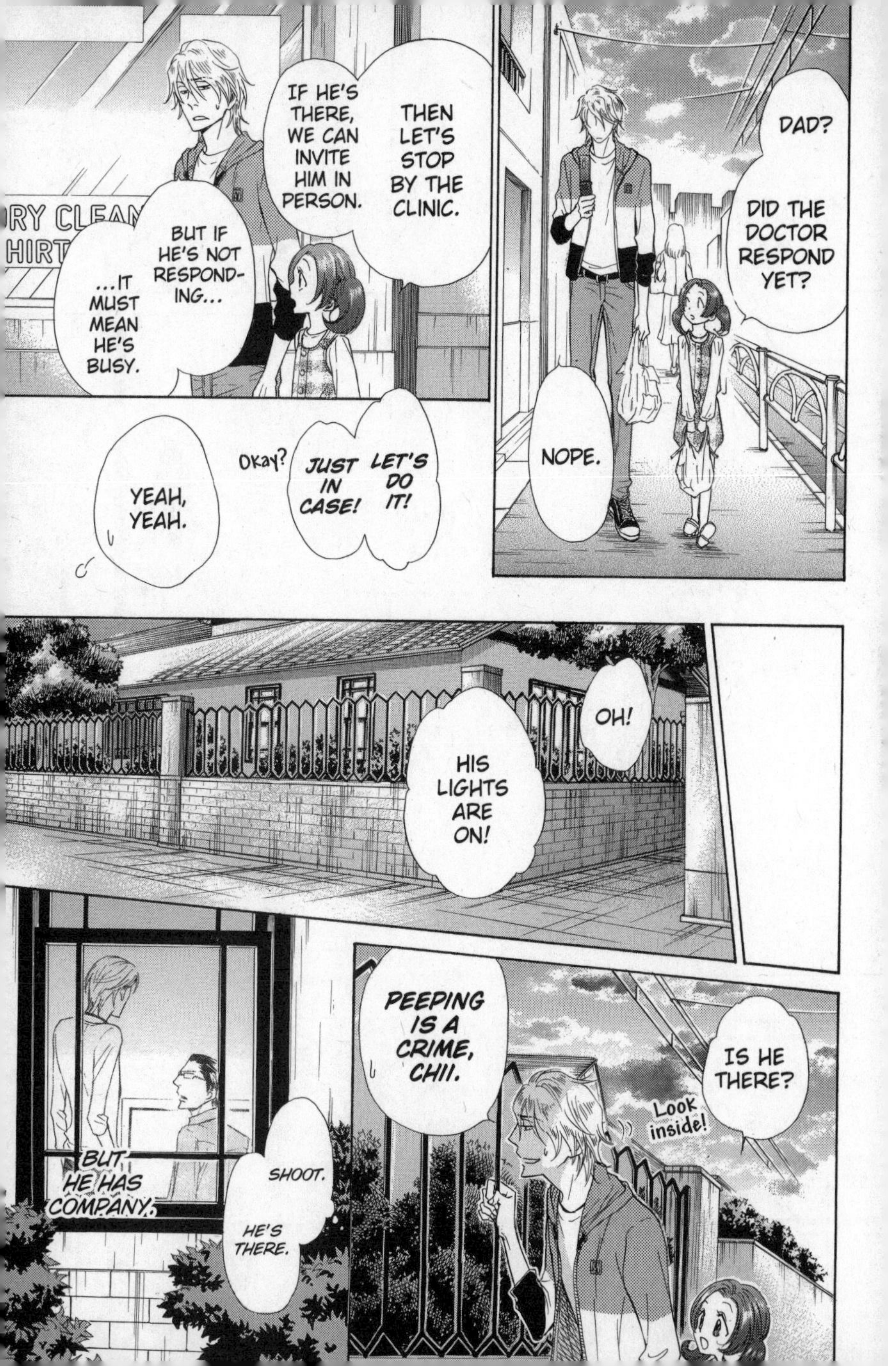
DAD?
DID THE DOCTOR RESPOND YET?
NOPE.
THEN LET'S STOP BY THE CLINIC.
IF HE'S THERE, WE CAN INVITE HIM IN PERSON.
BUT IF HE'S NOT RESPONDING...
...IT MUST MEAN HE'S BUSY.
LET'S DO IT!
JUST IN CASE!
Okay?
YEAH, YEAH.
OH!
HIS LIGHTS ARE ON!
IS HE THERE?
Look inside!
PEEPING IS A CRIME, CHII.
SHOOT.
HE'S THERE.
BUT HE HAS COMPANY.

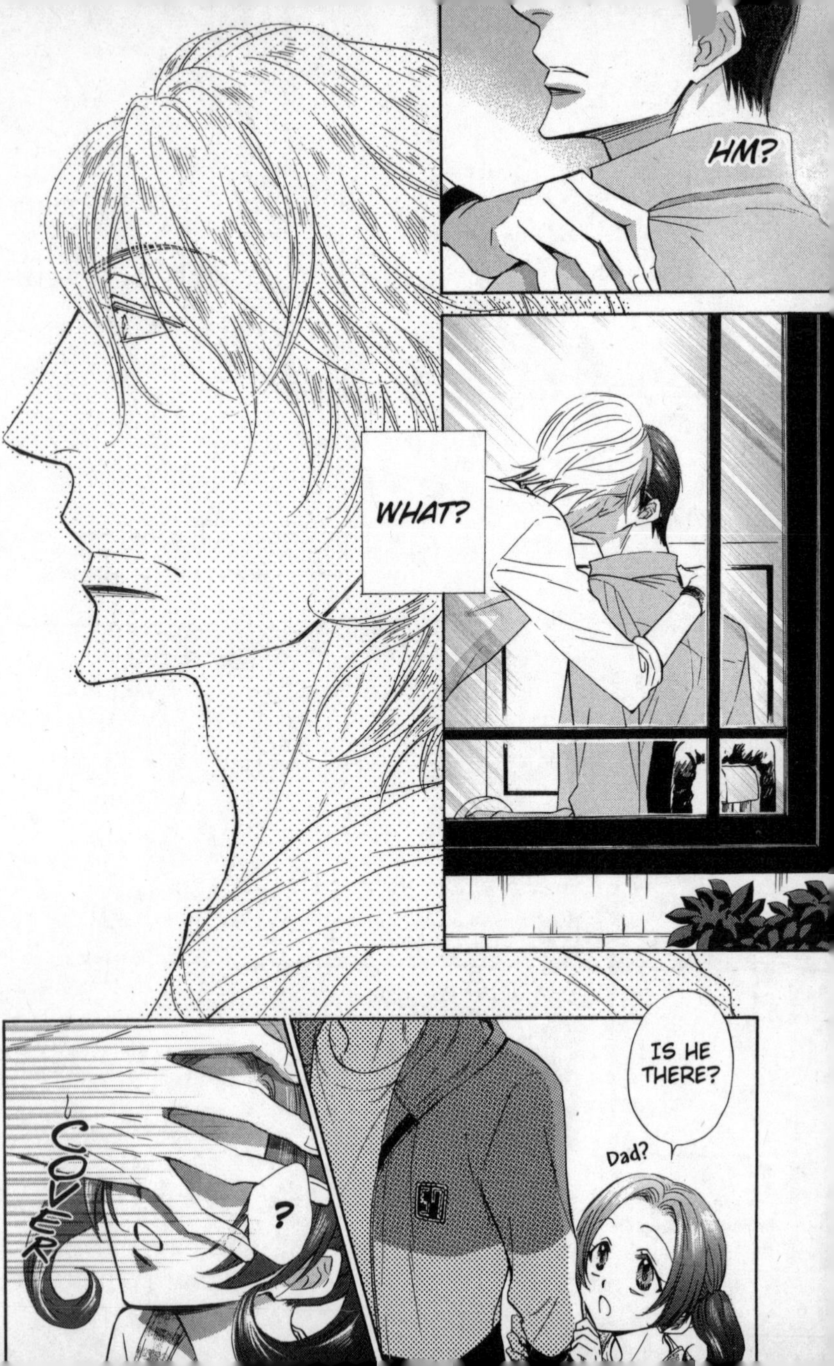
HM?
WHAT?
IS HE THERE?
Dad?
COVER
?

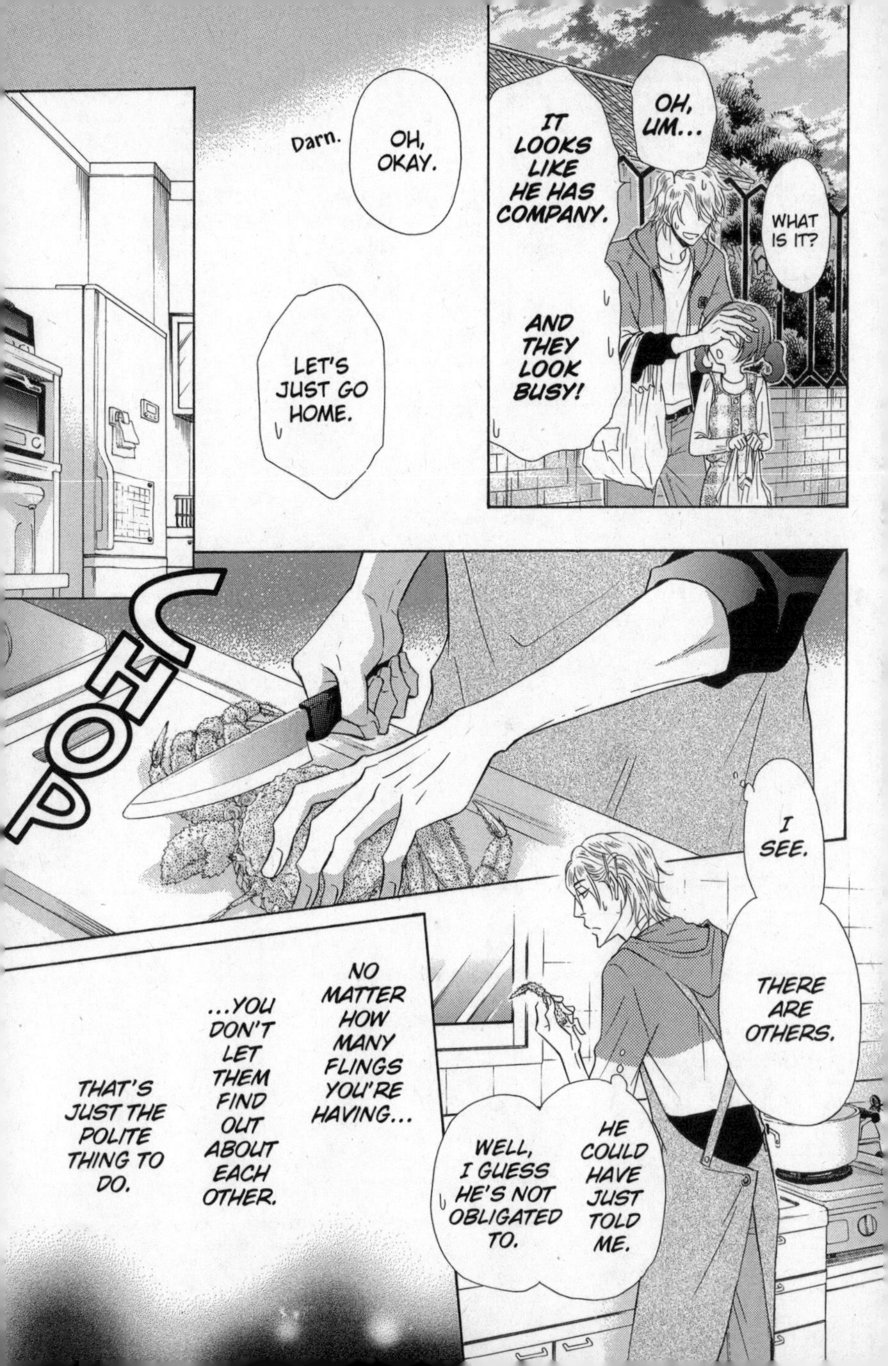
OH, UM...
WHAT IS IT?
IT LOOKS LIKE HE HAS COMPANY.
AND THEY LOOK BUSY!
OH, OKAY.
Darn.
LET'S JUST GO HOME.
CHOP
I SEE.
THERE ARE OTHERS.
HE COULD HAVE JUST TOLD ME.
WELL, I GUESS HE'S NOT OBLIGATED TO.
NO MATTER HOW MANY FLINGS YOU'RE HAVING...
...YOU DON'T LET THEM FIND OUT ABOUT EACH OTHER.
THAT'S JUST THE POLITE THING TO DO.

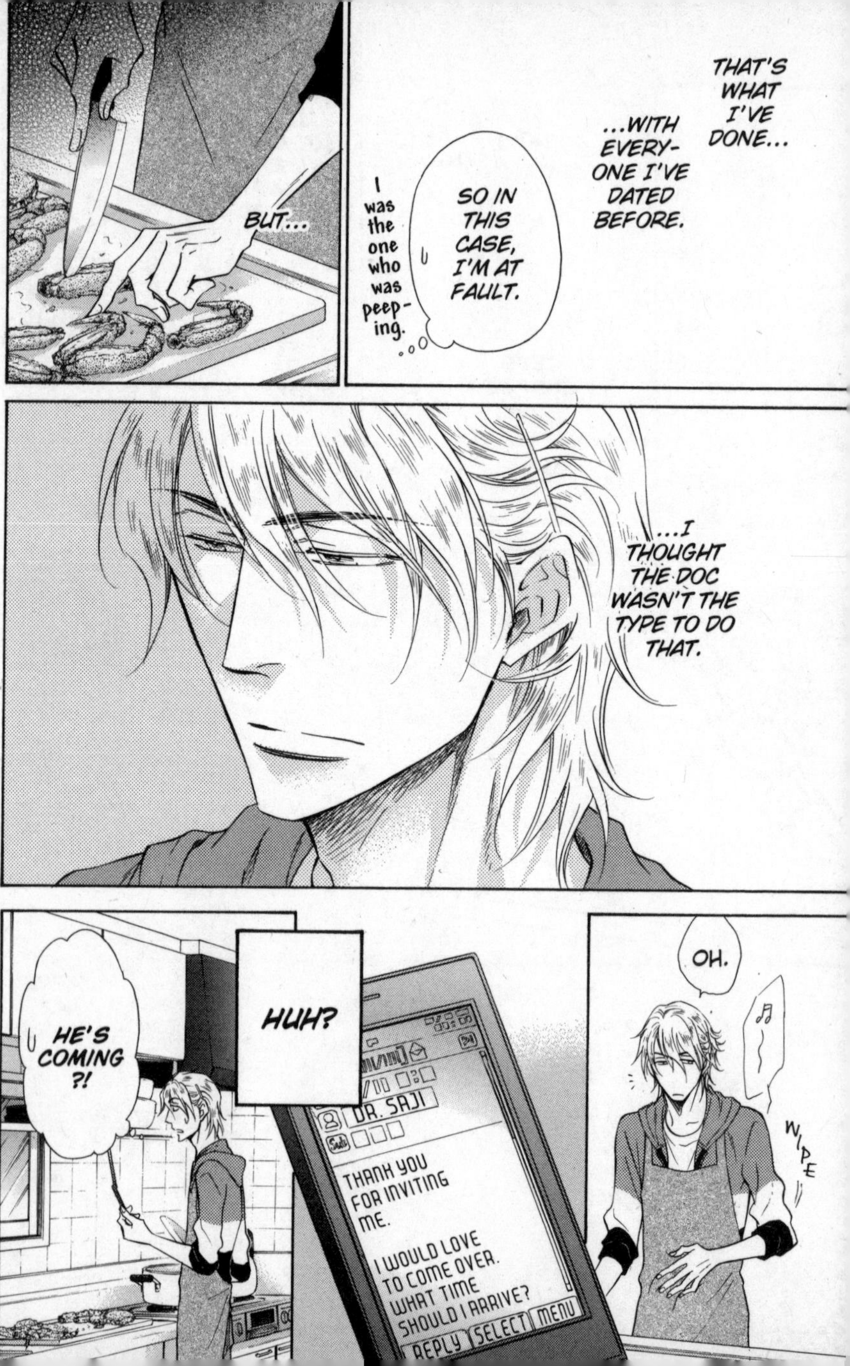
THAT'S WHAT I'VE DONE...
...WITH EVERY-ONE I'VE DATED BEFORE.
SO IN THIS CASE, I'M AT FAULT.
I was the one who was peep-ing.
BUT...
...I THOUGHT THE DOC WASN'T THE TYPE TO DO THAT.
OH.
WIPE
DR. SAJI
THANK YOU FOR INVITING ME.
I WOULD LOVE TO COME OVER. WHAT TIME SHOULD I ARRIVE?
REPLY
SELECT
MENU
HUH?
HE'S COMING ?!

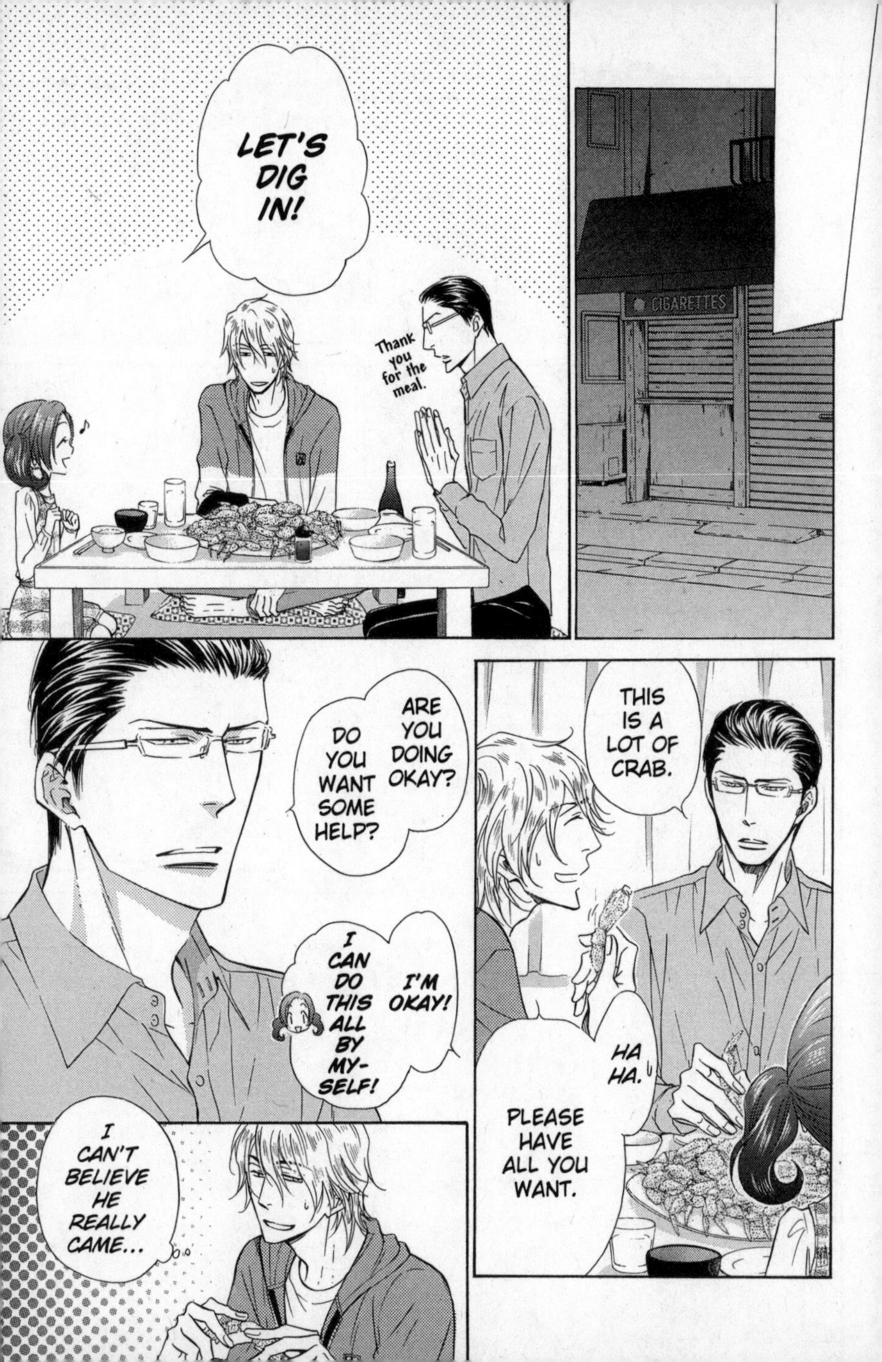
CIGARETTES
LET'S DIG IN!
Thank you for the meal.
THIS IS A LOT OF CRAB.
HA HA.
PLEASE HAVE ALL YOU WANT.
ARE YOU DOING OKAY?
DO YOU WANT SOME HELP?
I'M OKAY!
I CAN DO THIS ALL BY MY-SELF!
I CAN'T BELIEVE HE REALLY CAME...

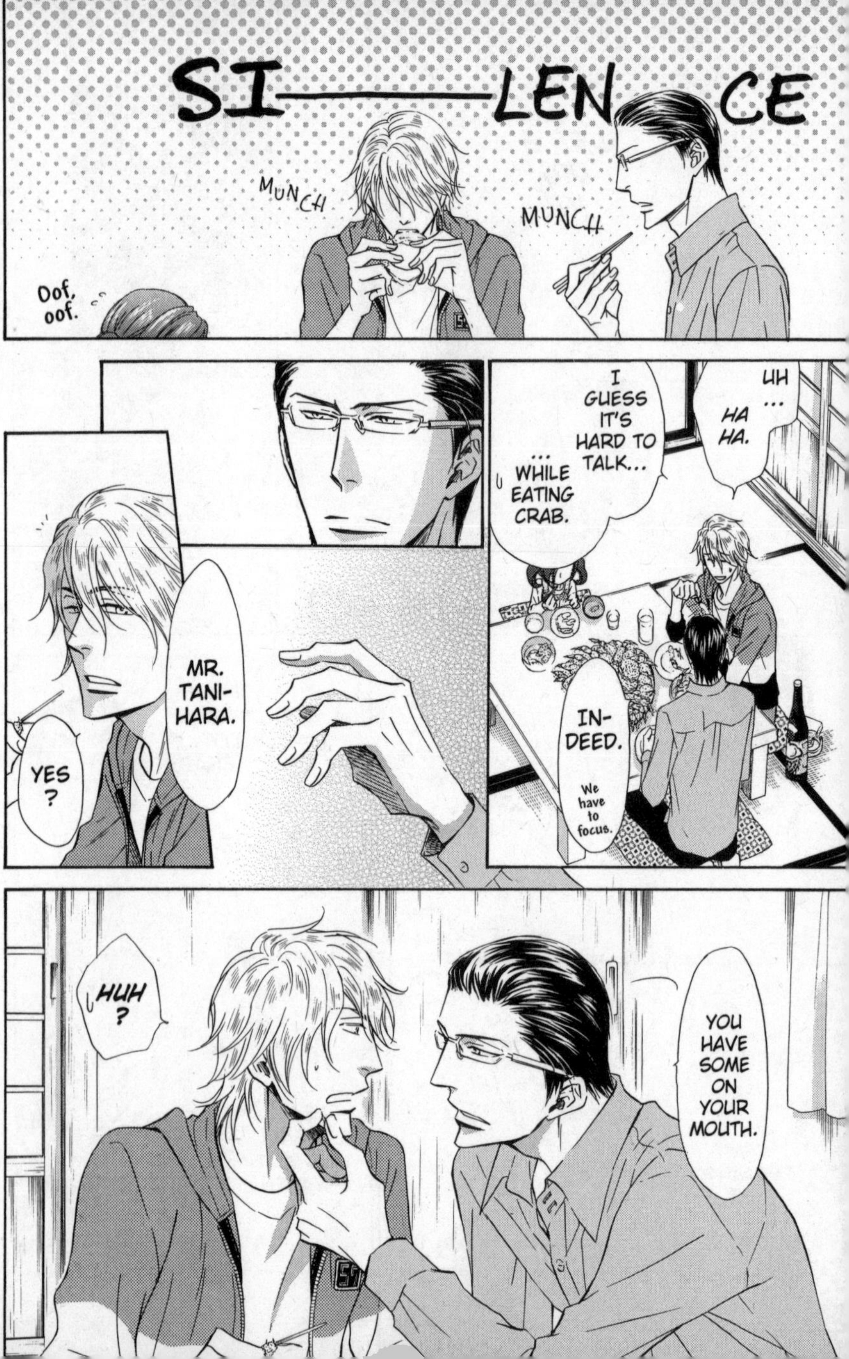
SI——LEN CE
MUNCH
MUNCH
Oof, oof.
UH... HA HA.
I GUESS IT'S HARD TO TALK...
... WHILE EATING CRAB.
IN-DEED.
We have to focus.
MR. TANI-HARA.
YES?
YOU HAVE SOME ON YOUR MOUTH.
HUH?

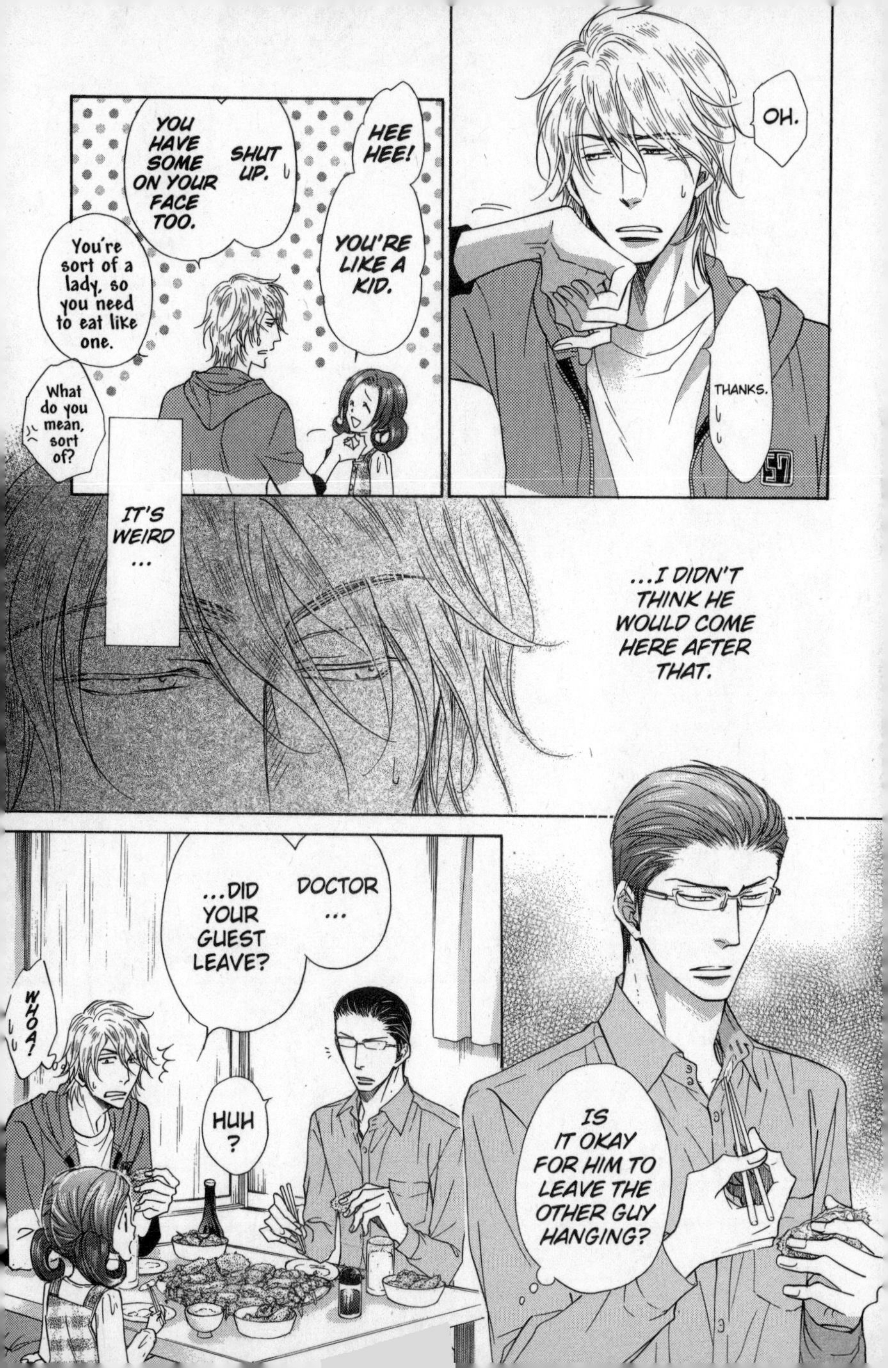
OH.
THANKS.
HEE HEE!
YOU'RE LIKE A KID.
SHUT UP.
YOU HAVE SOME ON YOUR FACE TOO.
You're sort of a lady, so you need to eat like one.
What do you mean, sort of?
IT'S WEIRD ...
...I DIDN'T THINK HE WOULD COME HERE AFTER THAT.
IS IT OKAY FOR HIM TO LEAVE THE OTHER GUY HANGING?
DOCTOR ...
...DID YOUR GUEST LEAVE?
HUH?
WHOA!

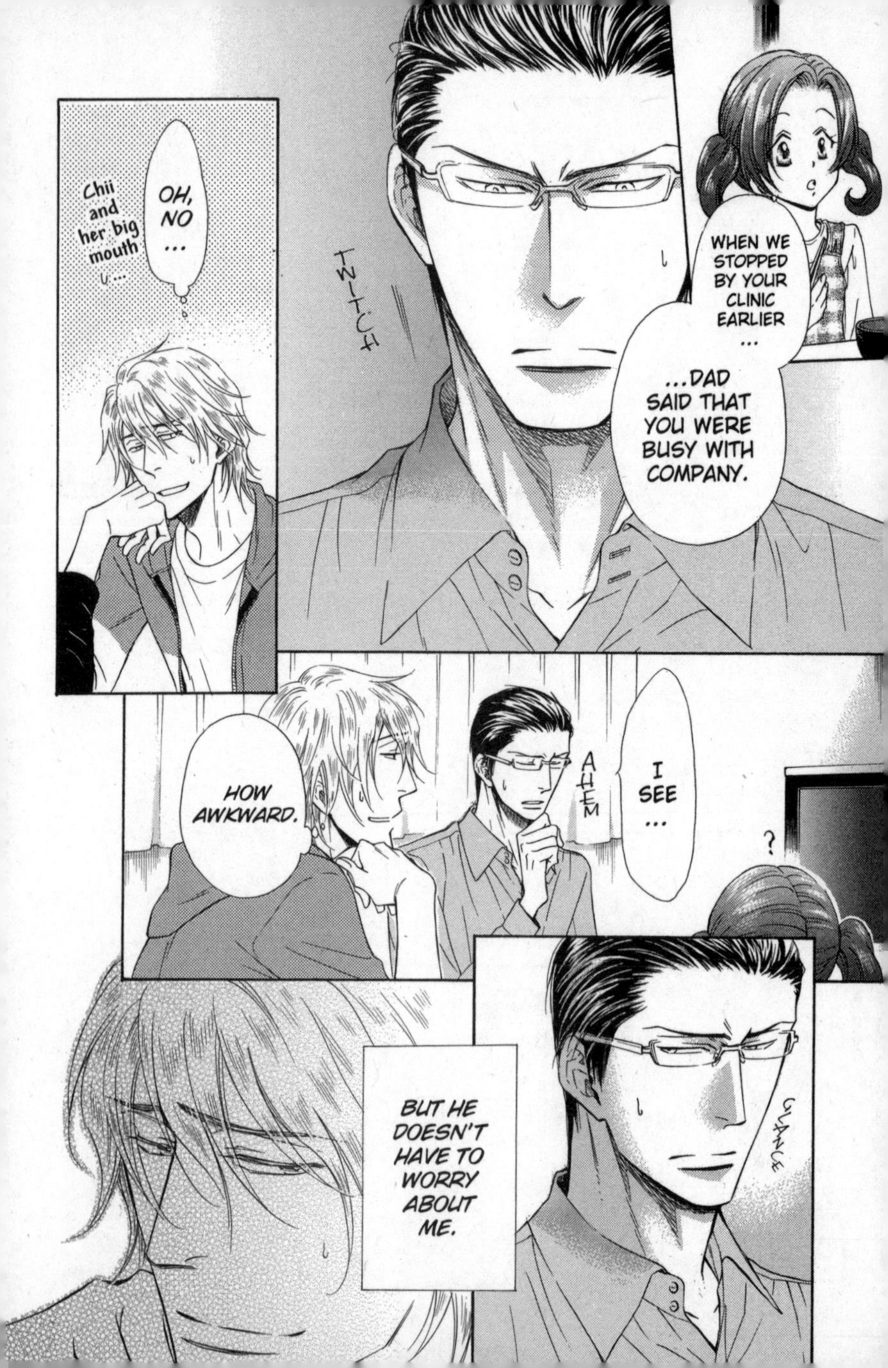
WHEN WE STOPPED BY YOUR CLINIC EARLIER ...
...DAD SAID THAT YOU WERE BUSY WITH COMPANY.
TWITCH
OH, NO ...
Chii and her big mouth ...
I SEE ...
AHEM
?
HOW AWKWARD.
GLANCE
BUT HE DOESN'T HAVE TO WORRY ABOUT ME.

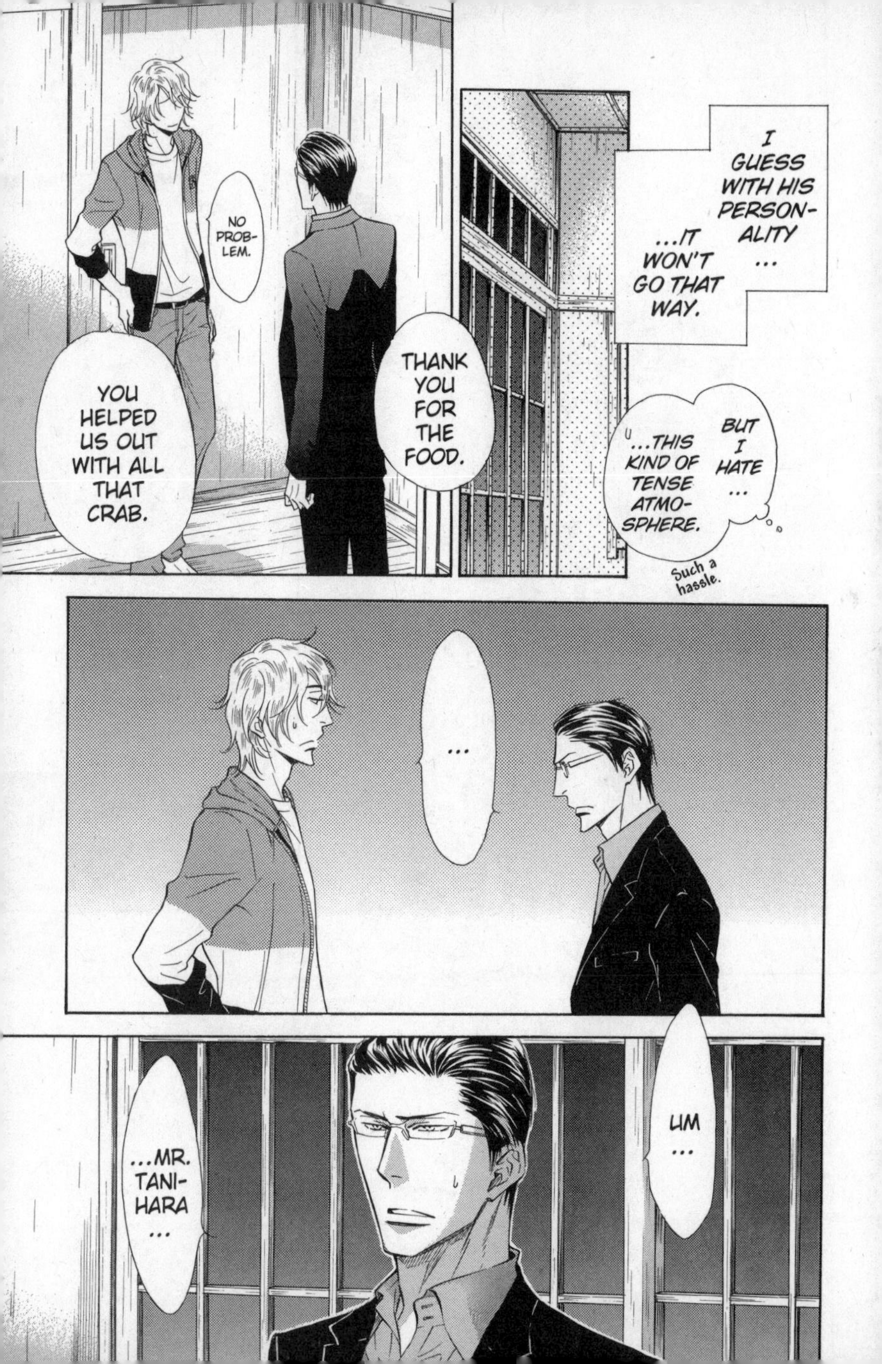
I GUESS WITH HIS PERSONALITY...
...IT WON'T GO THAT WAY.
BUT I HATE...
...THIS KIND OF TENSE ATMOSPHERE.
Such a hassle.
THANK YOU FOR THE FOOD.
NO PROBLEM.
YOU HELPED US OUT WITH ALL THAT CRAB.
...
UM...
...MR. TANIHARA...

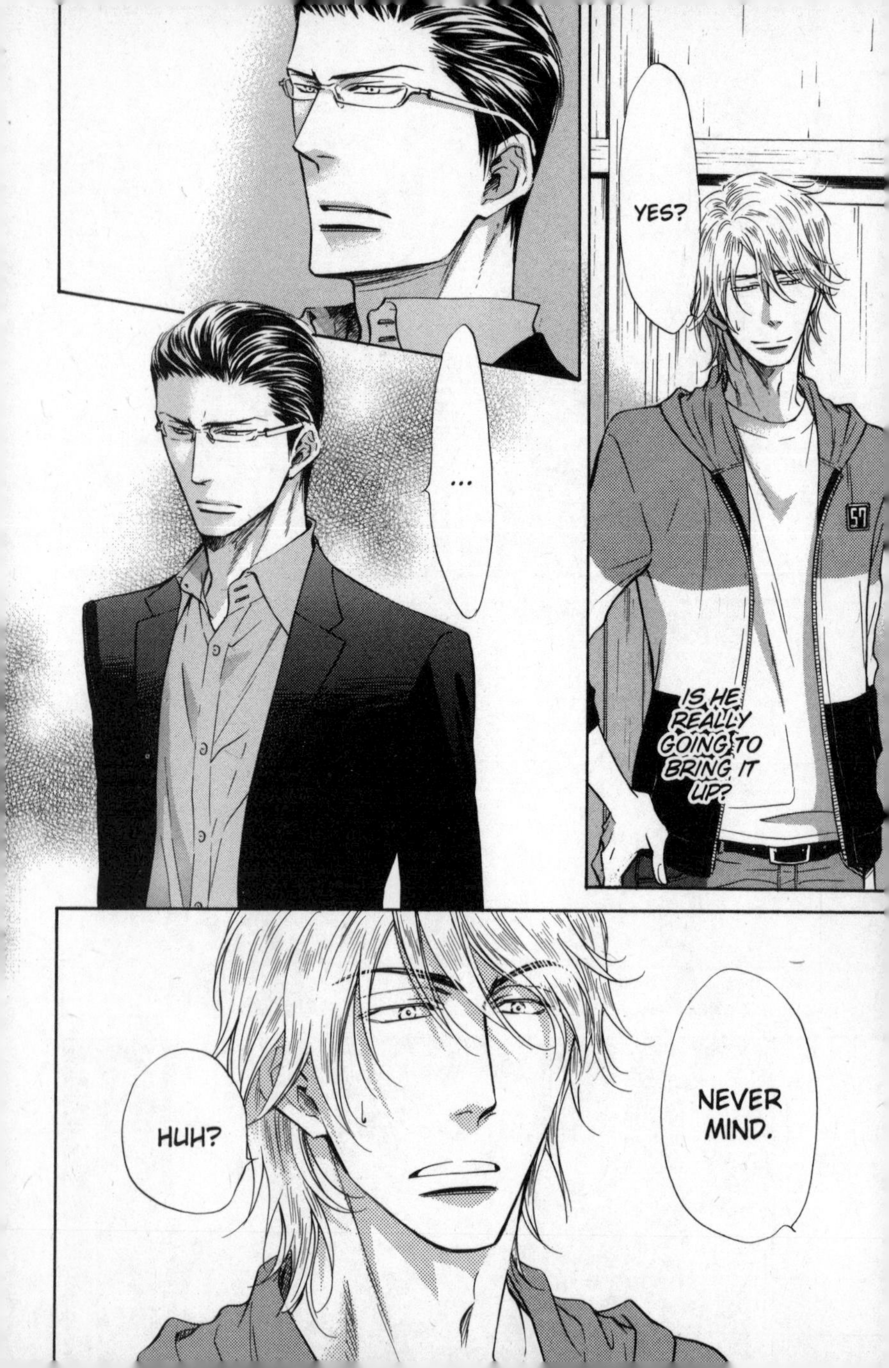
YES?
IS HE REALLY GOING TO BRING IT UP?
...
NEVER MIND.
HUH?

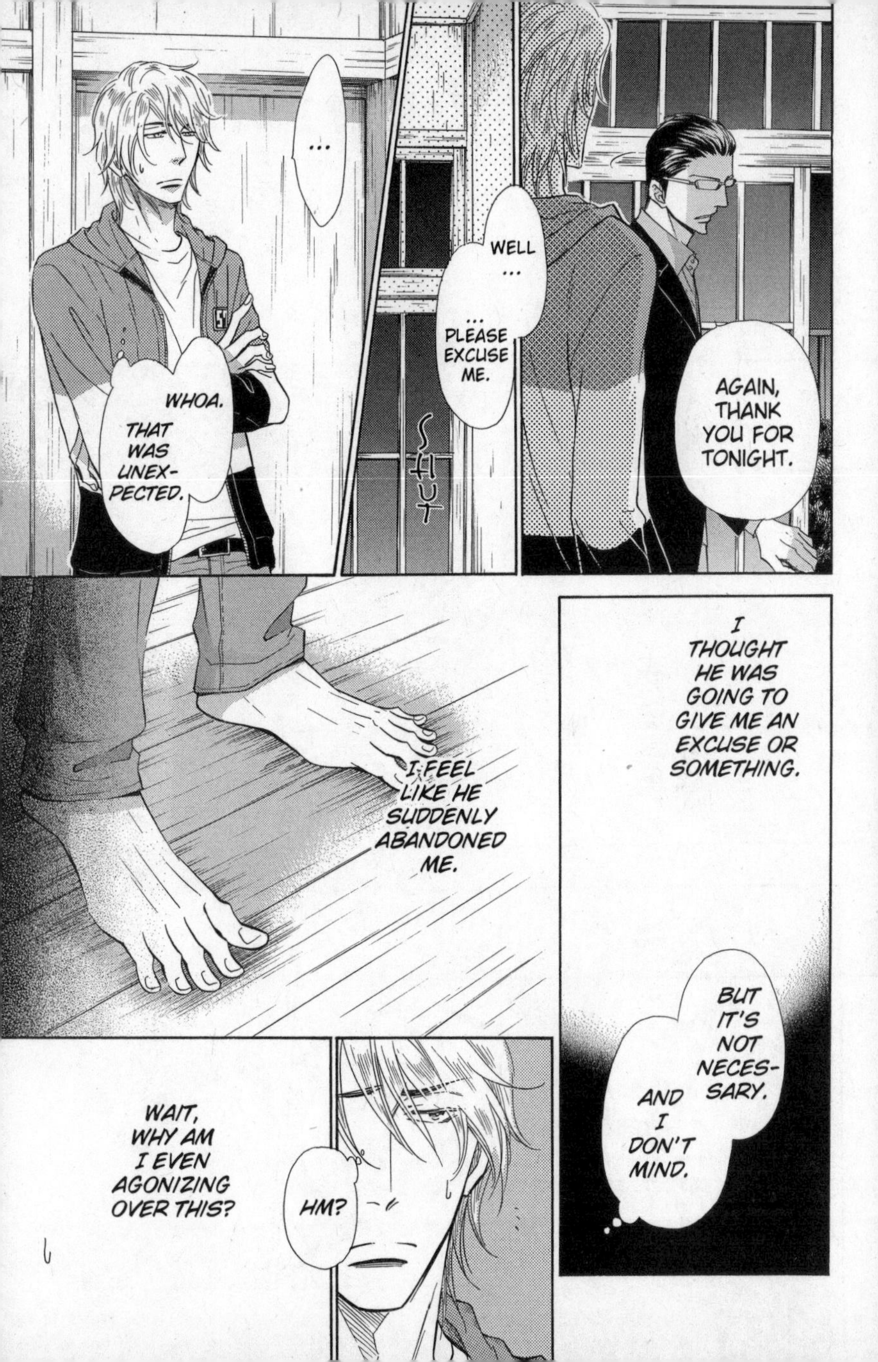
AGAIN, THANK YOU FOR TONIGHT.
WELL...
...PLEASE EXCUSE ME.
SHUT
...
WHOA.
THAT WAS UNEXPECTED.
I THOUGHT HE WAS GOING TO GIVE ME AN EXCUSE OR SOMETHING.
BUT IT'S NOT NECESSARY.
AND I DON'T MIND.
I FEEL LIKE HE SUDDENLY ABANDONED ME.
HM?
WAIT, WHY AM I EVEN AGONIZING OVER THIS?

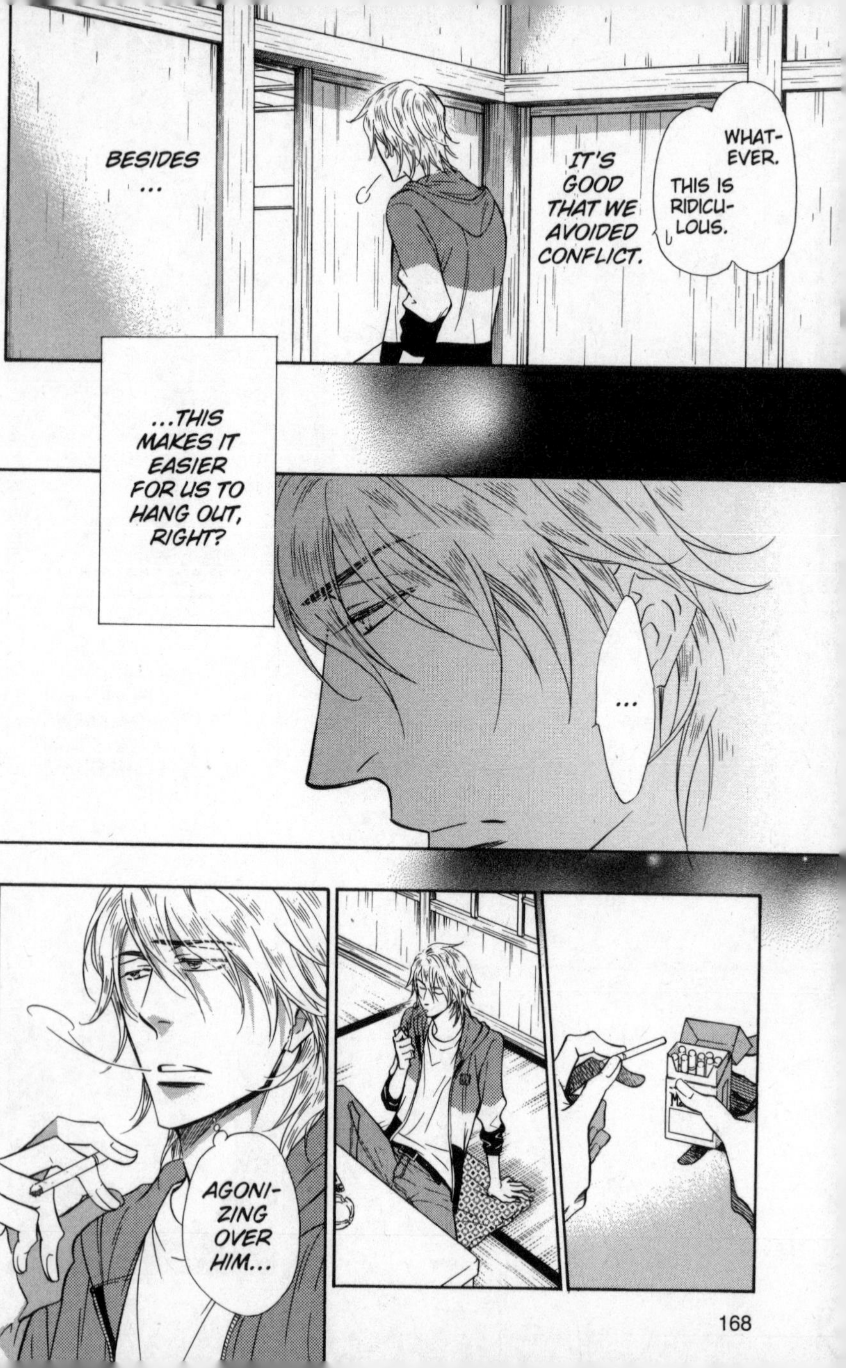
WHAT-EVER. THIS IS RIDICULOUS.
IT'S GOOD THAT WE AVOIDED CONFLICT.
BESIDES ...
...THIS MAKES IT EASIER FOR US TO HANG OUT, RIGHT?
...
AGONIZING OVER HIM...

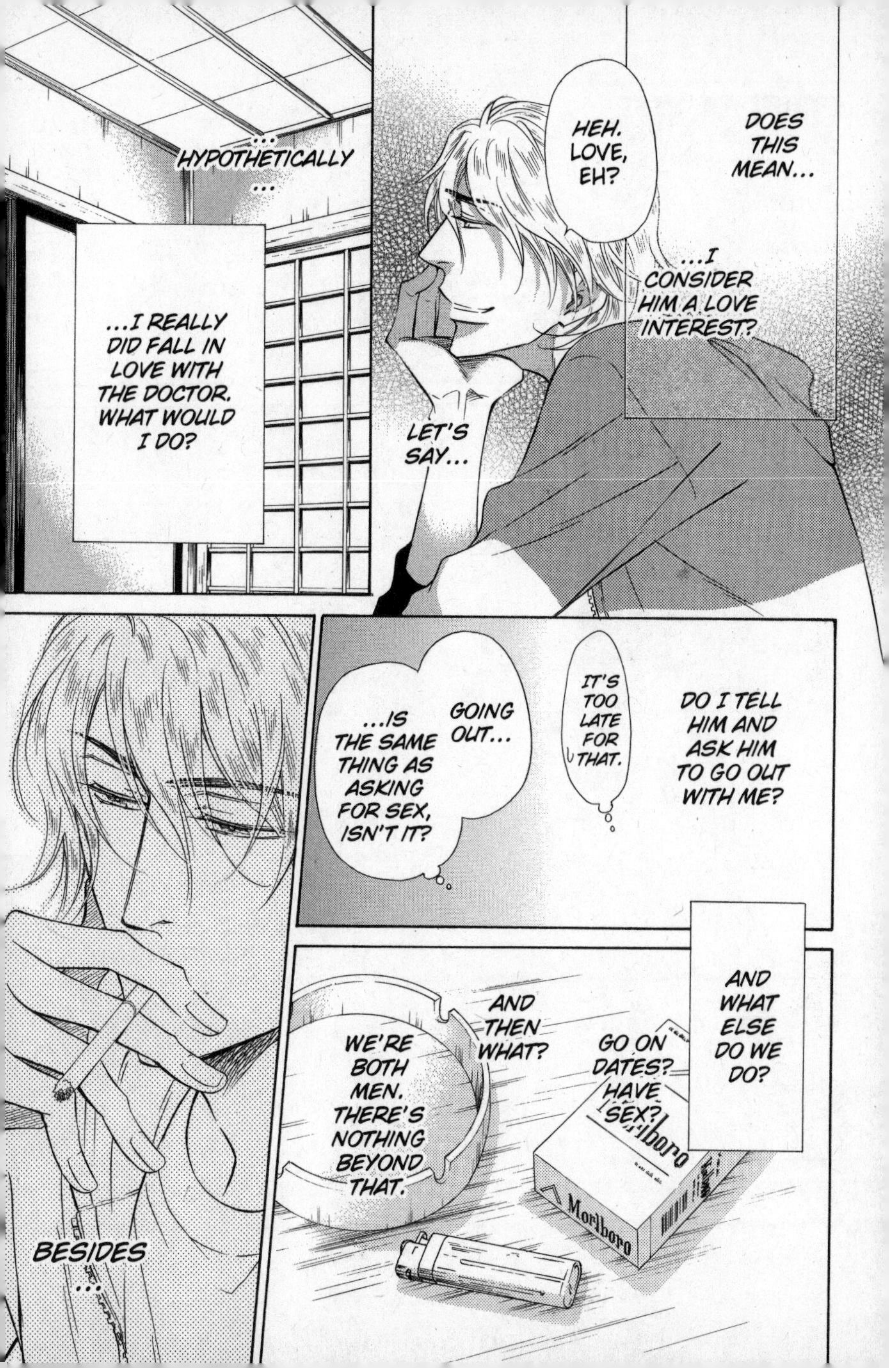
DOES THIS MEAN...
...I CONSIDER HIM A LOVE INTEREST?
HEH. LOVE, EH?
LET'S SAY...
...HYPOTHETICALLY...
...I REALLY DID FALL IN LOVE WITH THE DOCTOR. WHAT WOULD I DO?
DO I TELL HIM AND ASK HIM TO GO OUT WITH ME?
IT'S TOO LATE FOR THAT.
GOING OUT...
...IS THE SAME THING AS ASKING FOR SEX, ISN'T IT?
AND WHAT ELSE DO WE DO?
GO ON DATES? HAVE SEX?
AND THEN WHAT?
WE'RE BOTH MEN. THERE'S NOTHING BEYOND THAT.
BESIDES...

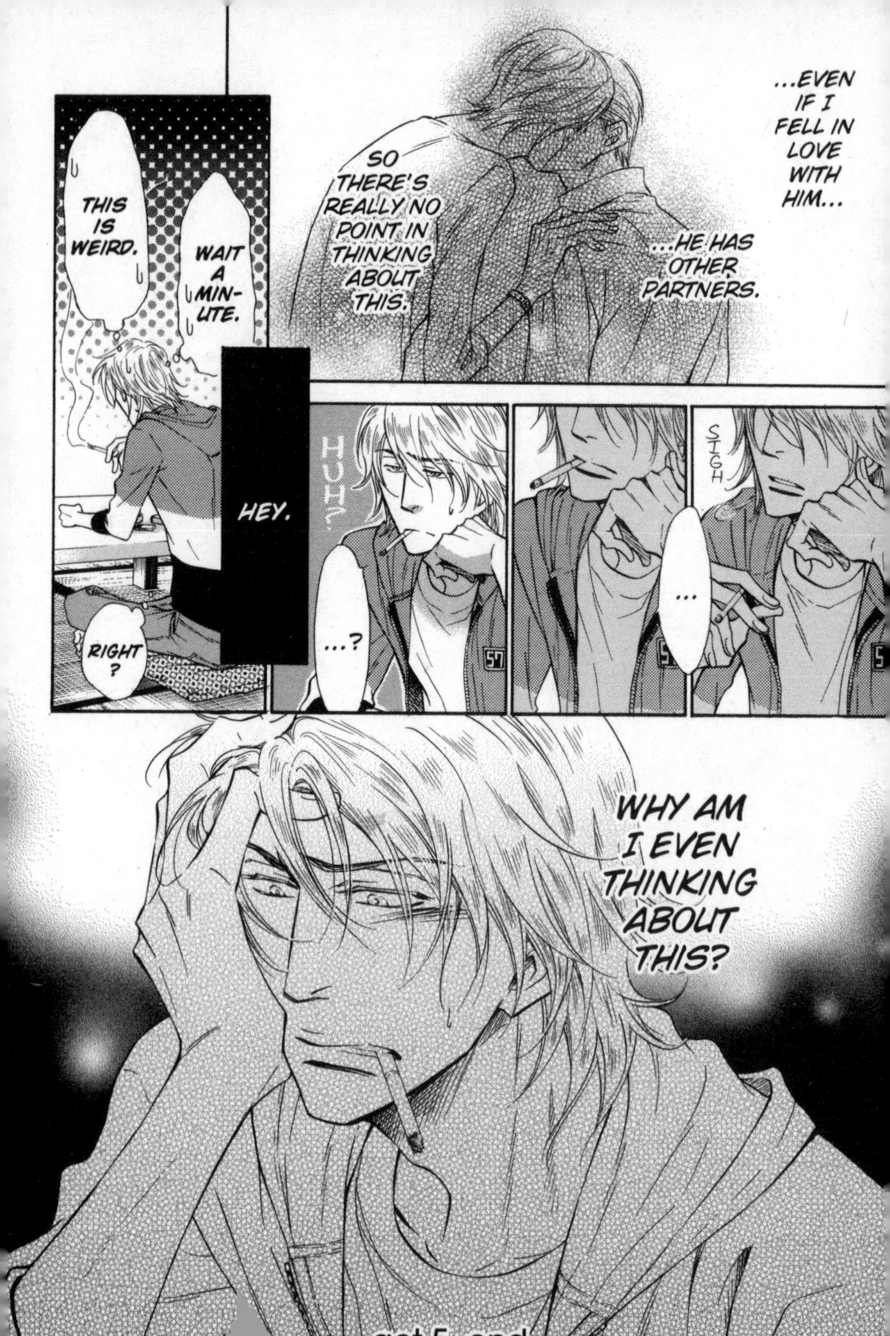
...EVEN IF I FELL IN LOVE WITH HIM...
...HE HAS OTHER PARTNERS.
SO THERE'S REALLY NO POINT IN THINKING ABOUT THIS.
SIGH
...
...
HUH?
...?
WAIT A MINUTE.
THIS IS WEIRD.
HEY.
RIGHT?
WHY AM I EVEN THINKING ABOUT THIS?

act.5 end

秘めごとあそび

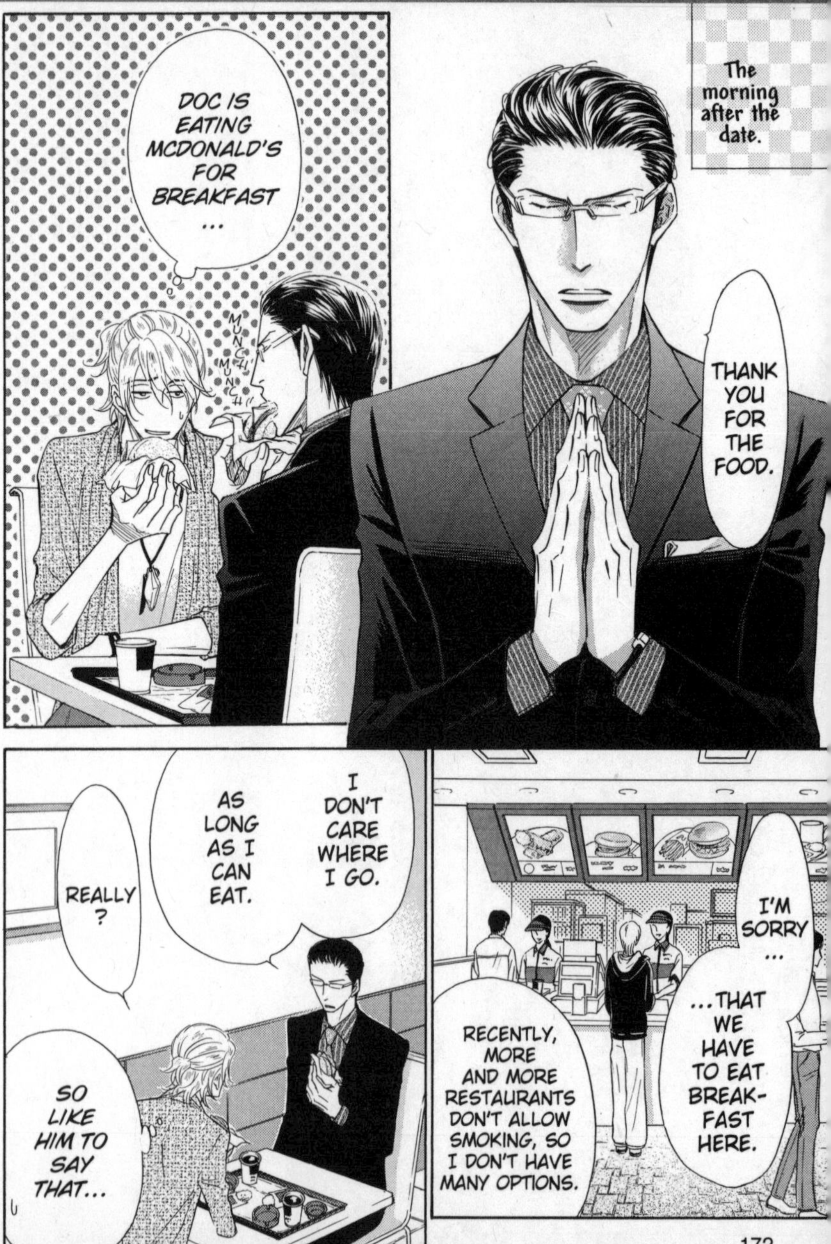
The morning after the date.
THANK YOU FOR THE FOOD.
DOC IS EATING MCDONALD'S FOR BREAKFAST...
MUNCH MUNCH
I'M SORRY...
...THAT WE HAVE TO EAT BREAKFAST HERE.
RECENTLY, MORE AND MORE RESTAURANTS DON'T ALLOW SMOKING, SO I DON'T HAVE MANY OPTIONS.
I DON'T CARE WHERE I GO.
AS LONG AS I CAN EAT.
REALLY?
SO LIKE HIM TO SAY THAT...

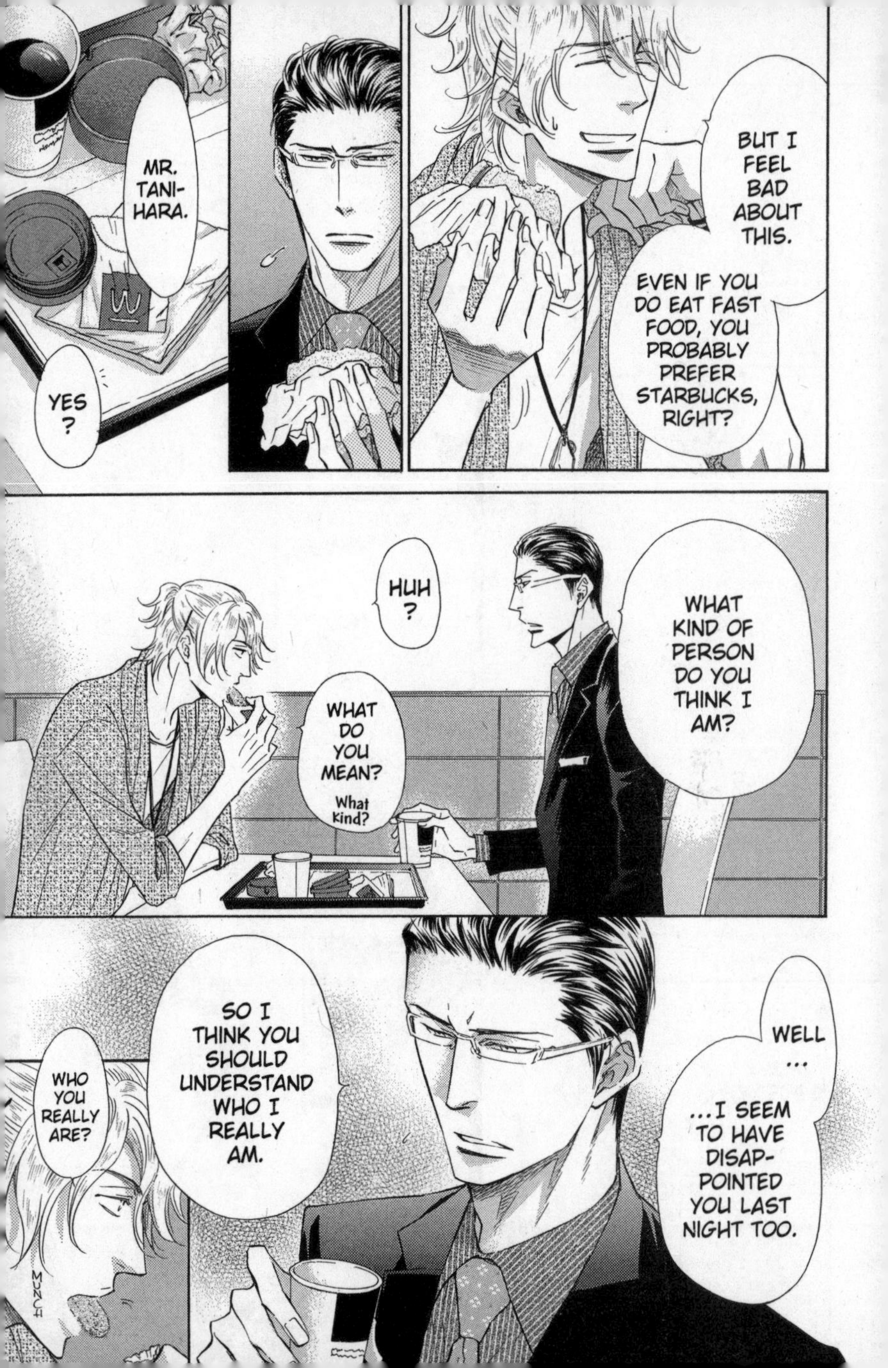
BUT I FEEL BAD ABOUT THIS.
EVEN IF YOU DO EAT FAST FOOD, YOU PROBABLY PREFER STARBUCKS, RIGHT?
MR. TANI-HARA.
YES?
WHAT KIND OF PERSON DO YOU THINK I AM?
HUH?
WHAT DO YOU MEAN?
What kind?
WELL...
...I SEEM TO HAVE DISAP-POINTED YOU LAST NIGHT TOO.
SO I THINK YOU SHOULD UNDERSTAND WHO I REALLY AM.
WHO YOU REALLY ARE?
MUNCH

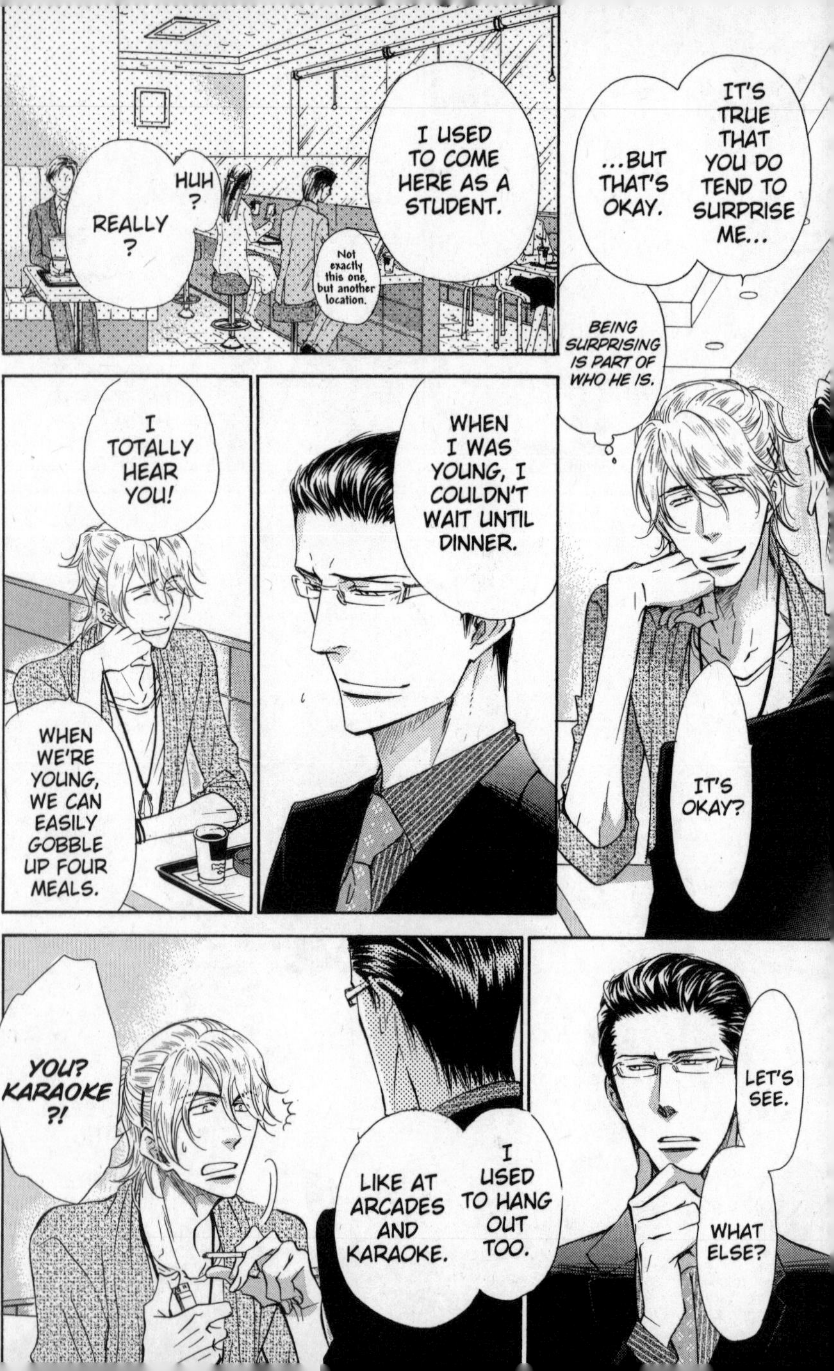

IT'S TRUE THAT YOU DO TEND TO SURPRISE ME...
...BUT THAT'S OKAY.
BEING SURPRISING IS PART OF WHO HE IS.
IT'S OKAY?
I USED TO COME HERE AS A STUDENT.
Not exactly this one, but another location.
HUH?
REALLY?
WHEN I WAS YOUNG, I COULDN'T WAIT UNTIL DINNER.
I TOTALLY HEAR YOU!
WHEN WE'RE YOUNG, WE CAN EASILY GOBBLE UP FOUR MEALS.
LET'S SEE.
WHAT ELSE?
I USED TO HANG OUT TOO.
LIKE AT ARCADES AND KARAOKE.
YOU? KARAOKE?!

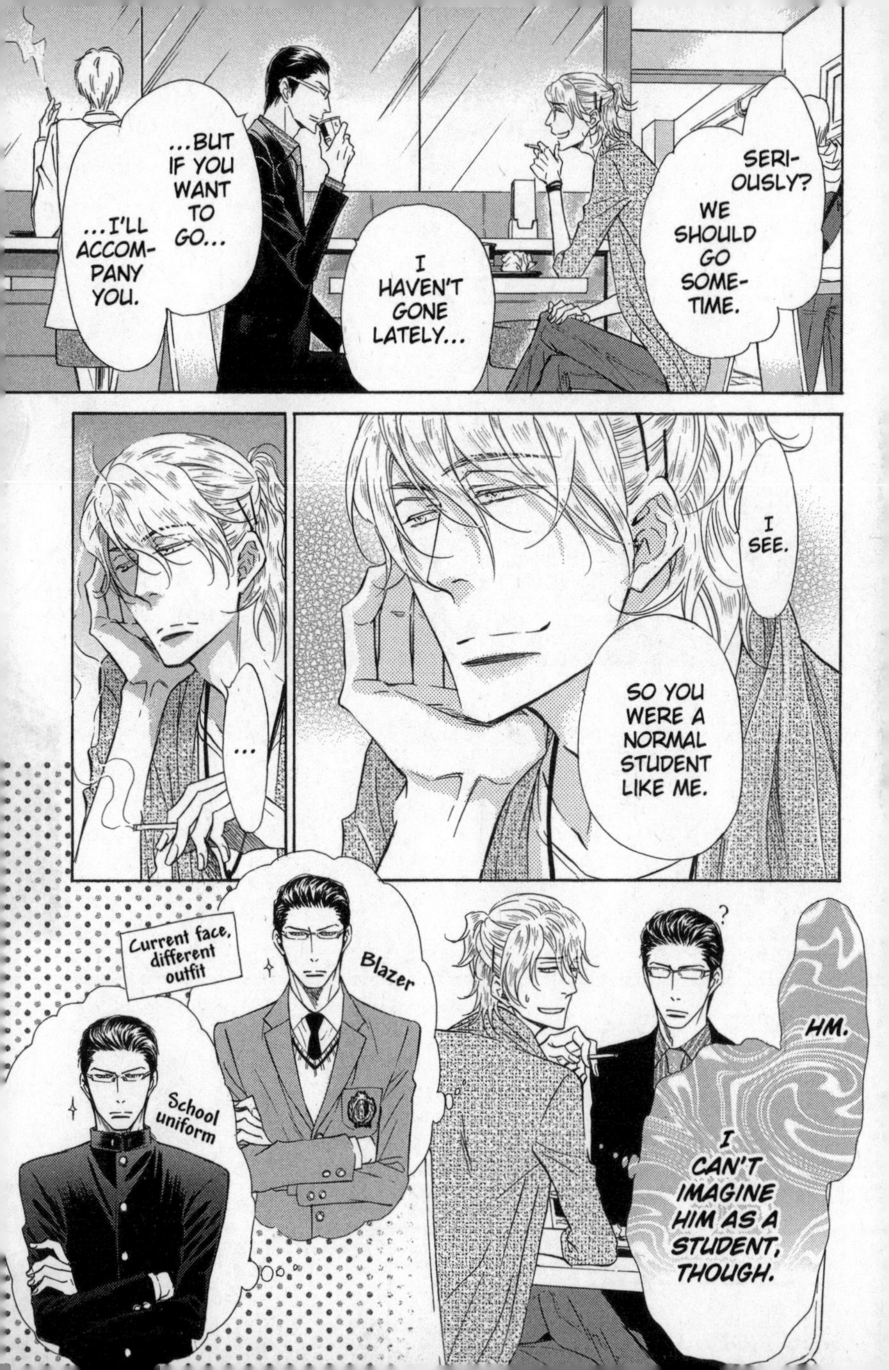
SERI-OUSLY? WE SHOULD GO SOME-TIME.
I HAVEN'T GONE LATELY...
...BUT IF YOU WANT TO GO...
...I'LL ACCOM-PANY YOU.
I SEE.
SO YOU WERE A NORMAL STUDENT LIKE ME.
...
HM.
I CAN'T IMAGINE HIM AS A STUDENT, THOUGH.
?
Current face, different outfit
Blazer
School uniform

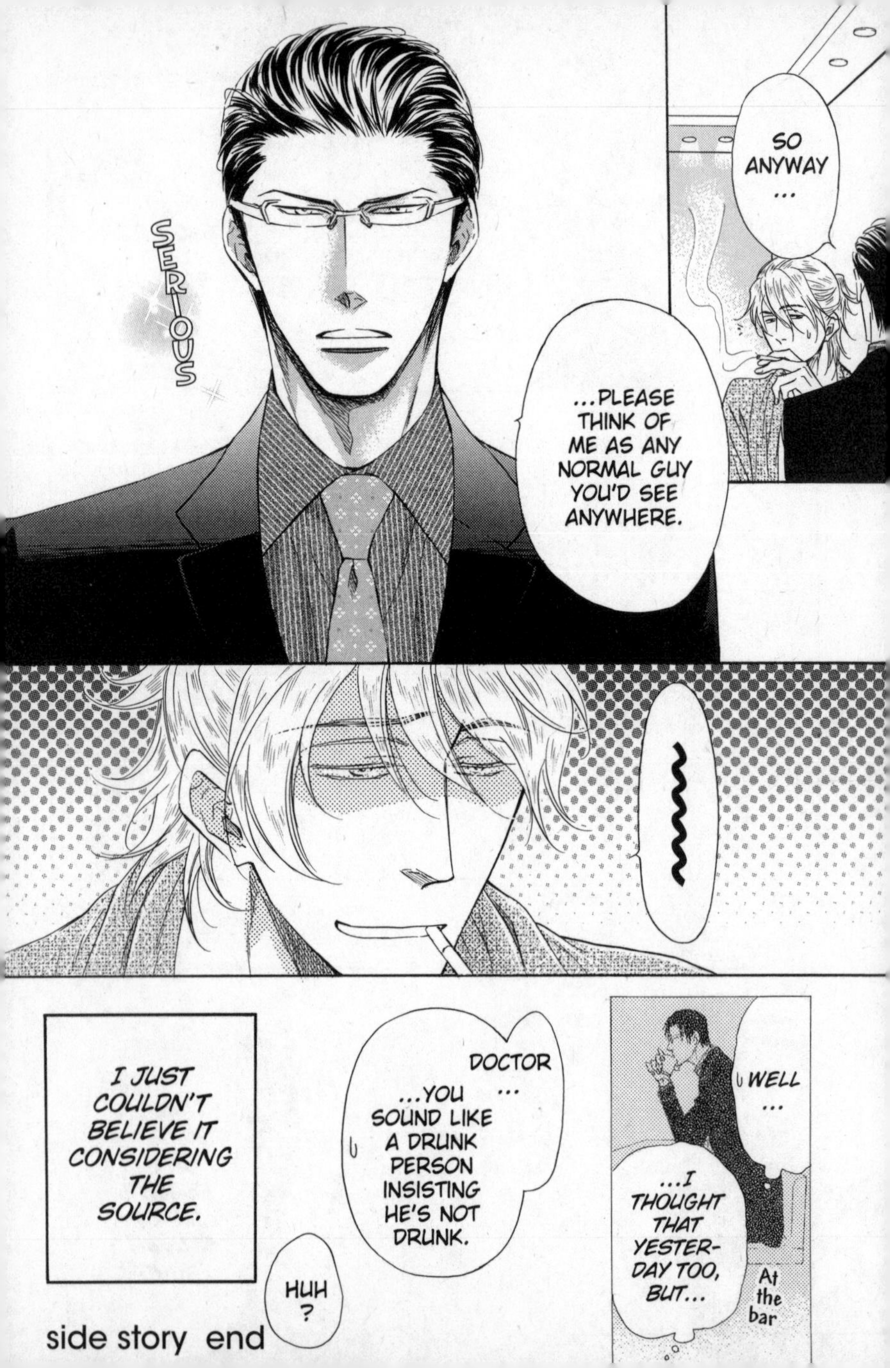
SO ANYWAY ...
SERIOUS
...PLEASE THINK OF ME AS ANY NORMAL GUY YOU'D SEE ANYWHERE.
......
WELL ...
...I THOUGHT THAT YESTERDAY TOO, BUT...
At the bar
DOCTOR ...
...YOU SOUND LIKE A DRUNK PERSON INSISTING HE'S NOT DRUNK.
HUH ?
I JUST COULDN'T BELIEVE IT CONSIDERING THE SOURCE.
side story end

This series is a spin-off of my last work, *Bond of Dreams, Bond of Love.*

Even if you haven't read it, it won't affect your understanding of the story, so don't worry.

In that story, Shuji is the go-to person for advice for the main couple, so please read it if that interests you.

(Shameless plug)

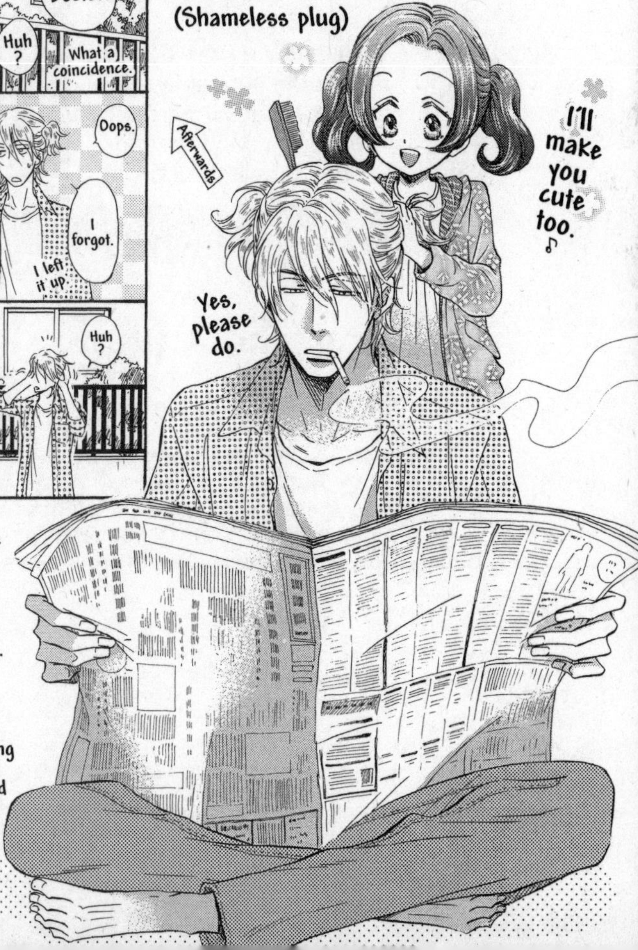

I'll make you cute too. ♪
Afterwards
Yes, please do.

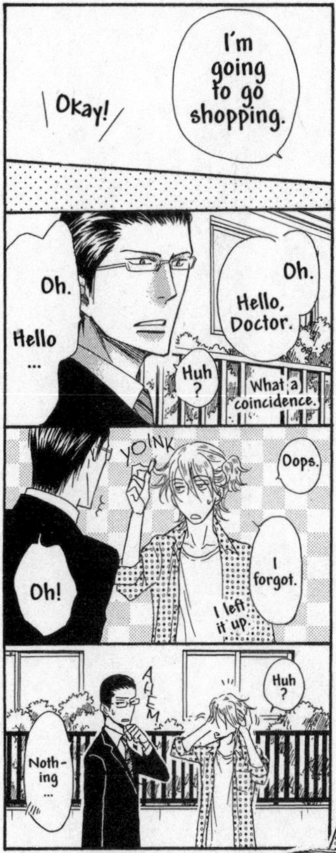

I'm going to go shopping.
Okay!
Oh. Hello, Doctor.
Huh?
What a coincidence.
Oh.
Hello...
Oops.
YOINK
I forgot.
I left it up.
Oh!
Huh?
AHEM
Nothing...

The character of the doctor is a mix of the doctors in my neighborhood.

It really touches me when a doctor speaks to adults like a child... (*laugh*)

Doctor! (*cry*)

The area I work in is blessed with interesting doctors. And we also have an old-fashioned mom-and-pop candy store like Shuji's too! Yay!

> As far as cheap candy goes, I used to like chocolate rounds. (Is that what they're called? The sponge cake covered with chocolate?) You can buy them in convenience stores now, but it's the atmosphere of the store that's important! I'm truly a child born in the Showa period.

About the Author

Yaya Sakuragi's previous English-language releases include *Tea For Two*, *Hey, Sensei?*, *Stay Close to Me*, and *Bond of Dreams, Bond of Love*. Also a prolific novel illustrator, she was born July 6th and is a Cancer with an A blood type.

Hide and Seek
Volume 1
SuBLime Manga Edition

Story and Art by **Yaya Sakuragi**

Translation—**Satsuki Yamashita**
Touch-up Art and Lettering—**Annaliese Christman**
Cover and Graphic Design—**Courtney Utt**
Editor—**Jennifer LeBlanc**

HIMEGOTO ASOBI Volume 1 © Yaya SAKURAGI 2012
Edited by KADOKAWA SHOTEN
First published in Japan in 2012 by KADOKAWA CORPORATION,
Tokyo.
English translation rights arranged with KADOKAWA
CORPORATION, Tokyo.

ASUKA
COMICS
CLX^D

Printed in the U.S.A.

Published by SuBLime Manga
P.O. Box 77010
San Francisco, CA 94107

10 9 8 7 6 5 4 3
First printing, July 2013
Third printing, November 2019

SUBLIME
www.SuBLimeManga.com

For more information

on all our products, along with the most up-to-date news on releases, series announcements, and contests, please visit us at:

 SuBLimeManga.com

 twitter.com/**SuBLimeManga**

 facebook.com/**SuBLimeManga**

Downloading is as easy as:

A sweet story of not-so-unrequited love.

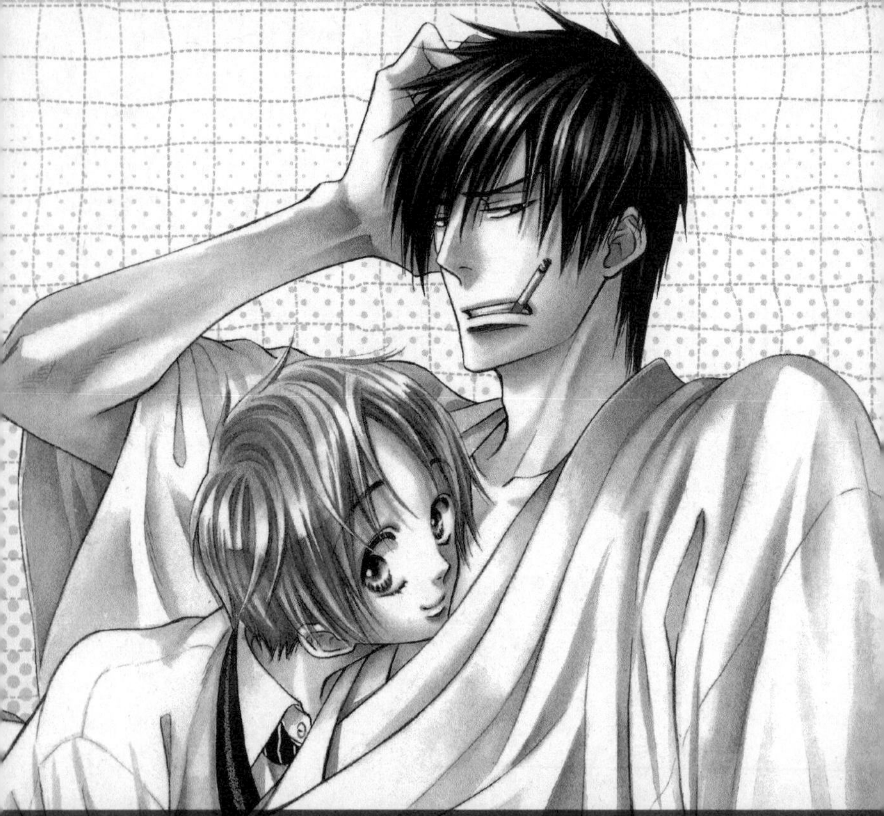

Bond of Dreams, Bond of Love

Story & Art by Yaya **SAKURAGI**

High school student Ao has been dreaming about his longtime neighbor Ryomei, a priest at the local Shinto shrine. A little freaked out—and a lot excited—at the prospect of having a relationship with Ryomei, Ao gathers up his courage, confesses his feelings...and gets turned down flat. Luckily, Ao's not the kind to give up easily. Thanks to some creative persistence (and Ryomei's weakening resolve), he finally gets a kiss. But one single kiss won't satisfy him for long!

M MATURE

On sale now at
SuBLimeManga.com
Also available at your local bookstore or comic book store.

SUBLIME